Ephesians

Reformed Expository Commentary

A Series

Series Editors

Richard D. Phillips
Philip Graham Ryken

Testament Editors

Iain M. Duguid, Old Testament
Daniel M. Doriani, New Testament

Ephesians

BRYAN CHAPELL

P&R
PUBLISHING
P.O. BOX 817 • PHILLIPSBURG • NEW JERSEY 08865-0817

Italics within Scripture quotations indicate emphasis added.

Page design by Lakeside Design Plus

Printed in the United States of America

Library of Congress Cataloging-in-Publication Data

Chapell, Bryan.
Ephesians / Bryan Chapell.
p. cm. — (Reformed expository commentary)
Includes bibliographical references and indexes.
ISBN 978-1-59638-016-5 (cloth)
1. Bible. N.T. Ephesians—Commentaries. I. Title.
BS2695.53.C43 2009
227'.507—dc22

2009017034

Contents

Series Introduction vii
Acknowledgments xi
Introduction: Author, Setting, and Themes xv

1. Our Calling (1:1–2) 3
2. The Father's Purpose (1:3–6) 17
3. The Son's Mission (1:7–10) 32
4. The Spirit's Assurance (1:11–14) 44
5. The Church Triumphant (1:15–23) 59
6. The Gift of God (2:1–10) 77
7. Identity Found (2:11–13) 91
8. Breaking Down Barriers (2:14–18) 105
9. Built Tough, Built Together (2:19–22) 120
10. Counterfeit Callings Exposed (3:1–13) 134
11. The Prevailing Power of a Supreme Love (3:14–19) 149
12. He Is Able (3:20–21) 167
13. Owner's Manual for the Church (4:1–16) 181
14. The Life of Lizards and Stallions (4:17–24) 201
15. Witness of Grace (4:25–32) 217
16. The Smell of Jesus (5:1–7) 235

17. The Light Bearers (5:8–21) 250
18. The Sacrificial Head (5:21–33) 270
19. The Submissive Wife (5:22–33) 290
20. The Godly Household (6:1–9) 305
21. The Armor of Faith (6:10–24) 327

Index of Scripture 351
Index of Subjects and Names 373

Series Introduction

In every generation there is a fresh need for the faithful exposition of God's Word in the church. At the same time, the church must constantly do the work of theology: reflecting on the teaching of Scripture, confessing its doctrines of the Christian faith, and applying them to contemporary culture. We believe that these two tasks—the expositional and the theological—are interdependent. Our doctrine must derive from the biblical text, and our understanding of any particular passage of Scripture must arise from the doctrine taught in Scripture as a whole.

We further believe that these interdependent tasks of biblical exposition and theological reflection are best undertaken in the church, and most specifically in the pulpits of the church. This is all the more true since the study of Scripture properly results in doxology and praxis—that is, in praise to God and practical application in the lives of believers. In pursuit of these ends, we are pleased to present the Reformed Expository Commentary as a fresh exposition of Scripture for our generation in the church. We hope and pray that pastors, teachers, Bible study leaders, and many others will find this series to be a faithful, inspiring, and useful resource for the study of God's infallible, inerrant Word.

The Reformed Expository Commentary has four fundamental commitments. First, these commentaries aim to be *biblical*, presenting a comprehensive exposition characterized by careful attention to the details of the text. They are not exegetical commentaries—commenting word by word or even verse by verse—but integrated expositions of whole passages of Scripture. Each commentary will thus present a sequential, systematic treatment of an entire book of the Bible, passage by passage. Second, these commentaries are unashamedly *doctrinal*. We are committed to the Westminster Confession of Faith and Catechisms as containing the system of doctrine taught in the Scriptures of the Old and New Testaments. Each volume will teach, promote, and defend the doctrines of the Reformed faith as they are found in the Bible. Third, these commentaries are *redemptive-historical* in their orientation. We believe in the unity of the Bible and its central message of salvation in Christ. We are thus committed to a Christ-centered view of the Old Testament, in which its characters, events, regulations, and institutions are properly understood as pointing us to Christ and his gospel, as well as giving us examples to follow in living by faith. Fourth, these commentaries are *practical*, applying the text of Scripture to contemporary challenges of life—both public and private—with appropriate illustrations.

The contributors to the Reformed Expository Commentary are all pastor-scholars. As pastor, each author will first present his expositions in the pulpit ministry of his church. This means that these commentaries are rooted in the teaching of Scripture to real people in the church. While aiming to be scholarly, these expositions are not academic. Our intent is to be faithful, clear, and helpful to Christians who possess various levels of biblical and theological training—as should be true in any effective pulpit ministry. Inevitably this means that some issues of academic interest will not be covered. Nevertheless, we aim to achieve a responsible level of scholarship, seeking to promote and model this for pastors and other teachers in the church. Significant exegetical and theological difficulties, along with such historical and cultural background as is relevant to the text, will be treated with care.

We strive for a high standard of enduring excellence. This begins with the selection of the authors, all of whom have proven to be outstanding communicators of God's Word. But this pursuit of excellence is also reflected in a disciplined editorial process. Each volume is edited by both a series editor and a testament editor. The testament editors, Iain Duguid for the Old Testament and Daniel Doriani for the New Testament, are accomplished pastors and respected scholars who have taught at the seminary level. Their job is to ensure that each volume is sufficiently conversant with up-to-date scholarship and is faithful and accurate in its exposition of the text. As series editors, we oversee each volume to ensure its overall quality—including excellence of writing, soundness of teaching, and usefulness in application. Working together as an editorial team, along with the publisher, we are devoted to ensuring that these are the best commentaries our gifted authors can provide, so that the church will be served with trustworthy and exemplary expositions of God's Word.

It is our goal and prayer that the Reformed Expository Commentary will serve the church by renewing confidence in the clarity and power of Scripture and by upholding the great doctrinal heritage of the Reformed faith. We hope that pastors who read these commentaries will be encouraged in their own expository preaching ministry, which we believe to be the best and most biblical pattern for teaching God's Word in the church. We hope that lay teachers will find these commentaries among the most useful resources they rely upon for understanding and presenting the text of the Bible. And we hope that the devotional quality of these studies of Scripture will instruct and inspire each Christian who reads them in joyful, obedient discipleship to Jesus Christ.

May the Lord bless all who read the Reformed Expository Commentary. We commit these volumes to the Lord Jesus Christ, praying that the Holy Spirit will use them for the instruction and edification of the church, with thanksgiving to God the Father for his unceasing faithfulness in building his church through the ministry of his Word.

Richard D. Phillips
Philip Graham Ryken
Series Editors

Acknowledgments

The book of Ephesians celebrates the church of Jesus Christ, and I must do the same. I have certainly seen the church at her grumpy and mussed, irritable and tear-stained worst. But I have also seen her nobility in the courage and compassion of those who have shown integrity under pressure, displayed respect despite differences, returned good for evil, distributed mercy instead of revenge, displayed humility where pride was due, and shown me Christ's love when there was no cause. Contributing to my life and soul from my youngest years are the Cane Creek Primitive Baptist Church, First Evangelical Church, Glen Ridge Presbyterian Church, Winnetka Bible Church, Woodburn Presbyterian Church, Bethel Reformed Presbyterian Church, Covenant Presbyterian Church, and the collective churches of the Presbyterian Church in America. All are of the body of Christ and, despite their rich diversity and significant differences, each has contributed to his ministry in my life. I praise God for each and all.

I am thankful for the students, colleagues, and trustees of Covenant Theological Seminary. Their encouragement and support have made my life very rich as we have walked and worked together in preparation of the next generation of church leaders. I know of no greater fulfillment than preaching to such eager, loving, and discerning hearts. By preaching the messages of this book in our weekly chapels, I have learned more of the gospel and grown in my love for the Savior we serve and the church he loves.

I am thankful for Mrs. Mary Beth McGreevy who shared her considerable talents of mind and heart to help me convert these messages from their original sermonic form to a commentary format. Mary Beth's similar work for Dr. James Boice and Dr. George Robertson, as well as her magnificent teaching abilities, have made her a major contributor to the gospel efforts of this generation.

I am thankful for my colleague, Dr. David Chapman, whose New Testament scholarship far exceeds my own. He graciously and carefully analyzed my exposition and offered much exegetical insight, counsel, and occasional correction. His help with the footnotes was extensive and invaluable. On rare occasions, we saw a passage somewhat differently. Thus, where defects are discerned they should be attributed to me.

Because this is a homiletical rather than an exegetical commentary, I have retained the sermon structure through which I first presented the exposition of the passages that follow. Though these messages have been expanded to handle additional exegetical content, I have kept the original divisions to help pastors with the duties of regular congregational preaching. This means that I have often chosen not to debate exegetical intricacies within the body of the text. I have tried to follow the preachers' old mandate to display the fruit of my labor rather than the sweat of my labor. At the same time, where there are important exegetical ideas that may further pastors' understanding of issues in the text, I have included relevant details either in expanded discussions or in footnotes. These are not meant to be exhaustive (nor exemplary of what should be said in sermons) but rather to point pastors to areas where important issues lie that may require special care or study. Since this material will receive wider distribution than the original sermons I preached, I have also occasionally changed illustrative names or details to protect identities.

I am a preacher who depends upon the scholarship of others. As I have prepared the messages and chapters that follow in this commentary, I have studied other commentaries. I am mindful that God blesses neither the ministry of preachers who think they do not need wisdom from others, nor the ministry of those preachers who will never think for themselves. So as I have sought to pray, think, and preach through these rich passages of Paul's letter to the Ephesians, I have also benefited from the wisdom of many others. Since these messages were prepared as sermons rather than as essays, I rarely give precise citations for quotations or commentary information. Still, I want to acknowledge my debt and gratitude to these scholars whose work I consulted to produce the messages that appear in this book:

Bruce, F. F. *The Epistles to the Colossians, to Philemon, and to the Ephesians.* Grand Rapids: Eerdmans, 1984.

Eadie, John. *Commentary on the Epistle to the Ephesians.* Original 1883. Grand Rapids: Zondervan, rpt. 1977.

Ferguson, Sinclair. *Let's Study Ephesians.* Edinburgh: Banner of Truth, 2005.

Hendriksen, William. *New Testament Commentary: Exposition of Ephesians.* Grand Rapids: Baker, 1967.

Hoehner, Harold. *Ephesians: An Exegetical Commentary.* Grand Rapids: Baker, 2002.

Hughes, R. Kent. *Ephesians: The Mystery of the Body of Christ.* Preaching the Word. Wheaton, IL: Crossway, 1990.

Lincoln, Andrew T. *Ephesians.* Word Biblical Commentary. Edited by Bruce Metzger, David A. Hubbard, Glenn W. Barker. Volume 42. Dallas: Word, 1990.

O'Brien, Peter T. *The Letter to the Ephesians.* Pillar New Testament Commentary. Grand Rapids: Eerdmans, 1999.

Introduction: Author, Setting, and Themes

The opening words of this epistle attribute the authorship to the apostle Paul (1:1), and the author affirms his identity midway through the letter (3:1).

Critical scholars have sometimes raised questions about the Pauline authorship because the style (especially in the first half of the book) seems more abstract, more corporate, and more repetitive than other of his epistles. However, this revisionist thought not only denies the clear statements of the text, but naively assumes that an author cannot adjust styles for varying purposes. For example, while many themes and phrases of Paul's letter to the Colossians also appear in Ephesians (further confirming Pauline authorship), Paul writes Ephesians with a grander theme in mind.

Most Pauline epistles are directed to the problems or progress of an individual church, requiring an initial exposition of doctrinal truths that will drive later practical instructions. However, most scholars understand that Paul writes Ephesians as a general letter to the churches within the vicinity or cultural influence of Ephesus. For this collection of churches in a culture antagonistic to the gospel, Paul pens themes so grand they can still take our breath away, and often they move even the apostle to doxology and prayer.

Paul writes to the Ephesians during a time of his own imprisonment (see 3:1; 6:20), probably reflecting his A.D. 60–62 house arrest in Rome (described in Acts 28, and also mentioned in Col. 4:3, 10, 18). This two-year imprisonment itself follows two years of trials and incarceration subsequent to his initial arrest on trumped-up charges by his Jewish countrymen in Jerusalem. The circumstances surrounding Paul's arrest and appeal to Caesar have kept him from personal nurture of the fledgling churches hatched from his missionary journeys. Yet, despite four years of bonds, Paul's vision is never more free and expansive. He writes with the enthusiasm of a father and the vision of a prophet to inspire the infant churches he must love from afar.

Instead of following his normal epistle pattern of introducing doctrinal development that will be directed toward individual problems, Paul immediately moves from a personal salutation to a sweeping explanation of God's eternal plan of salvation. Paul says that God predestined his love for the Ephesians before the creation of the world and will culminate his purposes for his covenant people in the church's transformation of the world (chapter 1). God's eternal plan and sovereign power include and unite all races, bring the entire world under the reign of Christ through the ministry of the church, and are so certain as to have already secured the position of believers with Christ in heaven (chapters 1–2). Paul's scope runs to the past and future horizons of eternity, bridges earth and heaven, levels all human barriers, transcends all human effort, gives heavenly origin and purpose to differing gifts in the church, and yet is driven by such an intimate love that it compels unity, mercy, and purity in the church (chapters 1–4). Ultimately believers are not only assured of a transformed world, a place in heaven, and a purpose on earth, but they are also told how to have their lives and homes indwelt by the Spirit (chapters 5–6). Finally they are assured of the power of the resurrected Christ for the defeat of Satan (chapter 6).

The practical instructions in the second half of the epistle are reminiscent of other Pauline epistles, but given the grandeur of his opening subjects, the majesty and intimacy of the God he describes, and the hope these themes provide during the apostle's own peril, we should not wonder that his mind and heart would often fill with doxology and prayer. This epistle is rightly referenced as key for establishing the truths of God's sovereignty in our personal salvation. However, when we lift our eyes beyond personal borders to share even a glimpse of Paul's expansive vision, then we, too, will join his doxology for God's amazing grace that saves individuals, empowers the church, and through both, transforms the world.

Ephesians

The Glory of Christ in the Life of the Church

1

Our Calling

Ephesians 1:1–2

Paul, an apostle of Christ Jesus by the will of God, To the saints in Ephesus, the faithful in Christ Jesus: Grace and peace to you from God our Father and the Lord Jesus Christ. (Eph. 1:1–2)

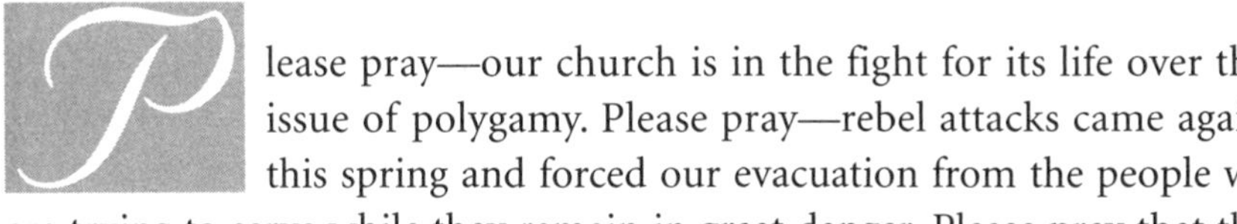

Please pray—our church is in the fight for its life over the issue of polygamy. Please pray—rebel attacks came again this spring and forced our evacuation from the people we are trying to serve while they remain in great danger. Please pray that the catechism being formed by this new church will truly reflect the primacy of the gospel of grace and not simply establish the authority of local leaders to set new rules in reaction to generations of pagan customs. Please pray for my habitual tendency to be activity focused—acting as though my self-worth and God's work depend on my ability to accomplish tasks."

These prayer requests are from Rick Gray, a missionary who serves in Bundibugyo, Uganda. When I read such reports in his mission letters, the challenges that Rick faces often leave me marveling at his faith—and longing for it. Consider the overwhelming odds against which he labors: an entire society crippled by extreme poverty and torn by civil war; an indigenous church caught in familial and sexual sin that is culturally sanctioned and generations old; church leadership that seeks to combat such evil with authoritarian legalism; and a heart that tries to do ministry amid all these problems with a reflex reliance on "what I can do to fix it."

The world outside and the world inside pose such imposing challenges that it would be understandable if Rick were to wilt or run, but he does neither. Somehow faith has granted him the ability to face the reality and the immensity of his challenges and still to serve with persistence, courage, and joy. What is the source of this ability to face a challenge greater than oneself with the expectation that God has a purpose in it—that one's efforts are not in vain? This is something all Christians want to know because we understand what it means to face challenges greater than ourselves, even if our mission field is not Uganda but our neighborhood, workplace, or home.

We know what it means to face shortages of resources and not know how or if God will supply as we wish. Many of us also know what it means to face families whose problems run through generations, to face companies or churches so influenced by the sins of our culture that they cannot even see what is wrong. And we wonder how we will make any difference because sometimes we do not see the wrong either. The challenges that are greater than we are not just outside us; they also are inside us. If we dare to look inside, we see our failures to overcome besetting sin, our persistent doubts about our capabilities to do what God calls us to do in our own homes and personal lives, and our own heart's resistance to the humbling freedom of the gospel. The immensity of the challenges outside and inside makes us want to wilt or run from God's calling, too. "The challenge is too much, Lord. I can't do this," our hearts cry. So how do we face the challenges that are greater than our resources and resistance? The apostle Paul answers for us in the opening words of his letter to the Ephesians. His introduction signals the responses of faith needed to meet the great challenges of an outside culture and our inner heart.

Affirm the Source of Your Strength (1:1)

Paul has an immense challenge before him. He is to be an apostle—a chosen messenger of the Lord Jesus to the Ephesian Gentiles (Eph. 1:1a and

Eph. 1:2a).[1] Not only is their culture historically opposed to the message of God's covenantal love, but the covenant people—the Jews—are opposed to the Gentiles receiving that message. Immense barriers of cultural, historical, and racial differences confront the apostle. And what can he do about it? He is in prison under Roman guard.[2] We would understand if Paul simply said, "I give up, Lord; the obstacles are greater than I. You'll just have to find someone else." Yet Paul refuses to quit because he recognizes that his strength to face the obstacles lies in provisions beyond him: God's Word and God's will.

God's Word (1:1)

When Paul says that he is an "apostle" of Christ Jesus, he is claiming to be an appointed messenger. The term is not incidental. The crucified Jesus who is the Christ—the Anointed One of the Jews, the long-prophesied Messiah, the One once dead but risen and alive with God, the King of the universe, the Lord who struck down the rampaging Saul on the road to Damascus to make him a redeeming voice to the Gentiles of the eternal love of God—this same Jesus Christ is the One for whom Paul has been called to speak. All of this means not only that Paul belongs to Christ Jesus, but also that Paul represents him so definitely that Paul's message is Christ's own message. When Paul speaks under the inspiration of God's Spirit, Christ himself speaks. When Paul speaks of grace and peace to the Ephesians, "God the Father and the Lord Jesus Christ" are bestowing their very own blessing on the people. What does it matter that Paul is in prison, that his deprivations are real, and that his opposition is great? He speaks for God, and knowing this fills him with courage and purpose for the challenges of his calling.

One might think that the special calling of Paul denies similar confidence to us. "After all," one might reason, "I am not an apostle. So what does his assurance have to do with me?" The answer is that all believers benefit from

1. A Gentile audience is clear in light of the references to "you Gentiles" in 2:11 and 3:1, and Paul emphasizes his role as an apostle to the Gentiles in this letter (3:1–12; cf. Rom. 11:13; 1 Tim. 2:7). This does not preclude the possibility that Paul also addresses Jewish members of the church, which would explain his emphasis on the unity of the church (Jew and Gentile alike) in 2:11–3:7.

2. Paul's imprisonment is implied in Ephesians 4:1 (cf. 3:13; 6:20). This would likely be the same imprisonment that Paul experienced during the writing of Colossians and Philemon, since the same messenger, Tychicus, bears the letter (Eph. 6:21–22; Col. 4:7–9; though note 2 Tim. 4:12; Titus 3:12; Acts 20:4) and also accompanies Onesimus (Col. 4:9; cf. Philem. 10–14).

his gift. Through the wisdom of his Lord, Paul provides a written record of God's message that is still available to us. So when we speak faithfully these truths, the Word of God is yet ours. We may face opposition, resistance, and deprivation, but the knowledge that God is yet speaking to and through us means that we are not dependent on our wisdom or authority. Whether we speak to our culture in the public arena or to a lost friend in a family room in the wee hours of the morning, God is still speaking his truth through us. We are not dependent on our words alone. His Word is here for us, and that is a source of strength when we face the limitations of our powers and the immensity of our challenges.

God's Will (1:1a)

Not only do we face challenges strengthened with the Word of God, but also with the will of God. Paul says that he is an apostle of Christ Jesus by "the will of God" (v. 1b).[3] Against the great challenges that he is facing, this phrase is his defense, his offense, and his confidence.

Because Paul's apostleship is the will of God, he can *defend* his right to speak. There was a time when Paul breathed out threats against those who confessed Jesus as Lord. He held the cloaks of those who stoned Stephen. We could rightly question, "What right did he have to speak for God?" None at all, based on his record. But Paul is not an apostle because of his record. He is an apostle because of Christ's redemption. Jesus had corrected him, claimed him, and commissioned him. Paul could well confess that he was the greatest of sinners, yet he could still speak for God, because it was God's will for him to do so.

What a message of comfort that is for us, too. When others who know about our past life question what right we have to speak for God—when they know the faults and failings in our personal history, we can say like the apostle Paul, "Were my speaking based on my doing, then I would have no right to speak. But God corrected me, claimed me, and commissioned me to speak of himself. Because God wants me to speak, I have a right to speak."

3. Paul's opening greetings often affirm that his apostleship is the result of God's will (1 Cor. 1:1; 2 Cor. 1:1; Col. 1:1; 2 Tim. 1:1). In the context of the opening verses of Ephesians this theme is all the more significant given the further stress on God's will operative in the predestination of believers unto adoption and glory (1:5, 11–12; cf. 1:9).

But the will of God was not only Paul's defense that he had a right to speak, it was also his *offense*. Because his apostleship is the will of God, Paul could say to his hearers, "I have a right to speak, and you have a responsibility to listen." Paul is about to say some hard things to the Ephesians. He knows how easy it is for them to belittle or ignore his words. But if his speaking is the will of God, then all must heed what he says. Because Paul's calling is the will of God, he has authority.

The will of God is Paul's defense, his offense, and, finally, his *confidence*. Not only does the "will of God" give Paul authority, it also creates a powerful expectation in him: "God has a purpose for me." That is power. When a person believes that he or she has been called from darkness to light by a power greater than any challenge this world can offer, then where others see opposition that person sees opportunity.

Paul's traveling companion, Luke, gives a wonderful picture of the power coming from the confidence that our calling is the will of God. Luke records that Paul did extraordinary miracles in his previous journey to Ephesus (Acts 19:11–12). As a result, many people began to believe on the Lord Jesus, openly confessed their sins, burned their valuable sorcery scrolls, and stopped buying idols from the silversmiths. Then a silversmith named Demetrius convened his fellow tradesmen and incited a riot. He said that the message of Paul was demeaning the goddess Artemis. The whole city erupted into uproar. A maddened mob seized whatever Christians they could find, hauled them to the city theater, and for two hours threatened violence, shouting, "Great is Artemis of the Ephesians."

I have visited that great stone theater which seats twenty thousand people. Even today it is frightening to be there and to envision a huge throng screaming for the blood of these new Christians. But what was Paul doing in the midst of this great danger? He was confidently saying, "Let me at them now that they are all gathered together." Paul's friends had to hold him back from going before the mob. In God's providence the city clerk told the people that if they did not settle down, the Romans would come and punish them for the riot, and that disbanded the crowd. But we do not doubt the confidence of Paul, who looked at a mob breathing for his blood as a providentially gathered congregation (see Acts 19:30).

What is the effect of our believing that God's people are chosen for a divine purpose by the will of God? It is not simply affirming that some missionaries in far places speak because they believe that God has called them to that purpose. Instead, we believe that no challenge facing any of us is beyond God's plan. When my friend and New Testament scholar Hans Bayer returns from ministry in economically depressed areas of the former Soviet Union, he grieves at overwhelming despair that can envelop an entire culture. Still, he returns to those areas again and again, because he says that he believes that God's Word is real, and that it is yet God's will to use his people who believe his Word to overcome overwhelming challenges.

We may face similar cause for despair, such as decades of abortion acceptance in our culture of promiscuity. Yet when we believe that the Word of God has spoken and that it is the will of God to use his people to overcome the greatest challenges, we will not only still dare to speak—we will also bother to speak. When we face the consequences and devastation of generations in poverty, we still fight for justice because we know the Savior we serve still delights in mercy and ministers his grace through it. When we face unbelief, ridicule, and long resistance to the gospel in our own families, we will not give up because of the faith that God's Word can be on our lips. We will believe that God's will in choosing us as his servants is our defense (even though others know our weakness), our offense (even though others may say we have no right to speak), and our confidence (even when there is little likelihood of change from a human perspective).

From where does this confidence come that God's will and Word enable us to overcome such overwhelming challenges? The apostle's starting point is important. Paul himself is an apostle because of the will of God (again, v. 1a). What is before his own eyes is how distant and opposed to the gospel was his own heart when Christ called him. The greatest witness to Paul of the great power of the gospel is its claim on his own heart. When he was Christ's enemy, God called him. When there was no desire to seek Jesus, the Savior made this Pharisee of the Jews an apostle of Jesus. Paul has been transferred from one universe to another, and it is plain to him that this was not and could not be his own doing but, rather, the sovereign work of God.

Once when I was attending a church meeting, this sovereign work became apparent to me. We were facing some difficult issues that could have caused us to despair. But in the middle of our discussions one man recounted how he came to Christ. Then another did the same. Then another. One after another, more men told the story of their salvation. One told of how he grew up in a non-Christian family; another had lived a hard and rebellious life of thirty years in the military, laughing at men of faith; another acknowledged that his college days were marked by sin and the assumption that Christians were crazy. Each said that the only explanation for their new lives was that God had acted in their behalf and turned their world upside down. Many believers could say the same: "I was caught up in business pursuits . . . caught in a web of immorality and deceit . . . immersed in secular philosophy . . . raised in a non-Christian family . . . sinking in cynicism and despair . . . when God lifted me up." There is no other explanation. God did something that cannot be explained and no one else could arrange. God changes the world by his will. This is what Paul says, and the affirmation gives him confidence in the face of his challenges.

The greatest evidence to Paul of the power of God's Word and will to overcome overwhelming opposition is the work of God in his own life. His apostleship is not only for the attestation of the truths of God, it is testimony to the power of God—a message that life can be different, that change is possible, that the greatest challenges to the gospel can be overcome. Paul rejoices in words not unlike those from the hymn that reminds us God is "the power of my power." Paul starts with this testimony because he knows that the Ephesians (as well as we) need to know the source and strength of spiritual power in light of what he must say next.

Acknowledge the Strength of Your Opposition (1:1b-c)

Paul affirms the source of our strength, in order to help us properly acknowledge the nature of our opposition. Though it can seem overwhelming, it can be overcome.

The Opposition Seems Overwhelming (1:1b)

Our eyes do not make the appropriate U-turn at the second half of verse 1 because we are unfamiliar with the ancient world. When Paul says his letter is to the "saints" in Ephesus, we rarely catch the significance.[4] We do not

4. A few of the earliest Greek manuscripts omit the phrase "in Ephesus." This has led to three views: (a) the original letter included the phrase "in Ephesus," but it dropped out in some early copies; (b) the original epistle was intended as a circular letter to many churches in Asia Minor (including the church in Ephesus), and a space was left to fill in the name of the church as the letter was read aloud; (c) the original

recognize that in modern terms this is something like saying his letter is to the Christians in Iran or the evangelicals working at MTV. The phrases do not seem to go together because the challenges to faith in the place these believers live are so strong.

Ephesus was the fourth or fifth largest city in the world of Paul's time. The sheer numbers would seem to overwhelm any new faith message. A missionary who flew over Calcutta for the first time sensed similar futility. Seeing the sheer mass of humanity below made him wonder what difference he could make in the city. The only thing that made him stay, said the missionary, was the belief that God was in Calcutta ahead of him. Paul must have had some of the same sense of God's prior presence and purpose, because the challenges to faith at Ephesus were so massive.

Ephesus would overwhelm not merely because of numbers but because of contrary belief. As you walk into the city ruins today, remnants of a great statue to the Roman emperor Trajan can still be seen. Trajan ruled after Paul's time, but the statue still demonstrates the attitude of the Roman rulers Paul faced. It shows the foot of the emperor upon the globe of the world, demonstrating two things: the ancients were not ignorant of the shape of the world, and Roman rule so dominated the ancient world that the emperor portrayed himself as having the authority of a god.[5]

Not only did Paul face the opposition of the Roman emperor cult, he had to face the other cultish commitments that had captured many more hearts. Ephesus was a great port on the sea. Even today as you walk the street from the ancient docks into the city, there remains a sign carved in stone that guides will say was used to direct sailors to a brothel. But the sexual enticement was not merely for the diversion of those passing through. Ancient accounts and continuing evidence amid the archaeological ruins demonstrate that the economy and culture of the entire region were as mired in materialism, sensuality, and idolatrous diversions as any modern city.

---

contained no reference to the specific Asia Minor church (or churches) for which it was intended (but the Ephesian church later personalized the letter to themselves). Regardless of the position taken, the cultural environment of Ephesus in the first century certainly illuminates the type of Asia Minor social context Paul's audience experienced.

5. Trajan ruled after Paul's time, but the early practice of the emperor cult in Ephesus (even prior to Paul's day) is further evidenced by the construction of the Temple to the Divine Julius and the Goddess Roma around 29 B.C. (Cassius Dio, *Roman History* 51.20.6–8).

Ancient Ephesus was not more wicked than other cities. In fact, there were competing religious appeals for moral uprightness from the "solid citizens" of the city. But whether the efforts were to stifle immorality or exploit it, the city exhibited all the normal desperations of a culture in search of something divine. For example, as you walk down the main street of reconstructed Ephesus today, the most imposing ancient building is the city's library.[6] The building is a landmark not just of that culture's commitment to learning but to the Greek notion (embraced in Roman culture) that true enlightenment was about rising to higher levels of mysterious knowledge—not merely knowledge of philosophy but of experience (both ascetic and erotic). The city and its surrounding culture were addicted to forms of paganism both sophisticated and sordid. And to make the situation worse, Greco-Roman culture was capable of claiming that both were religiously good. Modern scholars debate the degree of depravity present at Ephesus, but we do not doubt the darkness of a culture whose pagan gods were worshiped despite accounts of their craftiness and perversions.

For Paul to address believers in Ephesus as "saints," a phrase of Jewish origins meaning "set apart" or "consecrated ones" (a phrase sometimes reserved for angels), would have been unthinkable—even offensive—to the Jews of that time.[7] One commentator writes that by this terminology "Paul bestows upon all his pagan-born hearers a privilege formerly reserved in Israel for special servants (especially priestly) of God."[8]

It was incredible to refer to those who were in Ephesus as "saints," and maybe it was a stretch of the imagination, too. For how could there be "holy ones" in a place where politics, philosophy, economics, and religion all intertwined to capture an entire culture in pervasive sin? This is a question not only for Paul's day. For once we face the pervasiveness of sin around us and in us today, we too may wonder if there can be any holy ones where we live.

6. The Library of Celsus in Ephesus was built soon after Paul's time but well reflects the priorities and philosophy of that Greco-Roman era.

7. Paul commonly calls his readers "saints" in his letters, especially in his opening greetings to the churches (in all epistles except Galatians and 1 Thessalonians). The word *hagios* is actually an adjective commonly used in the Old Testament of God himself, as well as of the temple, the priests, and those sacrifices, days, and objects dedicated to the Lord's service. The adjective was further applied to the whole nation of Israel in the Old Testament (e.g., Ex. 19:6)—a people called to be "set apart" for the Lord (e.g., Ex. 22:31; Lev. 11:44–45; 19:2; 20:7–8; Num. 15:40; Deut. 7:6).

8. Marcus Barth as quoted by Kent Hughes in *Ephesians: The Mystery of the Body of Christ*, Preaching the Word (Wheaton, IL: Crossway, 1990), 18.

Can there really be saints, consecrated ones, in a culture of pervasive sin? At one level the answer must be no. For if materialism pervades a culture, how can even Christians not misplace priorities about work, money, time, and family? Can a mother of small children not on occasion feel victimized by them for denying her a better career path? If pornography surrounds us, how can even those whose marriages are healthy and whose morals are right not be tainted by impurity? In a religious culture that worships numbers, affluence, and size, are there any who are not guilty of pragmatism for the sake of success or envy of those who apparently have more than we? In a political culture convinced that human power is a path to glory, have any escaped the lust for power? In a culture where sin is pervasive, there are none who are untouched, but that does not mean that the sin is overpowering. By some measures our challenges will always appear pervasive and overwhelming, but through the gospel we should also realize that they can be overcome.

The Opposition Can Be Overcome (1:1c)

Paul identifies only the earthly location of these saints as being at Ephesus; their spiritual status he will not bind to this place. With clever parallelism in the original Greek the apostle speaks of the people of God as "the saints in Ephesus"—giving their physical locale; and as "the faithful in Christ Jesus"—giving their spiritual status.[9] Surrounded by paganism they are nonetheless secure in Christ, not on the basis of their consecration, but on the basis of faith that unites them to Christ. Here once again, as is so often the case in the epistles of Paul, is the wonderful affirmation of the beauty and benefits of our union with Christ. Though troubles assail us and temptations attack us, yet they do not overcome us. We remain the holy ones of God because of our union with him. Again the apostle has taken us away from ourselves as the answer to the challenges that are greater than we. When sin is pervasive, we prevail not by our might but by virtue of the consecrating power of God that is ours by faith alone.

9. If the reading "in Ephesus" is deemed not to be original, then the Greek would read "to the saints who are also faithful in Christ Jesus." Even so, the readers are being called both "saints" and "faithful" (cf. Col. 1:2). The term "faithful" likely describes their status as those who believe in Christ Jesus (cf. 1 Tim. 4:12; also see 2 Cor. 6:15; 1 Tim. 4:3, 10; 5:16; 6:2; Titus 1:6; further cf. Acts 10:45; 1 Peter 1:21).

Recognize the Strength of Your Message (1:2)

In the opening salutation Paul gives the message that he wants to impart in the rest of the book: "Grace and peace to you from God our Father and the Lord Jesus Christ" (Eph. 1:2). These people are living amidst gross and powerful paganism. Their lives are threatened by it and touched by it, and yet the apostle is offering grace amidst sin, and peace amidst the storms of conscience and likely persecution. How can he offer such hope in the midst of such difficulty?

The Power of Grace (1:2a)

Paul can offer such hope because the grace and peace he offers are not of human origin. They are "from God our Father and the Lord Jesus Christ" and therefore do not have the limitations of human strength and effort. These words are common for the opening of Paul's letters (Rom. 1:7; 1 Cor. 1:3; 2 Cor. 1:2; Gal. 1:3; Eph. 1:2; Phil. 1:2; 2 Thess. 1:2; Philem. 3; also in an abbreviated form in Col. 1:2; 1 Thess. 1:1). It has often been noted that Paul combines the ancient Jewish greeting of shalom ("peace") with a Christian modification of the common Gentile salutation. The standard Greek greeting *chairein* (meaning "hello" or literally "rejoice") has been changed to *charis* (meaning "grace"). Thus, with these simple words Paul underscores the good news that God provides what we cannot provide for ourselves.

The divine origin of the grace in Paul's life pervades his message in many ways. Even the order of the divine names (Lord Jesus Christ) in his salutation reflects the progress of grace in the apostle's own life. When he was breathing out threats and seeking to earn divine approval by his zeal, this Jew formerly known as Saul was seeking to pacify God the *Father*. But then this zealot was struck down on the road to Damascus in a blinding light and heard a voice demanding, "Saul, Saul, why do you persecute me?" Paul responded: "Who are you, *Lord*?" "I am Jesus, whom you are persecuting" was the reply (Acts 9:4–5). And soon Paul begins to proclaim this Jesus as the "*Christ*" (9:22).

The Power of Peace (1:2a)

Paul's salutation to the Ephesians echoes the progress of his understanding of overpowering grace through the sequence of his experience with the persons of the Trinity. When Paul (as Saul) was God's enemy, the Father sent the Son to claim him. Through no effort on Paul's part—in fact, in the face of Paul's contrary efforts—the Son took the steps to make Paul a true child of God. For this reason Paul recognizes Jesus to be his Messiah, the Christ. The knowledge of a God who acts in behalf of his people without any merit of their own is the grace self-evident in Paul's life. He proclaims this grace to the Ephesians not simply as their hope but as their peace, because such grace means that God is not holding their sin against them. God has overcome the obstacles of the human heart and the powers of human evil. Because Paul knows this grace, he knows peace—and he shares both, knowing that when grace is understood as the compassionate and prevailing power of God in behalf of his people, then peace comes.

Peace is what enabled Paul to keep going when he suffered, when churches resisted his ministry, and when his ministry seemed incapable of overcoming the obstacles outside and inside the church. Even though Paul was in prison as he wrote to the Ephesians, he remained confident of God's love and purpose. Because he was at peace, Paul's ministry continued. Through his life we understand that peace is the power for ministry, as well as the fruit of grace. Perhaps this is the reason Paul began this letter with a promise of peace, since what he will say in the remainder of his epistle about the church's ministry will be so challenging.

We should be aware of this power in peace as well. The Lilly Endowment recently recorded statistics regarding the pastors of local churches: 30 percent are doing well—they are gifted for the task and seem to be effective in their efforts; however, 40 percent are "just muddling through"—they feel largely ineffective, see themselves as stuck in dead-end locations and ministries, treading water that feels more and more like mud; the remaining 30 percent are already on the edge—they are barely hanging on, under attack, believing that they are failures, looking for any way out that they can find. What this means is that 70 percent of pastors see themselves as ineffective in ministry. The obstacles have become too big. The pastors wonder if anything will ever change, and believe they have run out of options to make a difference.

One does not have to be a pastor to wonder if the ministry challenges are too great to expect change. Some of us work with young people who, despite being in church, seem hardened to the gospel and in bondage to their culture. Others face counselees whose problems are so deep, complex, prolonged, or evil that we wonder what we could possibly say or do that will help. Others of us work in environments where secular values are no longer questioned, making our Christian witness seem antiquated and even bigoted. We may even worship in a church compromised by generations of bitterness, license, and indifference.

If the problems are so great, the culture so wicked, the church so weak, and the people so human, then what basis is there to expect that any change is really possible?

The apostle teaches us the answer through caring opening words that reveal the key to our power. What Paul says has happened in him can happen for others in the church today. God overcame Paul's sin, his anger, his murder, and his war against the faith. If God can do that, then we can be at peace knowing that God can overcome any of the great obstacles of this life whether they are products of the culture's making or of our own weakness. We can be at peace regarding what cannot be accomplished in our own strength because God's work is not dependent on human strength. We need not despair simply because we are not strong enough to overcome our challenges. When the message of grace yields the fruit of peace, then we possess and reflect gospel power. Human weakness is not the end of the story. God is at work, so believers can be at peace and keep going. The personal peace that grace provides is the hidden power source of unvanquished ministry.

In the face of the overwhelming challenges in Uganda, Rick Gray wrote of a personal incident that reminded him of the source of his strength for facing the opposition and expecting change:

> While checking the first draft of the "Katekisimo" (the new catechism being written) I became intent on finishing a certain amount of pages each day. One afternoon as time was ticking away, and my dear Mubwisi co-translator struggled to come up with just the right Lubwisi word to express the English meaning, I grew impatient with him. I became harsh and unsympathetic, impatient for him to go faster. My penchant to get the job done blinded me to Christ's presence with us, and deafened me to the Spirit's conviction of my sin.
>
> Unless I maintain a Jesus-centeredness in the midst of ministry, I will be unable to love people well and bring the glory to God! Only as I realize my self-worth is determined by how awesome is the Savior's love for me, and not by how productive my work is for him, will I be free from my drivenness and need to accomplish tasks. When I gaze upon his nail-pierced hands and believe

> they are actually reaching out to embrace me, then I am empowered to reach out with similar compassion and care to those around me. It is gospel love flowing through me into the hearts of others that can alone change the folks with whom I am involved in ministry. . . .
>
> So while I believe the "Katekisimo" and Bundimulinga church discipline are all ministries that God can use to change people's hearts and lives, I am also convinced that unless these activities are done in partnership with Jesus, and steeped in a deep sense of Calvary's love, they can easily do as much harm as good.

What great challenges Rick faces: poverty, poor health care, poor education, immature Christians, inadequate catechisms, civil war, and personal danger. Yes, he wonders sometimes if his efforts will make any difference. But he answers such questions by embracing the truths of God's faithfulness.

The God whose Word and will overcame the obstacles in Rick's heart is not intimidated by opposing forces in this world. And this same loving God is still saying "grace and peace" to us, indeed, to all who call on his name. When we know his grace, then we can experience his peace no matter what challenges face us. Such peace keeps us from despair or surrender and thus is more powerful than the opposing forces in the world or in us. Peace is the evidence and expression of God's power. Nothing in this world is more powerful than the peace that is the power of the gospel to them that believe. With such peace the gospel conquers challenges greater than we, and grants us the confidence and compassion to face them in Christ's name and with his blessing.

2

The Father's Purpose

Ephesians 1:3–6

In love he predestined us to be adopted as his sons through Jesus Christ, in accordance with his pleasure and will—to the praise of his glorious grace, which he has freely given us in the One he loves.[1] (Eph. 1:4–6)

Some years ago my oldest son, then a senior in high school, fought his way through district and regional meets to win a berth in the state wrestling championships. We were thrilled with this blessing, but our happiness was tempered by what he had to give up to go to the state tournament. The weekend of the state wrestling tournament was the same weekend that he had to be at a college in another state to remain eligible for a prestigious scholarship for which he had also qualified. A lot of privilege and not a little money were being jeopardized by his not going to compete for the scholarship. But what could we do? As

1. By employing participial phrases and dependent clauses, Paul's Greek sentence extends throughout the whole of Ephesians 1:3–14. Although modern editions of the Greek New Testament sometimes insert periods before verses 7, 11, and 13 (each of which literally begins "in whom"; the NIV has "in him"), this punctuation actually separates these dependent relative clauses from their antecedent (i.e., Christ the Beloved of 1:5–6).

parents we could not say to this young man who had worked so hard for his sport, his coach, and his team, "You cannot compete in a state tournament because we want to save some money." He and we would regret that all our lives. So we devised a plan: If he did well in the state tournament, we would stay there all the way; but if he did not advance very far in the early rounds, then we would get in the car—no matter the time of day or night—and drive to the scholarship competition. Whatever happened, we would consider the outcome a blessing and praise God for it.

It seemed like a fairly good plan until we got to the point where my wife and I had to consider exactly what we should pray for. Should we pray for the blessing that he win the tournament, or should we pray for the blessing that he win the scholarship? We could not pray for him to lose his wrestling matches, but we did not want him to miss the scholarship. What should we do?

There was not any question at all what we should do once the wrestling match started. When you see your own son before thousands of spectators, wrestling with all of his strength against a well-muscled foe, there is no question what a father does. He shouts as loudly as he can, "Go Colin! Fight! Wrestle! Squeeze him! Squash him!" A father cheers as loudly as possible to encourage his son in such a match. The shouts are a father's way of saying, "I am here for you in your struggle, my son." Now when a father is shouting that kind of encouragement to a wrestling son, those around the father may not take it so well. His words are so loud and forceful, his voice so strident, that those who are not that father's children may not understand; they may even take offense. But children who need the encouragement do understand.

When we are wrestling against spiritual forces that are challenging and sometimes overwhelming us, we may wonder, "Is my heavenly Father still here for me? Does he still want me to win? Have my compromises and weaknesses turned him away?" So, to teach us the answers, here in this passage our heavenly Father shouts his encouragement to his children who are wrestling against great evil in Ephesus. The words he uses are as strong as any in Scripture. The Father says things like "I chose you. I predestined you. You are mine, no matter what." We cannot deny that these words are strong, and even capable of causing offense; but when we see their context and their purpose of blessing and encouraging God's children who are wrestling against great spiritual foes, then we will realize that these words are cause to praise our heavenly Father.

Praise of our Father is really the focus of this passage. The apostle says that we should praise God, because he blesses us as *our* Father.[2] Paul highlights this theme by the praise statements that form the borders of our text: "Praise be to the God and Father of our Lord Jesus Christ, who has blessed us . . ." (Eph. 1:3); and "He predestined us to be adopted as his sons . . . to the praise of his glorious grace . . ." (Eph. 1:5–6). Between these bookends of praise Paul tells us why such regard is warranted.[3]

Blessed with Christ's Blessing (1:3)

We should praise God, because he blesses us with Christ's blessing (Eph. 1:3). Paul says, "The Father of our Lord Jesus Christ . . . has blessed us in the heavenly realms with every spiritual blessing in Christ" (Eph. 1:3). We really need the last part of this verse to be able to explain the first part. The words "in Christ" remind us that our "spiritual blessing" includes several important elements.

We Are in Union with Christ (1:3a)

Twelve times in verses 3–12, Paul refers in various ways to believers' spiritual union with Christ. The words appear so frequently that we may grow numb to their significance. However, we will not miss the impact Paul wants to make on our hearts if we track to the end of the chapter. There Paul identifies the One with whom we are united. He is the Son of God the Father and was

> raised . . . from the dead and seated . . . at his right hand in the heavenly realms, far above all rule and authority, power and dominion, and every title that can be given, not only in the present age but also in the one to come. And God placed all things under his feet and appointed him to be head over everything

2. In Ephesians Paul delays his common opening thanksgiving (Eph. 1:15–16) in order to begin instead with these praises to God for what he has done (cf. 2 Cor. 1:3–4; 1 Peter 1:3–5). Such praise is strongly reminiscent of many Old Testament passages (e.g., Gen. 24:27; Ex. 18:10; 1 Chron. 29:10), especially from the Psalter (e.g., Pss. 28:6; 66:20; 72:18–19), and the form is paralleled in early Jewish liturgy (e.g., the Eighteen Benedictions). The Greek word for our praise to God (*eulogētos*) is cognate with the verb (*eulogēsas*) and the noun (*eulogia*) used for the blessings we receive from him; hence the New American Standard translation reads: "*Blessed* be the God and Father of our Lord Jesus Christ, who has *blessed* us with every spiritual *blessing*. . . ."

3. Note that a similar expression of praise also closes the whole section in verse 14: ". . . to the praise of his glory" (cf. 1:12).

> for the church, which is his body, the fullness of him who fills everything in every way. (Eph. 1:20–23)

Paul says that we are united to the One who is above every earthly power and authority in this age and the age to come. He is Lord. Yet we share his honor and blessings by being united to him.

Paul spells out the blessings: Christ is risen from the grave with power over sin and death; he is seated in the heavens with the Father; his power and privileges exceed anything on earth; and we share his glory. He is head of all things, and all that is precious in church and world is filled with him. All of these blessings we share by the marvelous grace of being united to Christ.

We struggle fully to apprehend all the goodness and glory of our union with Christ. The beauty of a sunset, the power of a storm, the purity of a child's prayer, the majesty of a hero's glory, the wonder of love's passion, and the hope of eternal glory when such earthly blessings fail—all these are of him, all are under him, all are by him, all reflect the wonder, majesty, purity, power, and beauty of who he is. And because we are in union with him, they are ours, too.

We Are in Heaven with Christ (1:3b)

If such wonder is ours to enjoy, then a song may come to mind: "Heaven, I'm in heaven. . . ." And that is just the point that the apostle makes in the first part of verse 3. There he reminds us the blessings of Christ not only involve being in union with Christ but, through that union, being in heaven with Christ.

Paul says that God "has blessed us [past tense] in the heavenly realms with every spiritual blessing" (Eph. 1:3). Does that mean that God is in the heavenly realms—up there—blessing us down here? Yes, but it means more also. Paul will later remind us with these same words that God raised Jesus "from the dead and seated him at his right hand in the heavenly realms" (Eph. 1:20). Jesus is in the heavenly realms; believers are united to him. So where are we? It is clear: we are also blessed with every spiritual blessing in the heavenly realms.[4] This is precisely what Paul says in the following chapter:

4. The Greek literally reads "in/among the heavenly." The adjective "heavenly" here is either masculine (implying "among the heavenly beings") or neuter (implying "in the heavenly realms"). The latter is more likely, given the positional nature of the phrase in Ephesians 1:20 and 2:6 (where Jesus is seated),

"God raised [past tense] us up with Christ and seated [past tense] us with him in the heavenly realms in Christ Jesus" (Eph. 2:6).[5]

Because we are in union with Christ, who is in heaven, then we are in heaven with God. The apostle urges praise for God not so much because the Father is in heaven blessing us, as because we are there with him being blessed by him. As hell is total, conscious separation from the blessings of God, so the spiritual dimension of heaven is total and conscious union with God. In our union with Christ, we are already partakers of this spiritual reality, even though it is not fully realized until we are in our glorified state freed of our mortal bodies and the constraints of our temporal existence. This means we are already experiencing aspects of heaven, although we are not yet there.

The benefits of this "already and not yet," Paul has already stated: grace and peace (Eph. 1:2). We face difficulty, danger, and the deceit of our own hearts, but heaven and all its benefits are already ours. The difference the "already and not yet" makes can be compared to an experience our family had some time ago. On our family vacations, we enjoy going to a cabin that adjoins a deep set of woods. At certain times of the year the woods are so dense that when we have been out hiking, it is difficult to find the path back to the cabin. As night closed in during one such hike, we knew that we would not be able to spot our regular landmarks. So we began to angle through the woods in the direction we thought the cabin was. It got darker and darker; no familiar landmarks came into view. The children assumed that we were lost. I kept a brave face, as if I knew where we were, but ultimately I turned around to tell them the real situation. But just as I turned, a light from the cabin caught my eye. In the dark and dense woods we had actually walked past the cabin, but seeing the light, I knew we were safe. We were not yet inside, but the light meant that we were already safe and secure. What was my reaction to being "home"? Relief, and peace.

It is a similar reaction that Paul intends for us. He does not promise that we will never have to walk through the dark and dense woods. Trials are still

---

as well as the way that spiritual beings (including evil ones) are also said to be "in the heavenly realms" in 3:10 and 6:12.

5. The English past tenses here (and in Eph. 1:3) represent Greek aorist verbs. While the aorist does not inevitably convey past time, here the very common past-referring "constative aorist" is implied (note that Jesus' resurrection and session were past events; see Eph. 1:20).

here, disease still comes, finances are still hard, jobs and relationships remain difficult, and next steps may remain uncertain, but in Christ we are already home. We do not have to worry that there will be no place for us or that our God will not receive us, because he has already united us to his household through his Son and included us in his purposes. This gives us the confidence to be courageous in the face of opposition whether inside or outside the church. We say with the psalmist, "The Lord is with me; I will not be afraid. What can man do to me?" (Ps. 118:6). Such confidence enables us to be less worried about the dollars and cents of a troubling bill, and more willing to consider how God is calling us to be faithful; less concerned with the wrath of a godless boss, and more willing to entrust ourselves to God's care. Because we have eternal security that the deprivations of this world cannot deny, we are able to stand for truth when peers demand compromise, or stand up to a child who claims that our discipline will erase his love for us. The reality of our heavenly status in Christ makes earthly challenges less intimidating even if they are not less real.

But what if we do not feel worthy of such honor, or capable of earning such blessing? What if we face the same trials and temptations as did the Ephesians?

Blessed with Christ's Status (1:4–5)

We should praise God not only because he has given us Christ's blessings; we should praise God because he gives us Christ's status. Spiritual blessings are ours because through our union with Christ, we have his sanctity and his sonship.

Christ's Sanctity (1:4)

The apostle says that God "chose us in him before the creation of the world to be holy and blameless in his sight" (Eph. 1:4). Paul's wording reveals God's purpose. God chose us to be "holy and blameless in his sight."[6] This dual description relates to us the tandem benefits of our union with Christ in terms of our sanctification before God. We have something *removed* from us and something *supplied.*

6. See also Eph. 5:27; Col. 1:22; cf. Phil. 2:15.

By virtue of our union with Christ we have our blame *removed*. What shames us and justly condemns us is not held against us any longer. As Christ is without spot, so also we are "blemishless"[7] (the origin of the word "blameless") by virtue of his work in our behalf.[8] Paul will explain this process later in the chapter, but for now he identifies the results of the Savior's work: our guilt and shame are taken away; we are made blameless.

The effects of shame and blame can be amazingly real and long-lasting. Recently a pastor confided that he discovered that he was great at doing funerals—but he added a strange confession. He said, "I have a knack for being able to distill the character of a person and tie it to the gospel, but I hate visiting the family afterwards. The visit cannot be scripted, and I know that I run the risk of looking bad. This discovery made me realize that I am more concerned with impressing people than helping them."

The discovery of his need to impress led the pastor to seek wise counsel. And in the course of the conversation with that confidant the pastor said, "The need to impress people became acute in my life after fourth grade. I was always the best student in class, but in fourth grade I got sick and missed material needed for a math quiz. I did poorly on the math quiz, and the teacher wrote my name on the blackboard as one who needed remedial work. When she wrote my name on the board, I got physically sick. My teacher had to take me home, thinking that I was ill, but the problem really was that I blamed myself for being unprepared, and I worked never to be so shamed again."

Life will not allow any of us to be free of shame. Our weaknesses, the world's uncertainties, and our sin, all have the potential to shame us before those in earth and heaven. But the glory of the gospel is that our heavenly Father has erased our names from the blackboard—the handwriting that was against us, he took away and nailed it to the cross (Col. 2:14). He no longer blames us for what shames us.

Not only does our union with Christ remove our blemishes; it also *supplies* his righteousness. We are "holy" and blameless before the Father. The righteousness that was Christ's through his perfect obedience is imputed to us. The holiness that God requires, he also supplies not by our works, but by our

7. Greek: *amōmous.*

8. "Blameless" was a category of purity employed to describe also the spotless lambs sacrificed in the Old Testament (e.g., Lev. 4:32), and thus "blameless" was applied by the apostolic church to Christ's sacrificial death (1 Peter 1:19).

union with his holy Son who shares with us his own status of holiness. This is cause for amazement: God sees me as being as holy as his own Son. Not only do I have my debt wiped away; I have the riches of Christ's righteousness applied to my account (see also 2 Cor. 5:21). God does not pay our debt and then leave us with a zero balance. Rather than have us destitute, he opens the vaults of heaven to give us the benefits of the storehouse of his grace made full by Christ's obedience. The Bible says, "He who did not spare his own Son, but gave him up for us all—how will he not also, along with him, graciously give us all things?" (Rom. 8:32). Having removed our sin, God also supplies whatever is needed out of his entire creation—present or future—to bless us in the best way possible with the riches of the righteousness of his Son. But we question, how could this be since we are so unworthy of such riches? The answer is that God not only gives us the benefits of Christ's sanctity, he also gives us the status of Christ's Sonship.

Christ's Sonship (1:5)

The Father "predestined us to be adopted as his sons through Jesus Christ, in accordance with his pleasure and will" (Eph. 1:5). This sentence explains the goal of God's predestination of us. It was God's will and pleasure to adopt us as members of his own family through the work of Jesus. We should not miss the remarkable statements of verses 2 and 3. First, we are told that grace and peace come from God *our* Father (Eph. 1:2), and then we are told to praise the God and Father of our Lord Jesus Christ. If God is the Father of Jesus and of me, then I am Christ's brother and also a son of the heavenly Father. Through no work of my own I have the status of my Lord Jesus, as a child of the Father. What this means is beautifully articulated in an account in theologian Robert Peterson's book on adoption. A woman named Lisa writes:

> Adoption is attractive to me because it is the perfect antidote to legalism. . . . [Legalism] was the driving force in my life. I kept trying to be good enough for God but despaired at how impossible the task was. At the very heart I was afraid of one thing. At some point I would do something terrible and consequently lose my salvation. Although the church I was raised in preached assurance of salvation, I often wondered if I believed it mostly because I wanted it to be true. The confusion came from the fact that although the churches I attended said they believed in the assurance of salvation, they preached a list

> of things one had to do to be a "good Christian." I got the feeling that if you failed in any of those areas you probably were not saved to begin with.
>
> The study of adoption has clarified the confusion I once felt. Adoption is a legal procedure which secures a child's identity in a new family. . . . God didn't choose to be our *foster* parent. We don't get kicked out of the family because of our behavior. We don't have to worry day to day whether or not we are good enough to be part of the family. In his infinite kindness, God made us a permanent part of his family. . . . Nothing can undo the legal procedure that binds me to Christ. He died to redeem me. He signed the adoption papers, so to speak, with his blood. Nothing can cancel the work he did for me. I am free from the fear of falling away. Hallelujah![9]

God loves us because we are in union with the Son that he loves. United to Christ, we are also adopted by the Father, and as such have all the rights, privileges, and affection that the Son of God himself receives from God. Adoption in the Roman world emphasized the rights and privileges of sonship, and the analogy to our spiritual lives was one of Paul's favorites (Rom. 8:15, 23; Gal. 4:5). In Paul's day the head of a family would adopt a son (often a grown man) in order to pass on the family name and inheritance. Note how the saints' inheritance is also important later in the opening chapter of Ephesians (1:11, 14; cf. 1:18).[10]

These blessings are truly amazing to our ears: Christ's sanctity and Sonship are ours. The status that he has before God, we have by virtue of our union with him. Because God makes provision for us to receive Christ's blessing and status, we have much reason to praise him.

BLESSED THROUGH CHRIST ALONE (1:5–6)

How do we get the blessings and status of Christ from the Father? Paul answers when he repeats his goal of having us praise the Father. "He

9. Robert A. Peterson, *Adopted by God: From Wayward Sinners to Cherished Children* (Phillipsburg, NJ: P&R, 2001), 76–78.

10. Paul also speaks of Israel as adopted by God (Rom. 9:4). Both the sonship of God's Old Testament people (e.g., Ex. 4:22; Isa. 1:2; Hos. 1:10) and Jesus' calling his followers sons of God (e.g., Matt. 5:9, 45; Luke 6:35) likely provided significant impetus for Paul's teaching about the sonship of God's new covenant people who are in Christ (e.g., Rom. 8:14–23; 9:26; Gal. 3:26; 4:4–7; 2 Cor. 6:16–18).

predestined us . . . through Jesus Christ, in accordance with his pleasure and will—to the praise of his glorious grace, which he has freely given us in the One he loves" (Eph. 1:5–6).

Salvation Comes without Human Cause at All (1:5)

How much do these blessings of grace cost? Paul says the blessings of salvation are "freely given," and what that really means is the primary message of this passage. God alone is to be praised for our salvation because it comes to us without any human cause.

Over and over in this passage Paul makes this point of divine cause alone: God chose us *in Christ* (Eph. 1:4), not because of anything *in us*. It was his choice to put us in union with his Son. In fact, human initiative seems to be purposely undercut when we also are told that God chose us before creation (Eph. 1:4). Before we could do anything of merit, God chose to love us (2 Tim. 1:9; Rom. 8:26–39, esp. 29–30, 33). And undercutting the prejudices of that day (and ours), going back before creation to identify the source of that love reveals that God chose before any national, family, or personal achievements would warrant his love (see also Rom. 16:13; Col. 3:12; 2 Tim. 2:10; Titus 1:1; 1 Thess. 1:4).

Some commentators debate whether the election in Ephesians 1:4–6 is corporate (a group is elected) or individual (each person is chosen). While a corporate dimension should not be ruled out, to insist that the election is merely corporate would be to overlook the way that the personal blessings of being "chosen" and "predestined" (Eph. 1:4–5) are part of the larger picture of spiritual blessings Paul describes in Ephesians 1:3–14; and these other spiritual blessings undoubtedly have individual dimensions (e.g., redemption, forgiveness, sealing of the Holy Spirit).[11]

Modern events may help us understand why God would reveal his everlasting love to believers in a place like Ephesus. Like all cities, Ephesus was full of wickedness, and the pervasive evil was as discouraging as it was tempting. The message of God's prevenient love must have been vital to this fledgling church that included supposedly "unworthy" Gentiles. I understood more of the vital nature of such love when I recently listened to a church planter

11. Concerning the plural pronouns in Ephesians 1:3–14, Peter T. O'Brien (*The Letter to the Ephesians* [Grand Rapids: Eerdmans, 1999]), rightly notes: "The plurals ('we', 'us') are common, not corporate."

describe his experience of planting a church in downtown New Orleans. The downtown church had only two intact families. The struggling congregation of forty people was facing the likelihood that fifteen of them would move away because they wanted to get out of the troubled city. Alcoholism is rampant in the community (he said that nursery school parties for his children have been hosted with kegs of beer available for adult attendees). The stranglehold of poverty grips generations. Corruption remains too common to be news. The last Fortune 500 company left town years ago—long before Hurricane Katrina ravaged what remained. The Christians in the city struggle to maintain any vision of God among them and any hope of change. Their situation should remind us of the seemingly hopeless plight of believers in Ephesus. Sensing that helplessness helps explain why Paul would seek to supply hope by writing of God's eternal and unchanging love. Were he writing today, it would be as though the lyrics of singer Dan Fogelberg were being addressed to the church:

> Longer than there've been fishes in the ocean,
> Higher than any bird ever flew,
> Longer than there've been stars up in the heavens,
> I've been in love with you. . . .

Wouldn't it make a difference to your heart, to your zeal, to know that God loved you forever, even when you as a church were wrestling to survive? The message of God's eternal and unwavering love for his church is as powerful an encouragement for struggling churches today as it was for the baby churches in Paul's day.

Paul uses the assurance of predestination to strengthen the church for her struggles against evil and discouragement. This perspective does not solve all our logical questions about predestination; however, understanding Paul's purpose helps us properly contextualize our presentation of this precious doctrine when we talk to others. Predestination was never meant to be a doctrinal club used to batter people into acknowledgments of God's sovereignty. Rather, the message of God's love preceding our accomplishments and outlasting our failures was meant to give us a profound sense of confidence and security in God's love so that we will not despair in situations of great difficulty, pain, and shame.

Salvation Comes through Divine Love Alone (1:6)

This relational focus is most clear where the word "predestination" is actually used. Paul wants us to understand that salvation comes through divine love alone. So he says that God predestined us to be adopted as his sons in accordance with *his* pleasure and will, not based on *our* pleasure and will (Eph. 1:5).

We have already heard this language of God choosing someone by divine will in the preceding verses introducing this letter.[12] There Paul said that he was an apostle of Jesus Christ according to the will of God (Eph. 1:1). What could be more obvious to this apostle formerly named Saul? He was going one direction to arrest and kill Christians with his heart and mind bent on hostility to Christ, when suddenly on the road to Damascus, Christ turned Paul around. Paul knows that it was not his own pleasure and will to become a light to the Gentiles. God did something in and to Paul that the apostle recognized was beyond his own desire or choosing. Now Paul turns this language of what made him Christ's apostle to what makes believers God's children.

Paul's turnabout reminds me of a winter when we had a sixteen-inch snow that kept us in the house for days. Finally, getting cabin fever, my wife and I ventured out in the snow in our vintage Ford Pinto. We tried to drive down the two-lane main street of our little town. The street had been plowed but still had a healthy topping of ice. I discovered one of the ice patches as we were heading north on the road. The car shuddered, and suddenly without any planning or effort on my part, we were traveling south in the other lane. My wife said, "What did you do?" I said, of course, "I didn't do anything." We went right on home. There was a force beyond my actions and intentions that sent us a way other than we had planned.

Think how often we hear the same sort of thing from those whom God has saved from deep sin. I think of the good friend of mine that God saved from a life of hard living and anger at the church. When he became a Christian, he wanted to stand in church and tell how God had saved him. But he was so new a Christian that he did not know what he was supposed to say. So,

12. The connection is even stronger in Greek since "predestined" is actually a participle adverbially connected to the verb "chose." This participle could convey purpose or causality, but more likely indicates means. How did God choose us? By predestining us unto adoption as sons through Jesus Christ.

in a speech laced with profanity, he said that it was a darn (but he didn't say darn) good thing that God had gotten a hold of him because he was on the sure road to hell. There were a few gasps in the congregation at the language that was used, but the really mature Christians were thrilled. They said to each other, "Look what God did. He plucked a brand from the fire and saved a man who obviously could not save himself because it was God's will and pleasure to do so. Isn't God's love great?"

This explanation of God's need to choose us because we cannot save ourselves, obviously does not answer questions about why some are plucked from spiritual danger and others are not. Those are hard questions, but Paul has not yet come to the point of addressing them in this letter. He is simply saying that God makes us his own and loves us, even though we know that we are not good enough and do not merit his affection. In fact, knowing that we are not good enough or able to save ourselves is one of the marks of God putting his Spirit in us. Salvation is not about earning; it is about grace. We need to know this so that when we fall short of God's love in our own eyes, we can remember that we never were God's because of what we did. God "graced us"[13] (v. 6, literally)[14]; we did not gain him by the merit of our doing, background, or choosing. "In love he predestined us to be adopted as his sons through Jesus Christ . . . to the praise of his glorious grace, which he has freely given [lit., 'graced'] us" (Eph. 1:4b–6).[15]

Paul is using the doctrine of predestination not to separate believers, not to instill pride in our being chosen, nor to vaunt any special knowledge of how God works, but simply to assure hard-pressed believers that God has loved them and does love them apart from any merit of their own. In other words, predestination is meant to bless believers' hearts. It is *not* meant for endless argument; it is *not* an excuse not to evangelize; it *is* our basis of comfort when we face the limitations of our actions, will, and choices. We make mistakes at times by making predestination the source of our pride (i.e., we have status others do not, we know something others do not, or we are superior theologians who don't dodge hard truths), rather than the basis for assuring the beleaguered who are wrestling with their sin and the

13. Greek: *echaritōsen hēmas*.

14. The Greek verb *charitoō* ("freely given") is clearly related to the noun for grace (*charis*).

15. The prepositional phrase "in love" can be read either as the conclusion to the clause in verse 4 (KJV, ASV) or as the beginning of the clause in verse 5 (NIV, NASB, RSV, ESV).

world's trials. To such God says, "I loved you before the world began, so don't doubt me now." Predestination is the heavenly Father's shout of eternal love that echoes in our songs of thankful praise as our strength is renewed by the assurance of his care. When predestination is properly taught, it accomplishes what Paul says is his goal: praise to God for his glorious grace and peace to his people (vv. 3, 6).

An alumnus of Covenant Seminary who has a special heart for evangelism related to me the account of a man who came to his office after attending a worship service. The man had actually been in the church for about six years, but he came after worship confessing that though he "knew" everything about the gospel, he was not a believer. In the pastor's office the man confessed that his greatest fear, and what had kept him from the faith, was his fear that he was not predestined. My pastor friend responded with great wisdom, "That is just like the Evil One to place something like that in your heart. He confounds us by putting what should be your last concern first. You are worried about predestination even though you are not a believer. Predestination is for those who already love Jesus to assure them that their failures do not destroy his love." This is plainly Paul's point as he writes to the saints in Ephesus. The pastor continued, "The goal of predestination is not to raise questions in unbelievers; it is to bring peace to believers. What you need in this moment is simply to respond in faith, to confess that you need Jesus and to love him. Later on God will confirm to your heart the wonder that he loved you first. Now just love him because he gave his Son for you."

Whether or not you agree that predestination is a subject more for saints than unbelievers, discerning the motive of Paul's writing reveals the wisdom of this pastor's comments. Before we answer all the questions of why some are predestined and not others, we need to discern why Paul spoke to these saints wrestling in such a difficult circumstance. God shouts to them, "I have loved you with an everlasting love; before the world was made, I called you my own. You are mine." No doubt you will continue wrestling with the logic of predestination, as everyone does from time to time; but the next time you are wrestling with sin, difficulty, or your own failure, may you hear this shout from heaven: "You always have been in my heart, no matter what happens. I have chosen to love you since before the world began. You are mine." Although such a shout may offend some, those who are children of the Father hear it as the greatest encouragement possible that brings grace and peace.

Our son did not make it past the first few rounds at the state tournament, so we went to the college, and there he won the scholarship. It was a head-spinning weekend. Yet, afterward, my son was able to say, "It's amazing, Dad. God had it all planned from the beginning." How good for my son to know that his heavenly Father had it all planned. We did not, and do not, know all the reasons why the events unfolded as they did, but knowing that the heavenly Father had it all planned from beginning to end gives us a sense of peace not only about those events but also about the unknown events ahead. As my son prepares to wrestle with other issues that are sure to come in his life, the knowledge that his heavenly Father is always there for him, is always in control, and always loves, is a wonderful source of grace and peace. We should praise God that in all the wrestling that he (and we) will do, the Father is still shouting:

> Longer than there've been fishes in the ocean,
> Higher than any bird ever flew,
> Longer than there've been stars up in the heavens,
> I've been in love with you.

3

The Son's Mission

Ephesians 1:7–10

And he made known to us the mystery of his will according to his good pleasure, which he purposed in Christ, to be put into effect when the times will have reached their fulfillment—to bring all things in heaven and on earth together under one head, even Christ.
(Eph. 1:9–10)

"You're in, you're out." During a recent National Public Radio interview, an author described his experience in a New York subway. A reasonably dressed, but apparently disturbed man walked through the crowd, pointing to individuals and addressing them with these words of choosing: "You're in, you're out." There was no apparent rhyme or reason to the choosing. One chosen to be "in" might be poorly or well dressed, black or white, male or female. Sometimes two or three in a row would be "in" and then abruptly someone else would be "out." "You're in, you're in, you're in . . . you're out." The crazed man making choices for no reason at all neared the author, whose heart involuntarily began to pound and his breath quickened in anticipation of the coming choice. It was silly. Apart from the potential danger of the crazed man, there was nothing to gain or to lose in being chosen. There was no competition to be won, no qualification to be met. Who cared if you were a loser in this game? The man came still closer, pointing a finger at young or old without distinction: "You're in, you're out." Finally he came to the author, pointed a finger at his chest and said, "You're in." The author said later that he could not help feeling a sort of euphoria. He was among the chosen. Chosen for what? He did not know. He knew it was senseless to be proud of being so chosen, but he couldn't help but feel that there was some privilege earned, some approval gained, or some reward deserved now that he was among the chosen. He felt special for being chosen, but at the same time he felt silly for appreciating such a distinction that had no apparent benefits.

The world must look at biblical Christians with some measure of bemusement, if not disdain, that we can appear so proud of being chosen. After all, if there is any truth in our message that God's love is unmerited, unearned, and unconditional, then our being chosen has nothing to do with our qualifying for it. The biblical message of God's choice should never inspire pride; it is supposed to stimulate gratitude and humility. And yet it is so easy to get caught up in theological pride about the correctness of our message that we can be tempted to act as though we deserve our predestination because we understand it so well. If we really understood at a heart level (as well as at an intellectual level) what predestination offers, our chests would not puff out in ecclesiastical pride; instead, our entire being would bow before God in deep humility and thankful service.

In the previous chapter we explored why the apostle Paul would present us with this difficult teaching about God's unmerited choosing of his elect. The answer was so that those who have no basis for hope in themselves or their situation will trust in God the Father's provision rather than their own. But you may remember that this was merely Paul's opening cause for praise. In this one long Greek sentence that is behind verses 2–14 in our English Bibles, there are three successive waves of praise. In verses 3, 6, and 14, Paul uses parallel words about God's praise to bracket the work of the Father, Son, and Holy Spirit in choosing us. We now turn to the second bracket where the work and benefits of the Son are described. The purpose here is not primarily to explain why predestination exists, but rather to show its benefits. Knowing that our salvation is from and to eternity is merely an abstraction for theological debate if there are not some benefits that affect our daily lives. What are the benefits that flow from predestination, and what response should they produce in us?

The Benefits of Reclamation (1:7–8)

Paul uses two key terms to speak of the work of God's beloved Son (v. 6) when we are united to (or "in") him (Eph. 1:7): redemption and remission (translated "forgiveness" in the NIV). Both contribute to the biblical concept of reclamation whereby something that has gone wrong is made right again.

Redemption—and Its Cause (1:7a)

The reclamation process Paul first describes is "redemption" (Eph. 1:7a). Redemption involves the payment of a ransom to reclaim something that has been taken away or is held captive. Sin (both our personal sin and the sin nature we inherited from Adam) takes away the righteousness God intended to characterize our lives and holds us hostage to Satan's purposes. Apart from Christ's provision, we would perpetually exist in a prison of guilt and shame. We cannot escape by our actions. They too are tainted by our sin. We have to be rescued from this sinful state by something outside ourselves. The price for our ransom from sin's captivity is the sacrifice of God's Son.[1] By the gift of his life, we are freed from our captivity to sin. Here, as elsewhere (e.g., Col. 1:20), this redemption clearly is tied to Christ's shed blood on the cross. Paul also emphasizes the redemptive nature of Jesus' "blood" in Romans 3:25; 5:9; and we honor this redeeming sacrifice in the sacrament of the Lord's Supper (1 Cor. 10:16; 11:25, 27).

We know the truths so well that it may be hard for them still to affect us as the apostle intends. We who were made in God's image, holy and privileged, through the fall of our first parents became slaves to sin and bound to its penalties forever. Yet God so loved us that he sent his own Son to die in our

1. Paul employs the concept of "redemption" elsewhere in this book (Eph. 1:14; 4:30). In this verse redemption is treated as a present possession, though in Ephesians 4:30 Christians look forward to a future day of redemption. This reminds us of the "now and not yet" reality of the Christian life. Other Pauline passages speaking of redemption include Romans 3:24; 8:23; 1 Corinthians 1:30; and Colossians 1:14. In the Old Testament the exodus formed a central paradigm for God's redeeming work (Ex. 6:6; 15:13).

behalf. We are purchased with a price, not with perishable things such as silver and gold, but with the precious blood of the Lord Jesus (1 Peter 1:18–19). With his blood the Lamb slain before the foundation of the world purchased persons for God from every tribe, and language, people and nation (Rev. 5:9; 13:8; and see Eph. 2:13).

Along a highway near St. Louis, a row of blossoming pear trees lines the border of a state prison. In the springtime all that highway drivers see is the appearance of beauty, but behind the blossoms are razor wire and imprisonment. We are to understand that this is the Bible's perspective on the condition of humankind. Each day we can put on the appearance that everything is fine, even beautiful, but behind the appearance is imprisonment to our sin nature from which release does not come except at the price of Christ's blood.

Remission—and Its Extent (1:7b–8)

There is an additional effect of this shed blood: forgiveness—or, more specifically, the remission of sins. When you remit something, you cancel a debt or remove a penalty. Because of Christ's death for us, we have no penalty to pay for our sins. In this passage the general term "sins" actually translates a word that could more literally be translated "trespasses." We trespass when we cross boundaries God has set for us to obey or veer off the path he has designed for our righteousness.[2] Because the blood of Christ also deals with our trespasses, we know that his blood redeems us not only from the original sinfulness of our human nature, but also from the guilt of our individual and daily transgressions. Every dimension of my sin—all my individual trespasses—was covered by the blood of my Savior.

Christ wants me to know how vast is the mercy that covers matters small and large. Helpful translators rightly note that this forgiveness is "in accord with," not *out of* the riches of, God's grace (Eph. 1:7c). The One who possesses the riches of the universe does not reach into his penny purse to provide a little grace to cover my sin. No, his grace is in accord with his vast riches. The

2. For *aphiēmi* with the meaning of cancel/pardon a debt, and its extension into divine forgiveness, see W. Bauer, W. F. Arndt, F. W. Gingrich, and F. W. Danker, *A Greek-English Lexicon of the New Testament* (Chicago: University of Chicago Press, 2000), s.v. Here Paul speaks of "trespasses" remitted, while the parallel passage in Colossians 1:14 speaks of "sins" remitted—testifying to the conceptual connectedness of the terms "sins" and "trespasses."

abundance of his heavenly goodness is raining down on me, immersing me, washing me, taking my sin away as far as the east is from the west, so that now, continually and forever, because I am united to Christ, I am clothed with the righteousness of God's own Son.

This redemption and remission are "lavished on us with all wisdom and understanding" (v. 8).[3] Commentators struggle over this phrase. Does God lavish on us "wisdom and understanding" (i.e., are the wisdom and understanding ours), or does he lavish us with grace through his wisdom and understanding?[4] I think that it is the latter. While wisdom and understanding (or insight) regarding himself and his ways are surely benefits that God grants to us when he redeems us, in this particular case he seems to be measuring the lavishness of his grace by saying that he grants it despite his insight into us. Think of that. In his wisdom he knows more about the nature and horror of my trespasses than I do—and he is wise enough to know what will be needed to compensate for my wrong. He understands that my trespasses will require the blood of his own Son to cancel my debt, and still he redeems me and remits my sin so that I have Christ's own righteousness to my credit.

This idea is exemplified in our friends who have adopted a child with fetal alcohol syndrome. They are wise enough to know that the background of this child will result in many problems. Enslaved to its birth nature, this child will tax them—they will pay as with blood for this child's future good. But, despite this insight, they offer themselves to one to whom they owe no obligation or debt. They simply give themselves to reclaim this child from the horror of her background, and the misdeeds of her present and future, purely for the good of this child. As our Savior gives himself to reclaim us, so they reflect his grace in their care of their daughter. This is truly rich.

Once I sensed a measure of the lavish richness of Christ's reclaiming blood in a phone call from a leader in our church. Though he was responsible for the spiritual oversight of others, he became enslaved to sexual sin. Cover-up

3. These two Greek words for "wisdom" and "understanding" are found together in several places in the Septuagint (4 Macc. 1:18; Prov. 1:2; 3:13, 19; 7:4; 8:1; 10:23; 16:16; Wis. 7:7; Sir. 1:4; 19:22; Jer. 10:12), though they are truly collocated only in Dan. 2:23. Here in Ephesians the distinction between the Greek terms is so slight as to make a hendiadys likely (i.e., both terms combine to form a single coherent concept).

4. This question is complicated by the fact that in context God both possesses wisdom (Eph. 3:10; cf. Rom. 11:33; Col. 2:3) and gives it to the church (Eph. 1:17; cf. esp. Col. 1:9; and also Col. 1:28; 3:16; 4:5).

lies further bound him in a web of deception which was eventually discovered and led to his discipline and departure from the church. He left very angry, but the Spirit was working in his heart. Years later he asked to enter a process of restoration. We allowed it with very strict conditions relating to confessing the sin, counseling, and accountability measures. He agreed to every condition. He even asked, "Dr. Chapell, is there anything else I should do, or anyone else I should tell, or anything you want from me?" How different were this tone and attitude from those of the one who had once hidden his sin and resisted discipline. He did all we asked and still wanted to know what else he could do to satisfy his debt. He was so changed. I told him as much. "Bill," I said, "you are so different. Why?" His reply reflected his knowledge of God's lavish mercy. He said, "I know now that I do not have to hide any of my sin. His blood paid my debt and canceled the wrong of my sins. Now a phrase from a Christian song has become the motto of my life: 'Jesus paid it all.' I can live free of guilt and shame because Jesus paid everything I owed."

My friend now wants to do more than anyone on earth requires. He is motivated by the love that reclaimed him through Christ's redemption and the remission of sins. The Lord has lavished such grace upon this man that he knows whatever has happened or will happen in this life, he remains God's beloved by Christ's provision.

The Benefits of Revelation (1:9)

How do we know that God has provided the benefits of redemption and remission? He has revealed them to us. The benefits of our reclamation would have no motivational effect on our heart if we did not know of them. Thus, in his wisdom God also grants us blessed revelation of his grace.

The Mystery of Revelation (1:9a)

The apostle says that God has "made known to us the mystery of his will" (Eph. 1:9a). In the New Testament a mystery is not so much characterized by complexity or intrigue, as by timing. A mystery is a truth once hidden that is now revealed (Rom. 11:25; Col. 1:26). It could not be seen before, but now it can. In Jewish literature a mystery is the secret plan of God that will become apparent at the end of the age. When Paul says that the mystery has been "made known," he signals to these people and to us that what the prophets and people of old had long anticipated has now been revealed. We are already in the latter days of biblical history. We are in the time of special privilege to know what others could only anticipate.

The Content of Revelation (1:9a)

What God has now revealed is "his will."[5] This is the content of the revelation. We know that God reclaims his people through the redemption and remission of sins purchased with the blood of the beloved. That was only foreshadowed in the past, but now the way to God has been revealed to us. There is more to what has been revealed of the mystery, as we will see, but even this degree of revelation shows how great are our privileges.

Always it was God's plan to deliver his people by the grace and power of his Son. But now we can see it. That is a great privilege. A friend of mine recently had surgery that has renewed his sight. He's a golfer and says, "It's wonderful. I can even see the dimples in the ball that I could not see before." The dimples had always been there, but were hidden by his lack of sight. Being made able to see something as insignificant as golf-ball dimples makes him feel whole again. How much better and more glorious we should feel when we see that God has made a provision for us to see the mystery of all ages prior to Christ despite the faults and fissures of sin in our lives.

The Condition of Revelation (1:9b)

What are the qualifications or conditions for receiving this revelation? There are none. The Bible says that God revealed this mystery to his people "according to his good pleasure" (Eph. 1:9b; cf. 1:5), and this good pleasure was purposed in Christ. These are amazing words. God revealed salvation to his people through the blood of his Son because it brings him pleasure. He delights to show mercy (Mic. 7:18). And there is no work or merit that is the condition of his doing this. He delights to show mercy to those who are undeserving. Why? What in us makes us worthy in his sight to receive this revelation? Nothing.

5. Viewing the genitive (mystery *of* his will) as objective or as a genitive of contents—both of which would have basically the same meaning here (indicating that the mystery revealed is God's will).

The Westminster Confession of Faith says that God is "without body, parts or passions" (2.1). People stumble over the word "passions" because they say, "Doesn't God hate sin? Doesn't God love his people? How can we say that he has no passions?" Our difficulty is that we substitute the word "emotions" for passions. The Confession's use of the term refers to outside control. God is not controlled by external forces. He is not even controlled by my goodness in deciding whether or not to show me mercy. That is an amazing feature of grace. If we were deciding who would get a special gift from us, how would we determine who would receive it? Would we evaluate the beauty of the persons, or how nice they are, or what they have done for us, or what they can do for us? God says that despite knowing that sin makes you impure before him, and that to cleanse you he would have to sacrifice his Son, and to equip you he would have to provide his Spirit, nonetheless it gives him pleasure to reveal to you the mystery of Jesus. When there was no goodness or ability in us, God loved us and enabled us to know his love. This too is a precious mystery that even a child can know.

Some time ago, my daughter found a tent worm crawling in our backyard. Tent worms destroy trees; they are brown and not very attractive as caterpillars go. Still, she got a collection jar to keep it. She put leaves and sticks inside to make it comfortable, and cried when we would not let her take it to church that evening. There was nothing special in that worm, but it brought her pleasure to care for it. If you do not like being compared to such a worm, then you are not fully prepared to take in the truth of this passage. As the hymn writer reminds us, it pleased God to wound the sacred head of Christ "for such a worm as I."[6] The mystery of the ages has been revealed to us without any good in us to merit it. Our privilege is all from his mercy.

The rich truth of God's unconditional mercy should humble us. Strangely the opposite effect can also occur. Once we know the truth, it is so easy to fall into doctrinal pride, to puff ourselves up with self-importance that we know what others do not. We can act as though the reason that God revealed his Son to us is that we were better qualified by our superior understanding. But if we really understood what God has done, we would realize that all that we understand is only his gift, and our having any knowledge of him has nothing

6. Isaac Watts, "Alas, and Did My Savior Bleed," 1707. For those who question this "worm theology," please understand that God does not want his redeemed people to feel like worms but to recognize the devastation of an existence without his mercy and care (see Job 25:6 and Isa. 41:14).

to do with us. Most of us must learn again and again to approach each other, as well as those who do know the mystery, with absolute humility: I know only because he let me know. I am no better than you, and yet I know his grace—so there is hope that you can know it, too, even if you feel that you do not qualify. I did not qualify either.

The Benefits of God's Rule (1:10)

The humility we experience in the light of the mystery of Christ produces additional fruit for his glory. By our humility we gain further insight into who is really in charge of all things. Thus, Paul speaks not only of God's reclamation and revelation, but also of his rule as a way of eliciting our praise for his grace.

He Will Unite All Things (1:10a)

The apostle says that it is the will of God at the time of the fulfillment of all things to bring together heaven and earth.[7] We will be with the angels and, because we are united to Christ our King, we will share his glory with them. This is an amazing thought. The inhabitants of heaven and earth and the domain of heaven and earth will be one. What we pray for in the Lord's Prayer will be done. The will of God will be as present here as there; saints and angels will exist together in glory (see Rev. 11:15). There will be a reunion of loved ones already with him and those of us who remain, and we will be co-inhabitants with beings whose glory we can scarcely imagine.

He Will Head All Things (1:10b)

This united kingdom will exist in submission to our Lord. All that God brings together will be "under one head, even Christ" (Eph. 1:10b). As I mentioned previously, as you enter the ruins of ancient Ephesus today, you will see the remnants of a statue depicting the Roman emperor Trajan with his foot on the globe of the world. Actually all that remains is the foot. His rule has long since ended and was never complete except in his dreams. But

7. The wording of this verse in Greek, "unto the administration of the fullness of times," emphasizes the temporal sovereignty of God, who has established a time for all time to be fulfilled under his management of creation. And the next phrase shows the sovereignty of God through the messianic rule over every place and people (whether earthly or heavenly), since all these things will be "summed up" in Christ.

the reality of Scripture is that one day every knee will bow and every tongue confess that Jesus Christ is Lord, and he will rule over all (Phil. 2:10–11). There will be no corner of the world or feature of heaven where his rule does not extend.

Why does God reveal to us this ultimate mystery of the culmination of all things? Because we are central to the plan. The plan to reveal the mystery to us was launched before the foundation of the world was laid (Eph. 1:4, 10); the fulfillment of the plan is at the culmination of the world; and the revelation of both has come to us now. We are at the center of the hourglass of the revealed purpose of God. Why? Because we are a part of the plan!

The purposes of God are our purpose. God's reclamation of, and revelation to, his people is not purposeless. As later verses will reveal, our life in Christ is to the praise of his glory because we are united to him whom all will glorify. Our destiny is integral to all that will come to pass, and we are to live in accord with that purpose now. What this means is that it is now our mission to live out the purposes of God, seeking to *unite* all things and to *submit* all to the lordship of Christ.

As we serve in Christ's kingdom, we are to be active reconcilers. We are to be working past our differences so that the unity provided by the gospel is present in our relationships. At a personal and family level this means we are to confess our sins to one another, to forgive one another, and to try to find ways to reconcile with those with whom we have differences—sustained animosity is never our option. At an institutional and church level this is why we are committed to racial reconciliation, newly committed to discovering the richness of cultural diversity in other nations and settings, and seeking to overcome socioeconomic barriers, political and educational differences, regional prejudices, and theological pride. We want to be what God has purposed in Christ. At every level this means that we seek to find ways to bridge differences, to overlook faults, and to confront weaknesses that limit our love. For we understand that if we cannot love the unlovely or desire reconciliation with those who have sinned against us, then we have no credibility in speaking the gospel to the world.

Not only is it our purpose to unite all things, but to submit all things to Christ's lordship. It is our purpose to be involved in redeeming the whole of life for the glory of Christ. We refuse to compartmentalize the secular away from the claims of Christ. As Abraham Kuyper said, "There is not one square inch of this world over which Jesus does not stand and say, 'This is mine, mine.'" Therefore we believe that the influence of the Savior is rightly expressed throughout culture in the arts, business, government, education, science, and all of society; and those who are united to him are to be salt and light for him in every place.

Since he is Lord of all—he is the ruler not only of culture but of cultures—Christians must be committed to seeing that all nations and peoples know his lordship. We must remind God's people of their obligation to unite all peoples in Christ through the proclamation of his kingdom of mercy.

This will not be easy. Uniting all and submitting all can sometimes seem to be competing priorities. Even in the church misunderstandings can divide and distract us. Such a misunderstanding led to my sin a few years ago. Some difficult events caused me to go to our church staff and say, "We need to be aware that some people have mistakenly voiced some concerns about our actions, but we also need to make sure that we respond lovingly. We cannot expect to advance the cause of our King of grace if we will not reflect his heart." That wasn't my sin. I then met with my fellow pastors and said, "We need to be aware of these concerns that are being voiced, but we also need to respond lovingly. We cannot expect to advance the cause of our King of grace if we will not reflect his heart." That still wasn't my sin. But later I went to our church board and said, "We need to be aware that some people have mistakenly made accusations about our actions, and these are the steps that I think we should take to protect ourselves." That was my sin. Did you notice something missing there? I forgot to tell the church board that God mandated our love.

As it turned out, the board was the one gathering of leaders where we debated and divided about what to do next. I do not think that I really perceived what had happened until later, when I thought back and realized my error. We got bogged down in seeking to advance God's kingdom when I forgot to insist that we seek unity in Christ and express love to others for his glory.

I confessed my error to the board. I reminded those leaders and myself that I do not have a right to seek to advance the kingdom without a commitment to seek to unite God's people. Love is not without the occasional need for confrontation as well as conciliation, but we may never move forward in God's purposes without the loving motive that God would make himself and his ways more evident among his people and in this world.

What truth should we take from these verses? We should now have a keen awareness of the redemption, remission, and revelation that are ours solely by the grace of God. Further, we should be so gripped by God's mercy toward us that we will delight to be proclaimers of his grace. And because it is his grace that we proclaim, we should recognize no barriers of cultural pride or personal animosity, but, rather, should take personal responsibility to express Christ's love and unity. In this way his kingdom will advance to others through us because his rule will already have begun in our heart.

4

The Spirit's Assurance

Ephesians 1:11–14

Having believed, you were marked in him with a seal, the promised Holy Spirit, who is a deposit guaranteeing our inheritance until the redemption of those who are God's possession—to the praise of his glory. (Eph. 1:13–14)

I am fighting mold. In the annual battle to clean and seal my deck against nature's elements, I have found that I cannot keep the wood-destroying mold from growing in the shaded areas of my deck. In past years, I have tried a variety of products that are supposed to kill the mold and seal the deck against its recurrence, but to no lasting effect. So I decided that I would have to devote some real effort to eradicating the problem. I took a day to power-wash every inch of that deck, and then went to the hardware store to get a chemical sealant. I told the store clerk that I wanted a sealant that would also get rid of mold and keep it from coming back.

"Have you prepared the deck?" he asked. "I power-washed it," I said proudly. "You're kidding," he said. "No," I replied. He said, "Don't you know that when you power-spray mold, you drive the spores deep into the wood where they can regenerate?"

"No, I didn't know that," I said.

The store expert said, "Now you have to put chemicals on the wood to kill the mold. Apply it in a strong enough concentration to kill the mold, but not so strong as to damage the wood. And leave it on long enough to kill the mold, but not so long that you bleach the wood. Remember also to let the chemical killer dry before you apply the sealant so that it will bond properly to the wood. But don't let the chemical killer dry too long, or the mold spores that haven't been fully killed will start to grow again. And make sure that you get a sealant with some color stain in it so that UV damage from the sun is blocked. But do not get a stain that is too dark or it will block out the sun that helps keep the mold in check."

By the time I got all of these instructions, there was one thing that I knew for sure: That mold was going to grow! I couldn't do everything that was needed to stop it. Even if I did everything right according to my understanding, I had no assurance that my understanding of the instructions was entirely correct.

Killing mold I discovered is a lot like trying to live the Christian life. We can do everything right as best we understand, and still we know that there are no guarantees that we can do all God requires. My weaknesses of understanding and will, the complications of life, and forces beyond my control keep perfect performance of God's will far distant. So, what confidence do I have that God will continue loving and securing me if I cannot do everything he requires? Our confidence, the apostle Paul says, should not be in our accomplishments but in God's character. To give us confidence of God's care, Paul points away from our accomplishments and to God's faithfulness through his Spirit's giftedness.

His Past Faithfulness (1:11–12)

The apostle says that "in him [Christ] we were also chosen" (Eph. 1:11a). Our first task is to determine the apostle's meaning for "we." The answer can be seen in the contrast that Paul is setting up for the Gentile Ephesians just a few verses later where he says, "You also were included in Christ" (Eph. 1:13). First, there is a "we," and then there is a "you." If the "you" refers to the Gentiles, then the "we" must refer to the Jews originally included in God's covenant with Israel. Paul makes this clear by applying the ancient designation of God's covenant people to the "we" who are "chosen" (or "heirs"). In this way, Paul distinguishes ethnic Jews from the Gentiles who later came into God's covenant by faith in Christ.[1] Paul makes this identification of the chosen Jews to underscore the nature of God's past faithfulness. By his covenant with the people of Israel, God reveals the beauty of his heart, his plan, and reasons for his praise that will all be powerful encouragements to the imperfect Ephesian believers.

God's Heart (1:11a)

"In him we were also chosen," says Paul (Eph. 1:11). The words echo what has already been said about all believers earlier in this long sentence: "[God] chose us in him" (Eph. 1:4).[2] Our tendency in English is simply to insert a form of the verb "to be" to make sense of this phrase, "God chose us (to be) in him." But the meaning is deeper and different than that. If we were chosen to be in him, then the focus is on the end of the process, or what results. And while that truth is present, the focus is more on the origin of God's choosing than its end results. Although the NIV offers the translation "chose" and "chosen" for the verbs in both verses 4 and 11, in actuality the words in Greek, while overlapping conceptually, are distinct. Here the Greek word (*eklērōthēmen*) indicates that "we are apportioned as an inheritance." The passive voice favors the notion that "we" are those who are made to be the inheritance rather than those who have obtained an inheritance. The apostle is making it clear that God's love is based on something in his heart rather than on anything that we would achieve or claim for ourselves—just as an heir does not inherit because of what he has gained but because of what his father gives.

The chosen people of Israel were not chosen because of anything in them. They were not more holy, more numerous, or more distinguished than any

1. The "you" clearly designates Gentiles in Ephesians 2:11 ("you who are Gentiles by birth") and 3:1 ("for the sake of you Gentiles"). Indeed the argument of 2:11–3:6 hinges on "you" constituting Gentile believers. This same contrast appears between the "you" of 2:1–2 and the "we" of 2:3. Here the "we" is identified as those who literally "hoped beforehand" (1:12, *proēlpikotas*); namely, those Jewish believers who either were waiting for God's redemption in Christ or who were the firstfruits of that redemption.

2. See the ASV and the commentators F. F. Bruce, *The Epistles to the Colossians, to Philemon, and to the Ephesians* (Grand Rapids: Eerdmans, 1984); Peter T. O'Brien, *The Letter to the Ephesians* (Grand Rapids: Eerdmans, 1999); and Harold Hoehner, *Ephesians* (Grand Rapids: Baker, 2002). For the opposing view see KJV, NASB, ESV.

other nation. Moses tells the people in Deuteronomy, "The Lord your God has chosen you out of all the peoples on the face of the earth to be his people, his treasured possession. The Lord did not set his affection on you and choose you because you were more numerous than other peoples, for you were the fewest" (Deut. 7:6–7); and, "It is not because of your righteousness or integrity that . . . the Lord your God is giving you this good land to possess, for you are a stiff-necked people. Remember this and never forget how you provoked the Lord your God to anger in the desert" (Deut. 9:5–7). As the Old Testament people of God were called God's inheritance (e.g., Deut. 4:20; 9:29; 32:8–9; Ps. 33:12; 1 Kings 8:51), so too his new covenant people are God's portion and inheritance (Eph. 1:18). This apportioning is according to God's own choice (he is the agent—implied in the passive verb—who apportions the inheritance), which is further emphasized by Paul when he discusses God's predestining purpose.

Why were the people to remember that their God loved them because of what was in his heart rather than what was in theirs? So that the people would "know therefore that the Lord your God is God" (Deut. 7:9). The concept of choosing, which sometimes raises questions about God's fairness, is actually being used here to comfort God's people. Paul wants everyone to remember that we are loved not because of what is in us but because of what is in God. The loving faithfulness of God that is revealed in Christ is the cause of our being his. The locus, or cause, of the covenant people being God's is moved from them to him; they are his because of what is in his heart.

God's Plan (1:11b)

Divine causation is emphasized in the words that follow the reminder of God's choosing. The covenant people were chosen "having been predestined according to the plan of him who works out everything in conformity with the purpose of his will" (Eph. 1:11b).[3] These words follow close on the heels of Paul's earlier statement that the will of God purposed in Christ is "to bring all things in heaven and on earth together under one head, even Christ" (Eph. 1:10). God plans to bring everything under his Son, and even now the Father

3. This reiterates much of the language from verses 5 and 9, emphasizing again God's predestination (also see Acts 4:28; Rom. 8:29–30; 1 Cor. 2:7), and that this predestination is according to God's purpose (and good pleasure) flowing from his own will.

is making everything work together for that purpose—everything! The scope of these words our humanity has not the capacity to contain.

One summer I took a group tour with a botanist through meadows in the shadows of the Rocky Mountains. In addition to showing us the marvelous colors of the wild flowers we so easily fail to notice, he also used a hand-held microscope to reveal the incredible design of violets, clover, and orchids at the cell level. And while these flower cells were whispering the glory of God, the mountains above us were at the same moment shouting his greatness. I was moved to awe in those moments by remembering that all things—as great as mountains and as small as flower cells—are being coordinated according to God's plan to bring glory to his Son as the head of all things.

God's Praise (1:12)

The specific design that God has for his people Paul identifies in the next words. Everything has been orchestrated so that "we, who were the first to hope in Christ, might be for the praise of his glory" (Eph. 1:12). This is a narrower "we" than the first "we." Out of all the nations, the Jews were chosen, so that out of them would be this "we," the first of Israel (i.e., early Christian Jews such as Paul) to believe in Jesus as the Messiah. What would be the result of God's designing all of world history, and all of Israel's history, so that these people of the covenant would be the first to bow the knee to Jesus? Praise, praise, praise at the amazing heart and plan of God.

In one of Tom Hanks's early movies, *Joe and the Volcano*, the hero played by Hanks goes through a number of incredible circumstances and trials that ultimately leave him adrift at sea on a raft. As he drifts he has much time to reflect on his losses, his mistakes, and his failures. In the expanse and emptiness of the sea, he despairs. Then, one night, in a delirium of exposure and dehydration, he awakes and looks at the stars. The spill of stars above his head somehow no longer looks random. In fact, looking like a child's dot-to-dot drawing book, the stars have all been connected in their constellations. Orion and Capricorn and the Pleiades are all drawn against the night sky. Hanks's character suddenly sees that there is an order and plan to the whole universe. His world is not random. He rises to his feet with this profound realization of purpose and, despite his dire circumstances, speaks to the heavens: "God, I thank you for my life. I did not know—you are so . . . big!"

It is a rather profound theology from a Hollywood comedy, yet when we see that the whole universe is put together with purpose—that even the trials and difficulties of our lives do not undermine God's ultimate plan—we also cannot help but praise him. Furthermore, our lives, in scope and detail, are part of his plan and, therefore, we are also included in the design that brings him praise. Even when we have failed, even when our sin is apparent like that of the stiff-necked people of Israel, the purposes of God do not go away. The lines of God connect the events of the past, the events of our lives, and the experiences of others, so that all might be to the praise of his glory.

But here we may seem to have assumed too much. We have applied to ourselves the promises that Paul is making to the covenant nation and to the first Jewish believers. He has not said that these promises apply to us—not yet. For the apostle will next make it clear that God assures us of his continuing care not merely through his past faithfulness to faithless people like the Jews, but also through his present faithfulness to weak people like us who seek his strength.

His Present Faithfulness (1:13)

After recounting God's purpose for "we [Jews] who were the first to hope in Christ," the apostle speaks to the Ephesian Gentiles and says, "And you also were included in Christ" (Eph. 1:13). Whereas the earlier portion of this passage was the "we who . . ." section, this is the "you, too" section.

Expanding His Covenant (1:13a)

"In Christ" we were chosen and you, too, were included, says the apostle. The plan that was worked through the Jews to glorify Christ has now been extended to other nations. In the Greek both verses 11 (focusing on Jewish believers) and 13 (focusing on Gentile believers) begin the same way: "In him also." Both Jew and Gentile are found to be "in Christ" (also see Eph. 1:12). This says much about how Paul conceived of the nature of salvation, of the Christian life, and of the covenantal promises to the Jewish nation extended to the Gentiles. This co-inclusion in Christ also serves as a theological basis for Paul's argument that Jews and Gentiles now are fellow members of the body of Christ (see Eph. 2:13–22).

The plan "to bring all things . . . together under one head, even Christ" (Eph. 1:10) is being worked out in this present age. This is Paul's reason for using the continuing present tense to say that God "works out everything in conformity with the purpose of his will" (Eph. 1:11). God's plan is for the present age, our time. We who hear the gospel now are as much in God's purpose of bringing praise to Christ as were the Jews. From the beginning God purposed to work everything together in order to bring all things under the headship of Christ. This includes past and present, heaven and earth, Jew and Gentile (as is stated more explicitly in Eph. 3:6).

Extending His Mercy (1:13b)

God's involvement of "all things" in his plan is more than an expansion of the covenant; it is an extension of mercy. What did the Jews do to be the chosen people? Nothing. God's blessing was based in his mercy, not on their merit. And what do Gentiles now have to do to qualify for this mercy and be granted the same privileged status as the covenant people?

Will Gentiles have to swim seven seas, perform feats of great sacrifice, or read a hundred books? No. The apostle's language is very precise. "You also were included in Christ when you heard the word of truth, the gospel of your salvation" (Eph. 1:13). The Gentiles' inclusion does not even rest on their doing what the Jews were supposed to do. But simply hearing—actually having the ears to hear and really hearing—the gospel marked these Gentiles as those included in the covenant. Note that they could not have heard spiritually, if God had not already worked in their hearts and tuned them to receive his Word (John 6:44, 65). Truly hearing the message of God's mercy was itself a sign of inclusion in the covenant before anything else had been, or could be, done.

This unconditional covenant inclusion is a great mercy. The greatness can be comprehended only by remembering the pagan context of the Ephesians' world. Human pride, false morality, and deceitful idolatry all thrived in Ephesus. For God to call people from this place his own before they had done anything to qualify for his love is a sign of great grace—of God's willingness to be faithful in the face of great human frailty and sin. And thus, just as Paul can say that it was for "the praise of his [God's] glory" that those who first believed were from the Jews, the least distinguished of the peoples of the world (Eph. 1:12), so also when Paul concludes his thought about the

Ephesians, he says that their inclusion in Christ is likewise to the praise of God's glory (Eph. 1:14). Christ is glorified both because more persons are subject to him and also because his caring for them signals the wonders of his mercy.

There are many ways that these truths apply to us. First, there is the *big picture*: if we are included in Christ, then we are part of the eternal plan that began with the covenant people of old. All things are being worked out so that we, too, will be for the praise of his glory. Everything is being worked out for our good and his glory.

Second, there is a *big mercy*. More are being included who do not get everything right. We are part of the big picture because of God's mercy, not our merit. Our accomplishments would never qualify us for his mercy. There are forces greater than we that are at work throughout history, and presently, to make us God's own. Our salvation could never be dependent on our getting everything right—not yesterday, not today, not ever.

Third, we are part of the *big plan* to make everything right. There is a type of Calvinism that so emphasizes God's sovereign eternal plan that it virtually shuts out any role of human participation in the spread of the gospel. But when we properly understand what the apostle says here, we are compelled to put our lives in God's service for the sake of the gospel. We are instruments of his glory, not mere observers of his sovereignty.

When Calvin preached in Geneva, he did not push merely for doctrinal understanding. Visit his church and you can still learn how the great expounder of God's sovereignty welcomed people from all over the world, and then prepared them to gush forth from Geneva to take the gospel to others. Where confidence in the sovereign working of God was greatest, there were the greatest delight and zeal to participate in God's plan.

Paul says that the Jews were chosen in order that they might be to the praise of God's glory, and that when those who first believed from among the Jews told others, they might help fulfill God's plan to bring all things under Christ. God's people can be a part of extending God's mercy and glory. Those who have apprehended how great is the mercy of God desire that his glory spread, and they recognize that God uses human means to do this. Those most aware of the eternal plan are those most anxious to be a part of it, because they know that their efforts are not futile and even their failures are not determinative of God's final intentions. God will still use people who believe that they are part of his design to bring glory to his Son—and who know that his design will prevail.

I am always chasing rainbows. When a rainbow appears in the sky, I will run for a camera as well as whatever family member or pet I can get to pose in the picture. The beautiful colors, the contrast of darkening rain and glistening sun, the wonder of light in nature's prism, the reminder of God's mercy and covenant—all call to me to pay attention and relish the glory of God's design. But my ability fully to appreciate the glory is always incomplete. Because of the way that rainbows are formed I will never see a complete rainbow from the ground. You may be thinking that you have seen a complete rainbow because you have seen either all its colors or a complete arc that touches the ground on both sides. But from the ground you have not seen a complete rainbow. Because of the sheering effect of the rain and the angle of the sun, a person beneath the rainbow cannot see all of God's design where the legs come together and the rainbow is a complete circle. As long as our view is from the ground, earth gets in the way and we never see God's complete design.

Yet, you can see a complete rainbow. I have. If you get above the earth in a plane or on a mountaintop, when the sun is just at the right angle, you can see the whole rainbow, the full circle—the completeness of God's design. When earth does not get in the way, you can see all of God's design.

In this portion of Scripture, Paul moves earth aside so that we can see God's entire plan. He lifts us above earthly perspectives and lets us see our lives from the perspective of heaven. There we see the whole design of human history. We are raised above the limitations of our sin and finitude so we will see that from the beginning God chose to love us. He made a people for his very own and promised that from them would come those who would believe in Christ. These would be his instruments for telling others, so that all the world would come together in praise of his glory. And just as it was from the beginning, so it is now: all things are being worked together in conformity with Christ's purpose so that by his mercy all is to the praise of his glory.

The Bible's claim of divine purpose in all things puts Christians at odds with differing earthly viewpoints. First, it puts us at odds with the secular world. We do not accept the premises of the secular scientist at the university who refuses to let students use language of purpose and design in describing the world around us. Everything is part of God's design—not random, not developed by chance, but divinely designed.

Second, a heavenly perspective puts us at odds with much in our personal world. Our limited and finite perspective does not always confirm divine purpose for us. We question and doubt God's design because the things of earth get in the way: our troubles, our questions, our sin—yes, even our pain and suffering. How can they fit into his purpose? It is so hard to see divine designs when your child is ill, when the church seems troubled by needless debate, when you are struggling to hold a family together, or simply to make financial ends meet. Yet when our eyes see the full rainbow in Scripture—the completeness of God's plan—and know by faith that our lives are a part of God's design no matter what happens, then we can take whatever comes because we know that *we are for the praise of his glory.*

Our hearts naturally and understandably question, "Is there really purpose in all of this?" The apostle answers by taking us to heaven's heights to let us see from God's perspective the complete picture of his working all things together for Christ's glory and our good through no merit of our own. From the beginning he made a world good and to his glory. But then, like a balloon punctured and deflated, the glory was left in crumpled remains of human misery and earthly corruption by the fall of Adam. But ever since, according to the nature that is in him, the Lord has been following a predetermined plan to refill the balloon with his mercy, ever expanding and extending the balloon to its original glory. First, the mercy was extended to a chosen people through no merit of their own. From them came those who were the first to believe in Christ, and they carried the message of mercy to other nations who now also are included in the plan of mercy until the expansion of the kingdom purposes of God are fulfilled.

Paul writes this epistle so that we would grasp that such a vast, intricate, and, at the same time, intimate plan is true and applies to us. What a difference it makes in my life and yours when we believe that the trials as well as the accomplishments, the difficulties as well as the joys, are not simply the products of brute forces in the universe but actually are all part of God's eternal plan for his glory and our good. Do we have any assurance that such astounding truths do apply to us? Yes. Our assurance of God's abiding care rests not only in his past and present promises, but also in his Spirit's faithfulness.

His Spirit's Faithfulness (1:13c–14)

Paul says to the Ephesians, "You were marked in him with a seal, the promised Holy Spirit, who is the deposit guaranteeing our inheritance until the redemption of those who are God's possession—to the praise of his glory" (vv. 13b–14). Those who are part of God's redemptive plan are marked with a seal that guarantees their receiving the full rights of God's heirs in a kingdom redeemed and made right.

The "inheritance" concept is found elsewhere in Paul's prison epistles (Eph. 5:5; Col. 1:12; 3:24) and in his speeches in Acts (20:32; 26:18). This is an important continuity. Jesus spoke of the inheritance of the kingdom and of eternal life (Matt. 19:29; 25:34), and his followers continued this expression (1 Cor. 6:9–10; 15:50; Gal. 5:21; Heb. 1:14; 9:15; 1 Peter 1:4). But Jesus' words do not originate the concept. The Old Testament people were also promised an inheritance from God. Now, as God's people, this inheritance is "ours," but we are not the sole recipients of blessing. God also has his own inheritance in the saints (Eph. 1:18; and see comments on verse 11 above).

The "seal" image that Paul is calling to mind is that of the wax that was affixed to an official document whose promises are guaranteed because of the authority of the one who marked the seal with a signet ring. The sign was the guarantee that what was promised would be fulfilled for those to whom it was promised.

But Paul is not ending the imagery there. The Holy Spirit is not just a mark of God that we are his possession; the Spirit also is a deposit guaranteeing the redemption that is to come.[4] This deposit is similar to a down payment on a house that secures your position as the buyer, or the first fruits of a crop that indicate that the rest of the harvest is coming.[5] The Spirit is the first evidence of the full grandeur of God's completed purpose in our lives.

4. Commentators debate whether the Greek phrase "unto the redemption of the possession" refers to God's possession (as in the NIV) or to the believers' possession (cf. a similar issue in 2 Thess. 2:14). The former is more likely given that God is the one who typically "redeems," and that there is a long Jewish tradition of God's people being called his possession (Ex. 19:5; Deut. 14:2; 26:18; and especially, using this same Greek word, Mal. 3:17 [Septuagint]; 1 Peter 2:9).

5. See also 2 Corinthians 1:22; 5:5. The Greek word for "deposit" is a Semitic loanword known in Greek translations from Old Testament Hebrew (Gen. 38:17–20), where it constitutes a pledge that a promised payment would come. See W. Bauer, W. F. Arndt, F. W. Gingrich, and F. W. Danker, *A Greek-English Lexicon of the New Testament* (Chicago: University of Chicago Press, 2000), s.v. *arrabōn*.

It all sounds so great. The Spirit marks us as God's own and serves as the guarantee of God's purpose for our lives. But does this satisfy all of our questions? No. We want to know how the Spirit marks us. What are the evidences of the deposit to assure us that God's plan applies to us? The answer lies in the portion of the text not yet addressed: "And you also were included in Christ, when you heard the word of truth, the gospel of your salvation. Having believed, you were marked in him with a seal, the promised Holy Spirit" (Eph. 1:13).

It is important to remember that in the original language (despite the periods in our English versions) this portion of our text is part of one long sentence that extends beyond this verse. If this sentence structure is forgotten, then one is likely to create a time sequence for this verse that reflects our preconceptions rather than what the words actually say. If one's preconception is that some special expression of the Holy Spirit, such as charismatic gifts, will arrive in a second blessing weeks or even years after conversion, then the words might be read this way: "You were included in Christ, when you heard the word of truth, the gospel of your salvation. Having believed that, then *at a later time* you were marked in him with a seal, the promised Holy Spirit."

But what if the words are put as close together in time as the Greek sentence places the terms? Then the words do not indicate so much a separation of time as a sequence of logic. In this case, the words would be read this way: "You were included in Christ, when you heard the word of truth, the gospel of your salvation. Having believed that, then you were *at that time* marked in him with a seal, the promised Holy Spirit." In this case, the proof of the presence of the Holy Spirit is not indicated by a distant expression of extraordinary charismatic gifts, but rather the immediate fact that God has brought the person to saving faith. Belief itself indicates the presence of the seal (mark) of the Spirit of God that guarantees we are God's children because without the Spirit we could not and would not believe (Rom. 8:6–9; 1 Cor. 2:14).[6]

6. In verse 13, the main verb ("you were sealed") is preceded by two participles ("having heard" and "having believed"). The parallel nature and similar tense of the participles, and the fact that both participles precede the main verb would imply that both participles should be taken to have the same grammatical import. If the first is taken to be temporal ("after having heard"), then so should the second ("after having believed"). As to the grammatical reason for their preceding "you were sealed," most commentators argue either that (1) aorist participles precede the main verb in time, or (2) participles

We fail to recognize belief as the indication of the seal of the Spirit when we fail to remember how supernatural is the gift of our faith. The gospel says you are a sinner, and Jesus, the Lord of all and Lamb of God, died for your sins. *The world doesn't believe that.* The gospel says that even when you are faithless, the faithful God has forgiven your past, laid claim on your life, and secured your future. *The world doesn't believe that.* The gospel says that though you were dead in your trespasses and sins, Christ died for you, rose from the dead as the victor over your sins, gives purpose to your life now, and is coming to claim you eternally. *The world cannot believe that.* Not until the Holy Spirit comes and supernaturally changes a heart can anyone believe the truths of the gospel. Thus, says the apostle, your believing is the evidence that the Holy Spirit is in you.

The Holy Spirit who has already enabled you to taste the sweetness of God in the gospel of your salvation is giving you a foretaste of the glory that awaits you, guaranteed by his mark of belief in you. Already by the Holy Spirit's using the gospel, your spiritual world has been turned upside down and made new. Your belief is the proof that the Bible speaks truth when it says that you are a new creation. In addition, this testimony of God's Spirit in your heart affirms that what the Bible says about God's work throughout creation can be trusted. The Bible says the entire creation is being conformed to God's purposes and for his glory. Because we have witnessed the re-creating work of God in our hearts, we are able to trust that what the Bible says about God's ultimate renewal of all things is also true.

These are precious truths that give meaning, purpose, and courage to our lives. I can know that nothing in my life is without purpose because I believe that the Savior died for me and now, as my risen Lord, he lives in me by his Spirit so that my life will be used for his glory. Such belief is itself the evidence (and guarantee) of the Spirit's presence in my life and God's purpose for my life. God has a purpose for me in all my weakness, frailty, sin, and fear. Does Paul say this because he does not understand the real challenges that we face? He is claiming that we can know everything will work out for

---

which come in the text before the main verb precede the main verb in time. Thus hearing and believing happen before being sealed. The seal is not the cause of belief, but belief demonstrates the presence of the seal. Good commentators differ on specifics, but all agree that the language shows that all believers have been sealed with the Holy Spirit (the language does not necessitate a later charismatic experience). Those who believe the gospel have the assurance of the Holy Spirit's work in them and of the inheritance he guarantees.

God's glory and our good simply because of the evidence of our belief as the Holy Spirit's claim upon us. Does Paul live in the real world? Yes, he writes this letter while under Roman guard and awaiting trial. He knows the real world. And because he believes the gospel, he believes that even his suffering is part of God's purpose of spreading the message of his faithfulness past and present until all of God's precious people are gathered in to the glory of his name.

Because our weakness before the world outside of us, and our sin caused by the world inside of us, are so evident, we need the blessed assurance that our lives are not fruitless and that what we fail to achieve is not disqualifying of God's love. Ultimately our confidence has to turn away from anything that we would offer and, instead, toward the faithfulness of our God that is confirmed by his Spirit's work in us. Without these assurances the things that we must face until Christ comes again would be unbearable. But with the assurance that his purposes are secure and that we are in that plan, we can face whatever he calls us to endure and be secure even when our weaknesses are apparent.

A friend of mine recently shared that the high school graduation of his son Robby was filling the family with "new degrees of terror." The reason for the terror was that Robby was born with multiple mental and physical handicaps. Once school was over, much of the government support for Robby would disappear, and it was not clear how the family would take care of him.

Robby was on my mind when, a few days later, the pastor of my church was pronouncing that Sunday's benediction—the promise of God to give his blessing to his covenant people. As our pastor finished the benediction, a slurred voice rose in the back of the sanctuary and joined him in saying the final, oft-repeated words: ". . . to our God is the power and authority, now and forever, amen." It was Robby, who, from his wheelchair, was testifying of the power and sovereignty of his God—past, present, and forever.

How could Robby believe such things, and how could his parents? His suffering and their anguish have been so great. There is little on this earth that would confirm the truth of the words he repeated. Only faith affirms that Robby's hope is not in vain. But such faith rises above the earth and sees all things from God's perspective. There he shows himself to be the God of all power who is able to conform all things to his purposes. There he promises that every valley shall be lifted, every injustice will be made right, every tear will be wiped away, hearts will be healed, bodies will be made whole, and all that now happens will lead us and others to an eternity of these blessings with our Savior. The weakest of vessels and the vilest of sinners are part of this eternal plan, as are all who believe in him. How do you know that you are included? Because you believe in him and, having believed, you have the testimony of his Spirit in your heart that he is able to bring all things together for his glory and your good.

The universe of your soul is already different, and this is the work of the Holy Spirit. He is the deposit of God of the full redemption that is ahead, given to assure you that what you face is not without purpose and what you most cherish is not in jeopardy. Neither is in your hands. Rather, all is in the hands of the wonderful God who called and made you his own out of his mercy alone. Even when you cannot do everything right, even when things seem all wrong, you are all right with God because he who chose you is working out everything in conformity with the purpose of his will, to the praise of his glory.

5

The Church Triumphant

Ephesians 1:15–23

And God placed all things under his feet and appointed him to be head over everything for the church, which is his body, the fullness of him who fills everything in every way. (Eph. 1:22–23)

ow do you follow a record-setting sentence? The apostle Paul has just poured 203 words into a single sentence that extols the eternal love of God the Father, Son, and Holy Spirit. How will he follow that? He will explain why he was so concerned that the Ephesians, and we, know of that love. With words no less beautiful than those already expressed, the apostle now uses the foundation of the eternal love of God to embrace the church and, as a father would send a child made secure by such approval into the challenges of adulthood, to commission the church to her grand purpose.

The importance of having a clear purpose was emphasized during a restricted meeting of our church. There a leader reported to us on the secret work of a missionary we support. The lifelong missionary serves in a country that persecutes Christians. Those who gathered to hear of his work were taken into the confidence of the missionary and were cautioned not to use his name or identify the country where he serves, lest his efforts and his life be endangered. As the report of personal courage and sacrifice unfolded, those present were overwhelmed with the profound commitment of this missionary and his family. Yet, though that kind of personal zeal is compelling, it is not a rare story in evangelical churches. Uncommon valor in special individuals is a common story we share to encourage and inspire one another.

What struck me as more unusual was the infectious nature of this missionary's zeal. We were made witness not only to the personal courage of this remarkable man, but also to the stunning willingness of ordinary Christians in his country to worship with him. The commitment of those ordinary Christians was made plain when the missionary described how his church conducted worship that their national government forbids. The church rents a tour bus, drives to a remote highway, parks the bus, posts watchmen down the road in both directions, and then conducts services on the bus.

It is clear to us why the missionary is there—his occupation and calling require him to be there. But why are the other people there? They could read the Bible without gathering. They could worship as individual families without great risk. Certainly they could pray on their own. Christians are not required to gather in groups to get God's attention. So what compels these ordinary Christians, and millions more like them throughout the world, to risk everything to gather in Christ's name?

If social convention, political leverage, and personal advancement are insufficient motives in this culture, and nonexistent motives in non-Christian cultures, then what rightly motivates God's people to gather for his purposes? The answer is evident in Paul's words from prison to his spiritual children in Ephesus. His own trials speak clearly of the risks, dangers, and sacrifices that may be required of those gathering in Christ's name. But his words speak even more powerfully of the forces that compel God's people to seek him corporately. What compels God's people to gather together as a church?

Spiritual Support (1:15–16)

Despite the secularism and materialism of our culture, there is a deep longing for spiritual support. How we Christian leaders express this spiritual support was a particularly important question for many Manhattan churches that burgeoned with new attendees immediately after the September 11 tragedy. Sadly the question was apparently not well answered by many churches. They returned to normal attendance in a few weeks. One downtown pastor, Tim Keller, whose church remained at capacity long after the tragedy, offered a simple explanation: "If you were not ready to offer spiritual support before the tragedy, trying to organize the church to offer such care after the tragedy was too late." So what does meaningful spiritual support include? Key dimensions appear in the words of the apostle to the Ephesians as he speaks of both his thanksgiving and intercession for them.

Thanksgiving (1:15–16a)

The *cause* for Paul's thanks is the Ephesians' faith and love (Eph. 1:15). The object of their faith is the "Lord Jesus" (Eph. 1:15a). The object of their love is all the saints (Eph. 1:15b).[1] Their faith in Jesus *separates* them from the surrounding idolatrous culture of paganism and multiple gods. Their love for all the saints *unites* them to each other in the midst of that culture. Commending the Ephesians for what both separates and unites them reveals Paul's wonderful pastoral gifts as well as what draws the Ephesians to a corporate life in Christ.

Paul first commends the Ephesians for their faith in Jesus, which means relying on his provision and living for his glory in the midst of a sinful and self-serving culture. Are the Ephesians doing this perfectly? No. While there have been healthy faith commitments, Paul must later remind the Ephesians that their salvation is by God's grace and not by their works (Eph. 2:8–9). The apostle also commends the Ephesians for loving all the saints without discrimination or resentment. Are they doing this perfectly? No. Much of the remainder of this book will be Paul's exhortation to the church to overcome the barriers to its unity, to "keep the unity of the Spirit through the bond of peace" (Eph. 4:3).

Is Paul, then, being dishonest or disingenuous in giving thanks for the Ephesians' faith and love when we know that these are hardly complete in

1. Paul often opens his letters with a thanksgiving for the believers (Rom. 1:8–10; 1 Cor. 1:4–9; Phil. 1:3–8; 1 Thess. 1:2–10; 2 Thess. 1:3–10; 2 Tim. 1:3–7). This opening thanksgiving has particularly strong similarities to the ones in Colossians (1:3–8) and Philemon (4–7). Several early manuscripts of Ephesians are missing the words "your love" (contrast Col. 1:4 and note that this would be the more difficult reading); if this omission were followed, it would imply that their faith in the Lord Jesus is also a shared fidelity among all the saints.

them? No, Paul is simply demonstrating the faith he commends. By giving thanks for the good in others he knows to be imperfect, Paul indicates that, with his eyes of faith, he sees them robed in Christ's righteousness. Further, he is giving us wonderful pastoral instruction on how we can offer spiritual support to God's people. We give thanks for the fruit of the Spirit that we can see, even when we know that it has yet to ripen. As the farmer gives thanks for the nubbin of corn long before the ear is full, so leaders in the church commend the good that we can see in God's people, knowing that there is much growth still needed. Paul tells the Ephesians that he thanks God for what is incomplete in them in order to mature and unite them.

Learning the pastoral art of commendation is important for all Christian leaders who desire to form churches of spiritual support. It takes no special skill to see what is wrong with people, and to criticize them. But to see people robed in a righteousness not their own and to encourage them on this basis to be more of what they should be powerfully communicates the heart of Christ. The best leaders are those who develop the ability to see the good that is sprouting in people and water its growth with commendation, even when it is obvious to the leader (and perhaps to everyone else in the church) that more growth is needed. We provide spiritual support by commending others for the good we can see despite the growth that they still need.

Even though I have been a church leader for many years, I feel as though I am just now learning the power of commendation and thanks. But I find that I am not alone. I recently listened to the confession of a church leader whose occupation involves teaching businesses how to encourage their workers. For twenty years he has taught that the five most important words for building morale are, "I am proud of you." But upon some recent reflection, he recognized that he had not said these words to his own son in many years. "I have not supported my son as Christ supports me," he said. He immediately scheduled a dinner with his son to offer the commendation that had so long been lacking, and immediately the father and son renewed a bond that had been tenuous for years. All church leaders must similarly realize that God's children come to the church—the family of God—for spiritual support. Saying to them, "I am thankful for you," is powerful spiritual work, and "not stopping" in doing it as the apostle says (Eph. 1:16a) deepens our bonds with one another and with Christ in ways that are truly powerful.

How does commendation work in the life of the church? Consider, for instance, how we might make a cold church warm toward outsiders. Will it help more for us to criticize our people for their coldness or to commend them enthusiastically for the occasional smiles of welcome among them? Or consider whether we will make teens less promiscuous by scolding them every week for their indiscretions, or by searching for sparks of courage in the face of peer pressure that we take care to congratulate?

Of course, rebuke and correction will be needed in the life of the church. Still, leaders who discover the power of openly thanking God for the good in fallible people will do much to strengthen them in the spiritual support that God himself offers. Yes, it is our responsibility to reinforce and pass along Christian values and critique societal idolatries, but the church that compels God's people to gather is not simply about moral scolding. God's leaders compel his people to come in by building up the body of Christ in faith and love so that it can face the world and endure its assaults.

Paul makes it very plain for us who would be leaders in the church that we must apply grace to our vision as well as to our messages. So much of ministering to God's people is simply being ready to see the good and to envision what will be (rather than what is) in people. People cannot grow in an environment where only their failings are seen and remembered. I consider with embarrassment my mistakes over three decades as a pastor and organization leader. How thankful I am for those willing to look past my immaturity and faults to enable me to grow in the grace that God intends to surround and cushion our growth in him.

Intercession (1:16b)

Paul applies grace not only in offering his thanks for the Ephesians, but also in offering spiritual intercession for them. Paul says that he is "remembering" the Ephesians in prayer (Eph. 1:16a). He continues, "I keep asking that . . . God may give you the Spirit of wisdom and revelation" (Eph. 1:17), and "I pray also that the eyes of your heart may be enlightened" (Eph. 1:18a). Before we turn to the content of those prayers, simply note that they are other-oriented. Paul prays for others, and he lets them know this. In verse 16, the "remembering you" is translated even more precisely as "making mention of you." Paul literally says, "I have not stopped giving thanks for you, and I have not stopped mentioning you in my prayers."[2] Knowledge of this kind of specific intercession is a great encouragement to God's people.

Here, again, we receive powerful pastoral instruction from the apostle. In order to provide spiritual support, we are to give thanks for the good we can see, while praying for the good that God has yet to bring into the lives of his people. Praying specifically and regularly for God's people, and letting them know that we are doing so, builds the church. When God's people know that one whom they respect is putting them before the throne of grace, they are encouraged and strengthened. Wouldn't it encourage you to know that someone you respect was praying for you in this way? What so many are looking for today in our churches is just such spiritual support. Educational and fellowship programs, glorious worship presentations—as important as they are—are not a substitute for such spiritual support yearned for by the heart made alive by the Spirit.

Spiritual Insight (1:17–19a)

Knowing that the deepest longing and greatest needs of the people of God are spiritual, Paul makes the content of his intercession a request for their spiritual insight: "I keep asking that the God of our Lord Jesus Christ, the glorious Father, may give you the Spirit of wisdom and revelation, so that you may know him better. I pray also that the eyes of your heart may be enlightened in order that you may know the hope to which he has called you, the riches of his glorious inheritance in the saints" (Eph. 1:17–18). If our world is not to overwhelm us, we must know that what we see is not the full reality. With this in mind, the caring apostle prays that the Ephesians will see the spiritual reality that is not apparent to ordinary sight.

Scientists have discovered that blue whales, previously thought to be mute, actually have voices of immense power. Their voices resonate at a frequency below the level that the human ear can register. But with modern instruments scientists have found that the whales' *basso profundo* call is so powerful that it can carry over hundreds and even thousands of miles.

2. The import of this truth is magnified when we see that Paul often mentions his unceasing devotion to praying for the churches (e.g., Rom. 1:9–10; Col. 1:3, 9; 1 Thess. 1:2; 2 Thess. 1:11; also Philem. 4), and he commends this trait in others (Col. 4:12; 1 Thess. 5:17).

Without a satellite phone, a blue whale can call from a New York harbor and be heard in an English port. This amazing power has been present throughout the ages but undetected until recently because our senses have been too limited to register it. What Paul now begins to do is to make sure that the heart made sensitive by the Spirit truly does begin to sense the blessings that God makes available to his people through the ministry of the church.

How do we gain insight into the hidden dynamics of the spiritual world? Both divine and human agencies have a role. Heaven must give and the heart must receive what is necessary for spiritual insight. Paul prays for both.

Heaven's Provision (1:17)

The apostle prays "that the God of our Lord Jesus Christ, the glorious Father, may give you [the Ephesians] the Spirit of wisdom and revelation, so that you may know him better" (Eph. 1:17).[3] Paul prays that God would give knowledge of himself to his people. There is some debate among the commentators whether the "Spirit" mentioned here is the Holy Spirit, or the human spirit made wise. I think that it is most likely the Holy Spirit as the apostle continues to use the trinitarian formula introduced in the previous verses (Eph. 1:3–14). Further evidence comes from the way that in Paul's teaching "wisdom" and especially "revelation" are dispensed by the Holy Spirit (Eph. 3:5; cf. 1 Cor. 2:6–16). The lack of the article with "Spirit" is consistent with other references to the Holy Spirit (e.g., Rom. 8:4–5, 9, 13–14; Gal. 5:5, 16), as is a genitive attached to the Holy Spirit (e.g., John 14:17; 15:26; 16:13).[4]

Regardless of where one lands on the "Spirit" being identified, there is no question that the wisdom and revelation that are needed are God's gifts, so Paul's example instructs us that Christian leaders are to pray for God to make himself known to his people. This must become part of the ministry of all church leaders. We do not rely on our wisdom alone but pray that God would give his wisdom and reveal himself to his people.

3. God is identified here, in keeping with 1:3, as the "God of our Lord Jesus Christ" (cf. 2 Cor. 1:3; 11:31; Col. 1:3; 1 Peter 1:3). He is also "the Father of glory" (translated in the NIV as "glorious Father"—a descriptive genitive), which reminds one how elsewhere in Scripture God is called "the God of glory"—see Acts 7:2; Ps. 29:3 [Septuagint 28:3]).

4. See further Harold Hoehner, *Ephesians* (Grand Rapids: Baker, 2002), 256–58.

Human Reception (1:18a)

Praying for God to act is only half of the prayer needed for the spiritual nurture of God's people. Leaders also must pray that human hearts would be receptive to God's gifts. By praying this way, Paul recognizes the need of God's sovereign intervention and petitions him to act in behalf of his people by opening the human heart to see divine truths. For the Ephesians, Paul graphically prays "that the eyes of your heart may be enlightened" (Eph. 1:18a).

Once I had the privilege of hearing caring parents describe how they proceeded as a family when they learned that their young daughter was deaf. They said that at first they had no idea what to do or who could help. They felt the desperation of having a great need that they could not fix, without the slightest idea of how to go about helping their child. Then the Lord arranged for them to meet another family who had a similar child. That family directed them to various services provided by the state that were immensely helpful. The searching parents said the experience was like being asked to enter a room that you did not even know existed, and when you got inside the room you found out that there was an entire world unseen by most in society. In that world were very dedicated and expert people who were giving their lives to the care of such children. The world inside that room exists always, but you do not see it until you have such a need.

Paul knows that the spiritual needs of God's people are profound. So he prays that the eyes of their heart may be opened so that they can see the world of provision that heaven has made available for their care. Paul uses the Old Testament language of "enlightenment" (cf. Pss. 13:3; 19:8) for the spiritual understanding that comes to the believer's heart (2 Cor. 4:6) because the heart in Jewish thought was the seat of thoughts and emotions. Paul then specifically describes what the eyes of the Ephesians' hearts will have the sight to "know" as they are opened to heaven's provision: hope, inheritance, and power.

Hope (1:18b)

Paul prays that the Ephesians "may know the hope to which he [God] has called you." We know what the hope is. As Paul has described the work of the Father, Son, and Holy Spirit in the preceding passage, he has spelled out our hope: the world is the Lord's and we are his forever. The universe is not random, and we are never abandoned. Our God is just and gracious, sovereign and saving.[5] This was the Ephesians' hope, and it is ours also.

You recognize the significance of that hope when you hear the voices of our world that do not have it. The pop lyrics of the spiritually seeking, but yet unseeing musical group Vertical Horizon speak of what it means to have run out of hope. Their song "Lines upon Your Face" laments, "Sometimes I wish that we all were immortal, and the game of life always had a happy end, but I know it's not true. . . ." But it is true. The truth of the gospel is that we are immortal. Our time is eternal. And for those who put their faith in the eternal God who controls this world there is a happy ending—always, always!

There is an end of futility—the realization that the world is not senseless and that your sin is not endless in consequence or compulsion. There are a purpose to the world, pardon for sin, and power over it provided by God. God, who provides each of these, has called you as a Father calls a beloved child, out of darkness into his marvelous light. This is the hope that the apostle prays God's people would see, and we should pray for the same.

Inheritance (1:18c)

Paul also prays that the Ephesians would know the riches of the spiritual inheritance God provides his children. Commentators debate whether "his glorious inheritance in the saints" is the inheritance that God provides to his people, or whether his people are being counted as his inheritance (Eph. 1:18c). I lean toward the latter; that is, understanding that God actually considers us his inheritance, his promised blessing to himself. It is glorious to think that as the Father is said to rejoice over us in other texts, here also he actually considers us to be the rich inheritance he provides himself. He wills us to himself since we are his treasured possession. There is strong exegetical support for this position in New Testament parallels speaking of

5. Christians have hope in this life—a hope that was not theirs before knowing Christ (Eph. 2:12). Jewish believers were the first to have this hope (Eph. 1:12 in Greek), now Gentile believers do as well (Eph. 2:12–13). This hope here in Ephesians focuses on God's calling activities (Eph. 1:18), which extend to his calling of the whole united Christian community unto salvation (Eph. 4:4, "calling of you"; cf. Col. 3:15). This calling is performed by God's sovereign election unto salvation, as is consistent with "calling" in Paul's other writings. For God's electing call see 2 Timothy 1:9; Romans 8:28–30; 1 Thessalonians 5:24; 1 Corinthians 1:26–31; cf. Romans 11:29. For calling unto salvation see further: Galatians 1:6; 1 Thessalonians 2:12; 2 Thessalonians 2:14; 1 Timothy 6:12.

an inheritance possessed by God (e.g., Eph. 1:11, 14; 5:5; Acts 7:5), and there are many examples of God's inheritance constituting his own people in the Old Testament, especially in the Psalms (e.g., Pss. 68:9–10; 74:2; 78:62, 71; 79:1; 94:5, 14; 106:5, 40).[6]

Some commentators interpret Paul to be saying, instead, that God is providing heaven's riches to us in our spiritual poverty. This would mean that all of the resources of heaven are our inheritance—his mercy, his providence, his provision, his promise, and eternal life—and are ours to claim because he is our Father. Further, this means that God provides us the treasures of heaven, whatever is needed, to fulfill his purposes in our lives. Thus, again, the riches of God are our sure inheritance, and as such we can leverage our estate against present trials and challenges, knowing that they are not greater than what God will provide for us. When we experience trials now, we need not despair. The Spirit gives us eyes to see beyond this world and into heaven itself to know of the provision that is surely ours. Therefore, when all this provision is taken into consideration, the message still remains that God treasures us—after all, if we are recipients of his inheritance, this means that we are God's children.

F. F. Bruce speaks of the spiritual encouragement God grants by telling how much he treasures us:

> That God should set such high value on a community of sinners, rescued from perdition and still bearing too many traces of their former state, might well seem incredible were it not made clear that he sees them in Christ, as from the beginning he chose them in Christ. . . . God's estimate of the people of Christ, united to him by faith and partakers of his resurrection life, is inevitably consistent with his estimate of Christ. Paul prays here that his readers may appreciate the value which God places on them, his plan to accomplish

6. It is hypothetically possible that the "inheritance of him" is a genitive of source ("from him") with "in the saints" being taken as "among the saints" (Acts 20:32 could be taken as support that *en* after *klēronomia* can indicate "among"); also one could potentially argue that all the genitives "of him" in vv. 18–19 are genitives of source. However, all of the many genitive pronouns in construct with *klēronomia* in the Septuagint and the New Testament appear to be possessive genitives (e.g., his inheritance, your inheritance, etc.—see especially Eph. 1:14). And in the New Testament we have examples of a prepositional phrase with *en* indicating the contents of the inheritance (especially Eph. 5:5; also Acts 7:5)—also in the Septuagint (e.g., Gen. 31:14; Num. 36:2; 1 Kings 12:16). All this to say, it seems that the most natural way to understand "of him" is possessive—"his inheritance in the saints." This is consistent with Ephesians 1:14, and it is also consistent with the use of "chosen" (i.e., literally "we have been allotted") in Ephesians 1:11.

> his eternal purpose through them as the first fruits of the reconciled universe of the future, in order that their lives may be in keeping with this high calling and that they may accept in grateful humility the grace and glory thus lavished on them.[7]

Power (1:19a)

The promise of God's affection is not our only hope; Paul also prays for the Spirit to give eyes to see God's "incomparably great power for us who believe" (Eph. 1:19a). The promise is not only of an inheritance to come, but of power, great power for us.

Paul emphasizes the importance of power in this section of Ephesians by (1) placing it at the last of the triad of things to be seen with the illumined eyes of the heart, (2) using the evocative emphatic expression "surpassing greatness" to emphasize God's power, and (3) piling up words for God's strength and work in verses 19–20 (four different nouns and one verb in Greek). Power is a repeated concept in Ephesians (see Eph. 3:7, 16, 20; 6:10). By drumming this theme repeatedly, Paul calls the Ephesians in their historical situation to reject pagan notions of cultic and magical power, and also to encounter the heavenly and earthly powers, which are at odds with Christ, in the strength of the Lord (Eph. 1:21; 6:10–18). This is consistent with the power themes in Paul's other epistles (e.g., Rom. 1:20; 2 Thess. 1:9; 1 Tim. 6:16). Christians can face opposition to their faith only by claiming the power God now avails to believers (Phil. 3:21; Col. 1:11, 29; 2 Cor. 4:7; 12:9; 2 Tim. 1:7) through the Holy Spirit (e.g., Rom. 15:13; 1 Cor. 2:4–5). Not all see it but this power is present. It is in a spectrum of light not visible to the eyes of the flesh. So Paul prays for the Ephesians' senses to be made receptive by the Spirit so they can face their earthly challenges with divine power.

How compelling are hope and power to those who are hurting spiritually? Putting the question in the context of our physical reality will reveal the spiritual dynamics. When the mother of the deaf child I described earlier saw that people in another town had the power to help her daughter, then this wonderful mother took her daughter on a four-hour roundtrip to therapy each weekday for four years. Why would she do such a thing? Because she had seen with her own eyes the resources of medicine, knowledge, and

7. F. F. Bruce, *The Epistles to the Colossians, to Philemon, and to the Ephesians* (Grand Rapids: Eerdmans, 1984), 270–71.

therapy that were offered in that distant place. She had seen the power of those resources to grant new hope of hearing, health, and wholeness. And seeing the power gave her hope for her daughter's well-being that became a compulsion lasting many years and miles. Hope is that strong.

The church of Jesus Christ should offer such hope. I have tried to alert my students in recent years to what seems to be the common denominator in great preaching throughout the ages. It is not a style of delivery, or organization, or even exposition. These vary greatly by era. But what seems to be the thread uniting all great Christian preaching is hope. Great preaching always offers hope. We are in God's family and that means that we are in the "family business." That business is hope. There is hope for our fallen condition, our sin-sick world, and our sin-bound souls because of the power of Christ that is for us. We are dispensers of hope—offering the hope that God's riches and power can make tomorrow brighter than today. Making plain the nature and location of the power that gives hope becomes the next focus of the apostle.

Spiritual Power (1:19–23)

How do you make spiritual power apparent to God's people who are preoccupied and oppressed by this material world? I am told that one therapy utilized by those who treat autistic children is to cloud the lower half of their eyeglasses. Certain kinds of autism apparently manifest themselves as a child becomes completely focused on some dimension of his experience. Such a child can become so focused on a habitual activity or familiar object that interacting with that single aspect of life becomes the child's entire world. Thus, glasses clouded on the bottom but clear in the upper lenses force the child to look up—to take his eyes off of his little world and to consider a greater, wider world. In like manner, the apostle who would give us hope lifts our eyes from this world and causes us to focus on another power from One above. Our hope resides in understanding the power above and the power here.

The Hope Above (1:19–22)

First, Paul says the power that is available to God's people is "incomparably great" (Eph. 1:19). Then he tells us the nature of that power:

> That power is like the working of his [God's] mighty strength, which he exerted in Christ when he raised him from the dead and seated him at his right hand in the heavenly realms, far above all rule and authority, power and dominion, and every title that can be given, not only in the present age but also in the one to come. And God placed all things under his feet and appointed him to be head over everything for the church. (Eph. 1:19b–22)

The power that is at work in our behalf is *resurrection power*, able to overpower sin and death.[8] For those once dead in sin, new life is possible; and because of this divine provision, maintaining our witness before adversaries and our hope in adversity is not futile or impossible. The power that is at work in our behalf is also the *sovereign power* that places our Savior and Advocate above all rulers and forces of this world. To explain this sovereign power Paul mentions virtually every dimension of authority and strength that we would recognize in this world, from political rule to physical might to spiritual forces in this age and in the age to come, and says simply that Jesus is greater than them all.[9] He is the head of everything. And this great power that is at work in our behalf is *church power*. What Christ is doing with his power is "for the church" (Eph. 1:22c).

We might expect the apostle to say that what Christ is doing with his power is "for believers" or "for you," instead of "for the church." He could have said such things and been perfectly consistent with what he writes elsewhere. Christ does express his resurrection and sovereign power in behalf of us as individuals, but that is not Paul's point here. The point that the apostle is making is that the power of Christ is expressed not merely for individuals, but for the church of which you and I are only a part. He who created all things and who is the head of all things and who continues to fill all things is ordering all things in the interest of the church. There are powerful implications for those who gather corporately to worship God and to learn to fulfill his purposes.

We cannot truly fathom the magnitude of the apostle's promise that Christ, who is head over all things, is filling creation with his purposes for

8. The power of God in raising Christ and believers is a Pauline theme also found in Romans 1:4; 1 Corinthians 6:14; 15:43; 2 Corinthians 13:4; Philippians 3:10; Colossians 2:12.

9. On the language employed for these earthly and heavenly rulers see also Ephesians 2:2; 3:10; 6:12; cf. Romans 8:38–39; 1 Corinthians 15:24; Colossians 1:13, 16; 2:10, 15. Commentators note that "rule and authority, power and dominion" are reflective of the ranks of demons in Jewish literature, whereas "every title" more naturally refers to the ranks of human authorities.

the church. The universe is being constrained in its course, bent in new directions, for the good of the bride of Christ. As much as our perceptions may seem to deny this truth, the battles that rage, the leaders that rise, the events that occur do not thwart his agenda. History inexorably marches forward toward the triumph of the church of Jesus Christ. He is using all things (including the tragedies of a fallen world) to shape and reshape the world for her sake. The whole creation is being conformed to purposes that serve the glory of Christ's church. This is a compelling reason to be a part of the church. The entire world is Christ's bouquet to his bride, the church. But how does he prepare this bouquet? What instrument is Christ using to fill up the earth with his eternal purposes? It is the church.

The Hope Here (22c–23)

Jesus is "the head over everything for the church, which is his body, the fullness of him who fills everything in every way" (Eph. 1:22c–23). That for which the universe is being filled is itself the instrument of his filling. Jesus is changing the world for the good of the church by means of the church. Jesus said, "Where two or three come together in my name, there am I with them" (Matt. 18:20). This is more than a wedding song sentiment; it is a battle charge. It is the declaration of the divine groom that he will be present to protect and promote his bride.[10] He who is head over all things and gives the universe its full purpose also fills the church that gathers in his name. As such the church, the body of Christ, is the present instrument of his filling the universe with his purpose. The eternal, universe-conforming power of God is present in the world through the church, and this power is working in the world for the church.

This filling of the world with Christ's purpose for and through the church is the corporate hope we alone possess. No other agency on earth has this promise. God gives no other institution the promise or the power that it will be salt and light in the world. The world will ultimately and eternally yield to the influence of the church, because it is the body of him who is head over all and, thus, it contains and exerts his power in behalf of his own glory.[11] Our

10. In the context of Matthew, for example, Jesus' presence avails to resolve conflict in the church (Matt. 18:16, 20).

11. As in Ephesians (Eph. 4:12, 15; 5:23–24), Paul elsewhere frequently refers to the headship of Christ (1 Cor. 11:3; Col. 1:18) and to the church as his body (Rom. 12:5; 1 Cor. 12:12–27; Col. 3:15).

mission does not end at the threshold of the church door, nor is it limited to matters the world calls "religious." All of culture is our domain, all enterprises are of our interest, and all that is beautiful is ours to enjoy and cultivate. All that is here he is head over. Therefore we have a right to be concerned for it and to bring it under the lordship of him for whom it was created and for whose glory it is designed.

The way that the apostle expresses this power and purpose of the church has caused no little consternation for commentators through the ages because of the uncompromising nature of his words. The church is the fullness of him who fills everything; thus she completes his purpose for him even as he designs everything for her. The complexity of Paul's "fullness" language can be seen especially in Ephesians (Eph. 1:23; 3:19; 4:10, 13) and Colossians (Col. 1:19; 2:9–10). In Ephesians 1:23, the term "fullness" most naturally refers to the "body," that is, the church (see also Eph. 3:19; cf. Col. 2:10). Similarly, because Paul elsewhere conveys that the fullness of God "fills" the believers (Eph. 3:19), it is apparent here that Christ is the one who fills the church (*plēroumenou* here being considered a middle voice). Thus the NIV accurately translates this phrase: "which is his body, the fullness of him who fills everything in every way" (Eph. 1:23).

The church is God's instrument for world transformation and renewal. Some have interpreted this to mean that the church should seek to amass financial, political, or even military power to impose Christ's will upon the nations. More instructive is Paul's own unfolding of these truths in the remainder of this epistle. His following words do not frame a political, marketing, or military strategy but, rather, are a blueprint for the ministry of local churches that will produce mutual love and personal purity so that believers are prepared for godly service in every dimension of their lives. The church is called to be the church so that by her proclamation of the gospel in word and deed her people will be prepared to advance his kingdom wherever he calls them to be salt and light in the world.

The role of the church in world transformation needs to be emphasized so that all will realize how noble is the calling to lead and support her. The church is the primary instrument of the glory of Christ in this earth. If you work within her to tell the world of the hope, the resources, and the power that he provides, then the Lord is conforming all of life and history to your purposes because the church you serve fulfills purposes for which the world itself was created. With the church's ultimate triumph before our eyes, we may understand more and more the corporate purposes to which our God calls us, and the mandates he gives.

First, the corporate purpose of the church indicates that we are part of a body, where there may be *no mavericks*. In an individualistic culture we can forget this. We can talk about changing the culture, being salt and light, taking the message of Christ into the marketplace and, with the best of intent, think almost entirely in terms of personal, autonomous efforts. In accord with our Western culture's habits and interests, we think primarily in egocentric terms: what I will do, how I will change an industry, an artistic field, or a political movement. While we do have individual responsibilities, we do not fulfill our calling if we seek to influence the culture without the church.

The corporate calling of the church also means that there can be *no deserters*. To move forward without her is not only to move beyond our spiritual supply lines; it is to declare the body of Christ, his bride, irrelevant to us or contrary to our causes. This can be quite easy to do because the church can be intolerant, intractable, tradition-bound, blind to her duty, and a pain to endure. She can be an ugly bride. But she is the beloved of Christ and the only instrument that will ultimately fulfill his purposes on this earth. That is why she is worth the effort, and worth the dedication of our lives.

The corporate destiny of the church means, too, that there should be *no despair*. For all of her weaknesses—including the carping of her people and the failures of her leaders—she is the means that Christ will use to fill the world with his glory. And despite her setbacks and her apparent losses, the church will not be stopped. Those who serve her can have no higher calling. Despite all of her weakness, there is no more powerful an organization of hope in the world than a body of believers loving one another, helping and forgiving one another, praying for the work of Christ in their midst, supporting each other in joy and in sorrow, equipping disciples, showing mercy to outsiders, and praising the God who enables it all. The cumulative effect of multiple churches so living is the world's greatest power for good.

Ultimately, the corporate promises to the church mean that there should be *no surrender*. Those who have the eyes of their heart opened to the heavenly purpose that God commits to the church are a power that the world cannot restrain. She is the fullness of him who is head over all things, whose power fills everything in every way. The riches of heaven are outpoured in her behalf. This is our hope and, by the power of God, it is the church's certainty. We are part of the movement of God that all creation bows to honor.

In the early days of the French Reformation, the Huguenots grew with a force that was supernatural. As many as three thousand churches grew within one seven-year period. It was easy to see the "incomparably great power" of Christ in those years. But soon the Catholic French monarchy had enough of this new Protestantism, and in a series of edicts, imprisonments, and massacres destroyed the movement. Tens of thousands tried to flee the country, but being a religious refugee was itself a crime punishable by imprisonment or death. So while thousands fled, many more were forced to stay and worship in secret.

This commitment to private worship, we readily understand. What is less clear to us is why during this time the people continued to insist on finding hidden places to worship corporately. They fashioned communion sets that could be ingeniously dismantled and hidden inside books or flour sacks. Pulpits were constructed out of wire and sheets that could be folded into nondescript piles of laundry when not in use. One pulpit from that time was fashioned so that it could be collapsed into the shape of a wine barrel and, then, like a modern child's robotic transformer, be unfolded into a massive wooden pulpit. But why would the Huguenots exert all that effort? After all, during those years, if a congregation was caught worshiping without the king's approval, the minister would be executed, the other men would be sent to the galleys for life, the women would be imprisoned for life, and children would be taken away to be raised in state-sponsored religious schools. At times, whole villages were tortured until the people as a whole professed their allegiance to the state church. Surely in those years the people wondered where was the "incomparably great power" for those who believe.

Today a little farmhouse nestled into the French countryside holds the modest museum that commemorates the Huguenots. Inside is a white marble wall. On that stark wall appear the names of men and women who were executed, condemned to galleys, tortured, or imprisoned for life. Many suffered greatly, and surely in their day it was difficult to see the prevailing power of Christ as their churches were exterminated. Who could have blamed the people if, for their individual safety, they had abandoned the worship and practices of the corporate body? We struggle today to see the purpose the eyes of their hearts so clearly saw as they committed themselves to the church.

Yet after I visited that farmhouse museum in France, I was blessed by a glimpse of what the French Reformers saw. I continued on to Budapest to minister to pastors from Hungary, Romania, and the Ukraine. Through their heroic efforts the work of Christ has endured in nations oppressed by atheistic Communist rule for two generations. I spoke to men who also were tortured, threatened, and had their children taken by the government. These men too had endured for the sake of a purpose larger than their own lives. And when I asked them their reason, they told me that they were the descendants of the Huguenots. They were the offspring of the faithful few who escaped from their French homeland four centuries ago, as God seeded the world with the salt and light of their testimony and his truth.

With this testimony, I suddenly realized what I was witnessing: "the incomparably great power for us who believe." In the time since the Huguenots' persecution, kings and kingdoms have come and gone, governments and philosophies have risen and fallen, dictators and oppressors have ruled and faded, but through it all the church of Jesus Christ carrying the message of his eternal love and final rule has endured. The gates of hell have not prevailed against it, and they shall not. Christ shall have dominion, and he will use his church to bring his rule to the hearts of his people throughout the world.

Now God calls us to be a part of this ongoing mission to take the church into the world, with the eyes of our heart opened to his truth and to his triumph. I will not pretend that the challenges will be small or without pain, but I can promise that our efforts will not be in vain. However small we may feel our influence, however opposed may be our efforts, however weak may seem our strength, those engaged in the work of the church are members of the agency that God has determined will exert his power for the transformation of this world. Our Lord calls us to a good and a great work. May the eyes of our heart be opened to what he is doing in and through us so that we always speak of the hope, the riches, and the power that are the possession of those God calls his own for the glory of Christ Jesus our Savior.

6

The Gift of God

Ephesians 2:1–10

Like the rest, we were by nature objects of wrath. But because of his great love for us, God, who is rich in mercy, made us alive with Christ even when we were dead in transgressions—it is by grace you have been saved. (Eph. 2:3–5)

redestination was always a key subject as I was growing up. Although the small church that I attended as a child sat amid Tennessee corn and soybeans, it prided itself on its being faithful to everything the Bible teaches—even the hard things like predestination. Sensing that it was one of the few churches that would unabashedly talk about such doctrines, the small denomination with which my father was affiliated became all the more zealous for its distinctives. Thus we spoke very frequently about predestination. Whether the text was New Testament or Old, Psalm or Gospel, the topic was the same. I knew that God had "chosen us in him before the foundation of the world" (Eph. 1:4) before I knew my multiplication tables. No one dodged the truth that I was "predestinated according to the purpose of him who worketh all things after the counsel of his own will" (Eph. 1:11 KJV). It seemed that a sermon was not a sermon if it did not somehow refer to predestination.

The truth that we are God's based solely on God's sovereign initiative got so much emphasis in my youth that I entered adulthood with huge questions about my role in God's work. Those questions even set the agenda for my seminary studies. While the Lord gave me many wonderful teachers and subjects, my main goal throughout seminary was to reconcile all the tensions between predestination and human responsibility. I am still working on that agenda. But reflection since that time has also led me to consider what I think to be the special calling of those who will honor God's sovereignty while respecting his use of human instruments to do his will and spread his Word.

The classic text to which we now turn speaks clearly of the sovereign gift of God's love *and* of his call upon our lives.[1] God's sovereign gift and our human calling wonderfully coalesce to bring him glory and to give us purpose.

Why God Must Be Sovereign: Our Status, Practice, and Nature (2:1–3)

Paul's point throughout this passage is that salvation is a consequence of God's sovereign initiative and not a result of our achievement or merit. Sovereignty is a way of expressing God's rule that is independent of external control. God would not be truly sovereign—in control of the universe, if he were subject to human decisions or controlled by our actions. Among other things, this means that salvation is a gift of God, not a product of human efforts. Though the names of Augustine and John Calvin are often associated with these truths for historical reasons, what the Bible says here confirms these convictions—and it must be the Bible not human authority that ultimately determines spiritual truth.

What does the Bible say here that confirms that our salvation must be a gift of God? It reveals the status, practice, and nature that characterize us and incapacitate us, thus making it necessary for God to take the initiative in saving us.

1. This passage (Eph. 2:1–10) is a single coherent sentence in Greek, emphasizing the grace of God (N.B.: it is possible to break the structure at verse 8, but the "for" clearly connects Eph. 2:8–10 to 2:1–7). In Greek the direct object of the main verb is introduced in verse 1 ("you") and modified in verse 5 ("us"). The subject in Greek ("God") appears in verse 4 and the main verb in verse 5 ("made us alive"). Thus the core sentence states that God is the one who sovereignly acts to make the spiritually dead alive by uniting us with Christ. All the other verses hang as clauses onto this core sentence to show the depth of the misery of our depravity and the greatness of the grace of our loving and merciful God.

Our Status (2:1)

What is our status? Making the Ephesians emblematic of us prior to God's regenerating grace, the apostle says that we all lack spiritual life. Speaking of their preconversion status, Paul says to the Ephesians, "As for you, you were dead in your transgressions and sins" (Eph. 2:1).[2] Prior to our salvation, although we were physically alive, we were spiritually dead, incapable of life with God. Our lack of holiness rendered us incapable of a living relationship with a holy God.

Our Practice (2:1–2)

Because we are spiritually dead prior to God's placing his Spirit in us, there is no godly restraint on what we do. Speaking to the Ephesians, Paul says, "You were dead in your transgressions and sins, in which you used to live when you followed the ways of this world and of the ruler of the kingdom of the air, the spirit who is now at work in those who are disobedient" (Eph. 2:1–2). The practice of those who were dead in their transgressions and sins was to live following the ways of the world and the leading of Satan, who continues to exert his spiritual influence over those who are disobedient. They live a life of spiritual death.

The Greek literally indicates that the Ephesians "walked" according to the ways of the world, thus employing a typical biblical expression (cf. Prov. 8:20) for how a person conducts one's life (see Eph. 2:10; 4:1, 17; 5:2, 8, 15; and e.g., Gal. 5:16; Rom. 6:4; 14:15; 2 Cor. 5:7; Phil. 3:17; Col. 1:10). The "ways [literally 'age'] of this world" is similar to Paul's use of the "present evil age" in Galatians (1:4); it constitutes the time when the "world" and the powers that operate in it are in opposition to God (on this use of "world" see also 1 Cor. 2:12; 11:32; Gal. 4:3; Col. 2:8, 20; and cf. 1 John 2:15–17). The "ruler of the kingdom of the air" is Satan, who is further mentioned in Ephesians

2. In verse 1 the word "you" is the focus ("you were dead in your transgressions"), but the same phrase is repeated in verse 5 with "we." Some have contended that by employing the pronouns "we" and "us" Paul is merely including himself alongside the audience ("you"). However, in light of the clear indication in Ephesians 2:11–14 that "you" refers to the Gentiles and "we" to those of Jewish descent, it is likely here that Paul also refers to the Jew/Gentile distinction. Paul insists that, before God graciously intervenes, both Jew and Gentile alike conduct their lives according to the flesh (Eph. 2:3), are spiritually dead (Eph. 2:1, 5), and deserve only God's wrath (Eph. 2:3). This also serves Paul's purpose of promoting unity between Jew and Gentile since Jew and Gentile alike are all entirely in need of God's gracious salvation (Eph. 2:1–10) just as they are now members together of one body (Eph. 2:11–22).

(Eph. 4:27; 6:11, 16).[3] All of this background indicates that when Paul says we were dead prior to our salvation, he contends we are spiritually dead not only because of our unregenerate status but also because that status results in evil practices that are under judgment.

Our Nature (2:3)

This status and practice of death are not simply a consequence of what people without God do; it is both a result and evidence of what they are. Paul says, "All of us also lived among them [i.e., those dead in their disobedience] at one time, gratifying the cravings of our sinful nature and following its desires and thoughts" (Eph. 2:3). Disobedience apart from God was not an aberration; rather, we were living in accord with our nature.[4] Paul takes for granted our understanding that we are by nature born dead in sin. We inherit the fallen nature of Adam by which we are spiritually separate from God and subject to the desires of the world and its way of thinking.

In this natural condition we, "like the rest," are also subject to the wrath of God. Echoing language that becomes crucial in Romans 9 to describe the destiny of those God does not save, Paul says that prior to God's work in our behalf "we were by nature objects of wrath" (cf. Rom. 9:22).

This picture of our pre-Christian state is devastating to any suggestion that we possess the ability to act or believe in such a way as to save ourselves. Our practice is simply to live in accord with the nature we inherit with the rest of the world that is at odds with the holy ways of God. The consequence is that we cannot have a living union with him. By nature and practice we are spiritually lifeless. Our status before God is that of dead people. Nothing convinces me more of the need for the sovereign initiative of a loving God in my salvation than this assessment in Scripture of my total inability to save myself. The dead cannot save themselves.

The Bible well supplies us with images to help us understand the total inability of our dead nature. Imagine being present at the time that Jesus

3. Satan is also called "the god of this age" by Paul (2 Cor. 4:4) and the "prince of this world" in the Gospels (John 12:31; 14:30; 16:11).

4. The word for "sinful nature" in Greek is literally "flesh." Thus the NASB: "Among them we too all formerly lived in the lusts of our flesh, indulging the desires of the flesh and of the mind, and were by nature children of wrath, even as the rest." Here this idea of "flesh" is correctly paraphrased by the NIV to indicate the "sinful nature" which is within people (see further: Rom. 7:5, 18, 25; 8:1–17; 13:14; 1 Cor. 5:5; Gal. 5:13–26; 6:8; Col. 2:11, 13; 2 Peter 2:10).

approached the tomb of Lazarus. None of us would have approached the one that was dead and said, "Lazarus, you need to get up because Jesus is here to help you. Lazarus, come on now. He is really a wonderful Savior. All you need to do is reach out to him and he will save you. Come on, Lazarus, if you will just take the first step, then he will do the rest." We would not have said any of those things because we knew that Lazarus was dead. But when Jesus said, "Lazarus, come forth," he responded. Do we say that this was because of any initiative or effort of Lazarus? No. Lazarus responded, but this was because Jesus gave him ears to hear, strength to move, breath to live, and the will to obey. Lazarus responded but Jesus was responsible for the new life, because Lazarus was dead.

Jesus alone raised Lazarus to life. He alone is the life-giver because Lazarus was dead and totally unable to do anything. Since we are spiritually dead prior to God giving us new life, the spiritual life we have must be his doing and is to his glory alone.

Why I Must Be Saved: His Love and Power (2:4–7)

The apostle Paul makes plain the necessity of a sovereign deliverance that is beyond our accomplishment not only by describing the magnitude of our natural inability but also by describing the magnificence of God's divine enabling. The measure of God's mercy is as convincing of its divine source as is the measure of our need of it. That is to say, Paul not only describes what was missing in us, but also what is provided by God, and both signal why God must supply what is needed for our salvation. These next truths explain not merely why I must be saved from the spiritual death of my original nature, but how God saves. His merciful love and divine power combine to deliver me so that I can spiritually respond to him though I am spiritually dead.

His Merciful Love: His Motive (2:4–5)

Paul first describes God's reason for saving his people even though they are originally dead and are by nature objects of his wrath. Why does God make us spiritually alive? Paul answers, "Because of his great love for us, God, who is rich in mercy, made us alive . . ." (Eph. 2:4–5). This love is not toward the innocent. God expresses his love to those who were disobedient, who by nature followed the ways of the world and of Satan. "God demonstrates his own love for us in this: While we were still sinners, Christ died for us" (Rom. 5:8).

John Van Tholen was a Christian Reformed Church pastor in Rochester, New York, who was diagnosed with a very dangerous cancer. Invoking the truths of God's sovereign mercy from Paul's letters, Pastor Van Tholen reflected on what this struggle with cancer meant in the process of making him more aware of the glory of God's provision:

> Paul writes that "while we were still weak Christ died for the ungodly." He wants us to marvel at the Christ of the Gospel, who comes to us in our weakness and need. Making sure we get the point, Paul uses the word ("still") twice . . . in a repetitious and ungrammatical piling up of his meaning. "*Still* while we were *still* weak, at the right time Christ died for the ungodly. . . ."
>
> I'm physically weak, but that is not my main weakness. . . .
>
> While we were *still* weak . . . still sinners, still enemies, we were reconciled to him through the death of his Son. I find it unfathomable that God's love propelled him to reach into our world with such scandalous grace, such a way out, such hope.
>
> No doubt *God* has done it, because there is no hope to be found anywhere else.[5]

This beautiful truth of God's unconditional love is the heart of the gospel that becomes most dear to us when by God's grace we see our own weakness so clearly that we know that there is nothing in us that warrants God's love. Time and again I have heard words of consternation from those whose sin is so plain to them that they believe God *should* not love them; the high school student whose dating life has become promiscuous; the churchman whose marriage is falling apart due to his own hardness; the seminarian who, despite his aspirations and location, is still caught in a cyclic web of addiction and guilt; the young mother who doubts that she can treat her children better than her mother treated her. Over and over, in these situations, I have heard desperate souls saying, "Because of what I have done, because of who I am, God should not love me." And these words are true. On the basis of justice alone, a holy God should not love the sinful. Yet, having dispensed his justice in the judgment of his Son, our

5. *The Best Christian Writing 2000*, ed. John Wilson (San Francisco: Harper, 2000), 258.

God not only delights to extend us his mercy, but by his power he enables us to respond to his love.

His Divine Power: His Means (2:5–7)

The power of God that claims us is expressed in dimensions that are difficult for us fully to fathom. Not only do those dimensions reveal the greatness of God's power, but they also make clear our helplessness apart from his working as the Lord of life, the Lord of eternity, and the Lord of love.

By his power God first *provides new life* (Eph. 2:5). We are dead in our natural state, yet we are enabled to love God. How does that happen? Paul says, "God . . . made us alive with Christ even when we were dead in transgressions" (Eph. 2:5a). Here is the amazing truth of our spiritual re-creation. Just as God breathed into lifeless dust to give life to Adam, the Lord gives spiritual life to those who were spiritually dead. This God alone can do. We do not have the ability to bring life from death. A dead person cannot will himself to breathe. A truly lifeless person will not do what we say no matter how passionate our exhortation for him to rise and walk. Yet we who were spiritually dead in our transgressions and sins, God made alive. This profound truth, that where there was death now there is life, will soon cause the apostle to pause and utter the first of two great affirmations of the cause of our salvation in this passage: "It is by grace you have been saved" (Eph. 2:5b). Since the dead are helpless, our spiritual life can be credited only to God. Our salvation is the gift of God.

By his power God also *provides eternal life* (Eph. 2:6). Now the nature of that gift of life is explained in words of true wonder. Paul says, "God raised us up with Christ and seated us with him in the heavenly realms in Christ Jesus" (Eph. 2:6). These are the words of resurrection. Just as Christ was raised from the dead, so also we are filled with the life that is from God.

Our spiritual death has been swallowed up in Christ's resurrection victory. The guilt and power of sin have been conquered by the Savior who now resides in us. Paul has already reminded his readers of the power of God evident in the resurrection and session of Christ (Eph. 1:20). Here he explicitly states that believers are united with Christ in his resurrection and exaltation in the heavens (see also Rom. 6:3–5; Col. 2:11–13; 3:1).

The resurrection power of God in us indicates not only that we are a forgiven people, but also that we are an empowered people since Christ lives in us. The sin that assaulted us yesterday can be met and overcome by the risen power of God in us. Tomorrow does not have to be like yesterday for those who are in Christ Jesus. This power over tomorrow is not limited, however, merely to our ability to make progress over sin as time passes. We are not merely made alive, but also have the status of the Risen One to whom we are united by faith. Our Savior has given us power over sin, and made us right with God.

How right we are is emphasized in the final dimension of power that Paul explains. He says that we are also seated with Christ in the heavenly realms (Eph. 2:6). Because our sin is pardoned and its power is annulled, we are counted as God's own children with the right to heavenly thrones beside his Son. But this heavenly seating is not merely for some future day. Paul writes to the Ephesians that God raised them (past tense) from their estates of death to life with Christ by resurrection power.[6] But now Paul also writes to these living and breathing New Testament Christians that God has already seated them (past tense) in the heavenly realms. How can this be? The answer is that although glory is ahead for the living, their enthronement is already accomplished. All God's children already have the status of his Son.

Eternity has been compressed into a present reality in God's accounting. I still see myself from the perspective of my present humanity and sin, but God has so secured my eternal destiny that he allows me also to see that I am already an heir of God and a possessor of the glories of heaven. My status as an enthroned heir of heaven—despite my presence as a finite and frail creature of earth—underscores my helplessness to secure what salvation provides. I do not have the power to give life or status the way that God grants it to those who are the objects of his mercy.

By his power God ultimately *provides a united life* (Eph. 2:7). How God grants Christ's status and secures our eternity is marvelously expressed in the words used to describe the provision of his power. The Greek verbs all line up with the same prefix. God "*together* made us alive with Christ," "*together* raised us up with Christ," and "*together* seated us with him in the heavenly realms." Here in concise form are the benefits of our union with Christ. We have life with Christ: with him we are spiritually alive, with him we are raised by res-

6. Commentators commonly understand this as a constative aorist, indicating a past-time event. This is in keeping with Paul's view that believers are united with Christ in his death and resurrection, which are themselves past events.

urrection power to victory over the guilt and power of sin, and with him we are enthroned in heavenly realms despite our earthly shell and shame. All the righteousness and glories of the Son of God are ours because we, by being in union with him, receive all the love of the Father now and eternally. Elsewhere Paul asks rhetorically, "He who did not spare his own Son, but gave him up for us all—how will he not also, along with him, graciously give us all things?" (Rom. 8:32). The implication is clear, that God's love is so expansive for those who are united to Christ that all that is due Christ is granted us.

Paul uses classic terminology to summarize this union in the following verse. He says that God grants life with Christ, resurrection power with Christ, and eternal love with Christ, "in order that in the coming ages he might show the incomparable riches of his grace, expressed in his kindness to us in Christ Jesus" (Eph. 2:7). Life, pardon, divine righteousness, and eternal glory are mine because I am "in Christ." All of these blessings are the fruit of my union with my Savior. Yet none of these is within my power to grasp or my right to claim by my righteousness.

Not only does God pardon my sin, but he also unites me to the glory of his Son, which is the promise of his righteousness and preciousness in exchange for my sin and worthlessness. These two aspects of the gospel of his love explain the magnitude and magnificence of my union with the King of the universe. They also convince me that my salvation must be the gift of a divine hand and not the product of any human effort.

This emphasis on the divine origin and proportions of our salvation underscores what the apostle mentions three times in this passage: that our salvation is by grace, a gift of God (Eph. 2:5, 7–8). Grace. Grace. Grace. "It is by grace you have been saved."[7] We are too dead to be the source of our salvation; we are too weak to be the maintainers of our salvation; we are too finite to be the eternal stewards of our salvation. The magnitude and magnificence of what our salvation involves indicate that it must be entirely a gift of God's grace.

Why I Must Proclaim His Grace (2:7–10)

Paul next gives us reasons why we must fulfill our God-given calling to make this gift of grace known. God certainly could work without us,

7. This "grace" is at the heart of Paul's message in his many letters (e.g., Titus 3:4–7; Rom. 3:22–24; 5:15; 11:5–6; 2 Cor. 8:9; Gal. 2:21; 2 Thess. 2:13–17; 2 Tim. 1:9–10).

but by working through us his kindness is made plain and our humility is made precious.

To Make Known God's Kindness (2:7)

God tells the Ephesians that though they were dead he has given them the gift of salvation so that his kindness would be revealed in the coming ages (Eph. 2:7). Note the importance of this pivot verse, telling us the reason for Paul's explanation of God's sovereign action (Eph. 2:1–6) prior to the summary of that sovereign activity (Eph. 2:8–10). God has acted, says the apostle, so that the kindness of God might be revealed.

These words obligate us to make sure that the doctrines of grace do not obscure the core message of the kindness of God. All too often those who use the phrase "the doctrines of grace" are ungracious people. Concern to defend predestination against the challenges of human choice and vainglory can create an unhealthy zeal for debate where virtually every gathering of the church is a forum for advocating God's sovereignty and for attacking those who differ. I have even attended funerals where the central theme of the message was predestination in order to convince the Arminians who were present among the mourners.

I in no way want to minimize God's sovereign choice that I believe is my only hope of heaven. But I must remember to make sure what predestination is really about: the revelation of God's kindness. Angry arguments and insistent harangues miss the mark when their goal is promoting the doctrine of predestination rather than advancing understanding of divine kindness.

The reason that our message must be Christ-centered and grace-focused is that consistent adulation of the love of God in Christ will not only move our hearts to love and obedience; it also will convince us more and more of our dependence upon his kindness rather than our performance, right actions, or right doctrine.[8] We are not saved by right thinking any more than we are saved by right actions. There is no cause for boasting among those who know that their salvation is a gift of God. Rather, greater humility, love for God, and love for his people flow from those who recognize that their daily existence and eternal destiny are entirely a gift of God.

8. For more extensive treatment of the role of grace in motivating our sanctification, see the author's *Holiness by Grace* (Wheaton, IL: Crossway, 2003).

To move the locus of faith from the kindness of God's grace to zeal for our arguments is to miss the mark. That is why even the great Presbyterian theologian Benjamin Warfield said that the heart of Reformed theology is not predestination but grace. To emphasize predestination over the kindness of God inadvertently turns a proper acknowledgment of how God acts into an improper qualification for the grace that God grants. God loving us entirely out of his mercy is the point we miss if we focus on the doctrine of his action rather than on the beauty of his kindness. We will never in this life fully understand the mysteries of his sovereignty, but we can grasp much of the love in his heart. Relishing the kindness of God is the goal that predestination rightly seeks and the emphasis that should remain our message. We will not in this life know why God chooses as he does, but we know enough about him to rest assured that his choices are good, just, and loving.

To Ensure My Humility (2:8–9)

So important is it to Paul that God's kindness gets full credit that his summary of this passage takes away every avenue of personal credit for our salvation. Paul says that we are saved by grace through faith, "and this not from yourselves, it is the gift of God" (Eph. 2:8). For centuries, commentators have put forth arguments about what the "this" or the "it" in this sentence means. Some have said, on the basis of their theology, "it" is grace. Others, on the basis of the nearest antecedent, say "it" is faith. Most modern commentators say that "it" is the whole package, grace and faith.[9] Grace is his unmerited favor; it comes to us through faith in what he has done. But even that faith is a gift, so that no one can boast (Eph. 2:8–9). For we are God's workmanship, a product of his hand, created in Christ Jesus—made by God through union with Christ—to do good works not of our devising, but that he himself planned in advance for us to do (Eph. 2:10). Grace is of him, faith is of him, our union with Christ is of him, the works we do are of him, and the intention to do them is of

9. Greek pronouns agree in gender with the nouns to which they refer; however, the pronoun "this" in "this not from yourselves" is neuter, while the nouns "faith" and "grace" are both feminine in gender. The best explanation for the neuter gender of "this" is that "this" refers not to just one preceding noun (faith or grace), but to the whole concept of salvation (including both the faith and the gift of the grace of God upon which salvation is predicated).

him. So there can be no boasting or pride, but only an acknowledgment of the kindness of the gift of God.

To reiterate, there can be no boasting or pride, but only an acknowledgment of the kindness of the gift of God, because this emphasis ensures our humility and clarifies our mission. The clear statement of Scripture and the witness of my own heart both affirm that my salvation is unmerited and unearned. Still, we must confess that no one but God can answer every question about predestination. I cannot take away all the mysteries of sovereignty or reconcile all the issues of justice and logic that it raises.

If, for instance, God is entirely sovereign, providentially controlling all his creatures and all their actions, how can we say in the Westminster Shorter Catechism that God left Adam to the freedom of his own will?[10] Justice demands, at least at that stage of human existence, that Adam have freedom of choice in order for God to be fair in imposing punishment for his sin. Yet how could even Adam have been free if God is entirely sovereign, "preserving and governing all his creatures and all their actions," to quote another portion of our Catechism?[11] Here our human logic reaches its limits, and we should not fear to say so even as we follow the clear teaching of Scripture in affirming both Adam's freedom and God's sovereignty.

We should be willing, as church historian David Calhoun taught his students was the practice of John Calvin in the *Institutes of the Christian Religion*, to acknowledge that when we come to the end of our logic we should not turn away from Scripture but rather affirm our humanity and humility by singing the Doxology. We do scriptural truth no disservice when we confess with the apostle Paul, "Oh, the depth of the riches of the wisdom and knowledge of God! How unsearchable his judgments, and his paths beyond tracing out" (Rom. 11:33). The reality of the ordinary progress of Christian understanding should not escape our notice: early believers "know no answers"; immature believers "know all the answers"; and mature believers "know the limits of our answers."

There are legitimate questions regarding fairness and logic that Calvinism will not fully answer because the Bible does not fully answer. If we are not interested in boasting, then it does us no harm to acknowledge this while at the same time affirming all that the Bible does say regarding God's sovereign activity in our behalf. Unending grace is my only hope and my deepest

10. WSC, 13.
11. WSC, 11.

comfort. That I do know and passionately proclaim to sinners as much in need of grace as I.

Why some people and not others receive this sovereign grace in election is a question not answered in Scripture; the Bible is a book designed to address God's people, not to answer all the questions of the world. But it is this totally unmerited choosing and enabling that further underscore the message of mercy that the Bible makes its main point. That point made clear in this passage and many others is that we can never stand before God and say, "The reason that I am yours is what I did or chose through my good actions, good sense, or good heart." Our salvation is entirely a gift of God—of his grace. The point of Scripture is not to explain why some and not others, but rather to comfort those who face the impossibility of being saved by their own works that God has sovereignly worked in their behalf to secure what they could not. There can be no boasting or pride in this, but only a growing appreciation for grace that is made more precious the more we understand the nature of our heavenly Father. This is why our focus must be more upon the person of God, rather than upon the nature of predestination.

In a personal letter theologian Robert Peterson beautifully responded to a question I had about the intricacies and tensions of God's sovereignty and human responsibility. This was his response:

> Knowing God (by his grace) permeates this discussion (and all of our discussions and more). It is easier to admit in humility that I don't have all the answers, indeed don't even know the right questions to ask, when I revel in the knowledge of God. He loves me and knows me and as a result, I know him. He is infinite and I'll never exhaustively know him or have all the answers that I might desire. But knowing him puts everything, even questions about the divine sovereignty/human responsibility tension in the Christian life, in a wonderful perspective. . . . I will never perfectly understand my wife and the workings of her mind . . . but I can rest in her love for me and in doing so put myself in a much better position to try to understand the inscrutable. We are all little children climbing into our Father's lap and asking him our heartfelt but (from his perspective) childish questions.

To Enable Ministry (2:10)

Certainly this insistence that our salvation (our hope) must be a product of grace—a gift of God—does not answer all of the questions about sovereignty and free will, especially the fairness questions, because as Pastor Van Tholen said earlier in this chapter, grace is "unfathomable."[12] But what the Bible makes plain is that even when we do not have all the answers, we do have responsibilities. The good that God wants to do he has ordained to do through us. "We are God's workmanship, created in Christ Jesus to do good works, which God prepared in advance for us to do" (Eph. 2:10).[13]

There need be no aloof sitting on the sidelines waiting for God to work because of his sovereignty and our finitude. He has already told us that he has prepared us for good works and, then, in this same passage describes what is good to him: making known his kindness to a world that must glorify him. This is not because God needs us to do so, but because he has so ordained to use us for such a glorious purpose. And the way that he has ordained for us to do this is the proclamation of who he is as he has revealed himself to us in the person of his Son. We do not have to know all the answers to divine mysteries to be able to proclaim him. If we are able to speak like the man born blind who was healed by Jesus, we will still fulfill our calling. When asked to explain how Jesus had healed him, the man could not. All he could say was, "One thing I do know. I was blind but now I see" (John 9:25). When all the credit was given to Jesus, the humility of the man and the glory of God were in the right place even when mysteries remained.

Yes, we are responsible to defend the faith and proclaim more than simple truths about God, but we are not ready to address the challenges of doctrine, church, culture, and world until we acknowledge that we will always be little children crawling into the lap of the Father to ask him how he works. Only in that attitude of humility, filled with the knowledge of his love and person, are we ready to speak to the world of a God who loved us when we could not love him back, and saved us when we could not save ourselves. For only as little children delighting in the opening of a gift beyond our highest hopes and fondest dreams can we really begin to "show the incomparable riches of his grace, expressed in his kindness to us in Christ Jesus" (Eph. 2:7). May God keep each of us such a child of his heart, and keep our heart humble before him, as the grace of the kindness of God in Christ becomes our greatest joy and eternal message.

12. See the comments of Pastor Van Tholen earlier in this chapter.

13. This new ability to do good works changes the "walk" of a person from one in allegiance to the world and the Devil (Eph. 2:2) to one in allegiance to the calling of God (2:10; cf. 4:17; 5:8). In this epistle Paul both claims for God all the sovereign glory for this new life of walking in good works (which God prepared beforehand; 2:10) and simultaneously commands the Ephesians actively to walk according to their new calling (Eph. 4:1; also 4:17; 5:2, 8, 15).

7

Identity Found

Ephesians 2:11–13

Remember . . . you who are Gentiles by birth . . . remember that at that time you were separate from Christ, excluded from citizenship in Israel and foreigners to the covenants of the promise, without hope and without God in the world. But now in Christ Jesus you who once were far away have been brought near through the blood of Christ. (Eph. 2:11–13)

emory knows before knowing remembers," writes William Faulkner in a passage from *Light in August*. The words are meant to remind us that there are experiences so deep, so profound in their effect upon us that even before the mind can consciously process all the reasons for certain reactions and emotions, our memories interact with present realities to inform us viscerally and instinctively how we should feel and react today. Such memories the apostle Paul presses to the front of our consciousness as he unrolls the implications of what it means for us to be God's workmanship, created in Christ Jesus to do good works that he prepared in advance for us to do (Eph. 2:10).

What are we to do as God's workmanship? The mind searches for the rational responses that will be supplied later in the epistle. But for the moment the apostle stimulates key memories, knowing that he must work at a level deeper than present consciousness to accomplish all his and his Savior's ends. Paul must bring the Ephesians and us to the realization that we cannot accomplish God's purposes unless we are united. Christians must pull together in a faithful direction to fulfill God's purposes. Christians in Ephesus who were of so many different backgrounds, nationalities, educational levels, and economic strata must have questioned this call to unity. How could they (and we in a culture no less mixed) all pull together? Not by reasoning—not at first, anyway—but by remembering. Paul points to memories that tell us not only where we have been but also where we must go in our hearts to fulfill God's purposes together.

"We are *God's* workmanship" (Eph. 2:10). That reminder of divine grace is supposed to trigger some profound recollections. That is why Paul begins these next verses with "Therefore, remember . . ."

Why does Paul tell us twice to "remember" so much? There can be only one answer: we too easily forget. Either because we do not want to face the pain of what we were, or because our pride tempts us to erase the shame of what we were, or because we do not want to confess that we are no better than those we judge, we press our past desperation from our memory. We forget the grace that God designed to bind our hearts to his truths and to the hearts of others also claimed by his grace. It is too easy to forget, too easy to be proud of our differences, too easy to embrace our prejudices, too easy to nurse our offenses—and so the apostle says, "Remember these things."

Remember the Nature of Your Past (2:11)

Remember Your Roots (Eph. 2:11a)

Paul reminds the Ephesians that they were pagans by birth. Literally, Paul says that they were once "Gentiles in the flesh." This is more than simply saying that they are from other nations; their foreignness is part of their flesh, rooted in their very nature. For those who are now Christian the reminder that they were born without the privileges of covenant status (so that even their bodies were considered impure and unclean) could not be pleasant.

Those of us who can be reminded of how unclean we felt when we used our bodies for unholy purposes can begin to get the sense of the impurity Paul is telling the Ephesians to remember. And their impurity is not simply a consequence of things they have done but also of being born outside the nation of Israel. Commentators say some Jewish rabbis taught that Gentiles were created simply to fuel the fires of hell, and Paul reminds the Ephesian Christians with pagan roots that such reproach was attached to them.

A compelling public service announcement that aired after the national tragedy of September 11, 2001, had one obvious purpose: to remind Americans that they share an identity despite their differences. With dark hair, dark eyes, and a Native American shawl over her shoulders, a young woman looks into the camera and says without blinking, "I am an American." With cowboy hat, dark mustache, and Hispanic features, a young man smiles into the camera and says, "I am an American." With a helmet that covers all but a few wisps of his red hair, a stoic-faced, middle-aged fireman speaks through wind-burned cheeks and with the hint of an Irish lilt: "I am an American." Softly, but with an unmistakable determination not to be excluded, a man with a chiseled chin, dark skin, and a white turban says the words, too: "I am an American." Beyond the constraints of regional cultures, deeper than the daily prejudices of birth and background, more powerful than the presumptions of color, class, and ethnicity that too easily divide, is a claim of common identity that should unite a nation. "Remember," says the commercial with the eloquence of visual image, "that we are a pilgrim nation, that we have come from many different lands, that prejudice has not helped us, that divided we will not stand. Remember that we are made one by commitments greater than our differences. Remember, because in a time of great challenge, it is easy to forget—and in forgetting to loose the threads that bind us together so that we can accomplish what our times call us to achieve."

What the commercial says in visual image, the apostle Paul says in penetrating words: "Remember you were regarded as pagans by birth and belittled by the religious elite. Remember that you were regarded as foreigners and deprived of hope. Remember what it meant for your sin to make you despicable in your eyes and in God's. Remember, for in those memories are the images that will make not only your salvation precious, but also will make those around you—including those once very different from you—seem very much like you *and* precious to you." But the message may not have the impact Paul wants, if those in the church consider only their past differences. It is just as important that they remember their mutual pain.

Remember Your Rejection (2:11b)

Rather than simply remembering the uncleanness of their former status, the apostle also wants all Christians to remember their former treatment. With your shame, Paul says to the Ephesians, remember the epithets with which the Jews rejected you. For the Jews the sign of circumcision was more than a physical distinction; it was the mark of covenantal privilege, social standing, and spiritual purity.[1] If you have ever been called by a racial slur, or put down for your looks, or your accent, or your parentage, or your origin, or your height—matters that caused you to be rejected simply as a consequence of the circumstances of your birth—then you have some idea of what the apostle is calling for the Ephesians to remember.

Once, early in my junior high years, I found my little brother crying uncontrollably in my mother's arms. He was born mentally handicapped. About the time he discovered that he was not like other children, they learned to taunt him with the word "retard." In sobs that could not find solace he wept to be called a derogatory name for a birth condition over which he had no control but which was used to cause him shame. Paul urges the Ephesians to remember the shame not only of their birth condition, but also of their rejection by those who thought themselves religious.

There is a leveling of all nations and peoples here. Paul reminds the Ephesians and us that apart from a covenant relationship with our God there is no escaping our shame. The uncleanness of the fleshly nature with which we were born, and the rejection such uncleanness warrants from the covenant community, make us all unworthy of the divine workmanship the apostle says we were designed to fulfill.

It is a curious leveling that seems to give privilege to a few: the Jews, the ones who are the circumcised. These are the ones who are calling names and deriding others. They seem to get special treatment simply because

1. Of course, circumcision itself was indeed ordained by God to designate his covenant people and to set them apart as pure unto the Lord (Gen. 17). Yet it was easy for a Jewish person to overlook Moses' caution that God is concerned not merely to call a people to put on a physical symbol, but to call to himself those who are his spiritual followers—those who are of a "spiritual circumcision" and who are "circumcised of heart" (Deut. 10:16; 30:6).

of their birth. But the apostle now does something to level all. The Jews who claim privilege simply because of a ritual—who "call themselves 'the circumcision'"—are basing their identity only on what is done "in the body by the hands of men." The apostle's words make it clear that although the Jews "call themselves" holy, their conclusion that they are right before a holy God is based only on what is done "in the body by the hands of men."[2] The reminder that they are relying on human efforts to give them spiritual status is Paul's way of saying that the Jews' fleshly status is no different before God than the Gentiles'. Paul uses the "in the flesh" echo to remind Gentiles and Jews that the natural state of all is merely of the "flesh." We are all remarkably human, and in our flesh this is inescapable.

We naturally assume that there must be some human community or design that would isolate us from the natural corruption of being finite. But everywhere there is the smell of rotting flesh. If, like a Margaret Mead or Paul Gauguin, you try to find a primitive community untouched by the corrosion of civilized man, even in the most Eden-like of communities you will eventually discover the faults of the flesh. And if, like a Karl Marx or the Khmer Rouge or a North Korean dictator, you try to reach perfection by the control of a society's natural impulses, you will discover that what humankind tries to control in the flesh only magnifies the worst of human corruption with the most horrible of results. Even among the religious in the best of churches—despite the veneer of religion and the formalities of faith—our humanity inevitably shows through in our pettiness, our quarrels, our lack of forgiveness, our envy, our lusts, our gossip, and our laziness. Inevitably we remain products of our birth, remarkably human—creatures in the flesh—with all the foibles and shame that nature involves.

These are not thoughts pleasant to consider. We do not like to acknowledge that what we despise and judge in others is really just our own human

2. The Greek term for "done by hands" likely has a negative slant, for it is actually used throughout the Greek Old Testament to designate pagan idols and their temples, which are useless because they are made by mere men's hands (e.g., Lev. 26:1, 30; Isa. 2:18; 10:11; 16:12; 19:1; 21:9; 31:7; 46:6; Dan. 5:4, 23). By way of contrast, in the New Testament the true temple of God is not made by men's hands (Mark 14:58; Acts 7:48; 17:24; Heb. 9:11, 24). Paul elsewhere transforms the idea of circumcision as an ethnic and religious dividing line by picking up the Old Testament teaching of "circumcised hearts" (Deut. 10:16; 30:6; Jer. 4:4; Rom. 2:25–29); he argues that the true circumcision is the spiritual one performed by God on the heart of every Christian (Phil. 3:2–3; Col. 2:11–13). Thus physical circumcision, though permissible, is no longer required of the people of God (1 Cor. 7:18–19; cf. Rom. 4:10–12; Gal. 5:2–6; 6:12–16; Col. 3:11).

identity. We may be appalled at business scandals, repulsed by the sin of molesters, ashamed of family alcoholics, and offended by the profane. Yet we ourselves are easily drawn to greed and tempted by perversions. We argue and rage with words and actions we thought would never erupt from us. We long for escape from our daily grinds and constant failures. But the apostle will not let our minds evade our sin or debate our guilt. He simply says, "Remember," as though our memories will confirm what our thoughts might rationalize away. And Paul is not yet done with what he wants us to remember.

Remember the Consequences of Your Past (2:12)

After forcing us to remember the leveling effects of our past shame, the apostle says with steely, unblinking objectivity, "This is what your past did to you." He then spells out the consequences for us to remember as well.

Paul first speaks merely in terms of the consequences of being Gentiles in a pagan, immoral culture apart from the covenant privileges of the nation of Israel. But the consequences quickly become more personal and more devastating. To the Ephesians, he says, consider these consequences of your past upon your identity:

Alienated from Community (2:12a, b)

As Gentiles, the Ephesians were separate from Christ (Eph. 2:12a). "Christ" is the New Testament term for the promised Messiah. Paul uses the term to remind these church people that, as a consequence of their birth, they were not natural parties to the rescue God had promised his people by the coming Christ. Although Isaiah had promised that God would bring light out of darkness by a coming Prince of Peace (Isa. 9:1–7), the spiritual darkness of the humanity of the Ephesians had no such promised light. They were separate from the promises of Israel.

They also were excluded from citizenship in Israel (Eph. 2:12b). As Gentiles, the Ephesians were outside the benefits of the commonwealth of Israel. God gave his theocratic state instructions for justice, worship, and mercy so that the grace of his character would have concrete expression in the laws of Israel. But no such protections of citizenship were available to the Gentiles.

Both in political status and in temple worship they lived outside the protections of God. By birth they were excluded from citizenship in his kingdom.

Some of you reading these words are living in a country other than your homeland. You know the loneliness and isolation that come from being away from your family in a foreign land. You know the ever-present fear that something might happen to deprive you of your security because your lack of citizenship gives you so little power and standing in a foreign nation. That sense of isolation and vulnerability Paul reminds the Ephesians was once theirs in terms of their spiritual citizenship.

Alienated from Intimacy (2:12c)

But the isolation is not merely from the larger community; it also creates alienation from intimacy with those much closer. Their natural status made the Ephesians "foreigners [strangers] to the covenants of the promise" (Eph. 2:12c). Commentators make much of the fact that the word "covenant" is plural in this verse. The word "promise" is singular, referring to the promise of God to be the God of the covenant people. But the covenants that compose this promise were many. In historical sequence we remember that God made a covenant with Adam, with Noah, with Abraham, with Moses, and with David. He renewed covenant promises with Joshua, Ezra, Nehemiah, and others. Through his prophets God covenanted to send a Redeemer. But these covenants of promise that united the nation to God also were woven into the fabric of the life of Israel. This was a covenant people. Land was divided and secured by covenant. The people covenanted to provide for priests, and priests to intercede for the people. A man and a woman lived in a covenant of marriage. A father covenanted to bless children, and children to maintain aging parents.

The covenants of promise were not only the basis of Israel's relationship to God, but also the social glue that united neighbors, worship communities, and families. To be foreigners to the covenants of promise was to live without intimacy in community, worship, and family. Paul's purpose is to remind us that any who live outside of covenant commitments are deprived of the most precious relationships this life can offer. In the subtlest of transitions the apostle is moving us from considering purely political associations to weighing spiritual consequences. By analogy he wants us to remember that living outside covenant commitments, in a state of sin and alienation from God, ultimately isolates us from intimacy with all we hold precious.

Christian psychiatrist Richard Winter once shared an article with pastors to help them understand how living outside of covenant commitments ultimately isolates men from intimacy with all that we hold precious. The article is a startlingly honest autobiography of a minister's struggle with sexual addictions. Midway through the article the minister writes of the alienation from intimacy caused by his sin:

> I have not mentioned the effect of lust on my marriage. It did not destroy my marriage, did not push me out to find more sexual excitation in an adulterous affair, or with prostitutes, did not even impel me to put unrealistic demands on my wife's sexual performance. The effect was far more subtle. . . .
>
> Because I have . . . gone over every inch of Miss October as well as the throng of beauties that Madison Avenue and Hollywood recruit to tantalize the masses, I start to view my wife in that light. . . . I begin to focus on my wife's minor flaws. I lose sight of the fact that she is a charming, warm, attractive woman and that I am fortunate to have found her. . . .
>
> Lust affected my marriage in . . . [a] subtle and pernicious way. Sex . . . . We performed okay. . . . But passion, ah, that was something different. Passion I never felt in my marriage. . . .
>
> We never talked about this, yet I am sure that she sensed it. I think she began to view herself as a sex object—not in the feminist sense of being the object of a husband's selfish greed, but in the deprived sense of being only the object of my physical necessity and not of romance and passion.[3]

These words are terrifying to any man. We know the power of the truth that underlies them. When we live outside of covenant commitments sexually, we ultimately deny ourselves intimacy with those we hold most precious because of our inability to look at loved ones, neighbors, brothers, and sisters as more than objects of our desires. The consuming power of sin to make others the objects of our desires rather than the partners of our hearts is obvious when we talk about lust. But we also should recognize that when we live outside of God's covenant commitments in order to pursue the goals of political ambition, business success, church recognition, or academic status, these too become tools of the Evil One

3. "The War Within," Anonymous, *Leadership Magazine*, Fall 1992.

to drive us from the intimacy our God desires us to have with those we are to love from the heart.

The reason that the Evil One is so zealous to distance us from covenant commitments is his ultimate aim of alienating us from God.

Alienated from God (2:12d)

Paul says that while the Ephesians were foreigners to the covenants of promise, they were "without hope and without God in the world." There is a sense in which we want to debate Paul here. Even before the Ephesians were justified, God was still with them, calling them to himself by his works of special and general providence. Yet there is a sense in which, when they were living outside of covenant commitments, his presence was not real to them. God was absent from their consciousness and thus not able to give them hope. The same remains true for those who live outside covenant commitments now.

The same pastor, who wrote about how his lust denied him deep intimacy in his marriage, also detailed the effect of his sin on his ministry. By harboring lustful habits while at the same time proclaiming the gospel and parading pastoral propriety, he became a divided person. Every day he lived a lie about the power of the gospel, and ultimately he doubted the reality of God's power, love, and mercy. Admittedly, a certain amount of spiritual schizophrenia is impossible to avoid in ministry. All those in ministry will at some point have an argument with a spouse right before counseling others on how to mend their marriages. We will harbor anger over personal offenses and speak of the obligation that Christians have to forgive. We will tell others to witness to their neighbors and retreat from the opportunities that God gives us. Our humanity remains inescapable; feet of clay come attached to each one of us. Still, we must understand that callousness to such sin—the willingness to live in a state of faithlessness to covenant commitments—will ultimately make God unreal to us. And then we, too, will have to live in the world that seems empty of him and full of darkness; more and more dependent on our flesh, more and more without hope.

The apostle's reminders of alienation are so heavy, so numerous, and so dark that we are left gasping for spiritual air. By nature we are only human, and with that status we are always vulnerable to alienation from communities of care, the people we love, and the God who gives us hope. When we read what Paul wants us to remember, it is as though we are in the roaring surf of despair, being hit by wave after wave of cold reality that pushes us deeper and deeper under the water of our spiritual devastation. We come up desperate for hope and relief from the memories that rob us of spiritual breath. And, at precisely this moment, the apostle throws us a lifeline.

Paul no longer says, "Remember the past," but instead identifies the reality of "now." While we are drowning in remembrance, the Word of God declares to us that the tide has turned with the simple phrase "But now." That was then, but this is now.[4] You and I now have a new identity that is not determined by memories of the past. We are not what we remember but whom God makes us. In the face of the memories that could haunt us, the apostle urges us to claim the reality of our new identity.

Know Your New Identity (2:13)

What are we to know that is more definite than memory and will heal our past with all of its consequences? What is different about us now?

In Christ (2:13a)

The apostle writes to those who were pagan by birth, separated from the covenant community and alienated from God, and says, "But now you are in Christ Jesus" (Eph. 2:13a). Paul often utilizes the language of union with Christ, but here he draws a contrast. Those who were pagan by birth and religious by ritual he has already identified as "in the flesh" (Eph. 2:11). Hopelessly human, they were imprisoned in their humanity, unable to escape the isolation from community, intimacy, and God. But now they are no longer "in the flesh." Instead they are "in Christ Jesus," not imprisoned in humanity but united to divinity. This sounds wonderfully freeing, but what does it really mean?

Brought Near (2:13b)

Paul explains first by use of a spatial analogy. "In Christ Jesus," he says, "you who were once far away have been brought near" (Eph. 2:13b). The

4. A similar contrast between the former times (2:11) and the "now" (2:13) is found in the preceding passage in Ephesians (former times in 2:1–3; now in 2:4–5). Paul is repeatedly emphasizing the deep misery of the churches' pre-Christian past in order to paint in brighter lines their present privileges.

language brings to mind the contrast of Jew and Gentile that has formed the backdrop of this passage. The presence of the glory of Yahweh in his temple meant that the Jews of the nation of Israel had the privilege of being near to God and, consequently, that the other nations were far off not only geographically but also spiritually. But now all are brought near in Christ.[5]

On his way to the cross, Jesus grieved with this image: "O Jerusalem, Jerusalem, you who kill the prophets and stone those sent to you, how often I have longed to gather your children together, as a hen gathers her chicks under her wings, but you were not willing" (Matt. 23:37). But now, in Christ, people of all nations are gathered under his wings. This means that they are gathered close not only to him, but also to each other.

The fleshly corruptions that separate us from community, intimacy, and worship are overcome by our union with Christ. In him distinctions of race and nationality, pagan and pious, young and old, sinner and saint, prideful and wounded, offender and offended, implode. In him we all are brought near.

The Westminster Confession of Faith expresses this unifying power of Christ this way: "The visible church which is also catholic or universal under the gospel . . . consists of all those throughout the world that profess the true religion, and of their children, and is the kingdom of the Lord Jesus Christ, and the house and family of God" (25.2).

In Christ we are part of the same family despite our pasts and their consequences. Being one in Christ has consequences for our community. This shared identity means that national identity does not take precedence over our identity as Christians. Racial prejudice cannot be justified and must be resisted. And, in contrast, racial identity that leads to a chip-on-the-shoulder judgmentalism toward other believers who have not fully realized their sin must also be swallowed in family understanding.

Being one in Christ has consequences for our intimacy. Our shared identity means that the respectable and the despicable are one. We do not divide our pews or our perceptions into those deserving of grace and those not. We are pushed together into the arms of Christ with equal recognition of our

5. The imagery of distance and nearness (also see Eph. 2:17–18), though employed in later Judaism with regard to Gentile proselytes, was also deeply grounded in Old Testament thought (e.g., Isa. 57:19; Deut. 4:7; Ps. 148:14; cf. more widely Ex. 19:22; 24:2; Pss. 34:18; 119:151; 145:18; and many other places).

total need of him, and equal dependence upon his grace, regardless of what has characterized our flesh in the past.

Being one in Christ has consequences not only for our relationship with each other but also for our relationship with God. Despite our weakness, arrogance, coldness, or ignorance, we are in union with him. When I may want to call myself "failure, liar, hypocrite, pervert, or betrayer," my God calls me "my child," because I am in union with his Son.

In essence, God says, "Take all of those other labels of the flesh and paste this one on top of them: 'God's Own Child, Heir of the Promises and Glory of Heaven.'" How can it be that you and I, whose identities are so much a product of our birth and our past, could have this new identity? The answer lies in the cleansing and uniting power of Christ's blood.

Through Blood (2:13c)

Paul says, ". . . you who once were far away have been brought near through the blood of Christ" (Eph. 2:13c). When we read these words, the first (and very appropriate) thought that comes to our minds is of the cleansing power of the blood of our Savior when he took the penalty for our sin upon the cross. This is the glorious truth of the forgiveness that is ours because he purchased us with the currency of his own blood. We are brought near to the holiness of the temple, reconciled to our God by the blood of sacrifice—the sacrifice of our Savior.[6]

But there is much more to learn. The context is not merely that of the temple but also of our union with the Son of God. We are in him. To be in union with him means that his blood is ours, too. We are not merely the beneficiaries of the blood of his death; we are recipients of the blood of his life. His blood, his life, flows through us. We draw near to the holy temple because his blood empowers our hearts, fills our bodies, and grants us the divine life that is his.

We are not merely forgiven of our sin; we also are filled with the benefits of his righteousness, holiness, and redemption. What he is, I am. My identity is no longer fixed by my birth, determined by my heritage, or spoiled by my sin, but is renewed, transformed, and reborn by my Savior's blood.

6. Paul already highlighted the redeeming blood of Jesus in his opening eulogy (Eph. 1:7; see the notes above on this verse for further cross references to Christ's blood in Pauline theology).

Yes, I have a racial identification, but more than that, I am a Christian. Yes, I have a family name, but more than that, I am a Christian. Yes, I have failed to be all that my God requires, but I am not my sin. I am a Christian, washed in the blood of Christ, and filled with its life through the grace of my Savior alone.

A friend of mine has served faithfully and courageously as a pastor in a neighboring state for most of the last decade. His courage showed when he moved his historic church from a denomination that had drifted from faithfulness to God's Word. Although he was faithful to God, some did not appreciate him. Because his own roots were in that community, some deemed his actions as a betrayal of his heritage. He was called names and threatened with the loss of his career through community prejudice. It must have been very painful to be given that identity in his own community, but he knew he was a child of the King, and that—his true identity—gave him both courage and solace. Whatever he was called, whatever anger and prejudice he faced, he knew that his identity in Christ was secure because of his Savior's blood. And that realization enabled him to serve in that community with courage for his God and compassion toward others.

But now my friend battles a very different enemy of confidence. In recent years, an illness that has long been present has become far more aggressive. He has had seizures in the pulpit, he has lost large parts of his memory, and he has lost the ability to drive. When the seizures began to come numerous times every day, something had to be done. A dangerous and complex surgery was performed at one of the nation's leading hospitals, and he has been free of the seizures—until recent days.

I talked to him one day after the first recurrence of the seizures. He was totally drained, not only by the previous day's seizure but by his new reality. He now knew that despite the great hardship and risk of the preceding year, everything might begin to spiral downward, again.

"Bryan," he said, "the seizures rob me of me. I cannot talk, I cannot think, and I cannot remember. But even though the seizures rob me of me, they are not me."

What did he mean? Somehow we know. Yes, the seizures are part of his life—they erupt from some reality of his past, and they presently exist in his body—this is true. But these seizures are only assaults on his life; they are not his life. He will not let them be. Without denying their reality, he claims the truths that establish the identity by which he will live. He is a father, a husband, a pastor, but even if all of that is taken from him, he is a beloved child of God. This is the identity that cannot be taken from him because it is provided by the blood of his Savior. My friend may suffer much in this life and know much failure of body and heart, but he is united to divinity eternally. He is a Christian, precious to God and created in Christ Jesus to do good works which God prepared in advance for him to do. That is his truest and most enduring identity, and remembering that identity gives him joy, purpose, and strength for each day—even the ones that are robbed of other memories.

Yes, we all face the corruptions of our births, our bodies, our pasts, and our relationships. We remain remarkably human—creatures of flesh. But now we are in Christ Jesus through his blood. And although we remain full of weakness, lies, lust, pride, and prejudice, we are God's beloved children now and forever. Beyond all our trials, disappointments, and failures, this kinship with God is our life, our hope, and our identity, because the blood of Jesus cleanses us and equips us for his glory.

8

Breaking Down Barriers

Ephesians 2:14–18

For he himself is our peace, who has made the two one and has destroyed the barrier, the dividing wall of hostility, by abolishing in his flesh the law with its commandments and regulations. . . . He came and preached peace to you who were far away and peace to those who were near. For through him we both have access to the Father by one Spirit. (Eph. 2:14–15, 17–18)

In the preceding verses, the apostle has redefined human distinctions by reminding the Christians at Ephesus that whether they are Gentile or Jew by virtue of their birth, the blood of Christ has given them one new identity. They are Christians. Now he begins to unfold for them and for us what it means to live before God with the consciousness of being a single people—despite race, ethnicity, class distinctions, and past offenses—to honor him.

Paul will no longer allow any sense of "you" versus "us"; it's all "we" and "us." Although at several places earlier in this letter "we," "our," and "us" have designated the Jewish race (and although here "you" still indicates the Gentiles; see Eph. 2:17), it is clear in this passage that "we" includes all believers

(Jew and Gentile alike), since "our peace" now extends to both groups (Eph. 2:14; also see 2:4–5, 10). With these words Paul not only reminds us of our unity, he also underscores the consequence of living as though persons once different and distant are all close to God: peace!

Perhaps you remember the song that contains these words:

Imagine there's no countries;
It isn't hard to do.
Nothing to kill or die for,
And no religion too.
Imagine all the people,
Living life in peace.

The secular conclusion of Western culture toward the end of the twentieth century, stated so artistically by John Lennon in his song "Imagine," was that faith divides the world and peace would come with the end of all religion.

But the conclusion more commonly found in our culture today is different. You will find it well stated in a seventh-grade social studies textbook, *Across the Centuries*, published by Houghton Mifflin and used in public schools across this country. In that textbook, students are urged to imagine "you are a Muslim soldier on your way to conquer Syria in A.D. 635. Write three journal entries that reflect your thoughts about Islam." The reason, according to Vincent Ferrandino, executive director of the National Association of Elementary School Principals, is, "It's only by having that kind of understanding that we can better work with people from different backgrounds." What is the understanding that we are to share with others? The textbook reveals its purpose in its description of the teachings of Islam: "These revelations confirmed both Muhammad's belief in one God, or monotheism, and his role as the last messenger in a long line of prophets sent by God. The God he believed in—Allah—is the same God of other monotheistic religions, Judaism and Christianity."[1] And so as not to give discriminatory favoritism to the monotheistic religions of Islam, Judaism, and Christianity, school districts where this curriculum is used also urge students to imagine being in a tribe and dancing to African gods.

1. "Parents Say Textbook Reads like Recruitment," *USA Today*, March 4, 2002, 6D.

The secular conclusion of today's culture is that peace will come between all peoples not with the end of all religion, but with the blend of all religion. The conclusion is not without effect upon the church. A religious scholar at Harvard recently wrote that the great task of the twenty-first century is to "create a positive multireligious society out of the fabric of democracy, without the chauvinism and religious triumphalism that have marred human history."[2]

It becomes clearer every day that one of the greatest challenges for the preachers of this generation is confronting pluralism with an uncompromising commitment to the uniqueness of the Christian faith as God's way of salvation. Cultural accusations of bigotry and intolerance, and personal qualms against pride and insensitivity make us more and more resistant to religious claims that put barriers between people.

So how does the Bible help us resist the tide of religious pluralism that now washes over the cultural landscape and advocates obliterating all the boundaries of religious distinction that supposedly create conflict? The Bible responds by offering, in this portion of Paul's letter to the Ephesians, this remarkable claim: neither the end of religion nor the blend of religion but rather the blood of Jesus Christ removes the barriers between all peoples and brings true peace to this world.

Christ's Blood Brings Peace between People (2:14–15)

The claim that Jesus brings peace (Eph. 2:14) follows the earlier statement (in Eph. 2:13) that through the blood of Jesus, those who were far away have been brought near. The statement reminds us that from a Jewish perspective there were only two races of people: Jews and everybody else. Those who were near to the temple where atonement was made with God were distinguished from all the other nations of the world who were distant and defiled. The Jews considered themselves chosen and all others defiled pagans (Eph. 2:11). Such perspectives fueled antipathies already identified by Paul.

But how does throwing Christ's blood on this war of pride and prejudice create peace? The importance of the "peace" the apostle wants to bring is evident in this passage by the repetitions of both the word "peace" (Eph.

2. Diana L. Eck, *A New Religious America: How a "Christian Country" Has Become the World's Most Religiously Diverse Nation* (San Francisco: Harper, 2002), 383.

2:14–15, 17 [twice]) and its antonym ("hostility," Eph. 2:14, 16). In striking language, Paul goes beyond saying that Jesus brings peace, for Christ *is* peace. In the Old Testament the Messiah was to be the Prince of Peace (Isa. 9:6), who *is* Israel's peace (Mic. 5:5). Structurally in the New Testament language, Christ both "is" peace (Eph. 2:14) and he "preaches" peace (Eph. 2:17)—these are the main clauses. In his capacity as peace incarnate, Christ makes both groups one (Eph. 2:14a). He destroys the barrier between them (Eph. 2:14b–15a) with the dual purpose of reconciling all persons to each other and reconciling each person to God (Eph. 2:15b–16). Thus, Paul says that Christ's blood both destroys ancient enmity and creates a new humanity.

Destroying Ancient Enmity (2:14–15a)

Paul says that Christ himself became our peace by breaking down the barrier formed by the dividing wall between the races (Eph. 2:14). There are various events and practices to which the apostle may be alluding. The one that most commonly comes to mind is the partition that separated the Court of the Gentiles from the rest of the temple. The Jewish historian Josephus tells of this partition with its inscriptions in Latin and Greek that warned Gentiles not to enter upon pain of death.[3] These inscriptions can still be seen in a museum in Jerusalem, and I could not help but think of them when entering the court created by partitions around the Wailing Wall in Jerusalem. As the scores of Jews gather daily in traditional garb to pray with commandments bound to their foreheads and arms, and bend over their copies of the Torah to study in this place, I also covered my head to enter but, as a Gentile, had an eerie sense of being out of place—still resented and perhaps in some degree of danger (if my respect were not adequate)—for invading ground thought sacred for four thousand years of Jewish history.

With such ancient enmity between Jew and Gentile, how does Christ bring peace? Paul says, "By abolishing in his flesh [i.e., in his incarnate being] the law with its commandments and regulations" (Eph. 2:15a). The commandments referred to here (with "regulations") are not the moral law—the Ten Commandments—but the rites of ceremony and sacrifice that made the Jews come near to the temple.[4] When Christ offered his flesh upon the cross,

3. Josephus, *Antiquities* 15.417; *War* 6.124–28; 5.193–94; cf. Acts 21:26–32.

4. This point is disputed among some commentators; certainly Paul can refer to the moral aspect of the law as "commandments" (cf. Rom. 7:7–13; 13:9; and Eph. 6:2). However, Paul can also use "com-

he made irrelevant for religious distinction all the ceremonies and distinctions of the flesh that separated Jew from Gentile, that made some holy and some unclean, that created hostility between the privileged and ostracized. But whether the dividing wall is actually the partition between the Court of the Gentiles and the Jews is not really the issue. The real point is that the barrier of ceremonial law that kept the races apart and was the basis of their hostility has been demolished by the sacrifice of Christ's flesh that makes all distinctions of the flesh now irrelevant for religious privilege.

Even the division between the common Jew and the priests who could enter the holy places has been demolished because in Christ all those whose sins are atoned for are made pure. Paul wants us to catch the significance of this elevation of all persons (Jew and Gentile).

Creating a New Humanity (2:15b)

Christ's blood brings peace not only by destroying the ancient enmity, but also by creating a new humanity. Through the shedding of his blood, Jesus erased the distinguishing features of two races of humanity. He wiped out the features of those who were distinguished by their participation in temple ceremonies, and he wiped out the distinctions of those who were denigrated by their exclusion from temple ceremonies. Without the continued validity of the temple rites, the ceremonies can no longer create separation between Jew and Gentile. Thus Paul says that "by abolishing in his flesh the law with its commandments and regulations," Jesus' "purpose was to create in himself one new man out of the two, thus making peace" (Eph. 2:15b), no longer segregated by ceremony.

But the effect of Jesus' work is more than homogenization (making the two alike); it is renewal (making both new and better). Christ's purpose was "to create in himself one new man."[5] The Jew and the Gentile are now alike in being in Christ (Eph. 2:15b). With various allusions the apostle Paul's words now begin to work a wonderful biochemistry. By his blood, Jesus provides the

---

mandments" to mean distinctively Jewish teachings which set Jews apart from the Gentiles (see Titus 1:14), and he can call "regulations" those prescriptive legal requirements that constitute the debt of the Gentile apart from Christ (see Col. 2:13–14).

5. Paul returns to the notion of the created "new man" in Ephesians 4:24 (cf. Col. 3:10; 2 Cor. 5:17), although here in chapter 2 he most clearly emphasizes the implications of this "newness" for the collective Christian community.

sacrifice that makes the shedding of blood in the temple sacrifices no longer necessary and, thus, the rituals can no longer separate the races (Eph. 2:13). In his flesh, he not only met the requirements of the law but also accepted the punishment of others demanded by the law. And, by perfectly fulfilling all the law required, he made null and void the ordinances that distinguished Jew and Gentile by their flesh (i.e., circumcision and uncircumcision; see Eph. 2:15).

Through his blood and in his flesh the two races are now one, but this one race is different from what both were before. The Jew no longer must offer sacrifice for his atonement; the Gentile is no longer separated from the atonement. Both are made pure in Christ. They are a new man, as though a new Adam has been created to launch a new human race altogether. Chrysostom, the great preacher of the early church, says it is as though one took a statue of silver and a statue of lead, put them into a forge and they came out a statue of gold. They not only have become one, they have become better. This higher oneness that creates a new race of humanity in Christ is not only the joy of individual Christians, it also is meant to be the source of peace between them, as they perceive the oneness they have in Christ. Each is to see the other as holy in Jesus Christ and, thus, to see the irrelevance of human distinctions that would separate hearts.

Once when I was speaking for a mission conference, the host church showed a video of a ministry that it supports in Hungary that is led by a Korean who has been commissioned by Presbyterians in Romania. It is rather mind-boggling to hear it all together: North American Anglos were supporting an Asian Korean who was a missionary to the land of Attila the Hun, having been commissioned by a Presbyterian church from the historic land of Dracula. At first glance this is bizarre, but for the Christian who perceives the breaking down of barriers enabled by the blood of Christ that makes all races gloriously one new race in him, the construction of such Christian jigsaw puzzles is pure joy. It is as though we get to watch at the dawn of the creation of a new humanity, and recognize that this dawn reflects the dawn of the eternal day. In the coming together of different persons we have the delight of pre-glimpsing the heavenly scene where the great multitude from every nation, tribe, people, and language will gather as one before the throne of God to wash their robes in the blood of the Lamb (Rev. 7: 9, 14). We who see what kind of barriers God can demolish recognize the power of the gospel when there is peace between persons so different, and it brings us great joy.

Such joy can be the great motivation of this generation that will likely make the greatest strides against racism, bigotry, and prejudice. It is easy to condemn the church for its failings in a land where the gulfs between peoples remain great. It is also easy to become discouraged because the kingdom of God seems so distant from the indifference of oppressors and the resentments of the oppressed. What will change us? Guilt is justified but its conviction rarely corrects attitudes of the heart. Apologies are deserved but rarely bring healing when persons do not feel personally responsible. We must pray that God would grant us the unqualified joy and pure delight of seeing persons so different from each other becoming one in Christ. Rather than responding in fear or animosity, we must pray that believers will recognize their differences and with pure joy welcome the variety.

It grieves me that some in our church may occasionally feel excluded and unwelcome because of their minority status. What can I do to change that? Impose mandatory greetings of different persons? Search out offenders? Question the motives of the complainers? All such steps might be effective for a while, but what will move us from "got to" to "get to" in our attitudes about accepting others is the ability to perceive the joy of persons from different races, backgrounds, and languages coming together. Until we sense that overcoming barriers is our own foretaste of heaven, we will not have the energy to move toward those who are moving away, the willingness to endure insult, the grace to forgive, and the desire to reach out in love toward those different from us.

How will we stimulate the joy that has such power? We stimulate such joy when we teach others to recognize that the barriers that God destroys between others and us are ultimately the reflection of the barrier that he has destroyed between us and him. People overjoyed with the wonders of their salvation delight to see the power of the gospel overcoming the barriers of race because it reminds them of the power of Christ to unite all of us to him. Consistent preaching and teaching of Christ's gospel make God's people desire all the dimensions of Christ's peace.

Christ's Blood Brings Peace with God (2:16–17)

How Christ's blood brings peace with others makes sense only when you perceive how Christ's blood brings peace with God.

Putting Corporate Hostility to Death (2:16)

We are accustomed to thinking that God makes us each a new creature in Christ Jesus whereby our individual nature has the imprint of, and bondage to, sin removed (2 Cor. 5:17). We are told that we have been made like Christ in holy status and in the ability to resist sin. Here Paul is saying something similar about newness, but our individual nature is not the focus. Rather Paul says that it was God's purpose to create one new man out of the two previous kinds of man (Jew and Gentile), thus making peace between them, *and* also in this one body to reconcile both to God through the cross (Eph. 2:16a). The reconciliation is not just between the individual and his Lord. The reconciliation is corporate.[6] The full reconciliation that God intends occurs as the two different races—in one body—are reconciled to him by the cross.

With the limitations of our English language, we read Paul saying that in the one body both races are reconciled to God by the cross, by which he put to death *their* hostility (Eph. 2:16). We think therefore that Paul is talking about the hostility between the Jew and Gentile. In our mind's eye we think of God as a referee making two angry fighters shake hands after a bitter match. But the hostility between the races is the subject of an earlier verse (Eph. 2:14). This second reference to "hostility" points to the enmity between all humankind and God—between both boxers and the referee. By the cross on which his Son died, God put to death the hostility between heaven and earth. Through the cross the Son absorbed the righteous rage God had against us and thus put to death the hostility between heaven and earth. What we may not be accustomed to thinking is that God intends for this reconciliation to occur as we are in one body. God's purpose is "to create in himself one new man out of the two . . . and in this one body to reconcile both of them to God through the cross" (Eph. 2:15b and 16). God intends to relate to us as one race—so unified as to be considered one body—incomplete without one another. There is a sense in which the full experience of our reconciliation to God is incomplete until we are approaching God together as one.

I am not saying that our salvation is dependent on our unity with others, but that our experience of reconciliation with him in some measure depends

6. A similar corporate view of reconciliation is found in Colossians 1:19–23 (esp. v. 20; cf. Rom. 11:15). For other soteriological uses of "reconciliation" in Paul see Romans 5:10–11; 2 Corinthians 5:18–21. The need for reconciliation with God is apparent in Ephesians 2:1–3, where both Gentile and Jew alike are "by nature objects of wrath" (esp. Eph. 2:3; cf. Rom. 3:9).

on our expression of unity with others. This should not be a new thought to us. After all, we ask God to forgive us as we forgive others (Matt. 6:12). We enter communion corporately, and are cautioned not to partake if we are sinfully separated from others. God's purpose is to deal with us together.

When I was a boy, my whole family was involved in little league baseball. I was either playing ball or watching my siblings play ball almost every summer night. That was a lot of games and a lot of boredom. One of the ways to relieve the boredom was to play in the powder-fine dirt that gathered at the edges of the groomed infields. We discovered that you could take a paper cup, fill it with the fine dirt, crush the cup with only a little opening remaining at its mouth, and throw it as high as you could into the air. The dirt would pour out of the opening leaving a trail in the sky like a fireworks streamer. At least, that is the way it was supposed to work. One night two brothers were throwing their paper cup streamer and discovered that if you aimed well you could get the dirt to flow out of the streamer over someone's head. One boy launched the dirt streamer over the head of his brother. Doused in the dirt, the brother picked up the paper cup, quickly scooped dirt back into it, and in anger threw it back at his brother, who had ducked beneath the stands where most of the parents were sitting. On its return route the paper cup streamer worked "perfectly" and spewed dirt all over the parents in the stands—one of whom was the boys' father. Now with a degree of his own hostility the father turned toward the boys and motioned with a pointer finger, "Come here." The boy that was nearest to the stands came right away, but the one farther away stood frozen in fear. So the father used the pointer finger of the other hand to indicate, "Both of you come here. I want to deal with you together when I instruct you about what you have done and what I now expect of you."

Although a homely illustration, this anecdote conveys the right idea about the hostility the apostle is describing. Our heavenly Father also wants to deal with us jointly in our sin. Our sin is not just between man and man; it is between man and God. In fact the hostility between the races has itself become an issue between them and God. Yet on the cross Jesus Christ took the dirt and the filth of all our sin on his own body, and now he says to all parties, "I want to deal with you." But he makes it clear that his intent is to reconcile us to him. This divine intention makes it clear that we cannot know the fullness of all that God intends to do for and through us until we approach him together.

God chooses to do far more through our oneness than through our isolation from each other. I witnessed the power of God at work in our Christian unity when an African-American pastor, friend, and former student of mine took a courageous stand. The leadership of a major African-American denomination had decided to give Planned Parenthood entry to its local churches to talk about "safe-sex" and "the option of abortion." My pastor friend was then asked to address a convention of pastors from this denomination. He took the opportunity to address his leaders and peers about the authority of Scripture and the biblical view of life. As a result, many other brave pastors decided not to have Planned Parenthood come to their churches.

Had I, as a white man, determined to tell these African-American pastors what to do, I would have been perceived as either patronizing or insensitive. But because God had led this brave pastor to study and deepen his biblical commitments, the work of the gospel powerfully progressed against a societal evil in ways that neither he nor I could have done separately. The gospel moved forward because of the bond established between races that enabled us to function as one body.

What would occur more regularly if we were able to perceive that just as a bond between races helped the gospel to move forward in this social and political cause, it also helps the gospel to move forward personally? We would see that in the coming together of different persons, the gospel is known by each of us better and more fully. Consider what this means practically. On a visit to the United States, African scholar Zack Nidingeye reminded North American believers that while African Christians can learn from us more of the doctrinal requirements of Scripture, North Americans have much to learn from them regarding care for one another in community. We tend to be much too dependent on material blessing for personal fulfillment, and much too independent of one another to experience the body life Christ wants for his church. In other words, to learn what God has to teach us about the gospel requires that we know people—people different from us—whom he has taught the different things that we need to know at all levels.

When I preach in some inner-city churches, I speak to congregations that are largely comprised of women and children in a culture where two-thirds of the children are raised without a biological father. In these churches are pastors who are speaking faithfully with great courage and perseverance to single mothers and needy children about whom I need to learn as my own white suburban culture is changing. What do African-American pastors who have dealt for decades with Black Muslim movements have to teach me about the appeal of Islam that is just coming into my field of view? What do immigrant populations of Asian, Hispanic, and Sudanese Christians have that I need to learn about being a pilgrim in the world and worshiping Christ for his essence rather than for the expectations and with the accoutrements of my culture? What do Eastern European and Sudanese pastors know that I don't know about the suffering that enables them to share in fellowship with Christ?

Without input from Christians with very different backgrounds and experiences from my own, I will not know all of what the gospel should mean in areas of life that I have not yet explored. Thus I must examine my heart and life to see where I may be distant from those God intends to help me better know him. Others have described a hierarchy of hatred that I have found useful in checking my own attitudes against the commands of Scripture. The hierarchy moves from obvious bigotry to subtle racism to true unity:

1. We have reason to hate them, because of their race.
2. We will tolerate them, if they stay in their place.
3. We will accept them, if they become like us.
4. We will accept them, despite our differences.
5. We will love them, because God wants us to help them.
6. We will love them, because we need them to help us understand God.

Unless I realize that there are treasures of God that I will not discover until I am in union with brothers and sisters quite different than I, I will not pursue the bonds of humanity that enable me to know the fullness of the God who is my delight. I thought of this after reading the results of a survey that found that most evangelicals think of their faith only in terms of "Jesus and me." Love for the lost, concern for the evils of society, the plight of the poor, hunger in the world, the pervasive trap of illiteracy for two-thirds of all peoples, the injustices of racism and materialism, too often are deemed the social causes of "bleeding heart" liberals or distracted evangelicals. Yet to know Christ as God intends, I must realize that without concern for the plight of all persons, my heart deadens to the Word of God for me. Jesus said that whatever we do for the least of his people, we do for him (Matt. 25:40). I cannot dishonor him by shunning or disregarding any of his people, and at the same time believe that my heart will still fully experience his.

God intends to relate to all categories of people as one in order to have his holy purposes and truths realized in our unity. The cross does its work of ushering the love of God forward with transforming power as we come together.

This awareness—that when we bond together in our differences, the power of God is poured through us—is our ultimate motivation to unite across race, nation, class, and personal difference. Together the riches of all of our backgrounds get expressed for the sake of the gospel. Sensing this makes us want to bond with brothers and sisters quite different from us so that the power of God, unfettered by hostility, will pour through us. As we intentionally appreciate the differences between members of our corporate Christianity, we will see the barriers between heaven and earth removed. No other motivation will suffice. If we are motivated simply by guilt, then our energies will not last in the face of the time it will take to overcome ancient enmities. If we are motivated simply by political correctness or societal moods, then we will not maintain divine purposes when political winds and societal attention shift. If we are motivated simply by being appreciated, then we will lose our resolve when the very people we are seeking to serve resent our involvement, are suspicious of our motives, and take advantage of or even attack our efforts.

When we believe that putting hostilities to death brings to life the power of God in our experience, then uniting in Christ with those of different races and backgrounds is not a burden. Variations in style of worship and approaches to ministry fill us with excitement. We become anxious to innovate in ways that demonstrate the manifold wisdom of God rather than anxious about changes to traditions that merely comfort us. Looking for opportunities to unite spiritual efforts across lines of race and class must be more than political correctness; it must arise from our own conviction that we will grow in the knowledge of God and the understanding of the gospel that he intends for us when we break down the barriers that our humanity and society have placed among us.

Proclaiming Corporate Peace to All (2:17)

Christ came and preached peace to those near and far (Eph. 2:17).[7] Consider why he would do so. Why would he—who cared so much for the love of God to be shed abroad in our hearts that he would give his own life for us—preach peace among us? He did so because he knows that if there is not peace between us we cannot fully know the peace that he gave his blood to bring to us. "He came and preached peace to you who were far away and peace to those who were near" because without our peace, his peace will always be remote (Eph. 2:17). So he preached to those near: the Jews in Nazareth, Capernaum, and Jerusalem; and he commissioned Peter and other disciples to continue that ministry. In addition, Jesus preached to those far away: speaking to a Samaritan woman at a well, comforting a Syro-Phoenician, blessing an Ethiopian eunuch through Philip, and commissioning Paul for the Gentiles.[8]

Christ's actions are the great endorsement and exhortation to break barriers since "*he* came" to do so (Eph. 2:17).

Christ's Blood Brings Peace for Each Soul (2:18)

But from where does the corporate peace come that is so essential to knowing the peace that God provides between heaven and earth? It is derived from the personal peace we share. Thus Paul's ultimate leverage for uniting the races is the reminder that Christ's blood brings peace for each soul that has equal access to the Father.

Paul has pressed hard the theme that we have obligations to those quite different from ourselves, and that we have access to great blessing from God

7. Cf. Isaiah 57:19; 52:7. See also the previous chapter on Ephesians 2:13.

8. Commentators debate whether Christ's proclamation of peace involves his earthly ministry (either before or after his death/resurrection), his crucifixion itself (as emblematic of a proclamation of peace), or the ongoing proclamation of Christ through his apostles and disciples. Aside from the meaning of the Greek word (*euangelizomai*), which conveys an actual verbal preaching of the good news, there seems no other reason to limit Christ's preaching role to only one time in his ministry. It is part of the character of the Messiah (the Prince of Peace) and of those who are "in him" that they proclaim the good news of his reconciling work to Jew and Gentile alike.

when we honor those obligations. But he ends the exhortation on quite a different theme. The final reason why he urges peace between the races is that both Jew and Gentile share access to the Father by one Spirit through Jesus Christ (Eph. 2:18).[9]

In my life, a lot of ugliness has revolved around the issues of race. In the South, where I was raised, issues of race and religion often divided people with prejudice, name-calling, and hostilities between black and white, Jew and African-American, Catholic and Protestant. It was not uncommon to experience outbreaks of true hostility. One of the striking memories of my youth is of my mother gathering me and my siblings on the shoulder of Highway 51 in Memphis, Tennessee, to see a civil rights march, and then hearing later that day that the leader had been shot. I also remember the agony of my parents trying to resist the white flight of their peers and keeping their children in public schools when the Memphis schools were integrated; and I remember when they took my sister from public school when hostilities became so great that she was attacked merely for being white.

I also remember my consternation when my father told me that at the end of the hostilities of World War II, he served with the occupation forces in Japan in an integrated military police unit. And I remember with sadness my father, who was raised in the rural South, telling of his relationship with a particular black man in the unit. They had served together, enjoyed good times together, and faced great danger and hostility together, but when it came time for them to part and return home, my father said he felt uncomfortable shaking the black man's hand. Something deep in my father's culture and upbringing—something almost at the level of the soul—made it difficult for him to touch a black man without a sense of repulsion. My father was not defending his feeling, but simply identifying its reality in him. Knowing that reality about my father, as did my siblings, we all wondered how he would react when my sister—the one who experienced such racial hostility in school—adopted a child who is black.

In our home we have a picture that I count precious. It is of my father asleep with my African-American nephew also asleep in my father's arms.

9. Paul returns to this concept in Ephesians 3:12 (cf. Rom. 5:1–2). Although care must be taken in making etymological analogies, it is likely relevant that the cognate verbal form of "access" is frequently employed in the Greek Old Testament to indicate the access the priest had to present offerings before God (e.g., Lev. 1:3, 10 and many other times; cf. Christ's role in 1 Peter 3:18).

The arms of my father that once held me also held a child of a different race. Ancient enmities had been overcome, and I experienced a taste of heaven because one very different from me had as much access as I to my father.

Somehow, deep within all believers there is the understanding that peace between the races and with God comes when, through the sacrifice of Christ, we see ourselves as a child in the lap of our heavenly Father and also see other children—red and yellow, black and white, precious in his sight—held with us in his arms. And we also know that when we count these other children precious, too, because our heavenly Father gives them equal access to himself through the blood of his Son, then we will have understood more of the heart of our Father and thus will know even more of his love for us.

9

Built Tough, Built Together

Ephesians 2:19–22

Consequently, you are no longer foreigners and aliens, but fellow citizens with God's people and members of God's household, built on the foundation of the apostles and prophets, with Christ Jesus himself as the chief cornerstone. (Eph. 2:19–20)

In earlier verses Paul says that the blood of Jesus Christ has obliterated the barriers that separate Jew from Gentile. Both now have equal access to the Father by the sacrifice of the Son of God so that peace should rule between them and with him. But how can there be peace in a world of turmoil and uncertainty? How can we know peace of soul when our security seems so fragile and our world is so frequently in upheaval? Relationships change, jobs disappear, health deteriorates, careers sputter and tumble. What good is peace between persons when personal worlds crumble?

My family felt some of this crumbling when my father sold his father's farm. I think that my brother felt that loss most deeply. As had the rest of my family, my brother had changed residences a dozen or so times during his childhood through college years. My father's company transfers, improving income, and the transitions of early adulthood made us all mobile. But my brother's Air Force career eventually made him the champion of our game of "who's moved the most." His early training as a downed-pilot rescue specialist took him to wild and remote areas throughout the world as he learned to get himself in and get someone else out of virtually any terrain. Later, as an air combat director and then as a liaison officer between the Air Force and NATO governments, his work took him to places and situations both distant and difficult. Yet despite all those transitions and varied experiences there was always a fixed place in my brother's mind that equaled home. Orienting all his experience like an unchanging North Star of life was my grandparents' dairy farm, the place where as boys we picked wild blackberries, chased pigs in the woods, and shot bullfrogs with BBs for the delight of a dinner of my grandmother's fried frog legs.

Always my brother could return to that world of fields and woods, of family and fishing creeks—always, that is, until my father sold the farm after my grandparents died. Then, for the first time in his life, my brother's North Star blinked out. Life was suddenly more foreign and fragile than it had ever been because the place that never changed was suddenly and irreversibly never to be the same again.

The unavoidable transitions of our lives take their toll on us. We are called by events both painful and pleasant to move on, to take the next step, and to leave what is familiar. Although we know transition is unavoidable and may even lead to changes we have long anticipated or sought, the shift from the familiar is always decentering and disorienting. What should orient you when you face the major transitions of life? The North Star you determine to use to navigate through times of transition is important, for it will not only guide you into the future, such a star will also determine how you will guide others whose lives are sure to be filled with transitions of all kinds.

The apostle Paul helps us chart the stars needed for times of transition as he addresses the Christians at Ephesus who have been called from paganism to faith in the living God. He has commanded them to turn from the religion of neighboring friends and family to a separate life of faith in Jesus Christ. He has told them to unite in worship with persons from different races and a formerly hostile religion. That worship will be in house churches that have none of the mystery, ornamentation, and pleasures of the pagan temples, or the sophistication and respectability of the philosophical forum. Everything will be new, unfamiliar, challenging, and possibly even dangerous. How does

Paul prepare these saints for the transitions ahead? He does it by reminding them that whatever changes come we remain dear to God, secure in him, and vital to his future purposes.

We Are Dear to God (2:19)

Unfolding the implications of the preceding summary that "through him [Christ] we both [Jews and Gentiles] have access to the Father by one Spirit" (Eph. 2:18), the apostle says to the Gentiles now in the church, "Consequently, you are no longer foreigners and aliens, but fellow citizens with God's people" (Eph. 2:19). Paul puts before us the grand consequence of the cooperative work of the Trinity in our behalf. Through the cleansing work of Christ we can now approach the heavenly Father. The word Paul uses to describe our "access" to God is used in New Testament times to describe access to a throne room. Our Father is a King.

Paul's careful wording reminds us that we can enter the presence of the King of the universe and seek his favor because he loves us as his own children. By the sacrifice of the Son, the effects of our sin have been washed away. Now we—although of Gentile origins—can approach the Father with the same status as the covenant people of old. And the Holy Spirit himself ushers us forward, announces our presence, and carries our petitions.

Father, Son, and Holy Spirit unite in heavenly power and compassion to grant us purity, peace, and purpose. The trinitarian theology of this passage (Eph. 2:18; cf. 2:22) is reminiscent of other trinitarian texts in Paul's letters (e.g., 1 Cor. 12:4–6; 2 Cor. 13:14; Eph. 4:4–6), but here there is a special emphasis on the effect of their cooperative work on our corporate status.

No Longer Foreigners (Eph. 2:19a)

Having access to the Father means that we are no longer foreigners and aliens to the covenant (Eph. 2:19). This is the converse of what was previously said: "You who are Gentiles by birth . . . were separate from Christ, excluded from citizenship in Israel, and foreigners to the covenants of the promise, without hope and without God in the world" (Eph. 2:11–12). Alienation from God and isolation from his promises and privileges characterized our former status, so that we were without hope and the comfort of God in this world of loneliness, trouble, and transition. But it is "no longer" so. We are no longer aliens and foreigners.[1]

But Fellow Citizens (2:19b)

We are fellow citizens with God's people.[2] If you have been an alien in a foreign country, then you understand how important such citizenship is. In your own country, you conduct business, seek medical attention, participate in government, have legal protections, and do not even think of the privileges. But if you travel to another country where you have no automatic rights—you worry about whether your medical insurance will apply, or whether your currency will work, or whether you will have legal rights if you get in trouble. When you are a stranger in a strange land, you feel vulnerable, alone, and wary every day.

Having citizenship in the ancient world also meant that you had special rights and protection. This is why the city officials at Philippi, who had beaten Paul and Silas without a trial, became so alarmed when they learned the two were Roman citizens (Acts 16:38–39). The officials knew that the protection and power of Rome could be exercised against them for their treatment of its citizens. So when Paul here reminds us that we are "fellow citizens" with God's people, he is reminding us that we have the power and protection of heaven. We are as treasured as any of the covenant people. Countering the vulnerabilities we feel in our travel through this world, Paul says we have the privileges of our heavenly citizenship to protect us.

And Family (2:19c)

Our privileges are not exhausted in our citizenship. Paul says that in addition to having the rights of citizens, we also have the benefits of being in God's family. "You are . . . members of God's household" (Eph. 2:19c), Paul

1. The Greek terms used here by Paul overlap conceptually: the former (*xenos*) indicates a stranger in a foreign land, and the latter (*paroikos*) designates a resident alien. Both can be used metaphorically in the Old Testament and New Testament—Christians, like the faithful patriarchs (who literally dwelt in lands which belonged to others), are strangers in this world (Heb. 11:13; 1 Peter 2:11; cf. Lev. 25:23; 1 Chron. 29:15; Ps. 39:12 [Septuagint 38:13]). Paul had earlier remarked that the Gentiles were strangers (*xenoi*) to the covenants of promise (Eph. 2:12).

2. Paul elsewhere applies citizenship terminology to Christians (see the Greek terms in Eph. 2:12; Phil. 1:27; 3:20). Those Gentiles who formerly were excluded from citizenship in Israel (Eph. 2:12) have now been made fellow citizens with all the saints in God's new heavenly kingdom (cf. Phil. 3:20).

says to the Ephesian Gentiles. Here the apostle narrows the circle of intimacy for those now in the Ephesian church. Paul began by broadly saying, "You are no longer foreigners and aliens." Then he draws the relationship closer, saying, "You are fellow citizens." Now he tightens that relationship even further by saying to people very different in race, class, and origin, "You are part of the same family."

Paul makes this relationship even more special by reminding the church that it is not just any family of which they are members; they are members of God's family. We understand how special this wording is when we see that Paul uses this word for family (*oikeios*) to refer to actual family members in 1 Timothy 5:8 and in a metaphorical sense to speak of the family of God (the "household of faith") in Galatians 6:10 (cf. *oikos* in 1 Tim. 3:15).[3] Thus even the adopted children of God (Eph. 1:5) can be assured that God is their Father and they are his family. Paul wants us to understand the great privilege and comfort that come from knowing that God claims us as his own family no matter what our past difficulties or failures.

Humorist Garrison Keillor tells the story of a young woman named Lydia who tires of her staid and proper upbringing in Lake Wobegon. She moves to New Orleans and takes up in the revelry until it, too, becomes routine. She longs for something more. Eventually she discovers that the "something more" is to feel important to someone, to be cherished and loved. She takes up with a man that she has met amidst the parties. He moves in with her, but he cannot leave aspects of the revelry that have become compulsive in his life. He cannot keep a job, but gives her the job of picking up his beer bottles that daily litter the floor and the sofa. She eventually tires of him, too. One day she leaves a month's rent on the TV and leaves him asleep at midday to make life on his own.

She takes the bus back to Lake Wobegon. They whisper about her there. Her days of ill repute generate much conversation over coffee at the local café where she now works. Though she is back at home, she is a foreigner. Familiar surroundings only make her feel more alien, reminding her that she does not belong here.

She goes to her parents' home for Thanksgiving. She sits at the table but feels out of place, not at home, although she is at home. So, as soon

3. A similar idea, though with different wording, appears in Hebrews 2:11.

as the pie is eaten and the dishes are piled at the kitchen sink, she goes to a remote part of the living room to escape the relatives who now seem alien to her. Tracing her hand along the fireplace mantle, she glances over all the familiar objects in all the familiar places, and then sees an unfamiliar picture. It is her picture from her senior year in high school. There she is fresh-faced with every hair in place, but there is something different about the picture now. Beneath her image in the frame is stuck a little label typed from her father's old Remington typewriter. It simply says, "Our Lydia." How strange to be labeled in one's own house, and yet Lydia knows the purpose. Before the world and against all the whispers this was her father's announcement to everyone who came into the house and knew nothing or everything about her: "This is 'Our Lydia.'" The "our" meant so much. Those three letters were as jewels to her, each one a diamond that said she was treasured in this house. No matter how far she had traveled in distance or behavior, no matter how foreign her place or practices, no matter what had transpired, no matter the time passed, no matter the rumors told, or the truth revealed—amidst all the transitions and enduring beyond them she was a member of this family. She was "Our Lydia."

God says in this passage that we are his family. We are treasured in his house always, always. Whatever transitions come, whether they are transitions away from current location or away from his approval, whether they are transitions of success or failure, whether they are transitions of family or difficulty or career, the love of our Father will never waver. His heavenly power and protection are active in our behalf wherever we go—near or far, to places familiar or alien—because we are citizens of his kingdom and members of his family. Through Christ we not only have access to our Father's presence, we also have access to our Father's heart. There his Spirit advocates for us with tenderness beyond our provoking, and pronounces to our heart what the heavens announce to the world: "You are *our* child, and you will always be."

The words sound wonderful. But our fears, frailties, and failures make us wonder how confident we can be of God's unfailing love. How strong or fragile is our relationship with the heavenly Father? Can we lose it? How sure can we be of heaven's love in a world of transitions? Paul answers these questions too.

We Are Secure in God (2:20–21)

To the English reader, the apostle seems abruptly to change metaphors as he turns from speaking of being members of God's family to being built on the foundation of apostles and prophets. However, the change is really a beautiful development of Paul's thought. Members of God's family are literally referred to as the "house-ones," or "house-people."[4] The word for "household" in Greek (*oikeios*, Eph. 2:19) has the same root as the word for "aliens" (*paroikoi*) in the same verse, and as the four building terms found throughout Ephesians 2:20–22 (*epoikodomeō*—built, *oikodomē*—building, *synoikodomeō*—built together, *katoikētērion*—dwelling). Thus the "house-ones" term naturally leads to consideration of how solid and secure is this house. Paul describes two aspects of its construction to communicate how secure is the heart-home of God's people that does not change even if their circumstances do. He speaks of its foundation and its cornerstone.

Having an Inspired Foundation (2:20a)

It is a natural question: "How can I know that God will not change his heart despite the changes in my circumstances?" Paul answers that the heart-house of which we are members is built on a foundation of inspiration.[5] The covenantal inclusion of the Gentiles was not an afterthought or an unplanned by-product. Paul says that the Ephesians are the fulfillment of a building process with foundations laid by those whom God inspired to impart his will in both the Old Testament and the New. The words of the apostles and prophets coordinate.[6] Though there is some question as to

4. The Old Testament temple of God was known as God's "house" (2 Sam. 7:5–13), thus further linking together the building/temple symbolism of Ephesians 2:20–22 with the household language of Ephesians 2:19.

5. The metaphorical use of "foundation" here is somewhat different than Paul's designation of Christ as the foundation in 1 Corinthians 3. Naturally, Paul could use similar metaphors in more than one way.

6. The single article in Greek uniting "apostles" and "prophets" conveys the coordination of their foundational activities (cf. Eph. 3:5); the article does not indicate the two groups to be identical (Granville Sharp's rule does not apply here since the terms are plural, and the two groups specified are clearly distinct in Eph. 4:11). The term "apostles," while it can refer in Paul's letters to people "sent out" as delegates from a church (2 Cor. 8:22–23; Phil. 2:25), most often designates in his terminology a limited number of specially recognized followers of Jesus who had been commissioned as apostles by their incarnate/resurrected Lord (1 Cor. 9:5–6; 15:7; Gal. 1:19; 2:7–9). The very next generation of early Christians recognized that the era of the apostles had passed (1 Clem. 42:1–44:6).

whether the prophets in this clause refer to the Old Testament prophets, there is no question that Paul is saying that the inspired messengers of the New Testament are speaking in continuity with those of the Old (cf. Eph. 3:4–5).[7] This engrafting of many nations and new peoples was always in the plan. There is not a problem with the new misaligning with the old. The inclusion of the Gentiles was not a surprise or an afterthought; the foundation of the Scriptures was laid broadly enough to include us. God always intended for us to be part of his plan. Those that God inspires to lay the foundation for understanding his purposes have indicated that the Father's household was always intended to include many nations. The light to the nations was always intended to bring others to the Father's home. We are welcome despite our differing backgrounds.

Having a Divine Cornerstone (2:20b)

And if the foundation of the apostles and prophets does not itself assure us of the welcome God intends for us, our security in his home is shown to rest on the unshakable cornerstone of Christ himself. The household of God is "built on the foundation of the apostles and prophets, with Christ Jesus himself as the chief cornerstone" (Eph. 2:20b).[8]

In his death and resurrection, Jesus stands as the chief witness to the enlarging and enfolding intention of the Father. It is by his sacrifice once

7. In favor of the term "prophets" here referring to New Testament prophets: (1) the word order ("apostles and prophets") would likely be reversed if it designated Old Testament prophets (who preceded the apostles), (2) later in the same letter Paul mentions prophets alongside apostles and indicates that they both received God's revelation for the church in this New Testament age ("now"; Eph. 3:5), (3) Paul designates the apostles and prophets as living gifts to the New Testament church alongside evangelists and pastors/teachers (Eph. 4:11), and (4) elsewhere Paul refers to "prophets" in the New Testament church (esp. 1 Cor. 12:28–29; also 1 Cor. 14:29, 32, 37). Regardless of one's perspective on whether the term refers to New Testament or Old Testament prophets, however, Paul's use of the term clearly underscores his understanding that the work of the apostles and prophets is in continuity with the Old Testament prophets (Rom. 1:2; 3:21), even if the "men in other generations" could not fully comprehend the mystery of the gospel (Eph. 3:4–5).

8. Commentators debate whether the Greek term here (*akrogōniaios*) means "cornerstone" or "capstone." In favor of the former, Isaiah 28:16 mentions a "precious cornerstone" which is laid for a "foundation" (clearly indicating that the "cornerstone" is laid at the base of the building). This text is the only use of this word in the Greek Old Testament (whereas other passages mention a "head stone," which is likely a "capstone"; see Ps. 118:22; cf. Matt. 21:42; Acts 4:11). Isaiah 28:16 was also well known in early Christianity (1 Peter 2:6; Epistle of Barnabas 6:2), and Paul may be intentionally drawing on its imagery. In any case, the preeminence of Christ is clear in this verse in Ephesians, and Christ is the ultimate ground for unity in the body/family/building/temple of God.

for all that the barrier between Jew and Gentile is destroyed. No longer is there a ceremonial partition between those inside and those outside of God's house. Jesus, the One who exactly represents the will of the Father, indicates that the Father's home is for both those near and those far away, for those included and those excluded, for those once united to the covenant and those separate. His sacrifice is the ultimate testimony on which we can rest our claim of God's love. His is the cornerstone of our assurance, a divine stone that cannot be shaken, a rock upon which the hope of all who trust him is sure.

With greater clarity we now understand the words of Isaiah describing the ministry of the coming Messiah: "See, I lay a stone in Zion, a tested stone, a precious cornerstone for a sure foundation; the one who trusts will never be dismayed" (Isa. 28:16; cf. 8:14–16; Ps. 118:22; Matt. 21:42; Acts 4:11). The witness of the apostles and prophets and the unassailable testimony of the Lord who sacrificed himself in our behalf are the inspired foundation and divine cornerstone of our assurance of his love no matter the temporal transitions and earthly troubles this life may hold.

Seminary president David Sebastian tells the story of his son biking into their garage and saying, "Dad, you'd better come. There's a crazy lady in the field and she's drawing a crowd." As a pastor in a small town, David knew that whenever there was "a crazy lady in the field," it fit in his job description to go see what was up. The woman in the field had made it from Missouri to Oklahoma on the bus before her money ran out. The police had offered her a place in a homeless shelter, but the shelter would not accept the young woman with the puppy she carried. In desperation and fear that someone might take her dog, the woman ran until she ran out of breath. Then she just stood there in the field, out of breath and out of hope, while a crowd gathered around her.

When Pastor David arrived, he received a quick summary of the situation from the police and then asked the young woman her name. With downcast eyes and a voice barely audible she replied, "Mandy." "Where is your home, Mandy?" he asked. She said, "Missouri." And that's when a bell rang in David's mental register.

"You are Mandy from Missouri?" he said. "I have been expecting you! Your pastor is a friend of mine. He wrote me weeks ago to say that you would come. I have prepared a place for you."

Mandy looked up with unbelieving eyes and said, "You know about me?"

"Yes," he said, "Look. I have the letter right here."

When David showed Mandy the letter, she could hardly believe it. The troubled young woman had not fully understood or remembered why the pastor in Missouri had placed her on the bus. She had not planned to come to this town. But someone had planned for her, and it was there in writing. It was too good to be true, but it was true. And the truth that someone had so cared for her renewed enough hope in her to give her strength to walk out of the field, to show up for work at a new job a few days later, and to start life again.

Seeing in writing that someone had planned all along to care for her provided powerful new hope for Mandy, but the plan touched more than just her. David Sebastian told that story to a group of seminary presidents. This is a group of persons whose occupations make them sophisticated in the matters of faith, but also accustomed to hard realities and public scrutiny. There is not much that moves them. But when they heard the story of Mandy from Missouri, isolated in a field and encircled by gawkers—yet still within the plan and compassion of God—they were touched. I watched as heads went down and hands crept up to wipe tears from eyes. All knew what it meant to feel isolated, alone, and under the scrutiny of others. Something in that story of a girl alone in a field and isolated by the pressures of life touched them. It was for such as them, as well as for such as us, that Paul in essence writes, "God planned for you all along to be part of his household. He loved you, planned for you, and prepared for you. See, he wrote down right here through the apostles and prophets his plan to include you so that you would be sure. And if you were to have any questions yet, he wrote his love in the blood of his Son. You can rest on that foundation, and on that cornerstone you can build much new hope."

Rising to a Temple (2:21)

Knowing of God's provision of his Son, and seeing the eternal and holy purposes of the house that God builds on this divine cornerstone, Paul writes, "In him the whole building is joined together and rises to become a holy temple to the Lord" (Eph. 2:21). The household that rests on the foundation of the apostles and prophets, and depends upon the cornerstone for stability and design, is fulfilling a heavenly purpose so that it is not merely a house but also a house of God, a temple. When we rest on the foundation of God's Word and build on the cornerstone that is Christ, then we too are fulfilling a holy purpose, even when we may not seem to be achieving much of any purpose at all in the eyes of the world.

The way that God expresses his glory through us is beautiful and cause for his praise. God makes our lives a temple for his praise even when we may not think anything special is happening to or through us. Think again how this happened in David Sebastian's account: Mandy from Missouri, a man in a distant town writing a letter, a boy riding a bicycle, a pastor in a small town, and a group of seminary presidents—all had a role in expressing the assurance of which I now write for many more people. Their lives became a place of testimony for the God who moves across time, speaks through prophets, sheds his blood, and sends his Spirit to let us know that we are dear to him and that we are secure in him. Through God's plan, they have become a temple for God's glory, even when human eyes would have seen little significance in what they were doing.

We Are All Vital to God (2:22)

God's scheme is grand. The scope of the foundation and the strength of the cornerstone are impressive. But we should not overlook God's use of individuals to fulfill his purposes. Each has a purpose that is remarkably expressed by the apostle as he describes how we function together and how the Spirit functions within us.

Built Together (2:22a)

In the picture that the apostle has constructed, we are no longer foreigners and aliens, but family members of God's household. The house beneath us is laid on the foundation of the apostles and prophets. All rests on the cornerstone that is Christ, a rock so solid that the house rises heavenward as a temple to fulfill God's holy purposes. But what are the bricks that form the walls of this house of God as it reaches toward heaven and fulfills divine purposes? You are. I am.

Paul says to the people in the Ephesian church, "And in him [the cornerstone which joins the whole building together] you too are being built together to become a dwelling in which God lives by his Spirit" (Eph. 2:22).

We cannot help but think of Peter's similar image: "As you come to him, the living Stone—rejected by men but chosen by God and precious to him—you also, like living stones, are being built into a spiritual house" (1 Peter 2:4–5a). "You also," the apostles say, are part of God's temple of spiritual purpose. We can hear the question of the Ephesians in our own heart: "Who, me?" Yes, you also are being fitted into an eternal plan for the house of divine purpose that God is building. Each one has a purpose that is tied to the purpose of another as we rise to become what God is building.

Laura Dye, a missionary in Chile, wrote of one of the bricks on which she was depending as her family rose to do God's work. Laura described the way in which others far away were supporting their mission efforts:

> Sarah Moore Young is a good illustration of the way many of you lift us up regularly. I met Sarah at camp when I was 13 or 14. We still write every so often. One week I wrote an e-mail with such a heavy heart about a girl in our church that had attempted suicide several times. I finally decided that I wouldn't sleep that night until I was at peace with God about the girl's life. Having a new baby, I was already going without sleep plenty. . . . Sarah [got the message and] grasped that even praying for this girl was a bigger job than I could handle. She e-mailed that she was praying for the girl and had put her on a 24-hour prayer watch in her church, taking the load right off my shoulders. I slept that night knowing that we weren't the only ones bringing her before the Lord.

By such examples we understand what Paul says: "And in him you too are being built together to become a dwelling in which God lives by his Spirit" (Eph. 2:22). Each brick is supporting the other in prayer, in resources, in encouragement, in offering our lives in example and sacrifice for the sake of others. We are together rising to become a temple of God, and each one is vital for all the changes and challenges that we will face.

Spirit Indwelt (2:22b)

What makes us ultimately know the vital nature of our service to God? Understanding that not only are we being built together, we are also indwelt by his Spirit. Paul tells the Ephesians, "You too are being built together to become a dwelling in which God lives by his Spirit" (Eph. 2:22b).

At the end of the first chapter of Ephesians the apostle said that God is transforming the world for the church and by the church. Now we begin to see how. The church, that is, the body of Christ, is built upon the foundation of the apostles and prophets and has Jesus Christ himself as its chief cornerstone. Its construction rises to heaven through the interwoven destinies and duties of each of us. But inside the walls that rest on this foundation and cornerstone lives the Holy Spirit of God.[9] This building composed of dear and vital human elements is itself alive and filled with his power. God lives in the house he constructs by building our lives together. Perhaps we could compare this to a modern science-fiction drama that portrays an edifice of great beauty and complexity that ultimately reveals itself alive. But Paul is thinking of something else. He is remembering the entry of the Shekinah glory into the tabernacle of God at the time of Moses (Ex. 40:34–35) or into the Jerusalem temple at the time of Solomon (1 Kings 8:10–11). This is the image we must call to mind as we consider what God is calling us to do.

What Paul communicates is that the days of glory are not past. God did not work among his people only long ago. He did not cease working for his purposes in some ancient day. The God who brings us together indwells us for his purposes now. There is still a task for his church, and he dwells in us so that we may fulfill it. Until he comes we are in his plan for each other and for this world.

When our lives become painful or roll forward seemingly without purpose, we by faith must reaffirm the vital role each of us has in God's building. Each person, as well as each generation, must embrace the vital role that we have to fulfill in God's building program. We are supporting one another, the body in which the living Spirit of God is at work to change the world. It is not consistent with Scripture to believe that the really important work or the best times are somewhere behind us in history. Always God gives us a vital role to fulfill in Christ's church as he is building us together to rise as the temple of divine purpose. He prepares to use us by filling us with the Spirit of power to fulfill his calling for this generation. This sense of purpose is what will

9. The church as the Spirit-indwelt temple of God is also found in 1 Corinthians 3:16–17 and in 2 Corinthians 6:16, although perhaps neither of these texts projects the image as universally as Paul does in Ephesians. The Greek term for "dwelling" here (*katoikētērion*) is used repeatedly in the Greek Old Testament to designate heaven as the dwelling of God, or Zion as the earthly locale of his presence (1 Kings 8:39, 43, 49; 2 Chron. 6:30, 33, 39; 30:27; Pss. 33:14; 76:2).

inspire us to fresh courage, faithfulness, and zeal when the world and even our colleagues may view what God calls us to do as small or meaningless.

As long as we draw breath, we are vital to God's purposes. A pastor friend of mine witnessed this truth as he was ministering to an older woman who was a new Christian. Soon after joining the church, she discovered that she had a terminal cancer. One day he went to her in the hospital and she spoke very honestly to him: "I'm scared, Pastor."

He said to her, "Betty, you are dear to God, secure in him, and vital to his purposes." The words could have seemed empty and formal. Yet even as my friend said those words, he could not help but think of the new church building program that had also taken such a toll on him, his ministry, and his marriage. He had been stressed and despairing for weeks, but as he said to her, "You are dear to God, secure in him, and vital to his purposes," the pastor really heard his own words and was reassured by them. He saw that God was using Betty in her dying to minister new hope to her pastor. God was not done with her. And the pastor realized with new power that God was not done with him.

God is not done with us either. As long as we draw breath on this earth, he is fulfilling his purposes through us. He tells us that we are dear to him, secure in him, and vital to his purposes because there is still his work to do. With assurance of such love, security, and purpose, his Spirit still indwells us so that our life will be a temple for his purposes and praise.

10

Counterfeit Callings Exposed

Ephesians 3:1–13

Although I am less than the least of all God's people, this grace was given me: to preach to the Gentiles the unsearchable riches of Christ, and to make plain to everyone the administration of this mystery, which for ages past was kept hidden in God, who created all things. (Eph. 3:8–9)

A boy grows up in a wealthy family in a major city of a sophisticated culture. As a child he is immersed in the orthodox religion of his country and attends one of the most well known worship centers in the land. In that setting he becomes a disciple under one of the most influential leaders of his traditions. He becomes a zealot for his faith, passionately devouring its teachings and passionately pursuing its enemies. And, then, something amazing happens. Somehow he becomes convinced that the very persons he has been opposing were right about their faith. And though they are small in number and despised by his religious leaders and culture, this young man joins the ranks of those he had so zealously opposed. He enters into a period of intense study, praying and fasting in order to fulfill a calling he believes he now has to take his new faith to others. In subsequent years, although his convictions and his actions cost him his reputation, his comforts, his freedom, and ultimately his life, this man of faith never wavers from his calling. What was his name?

His name was . . . Jibreel al-Amreekee. He grew up in Atlanta and attended a well-known Baptist church before becoming a Muslim, joining allies of Osama bin Laden's Al Qaeda and dying in 1997 while participating in a jihadist attack intended to "plant a flag for Islam" in Kashmir.[1]

Before reading his name, my readers probably assumed I was describing the apostle Paul rather than a Muslim extremist. The parallels in the lives of these men of faith are quite striking. Each was from quite a different cultural and religious background than he eventually felt called to promote. Each was willing to study, strive, and sacrifice for the calling he believed his God had placed upon his life. But we also realize that these conflicting callings cannot both be of God. This realization presses us to identify what kind of calling is genuine and what is counterfeit. The pressure is greatest on those of us who may have a sense of being called generally to serve God, but are far from certain of the specific form, type, or place of that calling. Such persons rightly wonder if our calling is for real and want to know how Scripture identifies a genuine calling.

Does examining the calling of the apostle Paul have relevance to determining whether your calling is genuine or counterfeit? After all, Paul was given a bolt of lightning and a voice in thunder on the road to Damascus to confirm that he was really called. I am not suggesting the same kind of confirmation is necessary for us. But I am suggesting that we can see this calling of Paul—which is not in doubt—as a window God graciously opens for examining the effects of a true call on the life of a believer. Rather than looking for an initial call similar to Paul's, an examination of his call may reveal to us the impressions that a true calling leaves on one's life and heart.

Captured by God's Goals (3:1–6)

When compelled by a true calling of God, a believer is captured by God's goals. Although Paul resides under house arrest in Rome, he does not consider himself a prisoner of the Romans or of the Jewish officials who originally accused him. He identifies himself as "Paul, *the prisoner of Christ Jesus*

1. *U.S. News and World Report*, June 10, 2001, 17–18.

for the sake of you Gentiles" (v. 1). With these words of imprisonment to Christ, the apostle tells us that one called by God is willing both to die to self and to live for others.

Willing to Die to Self (3:1–2)

Paul's willingness to die to the priorities of his own glory is evident in the titles and tenses that he uses to describe himself. The first title is so familiar to us that it may escape our notice: Paul. Remember that this same man, prior to his calling, had the name Saul, a reminder of the first king of Israel who was chosen for his strength, bearing, and stature above his peers. What does the name Paul mean? Small.[2] In his calling this Jewish holy man has gone from "Big Saul" to "Small Paul," and the naming is not accidental.

Dying to self involves *a willingness to sacrifice privilege.* Paul's earthly privilege and prestige are constantly being whittled away by his calling. He is not merely Paul; he is a prisoner.[3] He has known prestige and power in life, but now as the prisoner of a pagan ruler he awaits the arrival of his own countrymen who intend to accuse him and demand his death. Yet even while destitute, despised, and forsaken, Paul views himself as fulfilling a calling.

Even while under arrest he preaches the gospel of his Savior and uses his incarceration as a means of proclaiming it to those who would not otherwise hear. In this sense Paul views himself at the disposal of his God. He calls himself not only "Small Paul" and "Prisoner of Christ Jesus" but also one who has received an "administration of God's grace" (v. 2). The words identify Paul as a steward, one who, rather than being in charge, has been given a charge to take care of matters for someone else.[4] This point is emphasized later when the apostle will identify himself as "a servant of this gospel" (v. 7).

2. This would be most evident to the native Latin speaker, where *paul(l)us* means "little" or "small."

3. The timing of the imprisonment (also see Eph. 4:1) is likely the same as that mentioned at the end of Acts (beginning with chapter 22), with the locale of imprisonment quite often linked with Paul's house arrest in Rome. On the expression "Paul, the prisoner" see also Philemon 1; cf. 2 Timothy 1:8; Philemon 9. Paul elsewhere also employs rhetorically the expression "I, Paul" (2 Cor. 10:1; Gal. 5:2; Col. 1:23; 1 Thess. 2:18; Philem. 19).

4. The Greek term (*oikonomia*) can refer either to a person who has the role of a steward (as it clearly means in Luke 16:2–4) or to an administration, and these meanings can overlap. Although the other two references in Ephesians indicate God's "administration" (Eph. 1:10; 3:9), this very fact serves to indicate that "administration" commonly belongs to God (also 1 Tim. 1:4), whereas Paul classifies himself more as a "steward" who stewards the revelation of God's administration (1 Cor. 9:17 and Col. 1:25; see more broadly 1 Cor. 4:1–2).

The title "servant" is not usually treasured by someone once ranked as a ruler in Israel, yet Paul embraces the term as one who delights to serve his master. Paul teaches us by the titles he ascribes to himself that one called by Christ is so captured by godly goals that he is willing to forsake his own privilege.

We can imagine what the apostle Paul, confined under house arrest, might think to himself. "What am I doing here? I once commanded soldiers and now I am guarded by them. Once I was admired, and now I administer a message of a crucified rabbi from a forsaken part of the world. Once I was somebody to be served, and now I am a servant. What happened?" The words might sound very familiar to some who previously had positions of prestige, but gave up their own gain to follow Jesus with the humility and integrity that he requires. Once they had disposable income, but now they wonder if they will be able to pay for rent. Once they commanded the respect of others in the workplace, and now they submit to others. Once their aggression was feared, but now their gentleness is mocked. And, though it might not have been hard to forsake privilege initially, the longer they are away from former prestige, the more alluring it becomes. Singing the words of the hymn that profess our hearts to "be content to fill a little space if God be glorified" is quite different from living that reality.

Genuine calling requires a willingness to forsake personal privilege. This is true whether the Christian is a pastor, a businessman, an athlete, an educator, or a mom. God may not require great sacrifice in our callings, but true devotion is always willing to dispense with privilege if God's glory requires it.

Yet there is a problem in identifying a willingness to forsake personal privilege as a mark of true calling. While a willingness to sacrifice self is a necessary mark of true calling, it is hardly sufficient to mark those truly called by God. Those whose callings we view as counterfeit may also be willing to sacrifice themselves, such as the Kamikaze pilots of World War II and the Middle Eastern terrorists of today who sacrifice themselves with dynamite backpacks in crowded marketplaces. So if personal sacrifice is necessary but insufficient to mark true calling, what accompanies the forsaking of personal privilege in a true calling?

Dying to self also involves *a willingness to deny merit.* Another way to evaluate a true biblical calling is by considering the various ways that people handle their loss of privilege. Some are willing to sacrifice as long as they believe their suffering will earn them something. Yet Paul's willingness to die to self included not only a willingness to forsake privilege, but also a willingness to deny himself any merit.

Paul will not claim credit for any aspect of his calling, even when he has sacrificed himself to pursue it. As he writes to the Gentile Ephesians, the apostle says that the administration of grace "was given to me" (Eph. 3:2). His ministry was not earned or deserved but simply "given" to him.

Paul's passive role in the reception and carrying out of responsibilities is stated over and over. The "mystery" of salvation for the Gentile nations was "made known to me by revelation" (Eph. 3:3). He seems to give himself a little credit when he speaks of "my insight" regarding this mystery, but then he quickly adds that the mystery "has now been revealed by the Spirit" (Eph. 3:5). Paul says that he became a servant of this gospel "by the gift of God's grace given me through the working of his power" (Eph. 3:7).

It is extremely difficult to get into this habit of thinking: to believe that we are always in every dimension of life a recipient of unconditional grace, and never deserving of it. Some people with counterfeit callings are willing to make great sacrifice because they believe that they are purchasing the mercy and blessing of their god. If the accounts are true, those responsible for the World Trade Center and Pentagon tragedies of 2001 believed themselves to be earning palaces and virgins in heaven by their sacrifice. In contrast, the apostle Paul denies that what he has done, suffered, and sacrificed earns him anything. He knows that his heaven will not come by the work of his hands.

Willing to Live for Others (3:3–6)

In a true calling there are both a willingness to die to self and an accompanying willingness to live for others. Paul says that he is a prisoner of Christ Jesus "for the sake of you Gentiles" (v. 1). He says that the administration of grace (i.e., the message that he has been given to steward) "was given to me for you" (Eph. 3:2). A called Paul sees himself as a prisoner and a steward for the sake of others.

These words are also the testimony of New Tribes missionary Martin Burnham, who was recently killed in the Philippines. Members of the Abu Sayyaf terrorist group had held the Burnhams as prisoners for 376 days. During that time Martin was often used as a servant to carry the terrorists' supplies in treacherous terrain. But while bearing their loads he never complained, viewing even his servitude as a calling of God and an opportunity for the gospel. Though the Burnhams were increasingly weak and malnourished, when relief agencies managed to get food packages to them, they shared their food with their captors for their sakes. At one point Martin even repaired a satellite phone for his captors. He said to his wife, "The Bible says serve the Lord with gladness. Let's go all the way. Let's serve him all the way with gladness." The evidence of that resolve became apparent even to his captors who would debate about who would chain him every night. Each hated to be the one to chain him, because every night he would thank them. Why would anyone submit to being a prisoner and a servant of others with joy? The answer lies in the fact that over and over in the evenings Martin would patiently explain the gospel to his Muslim captors. He was living for them, and viewed his situation as a calling of God to minister the mysteries of the gospel to these lost souls.

Living for others involves *a willingness to reveal gospel mystery.* The "administration of God's grace," which Paul is now responsible to steward for the Ephesians, he describes as a "mystery" (Eph. 3:3–4, 6). It comes to him "by revelation," as he has briefly written earlier (Eph. 3:3). Now he is writing again so that the Ephesians "will be able to understand my [Paul's] insight into the mystery" (Eph. 3:4), and know what "was not made known to men in other generations as it has now been revealed by the Spirit to God's holy apostles and prophets" (Eph. 3:5). Paul's calling is to be a fountain of knowledge poured out to others. He knows nothing of the religious status-seeking so common in his day and ours that is pursued by claiming special or secret knowledge. Paul's goal is to reveal what he knows.

But what is the "mystery" previously hidden that Paul wants the Ephesians to know? "This mystery is that through the gospel the Gentiles are heirs together with Israel, members together of one body, and sharers together in the promise in Christ Jesus" (Eph. 3:6). Here Paul expands what he has already written about the sacrifice of Christ eradicating the distinctions between Jewish and non-Jewish people. Because the blood of Jesus makes atonement for the sin of all believers, all have equal access to the Father. So Paul says we are now "sharers together in the promise." This is the apostle's affirmation that God's covenant with Israel (to be their God and for them to be his people) now extends to all who are in Christ Jesus.

The usual way that we think of the "mystery" committed to Paul and the other apostles relates to the unveiling of the Messiah. For centuries the Jews had wondered, "Who will it be? When will he come? What will be the nature of his reign?" The mystery of the Messiah was almost always considered in terms of something once hidden later being revealed for the benefit of the covenant people. But Paul says that the full mystery of the Messiah cannot be conceived unless we consider that the Messiah comes not only for the personal benefit of the Jews, but also for the nations. The real mystery of the Messiah is that he comes simultaneously as Lord of my soul and Lord for all nations.[5] The Jews would object to this because such a Messiah would allow covenant entry to the Gentiles (unclean people). Gentiles would object because it would require entry into the covenant of the Jews (an arrogant and hated people). From both perspectives the mystery of God is glorified by a covenant that makes one body from persons of many kinds by the blood of the Messiah.

Paul must know how difficult it is for Jew and Gentile to allow each other equal status before God, so he plays with the word "together" in Greek to create a triple echo of special emphasis. When the Hebrews wanted to emphasize a word, they doubled it; and when they wanted to thunder a word, they tripled it, as in the phrase "Holy, holy, holy is the Lord God Almighty" (see Isa. 6:3). In a similar way Paul now shakes the foundations of traditional prejudices and long-standing antipathies between the races by tripling the word (actually a prefix) "together."[6] Both Gentile and Jew—one pagan and the other orthodox, one a new people and the other an ancient nation—are "heirs together." This means they are part of the same family and will get the same blessings of the kingdom in the future. They are also "members together," meaning that they are part of the same body now and, finally, they are also "sharers together" of the eternal covenant that extends from the past into the forever future.[7]

5. The new relationship between Jews and Gentiles that comes with the advent of the Messiah is also connected with "mystery" in Colossians 1:25–27; Romans 11:25 (cf. the revelation this required in Gal. 1:11, 16). Paul elsewhere often uses "mystery" to refer to some aspect of God's plan of redemption previously hidden and now revealed in Christ (Rom. 16:25–27; 1 Cor. 2:1, 6–16; Eph. 1:9; 5:32; Col. 2:2–3; 1 Tim. 3:16). Paul "stewards" such a mystery (Eph. 3:2–6; cf. 1 Cor. 4:1; Col. 1:25–27), and he has become its herald (Eph. 6:19; Col. 4:3). Paul's diversity of applications of the term "mystery" (e.g., compare 1 Cor. 15:51 with Rom. 11:25) indicates that he sees a broad spectrum of (previously hidden) specific truths unveiled in the broader revelation of Christ; thus Ephesians 3 should be viewed as fundamentally consistent with the various "mystery" themes in the other authentic letters of Paul.

6. In Greek the threefold "together" is expressed by the prepositional prefix *syn* ("with/together") affixed to each of these three words.

7. Paul in each of these terms is summing up parts of his letter and expressing full mutual participation of Jew and Gentile in the benefits of Christ's salvation: "heirs together" (Eph. 1:14; cf. 1:18); "members

Living for others also involves *a willingness to relish gospel promise.* Yet even as Paul thunders, we can almost hear him simultaneously chortling in delight as he relishes being able to say in so many ways, "We are one in Christ Jesus since his blood makes us all equally holy and precious to our Father in heaven." He can say to Jew and Gentile, "You think that we are enemies, but when the gospel conquers you both, we will be together." This is a portion of the gladness of the gospel that Martin Burnham claimed as he spoke to captors who had abused him and his wife. He was able to think that when the gospel conquered the hearts of those who thought that they were using him, those same men would actually be together with him in the church of Jesus Christ. All the barriers and animosities and prejudices would be gone.

Relishing what the gospel promises to do and can do is the second major mark of a calling that is genuine. We are willing to die to self, to live for others, and to delight—not in a triumph over others—but in the triumph of the gospel that unites us to others. When compelled by a true calling of God, a believer is not only captured by godly goals but also enraptured by God's grace.

Enraptured by God's Grace (3:7–13)

While selfless sacrifice and concern for others are important and necessary aspects of a Christian calling, we must acknowledge they are not unique to a Christian calling. Men and women are willing to sacrifice themselves for any number of causes and concerns. What else marks a Christian's true calling?

Enraptured by Grace to the Called (3:7–9)

Paul reminds his readers that he became a servant of this good news by the grace of God and the working of his power (Eph. 3:7).[8] Again, we cannot help but think of the way that God's power arrested and transformed Paul on the road to Damascus. God reached down and turned this man from being Saul the persecutor of Christians to being Paul the apostle to the Gentiles

together of one body" (Eph. 2:16; 4:4–6; cf. 1:23; 4:12, 15–16; 5:28–30); "sharers together in the promise" (contrast Eph. 2:12; and compare 1:13).

8. The Greek relative pronoun that begins this verse ties it to the preceding sentence, but the content is also clearly transitional into the next sentence (vv. 8–13).

through no power or decision of the man. It was sheer grace that transformed Paul.[9] But, as astounding as that grace was, the apostle does not leave the work of God's grace in the past.

The apostle speaks of himself in the present tense, saying that he has been given the grace to preach to the Gentiles even though "I am less than the least of all God's people" (Eph. 3:8).[10] There are those who say that this is a bit of pious hyperbole. Paul is not *still* the least of all the saints. He is an apostle, a scholar, a missionary, a faithful servant, and a willing sufferer for Christ. Surely there are worse Christians than he! But such assertions expose a worldly way of reckoning our status before God that the apostle will not accept. If our best works merit us nothing, and therefore all of Paul's righteous deeds and sacrificial actions are not to his credit, then the only entries on Paul's spiritual ledger are those of debt. Without his good works counting to his credit, all that Paul still has in his personal account are such things as holding the cloaks of those who stoned Stephen and personal persecution of those who named Jesus as Lord (Acts 9:4). Only demerit is in Paul's account. There is no good that he can provide to cancel it, and yet to such a one "grace was given . . . to preach to the Gentiles the unsearchable riches of Christ" (Eph. 3:8), and "to make plain to everyone the administration of this mystery, which for ages past was kept hidden in God, who created all things" (Eph. 3:9).[11]

By juxtaposing his human status and his divine task, Paul makes the effect of Christ's sacrifice and the greatness of God's grace all the more obvious. Paul should have the least status, the least privilege, the greatest debt of any Christian, and yet God has called him to preach to the nations. The unsearchable riches of Christ (the word "unsearchable" implies "inscrutable"

9. Paul has now so repeatedly mentioned God's grace (Eph. 1:2, 6–7; 2:5, 7–8; 3:2, 7–8; cf. 1 Cor. 15:10), and so clearly indicated that his own ministry was a gift (Eph. 3:2, 8 and 3:7 twice), that we readily assent with Paul that the origin of his ministry was God's gracious gift done in accordance with God's sovereign "working of his power" (Eph. 3:8; cf. Eph. 1:19; Col. 1:29).

10. In what is certainly a rare form, Paul has taken the Greek superlative "least" and has added a comparative ending to it ("less than the least"), showing the magnitude with which he felt this. Cf. the sentiments Paul expresses in 1 Corinthians 15:9; 1 Timothy 1:15.

11. In Ephesians 3:9 Paul recapitulates the themes of "stewardship/administration" and "mystery"—these have been discussed in the commentary above. Here it is clear that the "mystery" works on a temporal or redemptive-historical frame of reference—it was hidden in ages past by the very God who created those ages (as he also created all things). Paul's job is now to enlighten people into the meaning of this mystery.

or "incomprehensible"[12]) that Paul is called to proclaim are evident in their application to his own account. The greatness of his debt makes the magnitude of Christ's riches all the more plain. That is why Christian maturity is never afraid of repentance and, in fact, desires it. Seeing our sin for its true magnitude makes the grace of God all the more great and precious to us. That is why, as the apostle Paul approaches the end of his life, he emphasizes his sin all the more, saying not only that he is the least of the saints, but that he is the chief of sinners (1 Tim. 1:15).

Being enraptured with grace is the nature of Christian calling. Such awe of grace certifies our calling as genuine and energizes it in the face of sacrifice. The truly called are so enraptured by the grace of God toward them that the attacks of others, the difficulties of their circumstances, their lack of worldly comfort, and their lack of recognition in the world do not dissuade them from the joy of proclaiming Christ.

This enraptured perspective and motivation can be quite elusive for us in our human weakness. Even though we may be willing to make great sacrifice and to serve others for a time, persevering in such a call *and* doing so out of a response to grace will test our faith resources and understanding to their limits. Many young adults have sacrificed to serve in such callings—for a time. Pastors cannot limit their desires to serve in a church as long as the people are pleasant and the salary is sufficient for cable TV and a wireless network. Others of us must not seek to serve the poor only so long as we do not have to become poor to do so. In Christ's service, we cannot limit our calling to institutions or positions that do not require long hours or financial pressure or dealing with a difficult boss or sinful peers.

No genuine calling is without genuine pain. But we endure such willingly because those truly called are so enraptured by God's grace toward them that they must proclaim it. God has applied to us the unsearchable riches of Christ so that we are able to call him our Lord and to proclaim him to other people who are just as needy as we. Grace toward us in our destitution enraptures our hearts and empowers our calling. But it is not merely grace towards called individuals that enraptures Paul.

12. See W. Bauer, W. F. Arndt, F. W. Gingrich, and F. W. Danker, *A Greek-English Lexicon of the New Testament* (Chicago: University of Chicago Press, 2000), s.v. *anexichniastos*. Cf. Rom. 11:33; Job 5:9; 9:10; 34:24 (Septuagint). Paul earlier calls these riches of Christ "incomparable riches of his grace" (Eph. 2:7). On God's "riches" see also Eph. 1:7, 18; Eph. 3:16.

Enraptured by Grace to the Church (3:10–13)

Paul says that the reason that he will make plain the mystery of the Gentiles' inclusion in the covenant promise is that God's "intent was that now, through the church, the manifold wisdom of God should be made known to the rulers and authorities in the heavenly realms" (Eph. 3:10). Much discussion has flowed through the centuries over whether these rulers and authorities are good or bad angels. Some commentators remind us that in Ephesians 6, Paul says that we wrestle not against flesh and blood but against rulers and authorities in the heavenly realms (Eph. 6:12). However, in the first chapter of Ephesians, Paul says that Christ is seated above all rulers and authorities in the heavenly realms (Eph. 1:20–21). What is clear in all of these passages is that God is using the church to display his glory to the heavens.

Paul beautifully describes how the church is *a witness to glory.* The words "manifold wisdom" reflect the idea of something that is multicolored or diverse (the word "manifold" was used to describe Joseph's coat in the Old Testament translation of Paul's time). In this one phrase Paul enfolds previously mentioned ideas of God's predestinating will, sovereign election, and unfolding mystery. All reflect a divine wisdom working to meld into the church sinners made perfect from every tribe, people, and nation.

This manifold wisdom of bringing together into one redeemed body those who were so universally fallen and so particularly different is "according to his [God's] eternal purpose which he accomplished in Christ Jesus our Lord" (Eph. 3:11). Thus God's "eternal purpose" (cf. Eph. 1:11), which is usually seen in Reformed circles as relating only to our individual predestination, must additionally be understood as our eternally determined corporate engrafting into the covenant of grace with many others from the nations of the world.

This engrafting of the redeemed is so amazing that it was God's intent to use it to display his wisdom to the heavenly beings. Thus Paul's words create a celestial stage to display the wonders of grace that we can scarcely imagine but must consider in order to fulfill our calling. From the first chapter we learn that Christ has been raised and seated at God's right hand above all rulers and authorities in the heavenly realms (Eph. 1:20). In the second chapter we learn that because we are in union with Christ, we are seated with him in the heavenly realms (Eph. 2:6). Now here in the third chapter we learn that in union with other sinners made perfect, and as members of one body, we who come from every tribe and nation, people and personality, are on display as a church before the heavenly hosts as a testimony to the wisdom of God, the Creator. The heavenly hosts are to look at those of us in the church with all of our sin, differing personalities, cultural prejudices, and color differences and say, "How did God do that?! How did he get such difficult and disagreeable creatures together in one body to praise him? The manifold wisdom of the Creator God really is great!" Just as Paul's sin makes the grace of God more apparent, the uniting of sinners in the body of Christ makes the grace of God more brilliant—even to the hosts of heaven. By our unity in Christ's body, the church, we are preaching to the angels about the power, wisdom, and glory of the God who made us.

This is the apex of Paul's thought about the church. Earlier we learned that the church is the culmination of an eternal plan (Eph. 1:1–14) and the means by which God will fill the world with his purposes (Eph. 1:15–2:22). But here we learn that the church is intended not only to transform the world but also to transfix heaven. This transcendent purpose is the cause of delight and determination in those who are truly called. We serve not for self but for the sake of uniting others in the church for the glory of God.

Paul also beautifully describes how those in the church have *an access to glory*. He has not finished his description of the heavenly scene. He adds that as we gather together before the angels, we also learn that, regardless of our differences, we all may approach God "with freedom and confidence" (Eph. 3:12). This is a continuation of the image that Paul introduced earlier when he said that we have "access" (a term for entering a throne room) to the Father (Eph. 2:18).[13] Weak and sinful, sick and sad, we nonetheless have freedom and confidence to approach the Creator God. Consider the strange juxtaposition of vision and experience in the apostle as he writes these words. He is imprisoned by Caesar, yet he says that we have (and he has) freedom to approach God.

The word translated as "freedom" in the NIV can indicate "freedom of speech," but more fundamentally it indicates "boldness" in approaching God (cf. Heb. 4:16; 10:19).[14] Paul is concerned about what will happen when his

13. See further the comments on Ephesians 2:18.

14. A more literal translation of this verse can be found in the English Standard Version: "... in whom we have boldness and access with confidence through our faith in him."

accusers arrive. He knows he will face false accusation and personal assault, yet he says that we can be unafraid before God. How can we have such boldness in the face of life's constraints and difficulties?

Paul gives both the reason and the means to claim these privileges. We have freedom and confidence to approach the Father "in him" (Christ Jesus our Lord, cf. Eph. 3:11) and "through faith in him" (Eph. 3:12).[15] Here is the corporate gospel in beautiful synopsis. In the heavenly throne room we—the whole church of redeemed sinners from every nation—are able to approach the Father in Christ. The words "in Christ Jesus our Lord" signify our union with him and remind us of the unsearchable riches of God's grace that Paul has already described in this epistle, and that are the reason for our freedom and confidence. By our being in union with the risen Lord, his victory over sin is ours together (Eph. 1:19–20). "Because of his great love for us, God, who is rich in mercy, made us alive [*together*] with Christ even when we were dead in our transgressions" (Eph. 2:4–5). Our sin is forgiven, we are redeemed by his blood, and *together* we are provided with his righteousness (Eph. 1:7).

By what means are we all made recipients of this forgiveness of our sin and provision of his righteousness? "It is by grace that you have been saved, through faith—and this not from yourselves, it is the gift of God—not by works" (Eph. 2:8–9). Paul summarizes here in similar words, "through faith in him," indicating that what God has done in our individual behalf by grace through faith we also may experience corporately. We have access together to our God by faith. We experience corporately and without discrimination the blessings that are ours individually. Thus the mark of a true Christian calling is a willingness to offer personal sacrifice in order to bring together in Christ the strands of humanity separated by sin, misunderstanding, and prejudice, so that we may together experience (and be a witness of) the greatness of the grace of our God.

With this in mind Paul encourages the Ephesians "not to be discouraged because of my sufferings for you, which are your glory" (Eph. 3:13). The meaning of these words is most clear when we consider the reason that Paul

15. The Greek of verse 12 literally reads the "faith of him," and commentators debate whether this is "faith in him" (as in the NIV) or "his faithfulness." Both are grammatically possible, although the former has been the majority position. Certainly in Ephesians Christians themselves have "faith" (Eph. 2:8; 3:17; 6:16, 23), and this is clearly "faith in the Lord Jesus" (Eph. 1:15).

is in prison. The charge that originated against him in Jerusalem (and eventuated in his extradition to Rome) was that he had "brought Greeks into the temple area" of the Jews (Acts 21:28). And the reason that this charge came was that Paul had been together with a Gentile named Trophimus who was an Ephesian (Acts 21:29). Paul is in trouble for supposedly bringing a Gentile Ephesian into the temple to worship with Jews (it is not even clear that Paul actually did this). The charge may have been unjust, but such a covenant expansion that puts Jews and Gentiles together is the very dynamic that Paul now advocates to awe the angels. Paul therefore tells the Ephesians not to be discouraged about his sufferings for them because these sufferings are the instrument by which Jews and Gentiles and angels see the grace of God that makes us one body in Christ.

Paul is able to see his sufferings from a heavenly perspective and to delight in what speaks of heaven even when it creates suffering for him. From an earthly perspective his sufferings hinder his ministry, endanger his life, and spoil his reputation; but from heaven's perspective he sees that God uses even suffering for the great glory of bringing us together for the praise of our Savior. This is the ultimate sign of our genuine calling: we are so enraptured by grace that we would be willing to die to self and live for God so that we might bring together many sinners of many kinds to be a witness to the Savior in heaven and on earth. Our witness should not simply be about "Jesus and me," or about gaining approval, or even about my living for the glory of God; it is about seeing the glory of bringing many people together of different and distasteful and even antagonistic backgrounds and having them together come freely and confidently before the Father to glory in the grace of the Savior. By loving the unlovely, showing grace to the angry, being forgiving toward the hurtful, and being bold without bitterness in the face of attack, we show the glory of the wisdom of God to men and angels.

In June of 2002 a group of nine coal miners made national headlines during a seventy-seven-hour ordeal to rescue them from a flooded underground mine in western Pennsylvania. When they emerged from the mine, restaurants and gas stations posted on highway signs the words "Nine alive, Prayers answered." It was a time of glorious celebration for their escape from death. But there were days of even greater glory ahead when the story of what happened in that wet darkness began to emerge. When the water began to come in on the men, they rushed for escape. But when they recognized that the path was closed, they saved the lives of others by shouting to those who were coming down on a shift change to run because of the rising water.

After that heroism, these trapped nine began their finest hours of glory. Everything that they had was to be shared. A sandwich and a soda they shared. They huddled together to share body heat. They even took turns sharing the little piece of dry space above the water. They tied themselves together to keep anyone from floating off in unconsciousness. They bound themselves one to the other with the commitment that they would live or die as a group. When the outside world learned all that had happened, we all said, "Glory!" Each of these men was willing to give his life to save the lives of the others, those that the worst of circumstances had thrown together.

We learn from Paul's words that our calling has many similar attributes if it is genuine. We—for no merit of our own—are willing to die to self and live for others. We vow to share with others everything that we have in Christ. We do this not knowing the circumstances or cultures into which we will be thrown, but committing our own lives to saving others, even when it may be to our own great hurt to do so. We wrap our arms around those who may by their own selfishness and neediness take life from us. Why would we do such things? Because we are aware of the watching world, and the heavenly hosts give glory to God when they observe the church exhibiting such grace.

11

The Prevailing Power of a Supreme Love

Ephesians 3:14–19

I pray that you, being rooted and established in love, may have power, together with all the saints, to grasp how wide and long and high and deep is the love of Christ, and to know this love that surpasses knowledge—that you may be filled to the measure of all the fullness of God. (Eph. 3:17–19)

In the tragic comedy *A Thousand Clowns*, a child tells his mother, "I love you six," because six is as high as he can count. He stretches to the extent of his knowledge to express the magnitude of his love. How would you measure God's love for us? The apostle Paul answers that question in this section of the book of Ephesians by stretching our minds to the limits of understanding to perceive the measure of God's care for those in his church. Paul says God's love for his people is as long as eternity past, so wide as to include all nations, so high as to ring praises from angels in heaven, and so deep as to cancel the claims of hell on our soul. Knowledge of such magnitude grants more than comfort, more than assurance, and even more than joy. Knowledge of this magnitude is power! Here in these verses of Ephesians, Paul tells us how to access the spiritual power of divine love as he completes the prayer that he began in the first verse of this chapter. Our need for such power becomes evident when we experience things like the following.

"It won't work." The words came from an older man who confronted me after a sermon I had preached on overcoming temptation. I had given what I considered helpful and biblical counsel on the need to recognize sin, turn from it, practice new habits, avoid old ones, and become accountable to other fellow believers. The older man faced me directly and said, "I work with young men who travel on business. They are bombarded with sexual temptation of all sorts, and they think that simply by sheer grit and will power they will be able to resist. I have to tell them that they must pray that God will change the nature of their hearts, or they won't be able to resist. People do precisely what they love, and until they have a greater love for the things of God than the things of this world, they will not be able to stop."

At the time I thought that the man simply had not listened to me closely, or that he was just a kook. I have never seen him again. But, in the years since he spoke to me, I have thought much more about what this man said, and I have more than once wondered if he were not a man but an angel sent to help me think and preach more clearly about the power of the gospel. Could it really be that simple? Is our power in our passions? Passions control the insane and the romantic but could this also be true of the rest of our being? Do we simply do what we most love to do, and thus the power for spiritual change is found in the affections of the heart? If that is so, then the love that motivates us is actually the power that drives us. Why we do what we do is also how we do what we do. If why I serve God is also how I serve God, then greater love always precedes greater power. And, in fact, since we will only and always do what we love the most, then greater love is the means to greater power.

If greater love is greater power, then this has a profound impact on how we try to minister, parent, and help others honor Christ. For years I have searched for the answer to what will give people power over their addictions, compulsions, and recurrent sin. I have preached on mutual accountability, the cultivation of godly habits, and the exercise of spiritual disciplines. And I do not want to take away from the practicality and necessity of all such means of grace. Our catechism rightly instructs that God communicates to us the benefits of our redemption through the Word, sacraments, and prayer.[1] But if what controls our affections controls us (our actions), then these disciplines themselves have an object—to renew our affections, and through them our power for holiness. This means that the ultimate goal (the *telos*, purpose or aim) of my preaching, or of my parenting, or of my own personal devotions suddenly becomes quite plain. I must ignite, cultivate, spark, renew, demonstrate, broadcast, signify, magnify, and preach *love* for the God of our redemption. What never must be absent from my spiritual instruction is that which stirs in the heart a prevailing love for the Savior. While I may have much knowledge to communicate regarding Christian obedience, thought, and duty, my greatest obligation is consistently and compassionately to fire a more profound love for God in those dear to him. Without love there will be no power to do what God requires. Only an overwhelming affection for him will produce an overcoming power to defeat sin. Love is power.

The apostle Paul uses the truth that what we love motivates and enables our actions to summarize all the doctrine presented thus far in Ephesians. And in uniting spiritual strength to the believers' knowledge of God's love, the apostle tells us what must take priority in ministry that will truly help others discover God's transforming power. What characterizes ministry that possesses the knowledge that love is power?

Prayer from a Position of Power (3:14–15)

The apostle continues the prayer that he began in the first verse of this chapter before a long parenthesis explaining his ministry (Eph. 3:1–13). In that first verse, Paul began with words that are paralleled here: "For this reason I kneel before the Father" (Eph. 3:14). As Paul now continues forward with the prayer that began the chapter, we must consider what precedes verse 1 to find the reason that he kneels before the Father.

Humbled before the Father's Glory (3:14a)

The reason that Paul kneels is found in the words that precede his prayer. He sees the church made up of living stones from every kind of people and indwelt as by the Shekinah glory with the Spirit of God (Eph. 2:21–22). He

1. Westminster Shorter Catechism 88.

sees this spiritual temple made up of all races, tribes, and nations rising to heaven on the foundation of the apostles and prophets with Christ Jesus himself as the chief cornerstone (Eph. 2:20), an image so lovely and profoundly expressive of God's manifold wisdom that even the angels give glory to God for the beauty and design of the church (Eph. 3:10). Paul sees the wonder and the goodness of God's plan to build such a heavenly church through the apostle's earthly ministry, and falls to his knees in awe and humility before his heavenly Father.

As happened with the prophets of old who could not stand before the revelation of the glory of God, Paul's knees buckle in prayer. Commentators remind us that the Jewish custom was normally to stand for prayer, and that kneeling was reserved for moments of greatest emotion and homage as when Solomon knelt at the dedication of the temple in Jerusalem (2 Chron. 6:13).[2] Seeing this new temple built of living stones of earthly beings evoking praise from heavenly beings, Paul kneels toward the Father. The apostle cannot stand before this grand expression of the great grace of the King of heaven toward all the nations of earth.

But, curiously, with this posture of humility there is also a striking boldness. Paul prays not only humbled by his heavenly King's glory, but also confident of his heavenly Father's care (Eph. 3:14b).

Confident of the Father's Care (3:14b–15)

This sovereign God who is not worshiped in temples made with human hands but in a spiritual temple constructed of human hearts the apostle Paul simply calls "Father." The God who is infinitely great allows himself to be intimately addressed by one kneeling before him who has already identified himself as less than the least of all God's people (Eph. 3:8). This divine allowance of such intimacy with one so humble is a great grace, and yet Paul will help us understand that the grace is even more expansive than our minds dare imagine.

The apostle recognizes that despite his humble position, he is part of a vast and glorious family. The One that he calls "Father" is also the patriarch from whom his "whole family in heaven and on earth derives its name."

2. Jews normally stood for prayer (Matt. 6:5; Mark 11:25; Luke 18:11, 13), but knelt to express greater fervor or urgency (Ezra 9:5; Matt. 26:39; Acts 7:59–60; 21:5; Phil. 2:10).

The phrasing is a little difficult for us in English. We can approximate Paul's intention by saying that the Greek used here for "family" is actually "the fathered." The Greek words for Father and family (i.e., a community under a father, a fatherhood) are actually very similar. Paul's willingness to let nuances of both terms echo in his usage causes much discussion among the commentators. Apparently Paul relies upon his readers' understanding that God is Father (i.e., the community head) of all beings of heaven and earth. Then Paul uses these family/father echoes so that his primary readers (i.e., the newly enfolded Gentiles) will appreciate that having God as their Father also means they share membership in a privileged family that has heavenly as well as earthly status.

By identifying God as his own Father, and then identifying this same God as the patriarch of an extended family in heaven and earth, Paul makes an amazing claim. He is a member of the divine household that includes both the residents of heaven and the redeemed of earth. And so are we.[3]

As the redeemed of the Lord, despite our personal undeserving and our personal differences, we are family—brothers and sisters in Christ, siblings of Christ, and members of the household of heaven. The angels rejoice when even one of us sinners comes into their household (Luke 15:10); and when they perceive the union of our souls with those of every tribe and nation, the heavens shake with the praise they thunder: "Glory be to God for the wonders he has done. He has broken down the dividing wall of hostility" (see Eph. 2:14). "He has made those so different into one body and reconciled them into one family" (see Eph. 2:15–16, 19). "Great is the Lord. Glory to his name" (see Eph. 3:10).

Paul kneels humbly before the glory of God, and yet his spirit rises to rejoice in the implications of calling him "Father." Although Paul has no personal right even to kneel before God, yet because of his heavenly Father's care the apostle has the status of the glorified saints and angels. This means that all who share Paul's faith also share God's favor and may approach him not as foreigners or aliens but as citizens of heaven and members of God's household (Eph. 2:19). Such family status despite being personally undeserving is the basis of the apostle's "freedom and confidence" in approaching

3. It is also possible to translate the Greek as "every family," given the lack of an article in Greek, rather than as "his whole family." The result is the same: Paul says that every family is rooted in and named after God's family.

God (Eph. 3:12). He wants us to know that we share this status also, for such understanding is the path to spiritual power. The apostle displays gospel power in beautiful shorthand before the Ephesians when he prays before them: "I am unworthy to appear before the Father, but I am confident of his care." This combination of acknowledged humility and absolute confidence forms the foundation of gospel power in the heart of the believer.

John Owen expresses the power of combined humility and confidence this way:

> Let him that would not enter temptation labour to know his own heart . . . his natural frame and temper, his lusts and corruptions, his natural, sinful or spiritual weaknesses. . . . But store the heart with a sense of love for God in Christ, with his eternal design of his grace, with a taste of the blood of Christ, and his love in the shedding of it; get a relish of the privileges we have thereby—our adoption, justification, acceptation with God . . . and thou wilt in the ordinary course of walking with God, have great peace and security as to the disturbance of temptations.[4]

Face your sin—how humbling this is! Then face your Savior—how assuring he is! And by experiencing both, we are made confident, emboldened, and enabled for life in his presence.

One summer my oldest son went on a mission trip to Romania. He spoke in a church where it was still the tradition for men and women to sit on different sides of the sanctuary, separated by a partition. At one point in the service a little girl decided that she wanted to take her father a flower that she had picked when she came into the church. She knelt and crawled hesitantly, humbly, almost apologetically across the barrier between herself and her father. When he saw her, there was no hesitation on his part. He reached down, pulled her onto his lap, and put his arms around her. In the confidence of that embrace she offered him the gift that she had brought to him. She stuck her little fist with the even smaller flower beneath his nose, and he breathed it in as if it were the most fragrant perfume.

In some respects, the actions of this child and father make no sense. She had been wrong. In that culture she was not to leave the women, not to cross

4. *The Works of John Owen*, vol. 6, *Temptation and Sin*, from the chapter "Watching against Temptation" (London: Banner of Truth, 1991), 131 and 134.

the partition, not to forsake tradition, perhaps not even to pick the flower. Yet she offered her humble gift with confidence because the one to whom she offered it was her father. The sweetness of his heart drew her despite her transgressions. Such is the nature of the gospel that Paul so simply presents. We rightly come crawling to our heavenly Father, humbled by our transgressions because even our best works contain too much of the mix of our humanity to stand before a holy God. Yet, even as we kneel before him, we seek his favor with confidence because he is our Father. Out of his mere mercy he has chosen to incline his heart toward us as a Father with his own beloved child.

Why in his prayer does Paul reiterate for the Ephesians and for us this simple understanding of the gospel of our humility *and* confidence before God? The reason is that he knows we do not have the innocence of a child when we kneel before our heavenly Father. Before his glory the wrong of our actions and the unworthiness of our best gifts become all too plain. We see that even in our love for our spouses we are guilty of wandering affections and unkind actions. We see that even in our love for gospel ministry we are tempted to shortchange our studies and deal uncharitably with the reputations of our peers, parishioners, and fellow preachers. We fail to be completely honest in expression or action because we are so anxious to promote our own glory and to keep from facing our own limitations. And, for some of us, there are matters of deep and besetting compulsion that we have long hoped to overcome, but that instead have seemed to increase in the intensity of their assaults.

Worse than any of these sins, we also must face the humbling truth of failure in the context of the premise that Paul is about to put forward—namely, that sufficient love of God is the power to overcome sin. If this is true, then the presence of such sins in our life reveals that we do not love God enough. In fact, we have loved our sin more than we love him, or it would not have a home in our hearts. This is not a truth that we want to face, or are accustomed to facing on these terms. On those occasions that we do face our sin, we most often say to ourselves, "I was weak," or "I messed up," or "I failed my Savior." But even in these expressions of guilt there is still the assumption that we love Jesus; we just messed up. Yet, if our sin is an expression of our true love, our words have the false and empty ring of a wayward spouse who says to a husband or wife, "That other person didn't mean anything; I still love you."

Yes, there is still love present, but in those moments of betrayal the love for another passion if not another person was greater than the love for the one to whom the spouse is committed. When we sin, love for sin competes with and supersedes love for Christ.

This understanding can be completely devastating to us as Christian leaders. "Oh, no," we cry. "If such sin is present in my life, then I don't love God enough. I have sought to serve God and his people because I thought that I loved him. But if I loved God enough, then this sin would not overpower me. Despite all of my past promises and commitments, I must not love God enough." To such a broken and humbled heart the apostle Paul says simply, "You are right. You do not love God enough, but he loves you more—you, and a world of others like you. Despite your humanity and humiliation, the Father unites you with the saints and the angels. He loves you as a member of his own family. He loves you."

Confidence in the love of a heavenly Father for humbled creatures encourages our return, stimulates our repentance, and increases the love for the Father that is the power that the gospel offers. Humbled by our need and driven to our knees, we can yet approach our God with confidence because of the sweetness and greatness of his mercy. Paul's prayerful reiteration of these truths places him in a position to proclaim the power of the gospel. Next, Paul identifies the content of the prayer that Christian leaders offer if they would promote the gospel's power in God's people.

Prayer for a Divine Expression of Power (3:16–17)

Paul prays for a divine expression of power in God's people. Verse 16 begins with the first of three *hina* ("in order that") clauses in the Greek text of this paragraph. Paul says he is praying "in order that he [God] may give from the riches of his glory . . ." (Eph. 3:16 literally), and "in order that you [the Ephesians] may have strength to comprehend . . . and to know the love surpassing knowledge" (Eph. 3:18–19a literally), and "in order that you may be filled with all the fullness of God" (Eph. 3:19 literally). The NIV reflects the repetition of the *hina* clause by repeating the words "I pray" so that it is clear what the apostle is praying for. Knowing that the power to overcome sin is from above, the apostle overtures each member of the Trinity to do his work in the hearts of his people.

The Father to Provide His Riches (3:16a)

Paul prays that "out of his glorious riches he [i.e., the heavenly Father already referenced in Eph. 3:14–15] may strengthen you . . ." (Eph. 3:16a). What are these "riches" that will strengthen? We can answer because these words already have a treasured history in this epistle. Earlier in this chapter Paul contrasts his own spiritual poverty with the unsearchable riches of Christ that the apostle has the privilege to proclaim to the Gentiles (Eph. 3:8). The riches of God are those that cancel spiritual debt. This is made more clear when Paul says that God, "who is rich in mercy," who made us alive even though we were dead in our transgressions, has already seated us in heavenly places and enables us to "show the incomparable riches of his grace, expressed in his kindness to us in Christ" (Eph. 2:4–7). God's riches are revealed in the currency of his grace and mercy that save us from death, give us eternal security, and enable us to proclaim his kindness to others.

What is the source of these riches of mercy? Paul answers early in this epistle: "In him [Christ] we have redemption through his blood, the forgiveness of sins, in accordance with the riches of God's grace, that he lavished on us . . ." (Eph. 1:7; cf. 1:18). The riches of God are his kindness and mercy provided through the blood of Christ, which has redeemed us from the debt of our sin. But the riches do not merely cancel debt; they also are so vast as to provide us the rights and privileges of the household of heaven. We may even call our God "our Father" (see Eph. 3:14).

The Spirit to Provide His Power (3:16b)

Paul continues his prayer with the petition that God would provide "power through his Spirit in your inner being" (Eph. 3:16b). Again, the words have a rich background within this book.[5] Paul has earlier spoken of power in our inner being as the resurrection power of Christ that resides in believers and makes us spiritually alive (see Eph. 1:18–20). The power of the Spirit that brought Jesus from death to life has also made us alive who were dead in our transgressions and sins (Eph. 2:1–5). Paul compares this power residing

5. The link of this passage to the resurrection power described in chapter 1 becomes apparent when noting that the three terms used to describe God's power in Ephesians 1:19 (*dynamis*—power, *kratos*—strength, and *ischys*—ability) reappear in various forms here in Ephesians 3:16, 18. These all contribute to the fullness (*plērōma*) of God first described in Ephesians 1:23 that also reappears in Ephesians 3:19.

in us who are the living stones of God's temple to the Shekinah glory that resided in the tabernacle of Israel (Eph. 2:21–22).

To possess such power is to acquire the hope that sin will no longer hold sway in our life, the knowledge that the grasp of besetting sins is broken, and the confidence real change is possible. While Paul has been reveling in the corporate identity of Jews and Gentiles, he now speaks of a direct personal consequence of the Spirit who makes us one. That same Spirit also endues us as individuals with the power to defeat sin. The Christian life creates individual responsibilities as well as family relationships that are both made possible by the Spirit of God.

The Son to Provide His Life—Through Faith (3:17)

After petitioning for the power of the Spirit, the apostle ultimately prays for Christ to dwell in the hearts of his people (cf. Eph. 2:22). It is important here to be reminded of a basic gospel question. If we are dead in our transgressions and sins (Eph. 2:1), and if Christ is alive in us (Eph. 3:17a), then whose identity do we have? In heaven's accounting, Christ provides his life in the place of my own. The reason that the riches and power of God are mine is that Christ grants me his identity. I am a coheir with Christ of the love and riches of our Father. Christ's blood redeems me from the debt of my sin, and his righteousness provides me with the riches of his holiness and inheritance (Eph. 1:14, 18; 5:5). His life is mine.

Our union with Christ is the culminating thought in the apostle's description of the participation of the Trinity in the life of the believer. Paul has prayed that the Father, out of his riches (Eph. 3:14–16a), will provide power through the Spirit (Eph. 3:16b), so that Christ may dwell in the believers' hearts (Eph. 3:17a). The Father wills for the Spirit to be the instrument by which Christ takes over our heart and provides our identity. This description of the progress of divine intimacy echoes the epistle's progressive revelation of our relationship to our Savior: Christ is seated above us (Eph. 1:20–22), then we are seated beside him (Eph. 2:6), then we rest upon him (Eph. 2:20), then he indwells us (Eph. 3:17), then he fills us (Eph. 3:19), then we grow up into him as our head (4:15).

Some persons fear that too much emphasis upon the mercy of God in Christ will lead to disregard for the standards of God, but the Bible's message is that full understanding of God's love so unites our heart with the person and character of Christ that he increasingly becomes our life and our path. St. Patrick's famous prayer well reflects these truths: "Christ be with me and within me, Christ behind me and before me, Christ beneath me and above me; May your salvation, Lord, be always ours this day and forevermore."

What must I do or give to receive the benefits of this life of union with Christ? What sacrifice, duty, or accomplishment must I offer? Paul answers by praying with beautiful simplicity that Christ would dwell in his people "through faith" (Eph. 3:17b). The power of the new spiritual life is ours not by our will or strength but solely through trusting in what he provides. In trusting that his righteousness will redeem from our sin and substitute for our destitution we find his strength is ours.

Some time ago I wrote a letter to a friend and former pastor who has been imprisoned for embezzlement. I spoke of the mercy of a sovereign Lord, of forgiveness, of the graciousness of lessons that can be learned even from the devastations of sin. I had no doubt that the truths were biblical, but the letter still seemed empty of power. I could not keep the words from creeping into my consciousness as I continued to work through that morning. Some hours later I asked my secretary if the mail had been collected that morning. She said, "No." So I asked her to retrieve the letter from the office mail.

I ripped open the envelope. Then, where I had written to my friend that one day he could yet stand forgiven before God, I now inserted the words "robed in Christ's righteousness." He will be able to stand with Christ's life in substitution for his own. My friend's sin has been great. Yet as a truly repentant child of God, he may possess the riches of the righteousness of Jesus. Was I being too easy on him? Some may think so, but I want him back—back in the knowledge of the Savior, back in the path of obedience, back as a trophy of the grace of God—and the only power that will bring him back is true faith in the loveliness of the Savior who yet provides his life for our life. So I pray for and proclaim the love of the Father to provide the power of the Spirit and the indwelling of the Son in order that faith may save where no human compensation ever could.

You may know all of these basic gospel truths, and the Ephesians knew them; but Paul repeats these essentials because he knows that until they sink to soul depth, we will rely on our own powers of perception and strength to combat sin. And, consequently, we will remain powerless before the assaults of the Evil One. Apart from God we can do nothing (John 15:5). Paul prays for divine power to equip God's people because he knows that we will have no ability to defeat sin until we recognize:

> Without God's riches we are poor;
> Without God's Spirit we are helpless;
> Without Christ's life we are dead.

As counterintuitive as it seems, our recognition of our utter helplessness is the path to spiritual power. I am now and always a helpless being in need of an endless supply of God. If I ever believe or act otherwise, then I am only made more vulnerable and helpless before the Evil One. Acknowledgment of my fallen condition is the starting point of a journey to discover the power of the gospel in justification and sanctification. Unless God's people come to the end of themselves, they will not continue to turn to their only hope. This is why if all we do is preach Christian behaviors and morals, we actually make God's people more vulnerable to sin because we deaden their senses to the fact that apart from him they are helpless.

But then what? Once we confess that we can do nothing—that we are powerless before the powers of sin without the work of a triune God—how then do we access the very power that Paul prays for God to provide? The answer is in the next element of his prayer. In addition to praying for a divine expression of power, as one concerned for others, he offers something more.

Prayer for the Personal Reception of Power (3:17b–19)

All previous discussions of divine power naturally have led to the question of how God's people receive his power. Paul now answers.

We Must Grasp How Secure Is God's Love (3:17b–18a)

Paul begins this portion of his prayer for the Ephesians with a statement of their position as believers. He says, "I pray that you, being rooted and established in love, may have power, together with all the saints . . ." (Eph. 3:17b–18a). "Rooted" and "established" are both terms relating to growth; the first refers to the growth of a plant and the second to the growth of a building. Before Paul's eyes may be the traditional image of Israel as a tree, and the glorious temple of living stones made of believers from all nations and races. These are quite different images but they have something in common: they best rise heavenward from good ground.[6] The ground that is the foundation of such heaven-rising growth is God's love.

Paul beautifully and carefully expresses the foundational nature of the love of the Trinity for unholy persons such as we. Paul does not say that the love is either above us in heaven or ahead of us in time. We do not acquire God's love through our present power or future achievements. Rather, we are standing on this love, rooted and established in it. When Paul speaks to the Ephesians in their pagan society, he says that they have as secure a grounding in God's love as do all the saints, including those in the heavens he has already described. Though this may sound like a simple gospel truth, it is our fundamental reminder that power for spiritual change comes from the assurance that we are loved as much as and in the same way as the saints before us who now dwell on high with God.

This past year Covenant Seminary hosted a marriage conference. A couple whose marriage had been broken and later healed led a portion of the conference. They expressed how the power for spiritual change results from a foundational assurance of God's love. Each reflected publicly on what had enabled them to face their sin against one another and against God. They said, "In each of our lives we came across persons who tried to help us. All of our counselors loved us. Some were tremendous in helping with self-revelation and reflected our thoughts well. A number gave us good reading and accurately explained what the Bible said about our choices. But no one was direct with us, and still hopeful. We could not change until we were given the freedom to see our sin, and go to the cross, and be safe."

Power over sin rises with deep assurance of the security we have on the foundation of God's love. If that foundational assurance is weak, then our power will erode. For this reason, Paul next makes clear something else required to have power over sin.

We Must Grasp How Great Is Christ's Love (3:18b–19a)

Paul says that faith in the security of God's love is the means by which we "may have power . . . to grasp how wide and long and high and deep

6. The mixing of plant and architectural metaphors occurs elsewhere also (see Matt. 7:15–20, 24–27; 1 Cor. 3:9).

is the love of Christ, and to know this love that surpasses knowledge" (Eph. 3:18–19). In Greek these spatial dimensions are nouns rather than adjectives (i.e., width, length, height, and depth), and they are united together by a single article. The Greek text does not explicitly state an object of these spatial dimensions, so we might wonder, "Is it the width, length, height, and depth of God's power, his salvation plan, his wisdom, or his love?" Some commentators debate these options (including other possibilities), but the NIV rightly identifies the clearest reference as the "love of Christ" for us.[7]

The image of the temple resting on Christ and rising to heaven was in Paul's mind just before he started this prayer. Now that image seems to govern his thoughts (see Eph. 2:20–21). The temple is rooted and established in love, and its foundation enables us to consider the dimensions of the Spirit-filled temple that also express the width and length and height and depth of God's love. The words of this beautiful verse crystallize all the thoughts that the apostle has expressed thus far in this epistle:

- Paul has described a temple built of persons of all nations and races—this dimension shows us that Christ's love is as wide as the world (Eph. 2:19).
- Paul has said the divine love that designed this temple extends to eternity past and keeps us for eternity future—Christ's love is as long as eternity (Eph. 1:4–5).
- Paul has pictured this temple of living stones joined together and rising to heaven where even the heavenly hosts gape at its glory—Christ's love is as high as heaven (Eph. 2:21 and 3:10).
- Paul has even related that this divine love reaches past the depths of our hell-deserving sin to give us family status before God—Christ's love is as deep as hell (Eph. 3:8).

7. There is much to commend the "love of Christ" translation of the NIV: (1) the immediate context speaks of love (Eph. 3:17, 19); (2) the notion in verse 19 that the love of Christ "surpasses knowledge" coheres well with the expansive spatial dimensions in this clause; (3) Paul elsewhere speaks of the depth and height of the love of Christ and the love of God (Rom. 8:35–39); and, most importantly, (4) "love of Christ" functions in Greek as the direct object of the second infinitive in verses 18–19 ("to know" in Eph. 3:19), which is clearly coordinated (via "and") with the infinitive "to grasp," and thus "love of Christ" can rightly be supplied as an object to both clauses. The parallel in Romans 8:35–39 (where "love of Christ" and "love of God" clearly mean "Christ's love" and "God's love") also strengthens the argument that here the "love of Christ" means "Christ's love for us."

Grasping the dimensions of the love of Christ is to know of a love that "surpasses knowledge" (Eph. 3:19a).[8] Despite the beauty and wonder of Paul's description, the love of God is greater than the dimensions of our human knowing. Even an apostle can describe God's love to us only within the limits of human expression. As a child may try to express his love's extent by relating it to the highest number he can count (e.g., "I love you six, Mommy"), Paul's expansive expression of God's love remains too limited. Despite the ways that he has stretched his imagination and our hearts to understand the greatness of God's love, Paul must still confess that the love of Christ "surpasses knowledge" (Eph. 3:19).

Our human tendency is to measure the dimensions of God's love by what we know from our experience. We add according to our blessings and we subtract according to our difficulties to estimate how much God loves us. But the apostle says that Christ's love surpasses knowledge. Yet, although the dimensions of divine love surpass our knowledge, we can still grasp that love—if only as one holding a leaf on an oak tree.

This love surpassing knowledge is the truth we cling to in moments of crisis or disaster. Those without biblical understanding will try to measure God's love on the basis of their circumstances and what they know about their experiences. But the Christian does not measure God's love on the basis of the circumstances he or she knows, but rather on the character of God that is revealed in the width, length, height, and depth of the love of Jesus. We measure God's love by a cross. We trust and serve our Savior because of his love that surpasses our ability fully to express or explain it.

We Must Grasp How Powerful Is Christ's Love (3:19b)

What are the results of grasping a greater measure of the surpassing love of Christ? Perception of the prevailing love of God in Christ is power. Paul prays for the Ephesians' grasp of the love that surpasses knowledge, "[so] that you may be filled to the measure of all the fullness of God" (Eph. 3:19b).[9] The words "filled to the measure" mean filled up. The following words, "fullness

8. Either we must presume that Paul speaks nonsensically when he prays that we would comprehend what surpasses (*hyperballō*—thrown beyond, exceeding) knowledge, or we can be thankful that by the Spirit we can grasp, at least in part, the vastness of divine love that is beyond natural perception.

9. "That you may be filled" is the passive form of *plēroō* to indicate God does the filling, and the filling is accomplished by his work. Our power is from him.

of God," are explained by their earlier reference in this epistle. At the conclusion of the first chapter, Paul says that the church is the transforming power of Christ in the world because it is the fullness of him who fills everything in every way (Eph. 1:23; see also Col. 2:9–10). The fullness of God is his sovereign power directed by his divine mercy. When we grasp the love of Christ that surpasses knowledge, we are filled up with the power that transforms our world for his sake. Let us make sure that we understand this: when we grasp the love of Christ, we are filled with the power of God (Eph. 4:13).[10]

Now we understand how our passions are connected to divine power. We do what we want to do because what we most desire, we most pursue. When Thomas Chalmers wrote of "The Expulsive Power of a New Affection," he was describing not merely the need to love Jesus more, but the power that flows with and through love.[11] Love for Christ drives out love for the things of the world. And our love for Christ must first spring from an awareness of his love for us.

Each spring my family returns to a cabin that we enjoy and that we have previously "winterized" for the winter cold. Prior to the cold we drain all the water pipes and the hot water heater so that they will not freeze. In the spring we turn the water back on. But in order to fill the water heater we have to open a valve at the top of the tank. As the water fills the heater, it drives the air out of the tank through the valve. Such is the nature of love for Christ. As his love fills our heart, the oxygen for our sin is driven out. The love for the things of this world cannot thrive in a heart that is filled with love for Christ.

Harry Ironside wrote:

> The secret of holiness is heart-occupation with Christ. As we gaze upon him we become like him. Do you want to become like Christ? . . . Let the loveliness of the risen Lord so fill the vision of your soul that all else is shut out. Then the things of the flesh will shrivel up and disappear and the things of the Spirit will become supreme in your life. . . . This is the

10. Paul prays that we may be filled "to" (*eis*) the fullness of God. The preposition indicates movement toward a goal and signals that our being filled with the power of God relies on our comprehension of the full love of Christ—a comprehension that is yet being accomplished. Thus God's fullness remains incomplete in us though we are in the process of being filled to the brim out of his supply. But the more complete is this comprehension, the more we are in possession of his power over sin.

11. Thomas Chalmers, *Sermons and Discourses*, vol. 2 (New York: Carter, 1846), 271.

> only way whereby we may be delivered from the power of the flesh and the principles of the world.[12]

When Christian leaders see this wonderful truth of Scripture—that power follows love—our calling becomes very clear. It is our duty, our privilege, our delight to engender in those that we want to grow in grace and holiness an ever greater love for Christ. How do we do this? We engender love the way that the apostle does: we proclaim how great is Christ's love for us.

Some fear, of course, that a preoccupation with the love of Christ will lead to license and the abandonment of God's standards, but this cannot be. When we explain that even God's discipline is evidence of his affection and that his law is an expression of the very character of the One who loves us so much as to give his Son in our behalf, then honoring him becomes the prevailing passion of our life. Jesus said, "If you love me, you will obey what I command" (John 14:15).

Christ's statement about keeping his commands as a consequence of loving him explains Paul's pattern in this epistle. Having spent the early chapters extolling the eternal love of God, the apostle next will turn to explaining the practical duties, obligations, and mission of those in the church. But now those duties have their proper context; they are rooted and grounded in God's love. Obedience is a loving response to God's affection. Our righteous conduct and thought are a result of doing what the Spirit-filled heart loves to do because we are responding to how wide and long and high and deep is Christ's love.

What we love to do the most, we will do. This makes the object of our Christian disciplines clear. When we pray, study the Scriptures, and unite in worship, our ultimate aim is neither to earn approval with God nor to build our strength by our willpower. Rather, the disciplines of grace are designed to fill our hearts with greater love for our God.

"Filling up" with love for God is the object not merely of our private duties but also of our ministries to others. When we understand that the primary obligation of our preaching is to have God's people embrace the wonders of his love so that they can serve Christ with power, then preaching becomes a wondrous and joyful task. Our mission is to reach the wounded and

12. *Discernment* 2, no. 8 (November 2005): 15, available at: http://discerningthescriptures.org/Documents/discernment%20magv2i8.pdf.

rebellious hearts with the compelling love of Christ. Our ministry becomes more appealing even in our own minds when we understand that our task is more to buoy God's people with his love than to burden them with his displeasure. Because the joy of the Lord is his people's strength, we always minister with the aim of providing the hope that enables others to progress in their walk of faith.

When to promote love for Christ is the true aim and joy of my ministry, then I am also transformed by Christ's love. I grieve for those who do not know his love. Rather than simply decrying their rebellion, I am driven by love for them to share his love for them.

What becomes the primary obligation of my counseling, if I want troubled souls to have the power to overcome their compulsions and despondency? My purpose is to penetrate the sin centers of the soul with the constraining love of Christ.

What becomes the primary obligation of my parenting if I want my children to walk in truth? I am compelled to provide a life context where the assurance of God's love is as instinctively known, commonly expected, and perpetually present as breakfast. Even as I fill up my daughter's cereal bowl with milk, my parental purpose is to fill up her heart with love for Jesus.

What is the primary prayer of my own heart if I want more power to overcome the sin and weaknesses of my own life?

> More love to thee, O Christ. More love to thee.
> Hear thou the prayer I make, on bended knee. . . .
> Once earthly joy I craved, sought peace and rest.
> Now Thee alone I seek. Give what is best:
> More love to thee, O Christ. More love to thee.[13]

When we understand how secure, great, and powerful is the love of God, the response of our hearts—now full of more love for him—is to join with him in the walk of faith to which he calls us. Paul's burden of joy for the Ephesians is that they would grasp how great Christ's love for them is so that his fullness would empower them.

13. Elizabeth Payson Prentiss, "More Love to Thee," 1869.

12

He Is Able

Ephesians 3:20–21

Now to him who is able to do immeasurably more than all we ask or imagine, according to his power that is at work within us, to him be glory in the church and in Christ Jesus throughout all generations, for ever and ever! Amen. (Eph. 3:20–21)

Some time ago, I needed to make a difficult financial announcement about our seminary because stock market dynamics were creating serious pressures on our finances. I was stewing about the announcement during my early morning jog around a neighborhood lake. Deep in thought, I came to the top of a hill just as some Canadian geese were approaching the lake from the other side of the rise. The result was that for a split second I found myself face-to-face with a flying goose. I ducked to my right but he dodged to his left so that we were still on a collision course. I froze anticipating the crash of our noggins. But then, in one of those sequences that seem to unfold in slow motion, he tweaked his tail and lifted a leg so that his body twisted, and he went by my shoulder with an outstretched wing grazing the top of my head.

Once I realized that I had been spared, I could not help being a little philosophical. "Oh great," I thought, "wouldn't that have been a sad way to go out!" I could imagine the headlines: "Seminary President Taken to Heaven on the Wings of a Goose." Though it may seem a bit silly, in a strange way being saved by that little flick of a goose's tail gave me a great deal of peace that day.

My peace came from considering the protection God provided for me on that day I was so worried about dear friends, the place I serve, and many months of pressure to come. I began to consider what God had to arrange in order to make that split-second event of reassurance happen. What kind of planning did it take for a person—raised in Tennessee over fifty years ago—and a goose—probably hatched in Canada three years ago—to simultaneously approach a rise in Missouri and come within two feet of one another on the very day that I needed encouragement because of a difficult announcement that I had to make as a result of stock market dynamics that had taken years to develop in a worldwide economy?

The sequence of plans needed to make all of those events and entities converge so precisely is truly mind-boggling. The wisdom and power of God that made that goose's tail twitch at the precise moment needed to fan into flame a flicker of hope in me were beyond anything I could ask or even imagine. In a world that whirls in an endless procession of unpredictable events and personal challenges, we lose track of what God does moment by moment to preserve us and his purposes for our lives. We know that our God loves us, but amidst the pressures of rents to pay, jobs to perform, medical results to await, tests to take, and transitions to make, we wonder still, "Is our God able to help *me here today*?" The Bible's message of a sovereign God who rules over all things in all places among all people and for eternity calms our hearts and stimulates our prayers with the simple affirmation: "He is able."

But how can we be assured that he is able? Paul unfolds the answer by "singing" this little doxology in the midst of his epistle (Eph. 3:20–21). Paul also breaks into similar doxology in Romans 11:33–36; 16:25–27; Philippians 4:20; 1 Timothy 1:17.[1] Shorter outbursts of apostolic praise such as "to God be the glory" appear throughout the New Testament (e.g., Gal. 1:5; 1 Tim. 6:16; 2 Tim. 4:18; Heb. 13:21; 1 Peter 4:11; 5:11; 2 Peter 3:18) and especially occur repeatedly in the Apocalypse (e.g., Rev. 1:6; 4:11; etc.). Such doxolo-

1. There is some textual dispute over Romans 16:25–27.

gies draw on themes reminiscent of many Old Testament hymns of praise. This doxology, focusing initially on the ability of God, opens in a manner quite similar to Jude 24–25 and to Romans 16:25–27. The term in Ephesians 3:20 for "able" (from Greek *dynamai*) is related to the strength vocabulary (e.g., *dynamis*) found later in this same verse (and elsewhere in Ephesians). Paul intends for this doxology to begin with the answer to a simple question related to God's power:

HOW MUCH CAN GOD DO? (3:20A-B)

The answer is, *more*—"immeasurably" more than we can ask, and more than we can even imagine. The Greek word for "immeasurably" (*hyperekperissou*) is the "highest form of comparison imaginable" and could even be translated as "infinitely more than."[2]

More Than We Can Ask (3:20a)

For children of all ages, Christmas is the asking time of year. While we may not be asking for "mutant turbo-blaster robo-dinosaurs" or "Diamond Dancing Barbies," we adults still have our "asks." The adult requests are more in the form of secure jobs, incomes adequate to pay for the turbo-blasters, good health, diplomas, peaceable families, and a world without war. There is no reproach in the apostle's words for asking. That we would ask is, in fact, a natural outgrowth of Paul's earlier conclusion that we have confident and free access to the Father by virtue of Christ's work on our behalf (Eph. 2:18; 3:12). We come to a Father who is able to do what we ask, and invites us to come to him (Phil. 4:6).

But the apostle does not limit the Father's care or ability to what we ask. There is too much of our humanity in our requests for them to govern God's responses. Because we are human our requests are feeble and finite. We want dessert when we need meat, success when we need humility, and safety when we need godly courage—or Christlike sacrifice. We ask within the limits of human vision, but he is able to do more. He sees into eternity what is needful for our soul and for the souls of those whom our lives will

2. W. Bauer, W. F. Arndt, F. W. Gingrich, and F. W. Danker, *A Greek-English Lexicon of the New Testament* (Chicago: University of Chicago Press, 2000), s.v. *hyperekperissos*; see also 1 Thessalonians 3:10; 5:13.

touch across geography and across generations; and, seeing this, he is able to do more than we ask.

In 1983 a childless woman named Mary Nelson was working in her garden in St. Louis, praying while she worked. She asked God to help not only in her grief for the absence of children in her life, but also in her bitter awareness of women who could have children but choose to abort them. The absence of a child in her home created such a longing for life in her heart that Mary asked God, there in the garden, to help her give life to children in whatever way he would lead. Nine months later, Mary "gave birth" to the first Pregnancy Resource Center in St. Louis, and since that time literally thousands of children have been spared due to the prayers and labors of Mary Nelson and others who have followed her. She, who once asked to be a life-giving mother to one, has become life-saving mother to thousands.

Our God is able to do immeasurably above what we ask. I know to ask only what I think is good for my immediate family; he knows what is good for my children's children, and what will bring multitudes into his kingdom from places I cannot name or imagine.

More Than We Can Imagine (3:20b)

The ways of our Lord cannot be limited to what we ask, because his wisdom and power—and, therefore, his intentions—are beyond our imagining.[3] Earlier in this chapter of Ephesians we were told that his love is so wide and long and high and deep that it surpasses our knowledge (Eph. 3:18–19), but now we are told that this is not a passive or powerless love. His loving surpasses our knowledge, but his doing surpasses our requests and even our imagination. "No eye has seen, no ear has heard, no mind has conceived what God has prepared for those who love him" (1 Cor. 2:9; Isa. 64:4). For those in Christ, T. S. Eliot says, "the impossible union of spheres of existence is actual. Here the past and future are conquered, and reconciled."[4]

He who loved us so much that he spared not his own Son to make us his children (Rom. 8:32) invites us to come to him freely and confidently, but

3. The Greek word (*noeō*) translated here as "imagine" refers essentially to the ability to comprehend something, especially on the basis of careful thought (see the first meaning in *Greek-English Lexicon*, s.v.; this context seems an extension of that basic idea). God's ability thus exceeds our comprehension and hence our thoughtful imagination.

4. T. S. Eliot, "Four Quartets."

he also promises to bring the full measure of the wisdom and powers of his Godhead to answer us. How do we measure what he can do? He holds the whole earth in his hand; he created the universe but continues to control the light in your room and the decay of an atom in the most distant galaxy; he makes the flowers grow and the snow fall; he rides on the wings of a storm and holds a butterfly in the air; and he who was before the beginning of all we know still uses time as his tool of healing, restoration, and retribution. Our thoughts are as a window to him; generations to come from us are already known fully to him who loves our family more than we do. He looks at the length of our life as a handbreadth, and makes our soul, though sinful, his treasure forever. Such is the God who hears our prayers and is able to do immeasurably more than all we ask or can even imagine.

God's greatness allows me to believe in his good will even when something I ask for is not answered when I desire or how I imagine. At this year's Thanksgiving service in my church I listened in fresh-found awe as believers gave their reasons for thanksgiving. One gave thanks for a child soon to be born after three different doctors said a child for this couple was impossible. But this thanksgiving came just after the words of a mother thanking the church for its ministry to her during the year that her husband had been dying of liver cancer. And while the one rejoiced in the coming of a child, I watched the eyes of another couple turn red and their eyes brim with tears because no such miracle child had come to them in their years of marriage. Days later I learned that one of our alumni families, who had just suffered their fourth miscarriage, yet prepared a meal in their home for college students to celebrate the coming of the Christ child.

If the world or any cynic were to look on all of these accounts at once, I can only imagine that the response would be: "Now wait a minute. This one gives thanks when a prayer for new life is answered. That one gives thanks when a prayer for continued life seems unanswered. Then this other couple grieves because a child does not come to them but also gives thanks to God because he let his Son come for us. Does all of this make sense?" No. It does not make earthly sense. But if the God of all things earthly and eternal were at work, would you expect him to be limited by our wisdom and perceptions? No, you would expect him to be at work in ways beyond our imagining. And that is just what he is promising: to do immeasurably above all that you would ask or even imagine.

It must be this way, for inevitably that for which we pray is limited by our human perspective. We think that we shall be happy if we see the perfect sunset, meet the right person, get the right job, or get relief from the person or disease that troubles us. But the One who sees beyond the sunrise, into the heart and after the disease, knows that in a fallen world perfect solutions do not exist and their dim reflections may only distract us from dependence upon him who must redeem us from all that falsely promises fulfillment. J. R. R. Tolkien wrote that our ultimate joy "lies beyond the walls of the world." Ultimate satisfaction is not in a lover, a landscape, or a livelihood; although they may rightly please us, they will pass. That which is eternal and on which the soul must rest is "higher up" and "further back" (as Cornelius Plantinga puts it) than those things we presently relish, and it can be provided only by the One who is able to do more than we would ask or even think. But how will he do such things?

How Will God Do More? (3:20c-d)

Sovereignly (3:20c)

Paul says that our Lord is able to do immeasurably more than all we would ask or imagine, "according to his power." These words already have a rich history in this epistle. Paul uses "according to" as a way of indicating that something will be expressed to its full extent. In the first chapter we are told that we have forgiveness "in accordance with" the riches of God's grace (Eph. 1:7). That is to say, God pours out his mercy from the fullness of his storehouses; he is not budgeting a meager supply for us and saving more till later. We have the fullness of his forgiveness and love. "Power" is the expression of God's sovereign force of creation. By his power he brought the world into being, brought us from death to life, and will transform this world into a new creation (Eph. 1:4, 10, 18, 19–23). He is the One who made our lovers, landscapes, and livelihoods, along with the universe and the eternity that contain them. Thus, when Paul says that God is able to do immeasurably more than all that we ask or imagine, "according to his power," the apostle urges us to believe that God can do more than we can imagine because he is God, and will use his sovereign power—the creative power of the physical and spiritual universe—in our behalf.

Personally (3:20d)

But how will God apply this sovereign power? The answer to that question will truly stretch our imagination—and our faith. For what the apostle claims is that God will work sovereignly according to his power that is "at work in us." God works in us personally.[5] This is a return to the theme that Paul began at the end of chapter 1 where he identified the church as the means by which God would fill and transform creation with his own fullness. Now Paul speaks to those in the church, and he says that God will do more than we can imagine through his power (yes, I can get my mind around this, so far) and that this power will be expressed through "us" (now that is a lot for a mind to handle). You and I are the instruments by which God is going to accomplish more than we can ask or even imagine.

This sounds more than a little far-fetched and perhaps rings a bit idealistic. After all, some of us enjoy places of security and esteem, while others endure great difficulty and depressing obscurity. Some see the effects of their lives in great brush strokes of glory and accomplishment. Others look back on the last twenty or thirty years of their lives and honestly question, "Did I do anything?" How can we honestly affirm that God is doing more than we ask or imagine through us? How could Paul say it while chained to a guard in prison at Rome while he is writing to the few people in the crude and simple house churches of Ephesus?

In a photograph displayed at Auschwitz, a Nazi guard points a pistol at the head of a child. Beneath the picture there is a caption: "He who saves one soul saves the world." Our temptation is to look for heroism, significance, and success in noteworthy deeds and great accomplishments. But faith accepts that God is working out his plan—for the world and for eternity—one moment, one act, one life at a time. Our finite wisdom in a mortal existence makes it hard to act with unnoticed integrity, to persevere without apparent results, to show courage when there is no gain and no one to cheer the sacrifice. But by such integrity, perseverance, and courage among his people in a church worldwide, God is changing the world.

5. This theme of God's power dispensed to those in the church was earlier hinted at in Ephesians 3:16, where Paul prays that God "may strengthen you with power through his Spirit in your inner being." Paul's ministerial call also serves as evidence of "the gift of God's grace given me through the working of his power" (Eph. 3:7).

Consider a woman who teaches prostitutes alternative employment as hairdressers in Thailand; a man who teaches a mentally handicapped adult to paint; a woman who offers comfort to a newlywed distressed by the unfaithfulness of her husband; a woman who gives up a holiday to spend an evening with high school girls needing a friend; a woman who changes the diaper of a disadvantaged infant saved from the uncertainties of the foster care system; a man who lingers over a catechism with an African in a remote village so that the man will be an effective elder in a church of ten; a man who refuses to pay a bribe from mission funds to a rebel leader in India; and a secretary in a government office who encourages her boss with a promise to pray for him today. None of these acts of persons I know can be counted on to make any difference in the eyes of the world, but collectively the power of God is at work in these Christians to change this world. In ways unseen, unheralded, and unknown, God is transforming the world *according to his power through us* even now.

It is beyond our imagining but necessary for our endurance to remember often that it is God's way to work his infinite wisdom and divine power through us. This is something that we will need to remember when we face obscurity while serving in a small church, when God chooses others for recognition, when failure knocks at our door, when we face anger or ridicule from foes or friends, when our envy of others in more prestigious or lucrative positions threatens to rob us of our commitment to our calling, or when we wonder if the spouse that God gave us is the right one. Because God is working sovereignly and personally we know that for the purposes of our own Christlikeness and his own glory he gives us the spouse he intends, the church he intends, the position he intends, and the challenges he intends. God's provision may not always be what we would ask, and often stretches what we can imagine. But God gives us what he does in order to prepare us, to strengthen us, to humble us, to bless us, and to grow in us a greater dependency on himself and a lesser attraction to this world, according to his power in us.

When God put his Son in a stable, it must have been hard to imagine that there was "the knowledge of the glory of God in the face of Christ" (2 Cor. 4:6). But what may be harder yet to imagine is that we too "are being transformed into his likeness with ever-increasing glory" (2 Cor. 3:18). In each activity of the Spirit, in each transition of our lives and in each challenge that makes us question how something so humble, difficult, or unnoticed could be significant, there is a new advent of the glory of God, a new incarnation of his presence and power. Think of that: no matter how obscure or insignificant the act, when we serve the purposes of the Savior, the glory of the Son of God shines in us with increasing glory because of his power that is at work in us.

How shall we treat a God who so dignifies and empowers the humble offerings of service that we give to him? If what we do is, in reality, the result of his power at work in us, then there is only one thing to do: give him glory.

What, Then, Is His Due? (3:21)

God does more—more than we can ask or imagine; and he does this according to his power—sovereignly and personally. Our response must be praise. He is deserving of more glory than we can offer. More glory is due him. Glory in the church, glory in Christ, and glory in perpetuity are due the One who is so able and so loving.

In the Church (3:21a)

Glory is due God "in the church" because he has chosen to use her as the instrument of his purposes on this earth and for eternity. Here his gospel is proclaimed, his law taught, and his people are nurtured in his grace and equipped for his service of world transformation. Thus, when Paul earlier pictured the temple of living stones rising to heaven where the angels sing glory, the apostle also pictured the Spirit indwelling as a Shekinah glory—the presence of God's power and glory.

Whatever is accomplished by us in the church, it is done because our God is able and has enabled us, and therefore the glory belongs to him. Thus the church throughout all time proclaims along with Paul that God is indeed "the glorious Father" (Eph. 1:17). This fits with the concept Paul began earlier in the epistle that God's grace and our redemption are to "the praise of his glory" (Eph. 1:6, 12, 14). And from God's "riches of glory" flow his inheritance in the saints (Eph. 1:18) and the Spirit's strengthening of our inner man (Eph. 3:16). There will be glory in the church because God is working his power through each of us.

In Christ (3:21b)

The church that has been in Paul's mind since the first chapter—that temple made of living stones that rises to heaven with the Spirit indwelling—is a natural place for giving glory to the enabling God. We readily understand what it means for there to be glory to God in the church. But what does it mean for there to be glory to God "in Christ" (Eph. 3:21b)? The answer involves understanding our position and our God's passion.

If there is glory in the church, then the thought naturally follows that there is glory in Christ. After all, we have learned in the first chapter of this epistle that the church is Christ's body (Eph. 1:23). So if there is glory in the church, there is glory in Christ. This is not merely an abstraction but, yet again, an affirmation of our union with Christ.[6] Those who are in the church are recognized by God as having the identity of Christ. As his body, we have his attributes accounted to us: his righteousness, his holiness, his life. We may approach the Father who is able to help us, and we may approach him with confidence, because we are recognized as having the privileged position in and of his own Son. Because we are his body, we have his position, and, conversely, whatever we do is to his glory. But there is more than a tie of words between glory being given in the church and in Christ; there is also progression of thought.

We need both of these truths—that we represent him and he represents us. Since his glory is reflected in what we do as his body, we must always consider if our actions actually are bringing him glory, and repent if they do not. At the same time, the realization that we have his position answers a question that has been hanging in the air since the outset of this chapter. Early on, as the apostle's thought unfolds, we may be willing to agree with him that our God is able to do immeasurably more than all we ask or imagine. The question that remains is whether "he who is able" is *willing* to do such things. The answer is, yes. Because we are in Christ Jesus, he is willing to do more in our behalf than we would ask or even imagine. We have Christ's position, and thus we have our God's love.

Yet there is something even more than love, and perhaps even stronger than God's love, that assures me that he is willing to do what he is sovereignly

6. This union "in Christ" is emphasized so often in Ephesians that we can scarcely list all its occurrences (e.g., Eph. 1:1, 3, 4, 7, 9–10, 12–13, 20; 2:6–7, 10, 13; 3:6, 11, 21; 4:21, 32). Moreover, the theme of union with Christ, and its specific expression in the phrase "in Christ," is one of the most central theological concepts in Paul's many epistles.

and personally able to do for those who are in Christ Jesus. The immediate subject of the apostle is not the love of our Savior but the glory of our Savior. The reason that I rest assured that my God is willing to use his power for those who are in Christ Jesus is that he is passionate for the glory of the Son who represents the wonders of his love and the beauty of his own nature.

We sometimes mistakenly think of grace as some material blessing or privileged circumstance that God provides to us. But grace is simply an expression of his character. His grace is evident in the glory that is in Christ Jesus. The One who loved us and gave himself for us is an expression of the character of the Father. The fact that there is glory to the Father in him means that the love that Jesus possesses and reflects is the nature of the Father. The glory that is in Christ is also in the Father. Thus the mercy, love, and compassion of the Son are the glory of the Father; they are the expression of the glory that is his chief passion.

Recently I received a letter from a good friend of mine, a pastor who had just resigned from a very difficult church situation. He had endured years of stress, financial sacrifice, family strain, and career jeopardy. Yet, through it all, this man has been one of my chief encouragers. However great his difficulties have been, he has always taken the time to write to me, to encourage me, and to remind me of the eternal promises of the gospel. In the letter in which he told me that he had submitted his resignation, he did so again. He wrote, "I rest in God's passion for his own glory." Whatever happens, whatever is required of sacrifice or success, this wonderful pastor trusts and teaches that God is not only able to do more than we can ask or imagine, but is also willing to do so because we are the body of Christ and our God is passionate for his glory.

Sometimes this is all that can make sense of things in the world. Today I worry about funds; my readers may be worrying about their jobs or relationships; but in many parts of the world there are faithful Christians in far worse circumstances. A Christian mother in the Sudan will hold a child dying of starvation, and she will remain faithful. While you read this, somewhere in this world a Christian is being tortured and is crying out to God for help. While we enjoy Christmas celebrations to commemorate the Savior coming to a stable two thousand years ago, other Christians will depart this life at the hands of persecutors and will see Jesus face to face. How does it all work together? I don't know. It's beyond what I would ask or even imagine. God's sovereign and good intent is more than I could believe were it not for the coming of the Savior to suffer and die in my behalf.

When tragedy and heartache come to believers, what evidence is there that God is truly sovereign and loving? The answer will not be found in our circumstances, but rather in the character of God revealed in Christ. Cancers do come; tragedies do strike; one baby of a faithful couple lives and another dies; capable people serve in difficult and obscure places all of their lives. There may be no evidence of the sovereign, personal love of God since what he is doing is beyond our asking or imagining, but there is yet glory to give to Christ in these situations. He is the One whose very life and ministry make evident that what God is able to do on an eternal plane, beyond what we can ask or imagine, is for his glory and for the eternal blessing of those who love him.

As I write these words, the longtime chairman of our board of trustees is fighting a very aggressive cancer that has already claimed one of his lungs. He once said this to me: "We are praying for God to heal, but I know that whatever he does will bring glory to God. God will reserve the glory to himself." That is a mature faith, and it is a sustaining faith: "My God is working beyond my asking or imagining according to his power at work in me, because he is zealous for his own glory."

I remember a pastor who told me of a man who, having just come to faith, said, "I always thought it would be great if God were like Jesus." He is. God's glory is in Christ, and that is the reason that we know that our God is able and willing to help us.

In Perpetuity (3:21c)

How long will God keep this zeal for his own glory? Forever. We should never limit God's glory to the time of our finite measurement. Perhaps that is why the apostle says that the glory due our God is throughout generations and throughout time. The expression "for ever and ever" (a Greek metaphor, literally "unto the age of ages") is often found in Paul's expressions of praise (Gal. 1:5; Phil. 4:20; 1 Tim. 1:17; 2 Tim. 4:18) and elsewhere in the New Testament (e.g., Heb. 13:21; 1 Peter 4:11; often in Revelation).[7] This is

7. The expression is also known frequently in the Septuagint Psalter, such as in Psalm 72:19 (= Septuagint 71:19: "Praise be to his glorious name forever [the Septuagint adds: "and for ever and ever"]; may the whole earth be filled with his glory. Amen and Amen").

not merely a redundancy. There is an intended emphasis that our hearts are meant to endorse.

With saints of old we thus proclaim, "Amen!" (Eph. 3:21). This word is frequently used in the New Testament to signal a wholehearted corporate endorsement of a prayer or praise (especially 1 Cor. 14:16; 2 Cor. 1:20; see for examples in Paul: Rom. 1:25; 9:5; 11:36; 15:33; 16:27; Gal. 1:5; 6:18; Phil. 4:20; 1 Tim. 1:17; 6:16; 2 Tim. 4:18).[8] Paul invites us to join our hearts with his in this reminder that God will continue working throughout this generation. He is not simply the God of a former people. There is still work for this generation and every generation to do, and he is able for this generation, even as he was able for the generations of the past.

And he is able for ever and ever. There will never be a moment that glory is not due him, and therefore there will never be a moment that he is not working through you to do immeasurably more than you would ask or even imagine. In your moments of great success, he is able. In your moment of greatest fear, he is able. When you have failed, he is still able. When the challenge ahead is too great, he is able. For ever and ever glory is due him, for he is always able to do immeasurably more than we can ask or imagine according to his power that is at work within us, and continues to be at work for the purposes of eternity.

At this year's Thanksgiving service I listened as the wife of one of our pastors gave glory to God. She spoke in the light of the recent murder of her brother. For some years this brother had lived in rebellion against God but, through the witness of his family and others, a glorious transformation had occurred. She reported how her brother had one day come to her father and said, "Now I know where I am going and Whom I trust." After that, the brother changed and the circumstances surrounding that change were already more than the family could ask or imagine; God had worked sovereignly and personally to bring the young man to himself. After so much pain before knowing the joy of his salvation, one would think that the murder of this young man would totally devastate this loving family. Of course, in many ways, it did. But this dear sister reported how, after her brother's death,

8. "Amen" is a transliteration from Hebrew of the Old Testament proclamation that "this is true" (*amen*, only rarely transliterated in the Septuagint; 1 Chron. 16:36; Neh. 5:13; 8:6), and thus follows the Old Testament practice of confirming the truth of a statement of praise (e.g., Pss. 41:13; 72:19; 89:52; 106:48—English numbering).

and even while her father held his dead son in his arms, the father said that he was at peace. He knew that God had preserved the son until the time that his eternity was secure with the Lord. But even this promise of eternity was not all that caused the sister to rise to her feet to give glory to God.

She rose to her feet to give the glory to God that her family was now praying for the salvation of the man who had murdered her brother. The Lord is using the family of a man recently saved to pray for the eternity of the man who killed him. Is this senseless? To the world, yes, it is. It is even more than I would normally ask or imagine could be right. But in the church, and for those who are in Christ Jesus, such amazing love is but another reason to give glory to God, for we know it is more evidence that he is able to do immeasurably more than we ask or imagine according to his power that is at work in us. We give him glory not only because he is able to work immeasurably above all that we would ask or even imagine, but also because in Jesus Christ we know that our God is willing to give supernatural blessing so that there will be glory due him in the church and in Christ, through all generations for ever and ever. Amen.

13

Owner's Manual for the Church

Ephesians 4:1–16

There is one body and one Spirit—just as you were called to one hope when you were called—one Lord, one faith, one baptism; one God and Father of all, who is over all and through all and in all. But to each one of us grace has been given as Christ apportioned it. (Eph. 4:4–7)

"Will Michael Dwight please come forward." Hudson Amerding spoke these words with great authority. At that time, he was the president of Wheaton College and then, as now, he had the bearing and manner of a naval officer who had commanded many men in times of great trial. He called the student Michael Dwight (not his real name) to the front of the chapel assembly. This was during an era when bell-bottoms were popular, along with long hair and a certain attitude toward authority. All of these marks of the era were much in evidence in the person of Michael Dwight. He was known as a leader among the malcontents at the college, and when he was called forward by the naval officer turned president, everyone in the chapel auditorium held their breath for whatever fireworks were about to fly. Michael Dwight came forward, and Hudson Amerding addressed him directly. "Michael Dwight, I want you to know that you are my brother in Jesus Christ, that I love you, and that I refuse to allow what others may think about our differences to come between us." Then the two men separated by so many apparent differences embraced each other.

Pent-up tension went out of an entire campus like air going out of a balloon. Hundreds still look back on that day as one of the most memorable of their college experience. The embrace of the two different men also remains a picture of what most of us wish the church looked like more often: persons quite different in appearance, demeanor, generation, emphases, attitudes, and gifts expressing love for each other—believing and acting as though each had something valuable and precious to contribute to the kingdom of God. We can readily smile at the scene, but it is very hard to reproduce. Inevitably the reasons for our differences are matters of differing backgrounds, cultures, and priorities that make us believe that our church is best when it best reflects us, and it is very hard to value or even tolerate those who are different from us.

Paul faces the problem head-on in this letter to the Ephesians. He knows that gathered in the various house churches will be people from different ethnic, social, and religious backgrounds—people with different personalities and priorities—who must work together in order for the church to fulfill the grand calling of spiritual and cultural transformation that he has envisioned in the opening chapters of this epistle. How will he get such different persons together in work and worship? He first reminds them of basic but essential truths.

In the opening chapters of Ephesians, Paul has shared his grand vision of the divine power available to the church for spiritual and cultural transformation. But now there is an important shift in focus. In the remaining chapters, Paul pours his efforts into describing how the church purchased by Christ's sacrifice must function in order to fulfill its mission.[1] The open-

1. This is Paul's upside-down perspective on the church. Thus far we have been shown the upside (or heavenly) view of the power and privileges of the body of Christ from an eternal perspective; now the apostle discusses the downside (or earthly) operations of the church as believers in local settings live daily in accord with the power and privileges Paul has revealed. The transition to a focus on Christian ethical instruction begins in a common Pauline way (*parakalō oun*, "therefore I urge")—see especially Romans 12:1; 1 Thessalonians 4:1; 1 Timothy 2:1. The call "to live a life worthy of the calling" (literally

ing verses of chapter 4 are a summary of what has preceded and what will follow. In the first verse Paul reminds the Ephesians of his humble position as a prisoner (cf. Eph. 3:1), and of their great calling to be part of Christ's church that will transform the world. The "calling" in Ephesians 4:1 is doubly emphasized in the Greek with a noun and verb combination, which literally reads "the calling with which you were called." The same is true in Ephesians 4:4, where the "calling" is explicitly tied to the Ephesians' unified "hope" (cf. Eph. 1:18). This calling apparently involves all the privileges and responsibilities of the Christian life (especially those connecting the first three chapters with Ephesians 4:4–6).

How will the Ephesians fulfill this great calling? Should they take up arms and assert their power? No, the power for transformation comes from each person being humble and gentle (Eph. 4:2a). These individual qualities are then described in terms of the way that they will affect relationships with others: "be patient, bearing with one another in love. Make every effort to keep the unity of the Spirit in the bond of peace" (Eph. 4:2b–3).[2] From his humble position as a prisoner, Paul says that the diverse believers gathered in the Ephesian church will fulfill their calling as each one humbly, gently, patiently, and lovingly bears with others' differences, and all strive to keep unity and peace. In other words, pulling together is the secret to the church's power. But in order for this unity to come, Paul must underscore truths that were difficult for the Ephesians and remain difficult for us in a church and world of very different people.

We Are All the Same (4:1–6)

In many ways, we are all the same. Realizing the ways in which we are the same enables us to share mutual respect as God intends.

"to *walk* worthy of the calling") likewise draws on Paul's typical ethical vocabulary ("walk"), which is indebted to Old Testament and Semitic expressions (see notes on Eph. 2:10). This mandate to "walk worthy" ties into the theme of the Christian "walk" repeatedly evident in this book (see also Eph. 2:10; 5:2, 8, 15; and contrast 2:2; 4:17).

2. In other letters Paul also appeals for Christian unity, especially in Philippians 2:1–11; 1 Corinthians 1:10–17. The Christian character traits mentioned here are likewise thematic for Pauline ethical discourse (esp. Col. 3:12–13): "humility" (Phil. 2:3; Col. 3:12); "gentleness" (Gal. 5:23; 6:1; Col. 3:12; 2 Tim. 2:25; Titus 3:2); "patience" (1 Cor. 13:4; Gal. 5:22; Col. 1:11; 3:12; 1 Thess. 5:14; 2 Tim. 4:2); and "bear with each other" (Col. 3:13). Jesus constitutes the ultimate model of humility and gentleness for Paul (Phil. 2:5–11; 2 Cor. 10:1).

We Share the Same Identity (4:4)

Just as an individual is made up of body and spirit, the apostle reminds the people that the church, despite its many different members, is one body indwelt by one Spirit (Eph. 4:4; 2:22).[3] And just as our body and spirit, although different, have the same hope of being redeemed by the work of our Savior, so also the church in both its physical and spiritual dimensions is called to the same hope of redemption in Christ (Eph. 4:4). All we are and shall be in body, spirit, and aspiration is the same for those in the church of Jesus Christ.

We Share the Same Testimony (4:5)

United in him, we share the same testimony: one Lord, one faith, one baptism. These are the terms that characterize the testimony of all who are truly Christ's. We testify that Jesus is Lord; we testify that faith in his work on our behalf is our only means of salvation; and, by our baptism, we testify that we are cleansed of sin and united to him by his grace alone.

It is not uncommon to hear these terms spoken in ecumenical settings to minimize the importance of the distinctions of our individual churches or denominations. And, in truth, there is an implicit calling here to recognize the ultimate unity of all those who are truly Christ's. But the proper emphasis is on *affirming* what is true. There *is* one Lord, one faith, one baptism. The call to unity is not a justification for "anything goes" and "nothing really matters," but rather a calling constantly to examine our church, our denomination, and our traditions to make sure that they cohere with and are directed toward the truths of Scripture.

We are called out of our separateness not to do as we please, but to direct our faith and practice toward the truths given to us by the testimony of Scripture. This calling also causes us to honor brothers and sisters of other churches and denominations who unite their thoughts and actions to Scripture. In doing so we must affirm that there are differences that are honorable but not vital; there are believers with whom we differ on matters important but not essential; and even as we are correcting ourselves by Scripture, we

3. Beyond this passage, see further Ephesians 1:23; 2:14–16; 4:25; 5:30. The imagery of the "body of Christ" is also especially emphasized in connection with unity and with spiritual gifts in Romans 12:4–8; 1 Corinthians 12:4–31 (cf. Col. 3:15).

are called to seek ways to come together with those who are with us in their testimony of one Lord, one faith, and one baptism. What we are not permitted to do is unite ourselves with those who have abandoned these truths affirmed in Scripture.

We Share the Same Family (4:6)

When Paul says that there is "one God and Father of all," he reminds us that despite our differences—even those as great as the ethnic and social differences that separated those in the church at Ephesus—we are all of the same family because we share the same Father (Eph. 2:18–19).[4] The God of all is even more clearly the Father of all who have been given the righteousness and identity of God's own Son. This means not only that we have the Father's affection, but also that we are brothers and sisters in Christ and should have family affection one for another. Knowing that we are of one eternal family should reduce all earthly hatred.

On a recent trip to Korea, I was told that during the Cold War, South Koreans were taught to hate North Koreans as devils. Now believers on both sides of the demilitarized zone have led their nations in learning to love one another as brothers. I met a South Korean who risks his life on his annual vacations by going into China with supplies and Scriptures that will be taken to starving North Koreans. The permeable, but dangerous, border between China and North Korea has become a conduit for both physical and spiritual food as this brother serves fellow Christians, some of whom he has never met. Ancient antipathies melt away due to the gospel, as shown by this man who risks his life for those he does not even know in earthly contexts because he knows they are his brothers and sisters by heaven's provision.

4. The Old Testament monotheistic declaration of "one God" (Deut. 6:4) is now continued into the New Testament era (1 Tim. 2:5) with the awareness that God is now rightly called "Father" through the blood of our "one Lord" Jesus (Eph. 4:5; cf. 1 Cor. 8:6). Note here the mention of all three persons of the Trinity in verses 4–6: one Spirit, one Lord (Jesus), and one Father God. Debate sometimes arises over whether the "all" here in the "God and Father of all" means just Christians (who clearly have a special relationship to God the Father indicated by their faith and baptism), or whether it refers to all creation (see similar confessions in Rom. 11:36; 1 Cor. 8:6; Col. 1:16). In the context of Ephesians 3:14–15 God is the Father who, as the creator (Eph. 3:9), names all of creation (and, in that sense, could be the "God and Father of all"). However, the emphasis here—whether derived from God's whole creation fatherhood, or from his being the Father of those whose faith and baptism indicate they are in Christ—clearly is on uniting the church family (Eph. 1:5–6; 2:19; 4:2–3; 5:1).

The example should challenge us. There are all kinds of divisions among God's people: race, social status, national background, personal differences and perspectives. All threaten the unity that Paul knows is necessary for the church to fulfill her grand mission of world transformation. How can we overcome these differences? The Bible encourages us to come together with persons quite different from ourselves by remembering that the God and Father of us all "is over all, and through all, and in all" (Eph. 4:6). We are dealing with brothers and sisters in whom our God dwells by his Spirit. However much we may differ with each other, we are dealing with a child of God in whom Christ dwells. Knowing that we are of one family should cause us to honor and love one another.

When I look at a brother whom I believe is wrong in his perspective, or has wronged me, I must look behind the eyes of one who has hurt me or is angry with me because he believes the offense is mine, and I must see Jesus indwelling. This is a person for whom Christ died and in whom the Son of God lives. My brother in Christ is infinitely valuable to God, and therefore I must honor him with regard from my heart, with the words of my mouth, and with the works of my hands. Each of us for whom Christ died is called to love beyond differences of race, or class, or perspective, or personality. I am called to say to all those in Christ Jesus, "You are my brother. You are my sister. We have the same Father. Come let us love one another beyond our differences, for we have the same identity."

We Are All Different (4:7–14)

Not only does the apostle want those of us in the church to know that we are the same—and that is a good thing; he also requires us to understand that we are all different—and that is a good thing, too. The emphasis on our sameness encourages equal regard for one another despite our differences. The emphasis upon the legitimacy of our differences encourages equal respect for our differences.

How are we different? One way we are different is that we have differing gifts.[5] Christ "gave some to be apostles, some to be prophets, some to

5. Again, there are immediate parallels with Paul's discussion of spiritual gifts in 1 Corinthians 12:4–31 and Romans 12:3–8. In Ephesians Paul refers to the gifts with the term *charis* (often translated

be evangelists, and some to be pastors and teachers" (Eph. 4:11). Almost every one of these terms has some ancient debate regarding its precise definition and place in the contemporary church: Do offices of apostles and prophets continue past the early church? Do the functions of apostles and prophets continue? Is "pastor-teacher" wording referring to one office in the church or two?[6] However, what nobody debates and what is essential for present purposes is the understanding that Paul says we are not all the same.

In this passage Paul clearly establishes that God has gifted the leaders of the church in different ways (Eph. 4:11) and in different proportions (Eph. 4:7)—and that this is all right. Also we should understand that if there are such differences in the church's leaders, then surely there are differences among the church's people as well. These differences are often an irritation to us. It seems as though the world and the church would be so much better if everyone were more alike. What's wrong with wanting most persons to be the same . . . just like us? The apostle deals with this question before he ever begins to describe the differing gifts (Eph. 4:7–10).

"grace") rather than his more typical word *charismata* ("gifts"), but this only heightens the gracious nature of God who gives "gifts" (Rom. 12:6).

6. Grammatically in Greek, a single article governs "pastors and teachers" whereas all the other offices have their own articles; i.e., apostles, prophets, evangelists (note that the article in the NIV translation is represented by the word "some"). This fact unites the roles of pastors and teachers in some way not shared by the other roles; these two roles are not necessarily identical, but clearly overlap.

On another issue, a strong case should be made that apostleship was limited to a first-century office in the church. Although Paul can refer less technically to some people as "sent out" to be representatives of a local church (2 Cor. 8:23; Phil. 2:25), generally "apostles" is a term Paul reserves for either (1) the original disciples of the Lord, who witnessed Jesus in the flesh both before and after his resurrection (1 Cor. 15:7) and who performed Jesus' signs (2 Cor. 12:12); or for (2) himself since he saw the resurrected Jesus and was commissioned by him (1 Cor. 15:7–9; although cf. Acts 14:14 with the inclusion of both Paul and Barnabas). The only possible exception in Paul (Rom. 16:7) is properly understood to mean that Andronicus and Junias are considered outstanding *by* the apostles. The term "apostles" certainly was limited initially to only the twelve who were so appointed by Jesus (Matt. 10:2; Mark 3:14; Luke 6:13; Acts 1:26; cf. Rev. 21:14). Furthermore, only the first generation of such special witnesses were called "apostles" by those in the very next generation of church leadership (Jude 17; 1 Clement 42:1–44:6; *Epistle to Diognetus* 11:1–3; etc.); in other words, the immediate followers of the apostles knew that the role had ceased. Paul considers apostles and prophets to be "foundational" for the church (Eph. 2:20; 3:5), perhaps implying their temporal responsibility to be the first witnesses to Jesus. However, Paul does expect that some form of prophetic ministry will continue in the church, at least during his lifetime (1 Cor. 12:28–29; 14:1–5, 29–37; 1 Thess. 5:19–22). This is not because of his expectation of more apostolic revelation (because that role of the apostles ceased), but because New Testament prophetic utterances varied in authority and type, including what we would think of as "preaching." Not all of these would cease with the passing of the apostolic authority that established enduring Scripture.

How should we regard our differences? Paul says that we should recognize that the differing gifts are *derived from Christ's authority* (Eph. 4:7–10). Our different personalities, abilities, and experiences are gifts that God provides us so that we will bring many different talents and perspectives for building and extending Christ's church. No one has all the gifts needed for every challenge the church will face. The Holy Spirit gives us different gifts for different purposes in the church. The sweet side of this reality is that we have complementary strengths, weaknesses, interests, and personalities. The distasteful side is that these differences cause us to get on each other's nerves. Too often we end up singing our personal versions of the song from *Cinderella*, "Why can't she be more like me?" The simple answer is that God did not make that person like you. Christ apportioned the gifts differently among us (Eph. 4:7), and he has the authority to do so (Eph. 4:8–10).

Speaking of Jesus, Paul says, "When he ascended on high, he led captives in his train and gave gifts to men" (Eph. 4:8).[7] Jesus is the risen and ascended Lord, the victor over sin and death. Paul borrows from the imagery of Psalm 68, which metaphorically describes God ascending Mount Zion with his enemies as captives, to portray Jesus as a conquering king. The apostle portrays captives in Christ's victory parade to indicate that Jesus has defeated our spiritual adversaries, making what captivated us in the bonds of sin his own captives. Sin, death, and Satan are now overcome by the power of our King. In this victory march our King also dispenses the gifts of his victory to his people. Paul makes it clear that he who in victory "ascended higher than all the heavens, in order to fill the whole universe" with his transforming

7. Paul invokes Psalm 68:18 (a psalm about God himself claiming Zion as the place for his abode and leading captives in procession) with a slight change in verbal mood and number (from the Septuagint) and more substantial variance from "*received* gifts" (as in the Masoretic text and Septuagint) to "*gave* gifts" (although the verb "gave" is found in the Psalter of the Syriac Peshitta and in the Targum on the Psalms). It is possible that the Syriac represents the earlier form of the text, or that the Targum indicates a rabbinic interpretation that Paul knew and revised, but it seems more likely that Paul is engaging in a deep exegetical reflection on the meaning of Psalm 68 as found in the Masoretic Text or the Septuagint (an exegesis that we must now infer from scant information). One recent attractive suggestion compares the psalm with Numbers 18:6–7, where the Levites are "taken" by the Lord to be his priests and then "given" back to the people as those dedicated to perform the services necessary to bridge the gap between God and man. This is exegetically possible in the psalm itself (although it requires the "captives" to be Israelites and especially Levites), and it is certainly consistent with the context in Ephesians 4 where church members (especially apostles, prophets, evangelists, and pastors/teachers) are dedicated to God and called to his service as gifts to the church. Also note that Paul's Christology was so high that he could apply here (as elsewhere) a passage about God to the Lord Jesus.

power (v. 10), is the same one who "descended to the lower, earthly regions" (Eph. 4:9).

The ascent of Jesus refers to his ascension as resurrected Lord (who "ascended higher than all the heavens" in Eph. 4:10; cf. Eph. 1:19–21), from which position he dispenses spiritual gifts (Luke 24:49). The more complex issue is what constituted Jesus' descent. The descent apparently occurs before the ascent (this seems to be the logic of Eph. 4:9 and corresponds to the word order of Eph. 4:10). Some have argued that the "descent" substantiates the claim that Jesus "descended into hell," but the simpler explanation is that it refers to Jesus' incarnation. This explanation seems best because: (1) it is similar to other patterns found in Paul's writings where incarnation precedes exaltation (Phil. 2:5–11); (2) it is consistent with the citation of Psalm 68, where God metaphorically ascends Mount Zion along with the captives of the land, requiring him first to descend metaphorically to earth to gather the captives; and (3) the logic of verse 9 likely implies that in order to ascend (to heaven) Christ must first have descended (from heaven) so that he has need of ascending again to his original abode (heaven), and such a reading assumes Christ's descent from heaven (to earth) rather than from earth to a lower underworld.[8] Despite these complex issues, the clear message is that Jesus has dominion over heaven and earth, and thus he has the authority to dispense gifts here as he wishes, to whom he wishes, in the proportion he wishes, and with the expectation that we will respect his authority to dispense his gifts among his people as he knows is best. The implication for us is also clear: to despise others' gifts is to disrespect Christ's authority.

Paul also says that we should recognize the differing gifts are *reflective of Christ's generosity* (Eph. 4:8). We also respect these differences because we have Christ's gifts through his generosity. Christ does not ask us to respect the gifts he grants merely because they reflect his authority, but also because they reflect his generosity. In his death, resurrection, and ascension Christ imprisoned the power of sin over us. Our bondage to Satan, sin, and death is itself made captive to the power of Christ so that it

8. It is also possible to read the noun "of earth" as an epexegetical or an attributive genitive as does the NIV ("lower, earthly regions"), and if the manuscripts that omit the Greek word *merē* ("parts") are followed (although this textual issue is complex), this view of the genitive would be even more probable.

has no hold over us (Eph. 4:8). Rather, we have been captivated by Christ's love and are pictured as trailing in his victory parade as he ascends to heaven.[9] The further implication of the apostle's words (indicating that the gifts we now possess are connected to Christ's victory and the defeat of sin) is that the gifts he dispenses to us are his means of restraining the power of sin now. In this sense our gifts reflect the most essential and precious aspects of our Savior's being. The gifts are not merely material objects or personality traits but rather are Christ's sharing of himself. The gifts given to you and me—we who are the body of Christ—are the extension of Christ's very heart and being to his people. He is offering himself in all the manifold riches of his glory in the various ways that he is gifting his church.

We gain fresh and tender appreciation of the Savior and those about us when we see that the variety of the gifts is an expression of the great generosity of Jesus. In this variety he is sharing more of himself than can be contained in any one of us. Not any one of us has to do all the work of the kingdom because Christ has not given all of his gifts to any one person. You will feel the generosity of this when you realize that the entire work of the church does not depend on you. A leader said to me recently, "When I sit down, I feel guilty." God has been generous to us in taking from us the need to feel that we can or must do everything by ourselves for the church to survive.

Finally, Paul says that we should recognize the differing gifts are *intended for Christ's purposes* (Eph. 4:12–15). The reasons for the Lord's authority and generosity in dispensing his gifts become evident in the purposes of the gifts. Paul says that Christ gives the gifts so that leaders may be able to equip others for the work of ministry (Eph. 4:12a).

Christ does not want us to spend his gifts upon ourselves, nor let them lie dormant; we are to use them to build up the body of Christ (Eph. 4:12b). Our lives are purchased with Christ's blood and are not our own (Rev. 5:9). Already in verse 11 the leaders themselves have been identified as gifts to the church. The leaders receive from the Lord the gift of the capacity to do

9. Other commentators would suggest that the "powers" and "dominions" (Eph. 1:21–22; cf. Col. 2:15) are made captive to Christ, but the clearest reference seems to be to Psalm 68 (also quoted in Eph. 4), which would picture us as Christ's "captives" with whom he ascends to heaven, just as Israel (and her priests) are the captives whom God leads in his train in the psalm (see also n. 7).

their roles, and thus these Spirit-gifted leaders are themselves equipped to embody God's gifts to the church.[10]

Leaders are expected to use their gifts to equip God's people for works of service, and these works of service build up the body.[11] Paul builds this understanding with a key distinction in the three prepositional phrases (v. 12) of this sentence. The sentence literally says Christ gave some to be pastors and teachers "*to* the equipping of the saints *unto* works of service, *unto* the building up of the body of Christ"). The first phrase states the purpose of God's giving the leaders; the second phrase indicates the consequence of the leaders equipping the saints; and the last phrase gives the overall result of the leaders and (other) saints working together in the body. This idea of leaders equipping others so that all are involved in works of service is consistent with Ephesians 4:16. There the focus on leaders combines with the body metaphor in requiring "each part" (not just the leaders) to work for the upbuilding of Christ's church (cf. 4:7). Each gift has triple ownership: ours, the church's, and God's. But the last owner is the most significant and worthy, and so it is most important that we steward these gifts for his purposes.

Those purposes are also spelled out. The first is unity. The body is to be built up for unity in faith and knowledge (Eph. 4:13a) so that we will not be blown about by every wind of doctrine and by deceptive teaching (Eph. 4:14).[12] As the thoughts of verses 13a and 14 are connected, we understand that Christ's intention is that the church be of one mind in the truth it believes.

The second purpose is maturity. The body is also to be built up so that it will "become mature, attaining to the whole measure of the fullness of Christ" (Eph. 4:13b). The "fullness" of Christ is his transforming influence over the world through the church which is his body (Eph. 1:23; 3:19–20). As the thoughts of verses 13b and 15 are connected, we understand that Christ's intention is that the church would express the truth in love so that all are

10. Compare the list in 1 Corinthians 12:28–30 with 1 Corinthians 12:8–10—the former emphasizes persons whereas the latter emphasizes capacities (although at times Paul will even intertwine persons and capacities in the same verse).

11. This interpretation follows the translation in the NIV (contra the KJV).

12. Paul's great passion here was not hypothetical, for in nearly every epistle Paul confronted wrong doctrine and false teachers (e.g., 1 Cor. 15:12–19; Gal. 1:6–9); thus he frequently cautioned Christians about following such teachers (e.g., 2 Cor. 11:13–15; Col. 2:8–23; 2 Thess. 2:8–12; 1 Tim. 1:5–7; 2 Tim. 4:3–4; cf. Phil. 3:2). See notes above for some parallel passages on the unity of the church.

growing up in (i.e., fulfilling) the purposes of him who is the head—not just of the church, but of everything (Eph. 1:22). We are to be united in mind, so that we can be maturing in ministry for the expression of faith that brings all things under the headship of Christ.

In summary, we have different gifts authorized by Christ to be used to build us up in unity of mind regarding his commitment to truth and to build us up in maturity of ministry for world-transforming expression of his truth, so that all will be under the headship of Christ. When we begin to understand how great is the vision that Paul has for Christ's use of the gifts that God has given us, we should be sobered and newly inspired to offer the prayer of Francis de Sales, champion of the ministry of ordinary people: "Lord, give me the grace to be wholly yours." When we pray in this way, we are asking that we would make a gift to him of the gifts he has given to us, and recognize that he has dispensed these various gifts to ordinary people with authority and generosity for the purposes of kingdom building that he alone knows, but that are more vast than we can imagine.

What attitudes are needed regarding these differences? Certain attitudes are implicit in the words of the apostle that we must take as lessons if we are to honor the Lord who gave the gifts and see them used in the church as he intends.

Paul urges us *not to despise others' gifts* (cf. 1 Cor. 12:21–26). A good deal of life's contentment comes from the realization of each soul that God did not intend everyone to be just like me. The world is richer and better because of the variety of persons, and the church is stronger because of the variety of persons Christ has gifted by his authority, out of his generosity, and for his purposes. Some time ago, I listened to some sermon tapes of one of the great preachers of the middle of the last century. His voice was raspy, his manner was harsh, his exegesis was simplistic if not flawed, and yet God greatly used him.

I have discovered over and over that God calls persons of a particular personality, or endurance, or vision just at the time he needs them. Some of those God uses are difficult persons that he needed to move the church past a particular challenge or make it face a sin or failing that courteous people will not address. The best evangelists I know are not very tactful. They have a boldness that I find hard to take, but God uses them. Professors are often introverted, preachers are rarely good administrators, and church planters are often too entrepreneurial to be satisfied with maintenance ministries. But if we were all alike, there is little doubt that the church would flounder.

I am told that once there were dozens of banana species in the world, but in our efforts to make everything the same for our taste, there are now only three dominant species. A good blight could wipe out bananas worldwide because there is so little variety among them. Jesus does not so risk his church; when he ascended, he took captivity captive and gave gifts to men. He made some more sympathetic than others, some more enduring than others, some more adventurous than others. Some are better ramrods for organizing the efforts of many; some are better counselors for the concerns of individuals, some better businessmen, some better administrators, some better youth workers, some better scholars, some better in public and some better in private ministries. All are vital for the building up of the church for the fullness of the purposes of Christ, and none should despise the gifts that Christ proportions by his authority, out of his generosity, and for his transforming purposes.

You will never be at peace in the church until you recognize that God has brought different kinds of people (with different gifts and levels of maturity) into the church not only to sanctify you, but to build up his church in the ways that he knows are best. Some of the hard-driving people with whom I have most struggled in times of the church's peace have been those I have most needed in times of challenge. Some of those I most wanted to "get moving" in times of growth have been those I most needed for counsel in times of distress. Those God puts in his church he intends to be our gifts—his gifts to us—and we must love them accordingly even if they are quite different from us.

Paul also urges us *not to despise our own gifts.* Not only must we respect God's authority by not despising others' gifts, we must diligently avoid the trap of disregarding or disdaining the value of our own gifts (1 Cor. 12:14–20). We may never fulfill the purposes that God has for our lives if we constantly want to be something God has not designed us to be. I am told that once Billy Graham was asked to speak at a college and he gave a history lecture. It was not appreciated. Friends told him later, "God gifted you to be an evangelist. Never again despise the gift that is yours."

It follows that if we are not to despise our gifts, we also are not to neglect our gifts. We disregard God's authority and generosity when we neglect the gifts he has given us. You know the phrase "What you do not use, you lose." It is often true. People who do not steward their gifts lose the opportunity to do and be what God has best equipped them to do and be for the church.

Why do Christians fail to make good use of the gifts Christ has given them?

1. Some Christians do not understand that we are obligated to use the gifts that God gives for the building of his church (Rom. 12:4–8). Western mindsets of self-fulfillment may cause us not even to consider our obligation to steward what God has given us for the purposes of the One who purchased us with his own blood and gives us to fellow believers in the church. Failure to steward Christ's gifts is simply sinful neglect of our calling.

2. Sometimes we do not want the obligation of our gifts. They may be in an area that requires sacrifice or does not bring worldly acclaim.

3. Neglect of our gifts can also be a result of our wanting others' gifts. Instead of living for the Lord's approval and purposes, we want the regard of other people in our particular setting. We may be gifted in business, but are envious of preachers because their life seems simpler, and the church offers them greater respect. We may be gifted in being a pastor, but want to be a professor, which seems to be a simpler life. We may be gifted in relationships but want to excel in academics because we would prefer to be known as smart rather than caring. We may be gifted in prayer but give it no time because the rewards are private and not public. There is nothing wrong with wanting to excel, but there is everything wrong with not approving the way that God made you and driving yourself to excel in ways he has not gifted you. Happiest are those who discover Christ's gift and give themselves to excel in what God has made them to do—whether that is preaching or teaching or evangelizing or writing or making music or making money or giving counsel or showing hospitality or creating art—according to the gift that the Lord God has given.

In light of God's gifting us for his purposes, we must ask ourselves these important questions: "Am I doing what God has made me to do or am I neglecting my gift? Am I delighting to be what God has made me to be, or am I despising my gifts?" The Christians that I know who have made the greatest shipwreck of their lives (for reasons other than blatant sin) are those who have not been satisfied with fulfilling the calling of their specific gifts. They always wanted to be someone else. If you despise what God has made you to be, you will never find the satisfaction that he intends for you. Love what God has made you to be and believe that he is using you even in difficult places. Such confidence that he is giving himself to the church through you will be the source of the deepest satisfaction of your life.

Finally, Paul urges us *not to neglect others' gifts.* I can still remember the anger of the woman who was very upset because I did not attend her committee's planning meeting in the church. "You do not believe that what we are doing is important," she said. Actually, I believed that what she was doing was very important, but I could not attend every meeting of every organization in the church. I tried for a while, but ultimately I realized that if I had to be present in every ministry, then the ministry of the church was limited by my ability to be present at all events and control their proceedings. This is not mature leadership. Mature leadership seeks to equip others to use their gifts for the work of ministry and to build up the body (Eph. 4:12). The work of ministry is not dependent on any one of us, even those who are leaders. Our task is to equip others for their ministry of service and building up of the church. Here is the message: if you try to do it all, you will die and the ministry will, too. There is simply too much to be done: Bible studies, youth groups, diaconal ministries, educational ministries, mercy ministries, campus ministries, singles ministries, outreach to the workplace and on the campus, Right to Life, political advocacy, art ministries, public school board meetings, Christian school meetings, home school meetings—the list is endless.

We who are leaders have the important job of making ourselves nonessential for the doing of all the church's ministries because we are to be so equipping others that their efforts will not be dependent on us. Our essential task is to equip others for the ministry of the church. This is an important educational concept for the church that often will expect the minister or paid staff or session to do everything (and we can feed that expectation by trying to do everything). Yet if we make ourselves essential to every project and activity, then the church can never do more than the leadership can stretch itself to do. Christ's goal is that the church leaders would prepare others for ministry by equipping every person to do his or her part.

Mr. Holland's Opus is a movie about a dedicated music teacher who dreams of becoming a famous composer. He does not have those gifts and, instead, makes an impact he does not fully appreciate in the lives of a generation of students in his high school music program. Mr. Holland never writes the musical opus that will make him famous but pours himself into the young people before him: a redheaded girl with pigtails who struggles to play the clarinet, a football player who cannot keep rhythm but needs a band credit to keep his game eligibility, a street kid who is mad at the world but who discovers the beauty of his own soul in music.

As the movie concludes, Mr. Holland is fighting budget cuts for the survival of the high school's music program. He loses. And he retires. The last day of school he cleans out his desk and, with shoulders slumped down, walks the school hall for the last time. He is a picture of dejection, reminding us of a life spent without a dream fulfilled. But as Mr. Holland walks, he hears noise in the auditorium. He goes in to see what is happening and faces a packed auditorium of students and alumni thundering an ovation and chanting his name. The little girl with pigtails is now the governor of the state, and she addresses Mr. Holland from the podium. "Mr. Holland, we know that you never became the famous composer you dreamed of being. But don't you see it today? Your great composition is what you did with us, your students. Mr. Holland, look around you. We are your great opus. We are the music of your life."

Each of us is the music—the great opus—of those who have used their gifts to equip us. And I pray that we will know the joy and fulfillment that comes from knowing that we have used our gifts for the equipping of others for their works of service in the kingdom of God. We may not become famous before men, but we fulfill the purposes of heaven when we use what God has given us for the purposes he has designed for us in equipping others for the work of ministry and the building up of the church. A couple whose marriage is healed, a young man in a distant nation brought to faith, a grieving mother next to an empty cradle brought comfort, a preacher boldly proclaiming the word—all these are the works of service that we are equipping others to fulfill as we minister with the gifts that Christ has given. Together we are the transforming power of the church, Christ's great opus.

We Are All Dependent (4:15–16)

For this opus to echo the majesty of Christ's music, every believer must do his or her part. While we are the same in some ways and different in other ways, in order to fulfill Christ's purposes we also must remember that we are all dependent.

We Are Dependent on Christ (4:15–16a)

Although each believer is differently gifted, we must all depend upon the Savior, seeking our strength in him and seeking our purpose in him. The last two verses in this passage describe a spiritual flow that we cannot miss. First, we are told that as we use our gifts to speak the truth in love, we will "grow up into him who is the Head, that is, Christ" (Eph. 4:15). The image that comes to mind is of stem, leaves, and branches, each exercising its function so that it grows up into a beautiful flower. In this verse, the flower is the glory of Christ that he intends for us to produce as we exercise our gifts and equip others to do the same. But in the next verse the flow reverses. We are told that "from him the whole body, joined and held together by every supporting ligament, grows and builds itself up in love" (Eph. 4:16a; cf. Col. 2:19). The image is of the human body with all of its parts coordinated and enabled by the head. More than an ancient anatomy lesson, this image is a timely warning of the human reflex that we must always guard against. That reflex is to try to do God's work in our own strength—to exercise God's gifts without dependence upon the Savior.

It is easy to work so hard to provide for our families that we neglect to pray, to become so concerned to do well in exams that we forsake biblical integrity, to become so busy in making sure our children perform well that we slight the spouse God sent to support us, and to become so accustomed to depending on our gifts that we do not stop to depend upon the One who gives them. I know what it is to hit the ground running at the beginning of a day and to think about a thousand things before I think of the Savior, to attack a crisis with my wisdom before I seek the Lord's. Over and over I have to be reminded that apart from Christ I can do nothing (John 15:5).

One of the most important events in my life occurred when I went to visit Frank Barker, the senior pastor of a very large church, to ask his advice about a leadership issue. During our lunch in a crowded restaurant I asked him my question. He started to answer and then stopped himself. "You know," he said, "this is an important issue. Before we talk about it, we need to pray about it." And right there in the restaurant, in a way that broke into our routine and turned attention away from himself, this pastor with great gifts prayed for God's help before answering my question. I try to remember his words often: "Before we talk about it, we need to pray about it."

This passage that begins by describing different kinds of leaders in the church and leads us to reflect on the nature of differing gifts for everyone in the church should not be read simply as a manual for tolerating differences and appreciating gifts. This passage should also be read as a list of warnings against the ego sins of leaders that are common in Christ's church—leaders who, because of their gifts, may forget that Christ is the Lord of all.

- The first such sin is believing or acting as though we do not have to accept different kinds of persons in our church. For this reason we are reminded of the unity Christ requires and the fact that we are all one in him (Eph. 4:2–6).
- The second sin is believing or acting as though everyone has to be like us. For this reason we are reminded that our Lord has gifted us differently (Eph. 4:7–11).
- The third sin is believing or acting as though we by ourselves are adequate to do what needs to be done. For this reason leaders are reminded that our task is to equip others for the work of ministry that we cannot complete on our own (Eph. 4:12–15).
- The fourth sin is believing or acting as though we can do what Christ needs done without Christ. So we are reminded of our dependence on him (Eph. 4:16a).
- One more sin remains: the belief that other people have the gifts that Christ needs for his church, so there is nothing for us personally to do. For this reason, Paul reminds us that not only are we dependent on the work of Christ; we have an additional dependency on others.

We Are Dependent on Each Other (4:16b)

Paul says that "the whole body [is] joined and held together by every supporting ligament . . . as each part does its work" (Eph. 4:16b). We have a deep obligation to one another—everyone must do his or her part. Each has a calling to make the body work. This runs against the grain of Western culture with its emphasis on personal autonomy, and even against much of evangelicalism with its emphasis on a personal relationship with Christ. As important as is a personal relationship with Jesus, biblical Christianity never teaches that faith is just about Jesus and me. We are part of the body of Christ. We are his presence now on earth as his Spirit lives within us and among us (Eph. 2:22). I am the expression of Christ's love to others, and they to me.

It is very important to note that the phrase "in love" in verse 16 hearkens back to the key mention of "in love" at the opening of this section (Eph. 4:2; also repeated in Eph. 4:15). Paul draws on the theme of Christian love throughout the epistle (Eph. 1:15; 3:17; 5:2) because he recognizes that love, as a central characteristic of God and of Christ (Eph. 1:4; 2:4; 3:19; 6:23), is therefore essential for those united to Christ (Eph. 5:2). The church community functions because we are all called to be love contributors, not just love consumers. Every spiritual community to which Christ will ever call us does not exist merely to serve us but to be served by us out of mutual love. We need each other's love. We are here together because Christ has made us one, so that our gifts will lovingly complement each other, and together we can grow to maturity in Christ both in what we understand and in what we do.

Christ makes us one and obligates us to work together so that we can use our different gifts to build his church. In this task, all gifts are needed and everyone must do his or her part. We must never rule ourselves out of the process of building the church that is Christ's transforming power for this earth and for the eternity of multitudes that he is drawing to himself. We grow and mature as each one does his or her part.

Gene Mintz was my third grade Sunday school teacher in a large church in Tennessee. Not many men volunteered to be third grade Sunday school teachers when I was growing up. And I confess that I remember very little of Mr. Mintz's classroom teaching. What I remember is that when my parents were struggling in their marriage, making our lives awkward in the church, Mr. Mintz always greeted me—a little third grader from a troubled family—in the church hallways. Even when I went on to fourth grade, and fifth, and sixth, Mr. Mintz never forgot me. And when my family moved away when I was in seventh grade, Mr. Mintz sometimes still would write and ask how I was doing. I even got a letter or two when I was in college. And when I became president of Covenant Seminary, I got a letter from Gene Mintz that I will always cherish. "Bryan," he wrote, "I have prayed for you all of these years."

I believe that I am a living testimony of the truth of Paul's words: "From him [Christ] the whole body, joined and held together by every supporting ligament, grows and builds itself up in love, as each part does its work." Because Gene Mintz did his part faithfully, I have been able to serve God and teach others to do the same. I believe that. I hope that others will, so that we will make every effort to keep the unity of Spirit in the bond of peace, and will use whatever gifts God has given us to further equip his people for the work of ministry.

14

The Life of Lizards and Stallions

Ephesians 4:17–24

So I tell you this, and insist on it in the Lord, that you must no longer live as the Gentiles do. . . . You were taught, with regard to your former way of life, to put off your old self, which is being corrupted by its deceitful desires; to be made new in the attitude of your minds; and to put on the new self, created to be like God in true righteousness and holiness. (Eph. 4:17, 22–24)

In his book *The Great Divorce*, C. S. Lewis tells the story of a character who is tormented by a red lizard that lives on his shoulder. The lizard, which represents the indwelling sin we all face, constantly mocks the young man. Then an angel comes and offers to remove the lizard. The young man is initially thrilled and thinks, "I can be rid of this thing that so torments me." But then the young man recognizes that the angel glows with a deadly heat, and the way that he will remove the lizard is by killing it. The young man suggests that maybe it really isn't necessary for the lizard to die, and perhaps another time is better for dealing with him. The angel will not be put off. "This moment contains all moments," he says.

The lizard, then recognizing the danger he is in, also begins to strive for his life from a new angle. He tries to unsettle the young man with doubts and suggestions that any of us who know the subtle seductions of our own sin will recognize. "Be careful," the lizard says. Then he continues,

> He [the angel] can do what he says. He can kill me. One fatal word from you and he will! Then you'll be without me for ever and ever. It's not natural. How could you live? You'll only be a sort of a ghost, not a real man as you are now. He doesn't understand. He's only a cold, bloodless, abstract thing. It may be natural for him, but it isn't for us. I know there are no real pleasures now, only dreams. But aren't they better than nothing? And I'll be so good. I admit I've sometimes gone too far in the past, but I promise I won't do it again. I'll give you nothing but really nice dreams—all sweet and fresh and almost innocent.[1]

"Almost innocent. . . ." With such assessment we often justify our sin and compromise ourselves. We reason, "It can't really hurt. And even if it is wrong, to be without such flaws is practically not to be human. Who could live that way? Only the warped and the legalistic would deny themselves such things. I have a better understanding of grace than that. God will forgive me, and I won't let it go too far again." With such words we choose to let our lizards live. We convince ourselves that the remnants of sin in our lives are not really dangerous, and that almost innocent is safe enough. Paul says instead that nurturing such lizards can only prove fatal to the joys of the Christian life.

Having told us in preceding verses of the world-transforming and heaven-glorifying mission of the body of Christ, in which members with very different backgrounds and gifts are accepted as each does his or her part, the apostle now begins to discuss how each person will function. This section of his letter is a study in contrasts of what we are to put off and what to put on in order to do our part for the church to fulfill her purposes. The contrasts will be readily seen in the portions of the letter that we will cover in the future: we are to replace falsehood with truth, sinful anger with righteous anger, stealing with sharing, corrupt speech with edifying words. But before he describes all

1. C. S. Lewis, *The Great Divorce* (New York: Macmillan, 1946), 99–101.

of these contrasts, Paul tells us why we must know them—the difference is really that of life and death. He warns us here that those who live according to the world's ways are the walking dead—they will move about the earth without the joy and power that is true life.

The seriousness of the apostle's warning is apparent at the outset of this passage. He says that the Ephesian Christians "must no longer live as the Gentiles do" (Eph. 4:17). The Greek wording actually indicates that the believers must "walk" differently, indicating that Christians must be on a different path than the rest of the world if we are to be faithful to God.[2] If we simply walk down the same paths as everyone else, then there is something amiss in our Christian lives. The gifts of grace do not annul the calling to a separated life. To make this clear the apostle not only "tells" the Ephesians to live differently (Eph. 4:17a), he "insists" on it (Eph. 4:17b). The "insist" word is from the Greek word *martyreō* (from which we get our English word martyr). The use of the term reminds us of the importance of our testimony. Paul may well lose the regard and respect of others when he testifies of the need for revering God in all the areas that he is about to consider. But instead of shying away from the command, he adds even greater weight to it by saying that his insistence is "in the Lord." The command to walk a different path is not merely Paul's suggestion or opinion; it comes with God's authority as the apostle speaks from the context of his apostolic union with his Lord.

The reason for the seriousness and weight of this command is then stated. Paul looks down the path that the Gentiles are walking and says that it leads to empty lives. They walk (live) in "the futility of their thinking" (Eph. 4:17d). They walk down a path that they think will bring fulfillment, but it is a dead end. Out of love for the believers, this spokesman for God marks a better path for us. Lest we ignore it or minimize its importance, he begins to compare and contrast what will characterize life when we walk down either path.

Paul first considers the path of pagans, those "Gentiles" (people without covenant promises) who live without Christ and thus without hope in the world.[3] Paul has already depicted the spiritual despair of the Ephesians' former Gentile manner of life (Eph. 2:1–2, 11–12). Elsewhere Paul decries

2. The verb "walk" is an important ethical term in Ephesians (see Eph. 2:2, 10; 4:1, 17; 5:2, 8, 15). See the notes on Ephesians 4:1.

3. This is consistent with Old Testament and later Jewish approaches to Gentile morality (e.g., Lev. 18). Also see 1 Peter 1:14, 18.

Gentile conduct with its futile thinking and foolish darkened hearts (Rom. 1:21 and context; cf. Col. 3:5–9). However, since we are removed from the life of the ancient world with its striking contrasts between covenant and noncovenantal peoples, the "Gentile" term may lose some of the bite, horror, and sadness that the apostle intended. So, using the words of C. S. Lewis, it may help us to understand that what Paul is describing is the life of lizards. It sounds odd, I know. But the bloodless, cold, and insensitive nature that such an image calls to mind is appropriate for what the apostle makes clear about the life of spiritual lizards.

To Walk with Lizards (4:17–19)

Paul says of those who are following futile thinking, "They are darkened in their understanding and separated from the life of God because of the ignorance that is in them due to the hardening of their hearts" (Eph. 4:18).

Darkened Minds (4:18)

The terminology of living with a darkened mind will be contrasted to words about learning the truth that is in Jesus (Eph. 4:21). The darkened understanding relates to spiritual ignorance, and the consequence is separation from the life of God. The words hearken back to Paul's earlier statement that those separate from Christ were also aliens to the covenant, without hope and without God in the world (see Eph. 2:12; cf. Col. 1:21).

One time my daughter and I caught some little gecko lizards at a place we stayed on vacation. These little lizards are able to walk about, observe our movement, breathe, eat, and reproduce, but they have no sense of the world beyond the screen porch in which they live. When I catch one and he latches onto my finger, he has no understanding beyond blind instinct. Even when I offer him freedom, he does not let go. His understanding cannot extend beyond the borders of his experience and the urges of his biology. Thus he is alive but without any sense of what is eternal, what is truly beautiful, or what gives life meaning or hope. We expect this to be true of lizards, but it is this lizard life that the apostle says characterizes people who live with their understanding darkened to God.

The language of the apostle is meant to startle and arrest, perhaps even to offend. But the offense is not merely because the apostle contends that the Gentiles are the living dead. Yes, they walk about and breathe but without understanding life with God, and thus they live in a world of challenge and tragedy without the hope of God. This we readily accept. But what is more startling is the realization that this characterization is in the midst of a command—not to the Gentiles—but to the Ephesian Christians. There is the implication that living without hope must be avoided even by Christians. If it is even a possibility that one can live this way, we want to know what leads to such a darkened mind, and the apostle tells us.

Hardened Hearts (4:18)

A darkened understanding and the spiritual ignorance that deprive life of hope are the results of something at the core of the life of spiritual lizards. What is it? Hardened hearts. The first sign and actual source of lizard life is a hardened heart.

Paul does not speak of merely a "hard" heart, but a "hardened" heart.[4] The word in Greek implies a certain stubbornness and reflects the consequences of opportunities being resisted. Repeatedly making wrong choices causes the heart to become callous, making it ever more insensitive to God's will and ways. This sclerosis of the heart is the result of deliberate choices repeatedly made against the life ordained by God, and it is possible for such disease to enter the Christian life.

Recently I sat with a pastor who understood intellectually, but still had trouble accepting in reality, the path that one of his elders had taken—an elder who until recently was considering a career in ministry. That elder left his wife in order to take up a relationship with a younger woman. At a lunch where the pastor sat across the table from the man and cautioned him not to presume upon grace if he was choosing to live in rebellion, the man showed no softening of heart. Instead, with unblinking eyes—a lizard look—he said to the pastor, "I have never felt more alive."

4. This Greek expression (in both nominal and verbal cognates) is also used for "hardened hearts" in Mark 3:5; 6:52; 8:17; John 12:40. Paul employs more broadly the negative concept of hardening in Romans 11:7, 25; 2 Corinthians 3:14. Various Greek words are used in the Septuagint for the same concept when people's hearts are hardened against the Lord (e.g., Deut. 15:7; 1 Sam. 6:6; 2 Chron. 36:13; Ps. 95:8 [Septuagint 94:8]; Prov. 28:14; Isa. 63:17; Dan. 5:20) with Pharaoh being the most prominent Old Testament example of a man possessed by a hardened heart (e.g., Ex. 4:21; and eighteen other times in Exodus).

There is a sense in which he spoke the truth. Certainly his urges and instincts were at high throttle. But how could his natural body be so alive and, at the same time, his spiritual understanding be so dark? The answer is that the numerous choices he had already made had hardened his heart. A popular novel aptly reminds us that "when the time of choosing comes, all the choices have already been made." "Almost innocent" choices have been allowed to rub against the heart so often that they have calloused it and then, almost as a natural biological consequence of a hardened heart, the mind grows dark. With a hardened heart no longer pumping life-giving blood, the mind itself grows dull and dark to the things of God. And there are consequences of a hardened heart and numbed mind that also are indicative of a lizard life.

Calloused and Insatiable Senses (4:19)

Hardened hearts lead to a deadening of the senses, that is, to a loss of "all sensitivity" (Eph. 4:19a).[5] Our humanity cannot survive, however, without the sensations that not only prove that we are alive but make our living meaningful. And when the path we are on is not God's path, the need for sensation turns to "sensuality" and seeks fulfillment in the "impurity" of sexual expression. But what happens when even the excesses and abuses of sensation do not satisfy because they increasingly harden the heart and further numb understanding? There comes a "continual lust" for more and more and more, which spirals into further hardening, creates greater insensitivity, and thus spurs lust for more that will only harden the heart more.[6] Paul explains the

5. The verb (*apalgeō*) occurs only here in the New Testament and Septuagint. Its literal reference is to "become calloused or dead to feeling." Various nuances have been associated with its metaphorical use here, from being "despondent" (W. Bauer, W. F. Arndt, F. W. Gingrich, and F. W. Danker, *A Greek-English Lexicon of the New Testament* [Chicago: University of Chicago Press, 2000], s.v.) to a loss of capacity for shame or embarrassment (*Greek-English Lexicon of the New Testament*, ed. Johannes P. Loew and Eugene A. Nida [New York: United Bible Societies, 1989]). Likely the increasing dullness to spiritual condition (cf. Rom. 1:18–32) leads to a callousness in one's self (note the reflexive pronoun in the Greek) and an abandonment of self into pleasure seeking. Here this "sensuality" (Greek *aselgeia*) indicates debauchery (see also Rom. 13:13; 2 Cor. 12:21; Gal. 5:19), where such pleasure seeking has thrown off all restraint. This term often indicates sexual sin, as can the notion of "impurity," but the Greek phrase for "in every kind of impurity" (literally "in every impure work") with its emphasis on "*every* work" likely moves beyond exclusively sexual connotations.

6. The Greek word (*pleonexia*), here translated as a "continual lust for more," is consistently found in the New Testament (and Septuagint) with negative connotations to indicate a strong desire for personal gain. Paul exhorts against such covetousness again in Ephesians 5:3 (cf. Rom. 1:29; Col. 3:5;

lizard life this way: "They have given themselves over to sensuality so as to indulge in every kind of impurity, with a continual lust for more."

Perhaps this could be explained in psychological terms as the hedonist dilemma: pleasures fully indulged cease to please. But Paul is not speaking in terms of psychology, but rather in terms of the pathology of spiritual disease. Some of us have sat with dying loved ones who urge us to squeeze their hands. They long for the sensation of human touch as this world's experience is ending. Then, when the heart begins to fail and the sensations that can reach the brain dull, the desire for human touch becomes all the more intense and the need more pressing. I sat with the family of a man who was dying because of a tear in his failing heart. "Hold my hand," he said, "harder, harder." And, then, when he could no longer feel that hold, he said, "Hold me." His family lifted him to hold him, not realizing that the embrace would complete the tear in his heart, and he passed away only moments later. Such a sad image actually is the kind of picture the apostle wants in our mind. Sensuality outside the path of God promises to satisfy, but it only destroys the heart, darkens the mind, and deadens the senses.

Intellectually and theologically we know the truth of these words, but the apostle speaks graphically, and gives his commands strongly, to make us face the realities of our experience when we harden our hearts to the truth of these words. Remember it is to believers that the apostle gives these warnings. Why do Christians need these kinds of warnings? The answer comes when we consider why temptations such as the sinful allures of the Internet are so great. Whether the temptation is of gambling, pornography, or time waste, these, too, can seem "almost innocent." "Nobody gets hurt," "nobody need know" (employer or spouse), and "we can stop at any time," we think. But what happens follows the biblical pathology of sin. The sin in which we indulge for a while hardens our hearts, darkens our minds to the evil of what we are doing, and ultimately makes us less sensitive to and less fulfilled by the profound satisfaction God provides by his blessings in our lives.

The same kind of heart hardening occurs in those who think that profit or prestige or power will fulfill. Such persons discover that simply getting what

---

also 1 Cor. 5:11; 6:10; Eph. 5:5; and see Paul's own example of rejecting greed in 1 Thess. 2:5). Although the wording is different, such "lust for more" is clearly condemned in the last of the Ten Commandments (Ex. 20:17), where such covetousness can be sexual ("your neighbor's wife") or financial ("your neighbor's house . . .") or a desire more broadly for anything that is not properly ours.

you want does not satisfy. Always there will be the need for more—more pleasure, more security, more prestige. When we want the embrace of the world to satisfy, we inevitably discover that we need it to squeeze us tighter and tighter until it drives tenderness and feeling out of our hearts.

Sometimes God graciously allows the disappointments of the world to show us its hardening effects, and to free us from its grasp. For example, I have been surprised to find that losses in the stock market have made me more generous. When I have already lost ten thousand dollars in my retirement plan, my son's request for twenty dollars and my wife's desire for some things to make our house more pleasant are less of a challenge to my miserly spirit. I do not fully realize how much I am driven by money or name or power until it is denied me. And then, though I usually hate the fight to free myself from its clutches, in a way that still surprises me I find it amazingly freeing and fulfilling to live without it—like smelling spring after the confining cold of winter.

Denying oneself the indulgence of sin, "mortifying our flesh," as the Puritans used to say, in a strange way is actually freeing. C. S. Lewis describes this phenomenon as he continues the account of the lizard in *The Great Divorce*. The angel does indeed attack the lizard. As truth aflame, he seizes the lizard with fiery hands and with great power chokes the life from it. The lizard falls to the ground, but surprisingly does not die. It changes. The ugly red lizard becomes a beautiful stallion. The beast that has ridden on the shoulder of the young man to mock him is now mounted and ridden by the young man. He who was the master is now mastered. He who was in bondage is now free. What was once ugly is now beautiful even though it is the same creature, transformed.[7] Knowing the freedom and beauty of this horse is the life Paul now describes for us. What would the life under the constraints of godliness look like? We need to know not only so that we can experience freedom from the pathologies of sin, but also so that we can do our part for the kingdom of heaven.

To Ride Horses (4:20–24)

The life of horses, as C. S. Lewis described the Christian life, is really the experience of the power of heaven. How do we experience this power, or, to

7. Lewis, *The Great Divorce*, 101–5.

use the thoughts of the prophet (Jer. 12:5), how do we "run with horses" for the glory and pleasure of our God?

Listening Differently (4:20–21)

In contrast to the darkened understanding that leads to an endless appetite to satiate the senses, Paul says, "You, however, did not come to know Christ that way" (Eph. 4:20). The word for "come to know" (Greek *manthanō*) here does not refer only to head knowledge—raw understanding—but also to relational knowledge.[8] This is an unusual expression. Paul is speaking of the Ephesians' early encounter with the gospel as a relational encounter with Christ himself (cf. Col. 2:6 where Christians "receive" Jesus and thus in accepting his message also accept relationship with him). In a similar way Paul does not merely preach about Christ, but proclaims Christ himself (e.g., 1 Cor. 1:23; 2 Cor. 1:19; Gal. 1:16; Phil. 1:15). These Gentiles have been striving after relationships that they think will satisfy, only to discover the emptiness of what they pursue. The emptiness compulsively drives them to seek to fill relationships with money, sex, power, or comforts that hopefully will satisfy—but never do. Paul offers a very different relationship, saying that is not how you come to know Christ.

"Surely you heard of him [i.e., Jesus]," says Paul.[9] Our understanding of the power of this phrase increases when we see that Paul's original wording does not have the "of" preposition (the "him" is accusative, not genitive). "Surely you heard him," says Paul literally. There is an immediacy of expression in Paul's words, as though there is no intermediary in the truth about Jesus, but, rather, he communicates himself. This Jesus that we worship is not merely a historical figure or a religious concept. He is real and living, and by his truth his Spirit testifies of his reality in our lives. Not as a history lesson but as the truth of a living personality, we can have a relationship with the One who created all things and loves us eternally.

Not only have you "heard him," says the apostle, "you . . . were taught in him in accordance with the truth that is in Jesus" (Eph. 4:21b). Here again is

8. A related use of *manthanō* portrays the Colossians as "learning" the grace of Christ (Col. 1:6–7).

9. The NIV translation "surely" corresponds to a conditional ("if") clause in Greek. Thus the NASB: "If indeed you have heard Him." The context implies a confident response to this conditional, thus permitting the NIV translation (cf. 3:2; note that these readers are called "saints" in Eph. 1:1).

the concept of our receiving truth with the authority of Christ in contrast to the darkened understanding of the Gentiles. But there is more than authority being communicated by the reminder of "the truth that is in Jesus."[10] The word heard from Christ carries us to teachings that are "in him." Jesus is in the truth of the gospel and the truth is in him. To know his truth is to know him. It is as though the truth that we hear from him envelops us and carries us into relationship with him.

At some point, many of us have been carried away by what we hear. A symphony by Mahler or a pop song from our youth can capture us and transport us to another time and place where we first experienced life associated with that music. As the truth from Jesus envelops us, it is meant to take us from lizard life to another plane of existence by uniting us to Christ. But being enveloped in a relationship of truth is not without challenges. Other aspects of the world keep intruding. Today you can purchase special headphones that both amplify the sound and exclude the other noises to protect the musical experience. Paul wants similar protection for the Christian life. Thus he reminds us that those who are experiencing the truth of Jesus must always be excluding static and amplifying the music of their Savior to know the full enjoyment of living in a relationship with him.

Live Differently (4:22–24)

Not only must we listen differently to ride with the horses of heaven, we must live differently. Paul says, "You were taught, with regard to your former way of life, to put off your old self, which is being corrupted by its deceitful desires" (Eph. 4:22).[11]

To live differently means we must *put off the old self* (Eph. 4:22). We ordinarily think of this verse in terms of the human wardrobe. There are those old habits of our former, pre-Christian years that must be shed, as a lizard

10. On the Greek syntax of the anarthrous abstract noun "truth" (cf. Rom. 9:1; Eph. 4:25) see Andrew T. Lincoln, *Ephesians*, Word Biblical Commentary 32 (Dallas: Word, 1990), 280–83. Truth is an important concept in Ephesians—the gospel is the "word of truth" (Eph. 1:13), and thus truth is to characterize the speech and disposition of the believer (Eph. 4:25; 5:9; 6:14).

11. The NIV translation accurately brings out the three parallel infinitives in verses 22–24 ("to put off . . . to be made new . . . and to put on"—which are connected to one another by conjunctions in Greek). Although these infinitives could denote purpose or result, or even act as imperatives, it is most likely that they provide the contents of what the believers were "taught" (v. 21; the NIV repeats the verb "taught" in verse 22 in order to make the connection clear in English).

sheds its skin. Indeed, the language of putting off and putting on does relate to a clothing image. But we need to be very clear on what is being shed *and* when. Paul says, "You were taught . . . to put off your old self."[12] Paul here refers back to the time that the message of the gospel came to the Ephesians. At that time they were taught to put off an old way of life and to put on the new life in Christ. This does not mean that they are held captive by their old self, or that the old self is still alive. Paul is not telling the Ephesians to keep putting to death the old man that is already dead. Yes, old habits and sinful patterns are in view, but the apostle knows that these are not now inevitable. The Ephesians were taught to put off the old man by faith in Christ. Though the human heart will still be adjusting to the new reality of life in Christ by shedding the influences of the old self, the Ephesians already have the identity and power of new creatures in Christ (see 2 Cor. 5:17; Col. 3:9–10).

This side of heaven the new self is always growing into the full reality of what it means to be "created to be like God in true righteousness and holiness" (Eph. 4:24b), even as the old self "is corrupted by its deceitful desires" (Eph. 4:22c).[13] We are learning to be what we are, and we have to be something that we were not. The Puritans called this process of shedding the influences of the old life that is dead "mortification." This process is never easy because the habits and patterns of the old self were not something purely extraneous to us, but were integral to our old way of living and thinking. That is why the red lizard of C. S. Lewis gets such a hearing from the man on whose shoulder the creature rides. The young man recognizes that if the angel kills the lizard, then the man himself—as he knew himself and was oriented to his world—would die. This is what is so threatening: to kill past sin patterns and practices is to lose the self and the world that we knew. Yet what makes a total reorientation, a "new attitude of mind," feasible for us

12. The Greek is literally "the old man" (contrast "new man" in 4:24). Paul employs the same expression in Romans 6:6 and Colossians 3:9 to designate the sinful essence within that is crucified with Christ or is put off. The "old self" is thus related to Paul's negative usage of "flesh" to designate the "sinful nature" (e.g., Rom. 13:14; Gal. 5:13–26; Eph. 2:3). As the fleshly sinful nature produces deadly sinful desires (Eph. 2:3), so the "old self" is "corrupted" (on this word compare 1 Cor. 3:17; 15:33; 2 Cor. 7:2; 11:3) by "deceitful desires" (Eph. 4:22). Employing his typical "already/not yet" eschatology, Paul approaches our "old self" as already crucified (Rom. 6:6) and yet in need of mortification in our present experience (Rom. 6:11; Eph. 4:22; Col. 3:9–10).

13. The tense of this participle does not necessarily indicate an ongoing process of corruption: (1) the tense of a participle does not principally convey time but "kind of action" and (2) here one could easily translate it as "the old self *which is* corrupted."

(and the Ephesians) is the realization that putting on the new self introduces the believer to the new reality of being "like God in true righteousness and holiness" (Eph. 4:23–24).

The same apostle who speaks of our union with Christ (Eph. 2:13), of our salvation by grace alone (Eph. 2:8–9), of our already being seated with Christ in heavenly places (Eph. 2:6), of our holy perfection before God because of the righteousness of Christ being applied to our account (Eph. 1:7), of his indwelling resurrection power (Eph. 1:19–20; 3:20), or our being loved as fully by the Father as Jesus himself (Eph. 3:18)—does not now speak of our present lives being hopelessly corrupted by the deceitful patterns of our past lives. He speaks of his past instruction about the old self to remind us that, though our life prior to Christ was powerless to resist the work of Satan in us, we do not now have to yield to the patterns of the life we once knew. If we choose to crawl into the casket with our old self (though it is dead to us), we can be corrupted by our past, but we are not casket-controlled.

Christians should not allow our temptations to convince us that we are enslaved to our old nature.[14] With our old nature we could not resist the influences of the world, but with our new nature we can put off sinful practices. Historic theological distinctions help: (1) in our old nature we were not able not to sin (*non posse non peccare*); but (2) as new creatures justified by Christ Jesus and indwelt by him, we are able not to sin (*posse non peccare*). This does not mean that we will live perfectly before Christ comes (when we will not be able to sin—*non posse peccare*), but because of the living presence of Christ now in us by his Spirit, we are not powerless before temptation. We can obey the instruction of Paul and "put off" the sinful practices the Holy Spirit reveals to us—a lifelong process. In Luther's famous words, we are simultaneously justified and sinful (*simul justus et peccator*)—eternally justified, positionally sanctified, infinitely loved, but not invulnerable to sin. And that sin is so corrosive, so dangerous, and so damaging to our lives that the apostle of grace warns us with words that cannot be ignored to see the compulsive sensuality and the futility of life to which old patterns lead so that we will rid ourselves of them.

There is a positive side to Paul's instruction. His admonitions to believers at Ephesus remind us that we are not alone in our struggle with sin. Chris-

14. John Murray, *Principles of Conduct* (Grand Rapids: Eerdmans, 1957), 207–21.

tians through the ages have wrestled for purity and righteousness, and we are not strange or unique when we do the same. There is actually a terrible pride in believing that we have risen above the paths of ordinary men and simply do not have the usual struggles of others. But the Christian life is a battle. The residue of the old nature persists (even though that nature is dead). The old man's patterns of thought, word, and deed have placed deep ruts in our lives. Until we are with the Lord, we will struggle with aspects of our fallen nature. Those who do not know this are either living according to some formula of holiness that precludes serious self-examination, or are unwilling to seek with real passion and zeal to live for the Savior. Or, perhaps, they are too terrified of consequences to reveal to others or themselves the true struggles within their souls. No one who struggles against sin is unique or strange or alone.

There is a negative side to this as well. Christians who believe that they need not struggle with sin are terribly vulnerable. Some years ago, I would have told you that those Christian leaders who were most likely to be forced to leave their ministries were those who were most harsh, domineering, and judgmental. So often those who are most judgmental and controlling of others are those who are battling most intensely for control of their own greed, pride, addictions, lust, or lack of integrity. And while these dynamics continue to be true, more of the ministry failures I have seen in the recent years have been among those who are the strongest proponents of the message of grace. I say this with no ill will but with significant grief: those who really understand grace know the weakness of the human heart that requires it. Those who "prove" their knowledge of grace by participation in the patterns of the world, by walking in paths indistinguishable from unbelievers, by indicating little concern for their Christian testimony and their impact upon weaker brothers—such persons may understand something of grace but they indicate little knowledge of the power of the gospel and little knowledge of themselves.

Paul says that you are "to be made new in the attitude of your minds" (Eph. 4:23; cf. Rom. 12:2).[15] Christians do not believe that fulfillment or real

15. Commentators debate whether the infinitive here (*ananeousthai*) is middle or passive in voice (i.e., whether Paul is calling the audience "to renew their own minds" or to allow them "to be made new"). The middle voice is found repeatedly in intertestamental Jewish literature (notably 1 and 4 Maccabees and the Additions to Esther), where it always appears to be *non*-reflexive even in the present

happiness will be found in the ways that the world walks. The pleasures and comforts of the world are futile. We should not be rejoicing that we have license and the impunity of grace to do what everyone else is doing. Their path is destruction.

A most gracious God tells us of the futility and wasted living that come from the indulgence of sin. Too often the mark of those who think that they "really understand" grace is that they widen their tolerance for questionable entertainments, leave differences with Christian brothers and sisters unreconciled, become more self-indulgent with their time and treasures, and become a little less concerned about holiness in speech and behavior. After all, these compromises are "almost innocent." Doing or not doing such things will neither make nor break a Christian. But those in love with the Savior will hear his voice, and it will break their hearts to know that they are hurting him. Christ's love is behind the apostle's warnings. Love for the Savior, regard for him, delight in him, and a desire for us to walk with him motivate all Paul says. That is why the apostle says we should not only put off our old self, but also put on the new self.

To live differently means we must also put on the new self (Eph. 4:24a).[16] We are to take on the patterns of life that are indicative of the new life and new attitudes of Christ in us. Since we are in Christ and he is in us, our lives are to reflect his holiness of life before God, and his love for the lost and needy around us. The pursuit of the old self or the license to do so is no longer the aim. Instead, we are to put on the lifestyle of those "created to be like God in true righteousness and holiness" (Eph. 4:24b). This is what the Puritans called "vivification" (i.e., the opposite of "mortification"), which refers to nourishing or empowering the patterns that God promises will give us fulfillment and—in the truest, richest sense—real life.

---

tense (1 Macc. 14:22; 15:17). However, each of these instances also takes an accusative object, which is not the case in Ephesians 4:23, and this slightly favors the passive translation here. Also debated is the referent of the term translated "attitude" in the NIV, which literally is "spirit" in the Greek (*pneuma*)—is this the Holy Spirit or a reference to the internal disposition of the person (i.e., one's "spirit")? The expression "of your minds" likely limits the "spirit" to an internal disposition (as per the NIV).

16. Literally "put on the new man" (cf. Col. 3:10), which contrasts (both conceptually and through parallel syntactical constructions) with the "old man" in verse 22 (see notes above). In Ephesians 2:15 the "new man" is a corporate unity of all Christians (Jew and Gentile alike), whereas here the reference is more to individuals in Christ. The reference to "putting on" is quite similar to the Pauline concept of being clothed with Christ (Rom. 13:14; Gal. 3:27).

When we understand that God created us to be like himself in true righteousness and holiness, we will no longer believe that "almost innocent" is acceptable, or that piety is optional, or that holiness is oppressive. Paul's reference to our being created to be like God is a reminder that "we are God's workmanship, created in Christ Jesus to do good works, which God prepared in advance for us to do" (Eph. 2:10). Now righteousness and holiness are what most satisfy our heart because before the world was made God designed us to be like him, and by doing the good that he designed us to do, we find our greatest satisfaction and fulfillment. Putting on the life of the new man, far from being an onerous sacrifice, is discovering life in its richest, most satisfying, and fulfilling dimensions. As a racehorse is fulfilled in running and a saxophone is made for jazz, we find our greatest glory when we do what we are designed to do. We discover the greatest potentials and joys of our humanity when we live most as God made us to be—like him. In godliness we find our truest and best humanity. Our marriages are the most fulfilling, our pursuits the most satisfying, and our accomplishments the most rewarding, when we live as our God in his grace has designed. He warns us of the ruin of any other plan, and proclaims the beauty of his path, so that we will walk in the beauty and health of life that he intends.

On July 30, 1945, the heavy cruiser USS *Indianapolis* was heading home across the Pacific, having delivered a cargo of enriched uranium that would be instrumental in the ending of World War II. A Japanese torpedo ended the return journey. In the first twelve minutes after the attack, three hundred men died. More than nine hundred men, some grievously wounded, ended up in the salt water without fresh water to drink or shelter from the sun, and with no protection from sharks. Of the nine hundred that entered the water only 316 survived the four days and five nights in the ocean.

The chief medical officer, Captain Lewis Haynes, was one of the survivors and reported on what happened:

> When the hot sun came out and we were in this crystal clear water, you were so thirsty you couldn't believe it wasn't good enough to drink. I had a hard time convincing the men that they shouldn't drink. The real young ones—you take away their hope, you take away their water and food—they would drink the salt water and would go fast. I can remember striking men who were drinking (salt) water to try to stop them. They would get . . . dehydrated, then become very maniacal. . . . There were also mass hallucinations. It was amazing

> how everyone would see the same thing. One man would see something and then everyone else would see it. Even I fought hallucinations off and on, but something always brought me back.[17]

This horrible account reflects the intentions of Paul's warnings in this passage. We, of course, are struck—and perhaps taken aback—by the urgency and stridency of his warning. But there is great grace in his sternness. He tells us that the sin that looks so enticing, so almost innocent to our spiritual health, is like the water of the ocean. It too looks clear and innocent, but once imbibed it not only fails to satisfy but makes us desire more and more of what is actually poison to us, and deadens our senses to what is good. And when our minds are clouded and darkened to its effects, we begin to see the hallucinations with the rest of the world, convincing us that there is hope where there really is none. Mass hallucination may even occur in a Christian community when brothers and sisters taste the water that seems almost innocent and declare it to be good.

The reason that sin does not satisfy is the same reason that salt water does not. We were made for what the Bible calls living water, the truth and life that are in Christ Jesus. Those who are redeemed will find only in him and in the life he designs the health and happiness for which we were made.

The reason that C. S. Lewis's stallion soars with his rider is that the horse represents the truest self of the young man. When the lizard is mortified, the real self of the young man finds his most rewarding and fulfilling life. It is the life of freedom that God offers to us as we mortify the old self and live the beauty that our God has so graciously designed for us. The Scripture calls us to recognition and repentance—recognition of the poison in what is almost innocent, and repentance of the sin it truly is. God never intends to harm us even though the expressions that warn us may hurt a great deal. The call to recognition and repentance is the call to a life of rich fulfillment as we soar in our souls to the places where God intends for us to find our truest selves among his greatest joys.

17. Naval Historical Center, "Recollections of the Sinking of USS Indianapolis (CA-35) by Capt. Lewis L. Haynes," http://www.history.navy.mil/faqs/faq30-5.htm.

15

Witness of Grace

Ephesians 4:25–32

And do not grieve the Holy Spirit of God, with whom you were sealed for the day of redemption. Get rid of all bitterness, rage and anger, brawling and slander, along with every form of malice. Be kind and compassionate to one another, forgiving each other, just as in Christ God forgave you. (Eph. 4:30–32)

"Get your head up." The shouted command jarred the morning calm as I ran down the street near the end of my jogging route. My doctor friend Jim was also getting his exercise and had seen me coming with my head down and shoulders curled as I chugged up a hill. "Get your head up," he shouted. When we got even with each other, he explained: "You feel like you are working harder when you bend over like that, but you are really just making things harder for yourself." To demonstrate his point he said, "Try this—keep your arms down at your side and see how well you run." I complied and found how exceedingly awkward it was to run with my arms down. He said, "We are built so that our bodies are either giving off inhibitory responses or stimulatory responses. When you run with your head and shoulders down, you are actually inhibiting your stride—just like when you run with your arms down. If you will get your head up, your shoulders will lift, your stride will lengthen, and you will run with greater efficiency."

The advice is good for both running on a morning jog and for running the race of the Christian life. Paul provides similar instruction here in Ephesians 4:25–32. The apostle tells those of us who are "God's workmanship" (Eph. 2:10) to work hard to honor God in what we say, think, and do. But as he gives this instruction, Paul stimulates obedience by saying, "Keep your head up." What we see when we lift our eyes is grace so sweet that it stimulates the motivation and power for obedience. When grace lifts our head, God lifts our heart to honor him.

Already in this epistle we have learned that the blood of Christ alone sanctifies us before God. Christians stand before God without the blemishes or distinctions of past background, performance, or ethnicity. We are one in Christ (see again here in Eph. 4:25c). But now the apostle deals with the concern that grace will be abused and used as a license to sin. He knows the encroachments of our humanity will always seek to use the beauty of grace to deny the ugliness of our sin. So already the apostle has told us to put on the new self—to live as the holy creatures God has already made us to be by grace alone (Eph. 4:22–24). We are not to live to secure grace but to live out the grace that he secured for us. And so that we will not simply let such a principle evaporate into abstraction, the apostle now begins to spell out plainly what it means to live as those renewed by his grace in how we speak, think, and act.[1]

Grace for Renewed Living (4:25–28)

Paul, the "apostle of the heart set free,"[2] is no legalist, but he begins this passage with instruction that teaches us how the grace that renews us also stimulates personal holiness. Later, he will shift to a discussion of how grace encourages personal witness.

1. Ephesians 4:22–24 and 25–32 are connected by "therefore" at the beginning of verse 25, and by the repetition of the verb "put off" in verses 22 and 25. God has created the "new self" to be like God in "true righteousness and holiness" (Eph. 4:24); and this new self overflows into holy living, especially "truth" to be spoken (Eph. 4:25; cf. Eph. 4:21 where "truth" is in Jesus).

2. From F. F. Bruce's magnificent book of the same name, *Paul: Apostle of the Heart Set Free* (Grand Rapids: Eerdmans, 2000).

Speaking as a Renewed Person (4:25)

Paul sets up this instruction with a negative/positive pattern that he will repeat several times in this passage. First he says what persons renewed by grace should not do, but like a good preacher, he does not leave things there. Next he says what those renewed by grace should do, and later he will explain why. We see this pattern begin as Paul describes the speech of believers.

What should the renewed person not do? Tell falsehoods. Paul says, "Therefore each of you must put off falsehood" (Eph. 4:25a).

What should the renewed person do? "Speak truthfully to his neighbor" (Eph. 4:25b). The phrase is quoted from Zechariah 8:16, and the "neighbor" in this context is probably not people in general (although Christians are certainly expected to speak truthfully in general society), but rather the covenant community.[3] Christians are not to tell lies but to speak the truth. It would seem to us almost unnecessary to say, but Paul writes against this sin repeatedly (cf. Col. 3:9–10) because the pressures to gain advantages and avoid consequences always will tempt us to lie, even in the Christian community. Christians, Paul has already declared, are "to speak the truth in love" (Eph. 4:15). The kinds of temptations to lying are too numerous to mention, but I can identify some of the kinds of falsehoods that particularly tempt contemporary believers.

The first is falsely representing one's work. Surveys that provide anonymity reveal that almost all college students acknowledge some level of cheating in their academic life. A nearby town is presently in turmoil because the principal and guidance counselor gave an entire class the answers to a test to enhance their college entrance exam scores. Academic pressures, requirements of authorities, anxiety about the future, the concern not to lose face, and the need to compensate for lack of discipline in preparation can combine to make cheating a very common temptation.

3. This focus on the Christian community is clearly evident in the statement that "we are all members of one body" (Eph. 4:25, on which see below). Similar to the inaugurated eschatology of Ephesians, where Paul emphasizes God's gracious salvation lived out unto good works (e.g., Eph. 2:1–10), Zechariah promises God's grace and faithfulness to the remnant of Judah in the new Jerusalem (Zech. 8:1–15), and then directs the remnant's proper response toward acting truthfully in their communal speech and judgments (Zech. 8:16–19). The Old Testament citation in Ephesians is quite close to the Septuagint of Zechariah 8:16, although the preposition "with" is nearer to the Hebrew text. Paul grounds his ethical instructions upon Old Testament teaching here and in Ephesians 4:26, and this indicates that he is not drawing his thought primarily from Hellenistic virtue/vice lists (even if there is some similarity in genre).

Plagiarism is a closely related problem that has affected many preachers. One does not get rich in ministry. Our currency is the regard of others. Thus, especially in the preparation of sermons and papers, the need to look good, to be thought of as intelligent, insightful, and articulate causes us falsely to claim that the work of others is our own. Such misrepresentation seems more pervasive than ever because of the easy access to such materials on the Internet and various media services. This pattern of misrepresentation is very hard to escape once entered. No preacher wants to hear that last week's sermon was better than this week's, and the consequence of congratulations for one plagiarized sermon becomes stimulus for another one. Some of my closest friends in ministry are either out of pulpits or under discipline because they claimed personal credit for work they did not do. All of us in ministry should realize that even if we avoid being caught, something in us dies a bit when we minister in Christ's name falsely.

Another temptation is falsely to represent one's self. We are a mobile society and often attend churches where most of the people do not know us or our backgrounds. How easy it is to present ourselves as having had positions of greater responsibility or backgrounds of greater significance than is really true. It is also well within our Christian psyche to present our past experience as more sordid than it really was so that our salvation testimony seems more impressive. We can easily slide into the temptation of bringing glory to ourselves while rationalizing that what we are saying is for the glory of Jesus.

Some also may be tempted to create controversy in the church by speaking of what they do not know or twisting what they do know. Personal currency sometimes inflates in church communities through competing ideas, relationships, and reputations. The temptation always exists to further one's perceived importance by presenting others in a way that devalues them. We might say words that approximate what a preacher said (without his nuance or qualifications) in order to make him look unreasonable, unbiblical, or foolish—and ourselves in contrast more spiritual, biblical, and wise. To question the integrity or intelligence of church leaders, we may presume and suggest without full knowledge why they took certain actions, and by undermining them elevate our own status or sense of importance. But to voice suspicions and to talk about what we do not know to be true contradicts biblical commands only to speak the truth.

Those who study persuasion speak of the need to "perfect the enemy," to portray others so negatively that no reasonable person can help but hate them and oppose them. It is a powerful form of propaganda, but a devastating force in the church where we are required only to speak what we know is true. James said that a person who thinks himself to be religious but bridles not his tongue deceives himself and his religion is vain (James 1:26).

A final temptation is misrepresenting facts. Falsehoods are so tempting when we face car trades, expense reports, tax returns, business dealings, library fines, due dates, rents, curfews, traffic citations, parental questions, spousal pressures, and so on. The opportunities to shade or hide the truth to avoid personal consequences or advance personal gain are constant challenges—and frequent causes of sin.

Now your head may be hanging down with mine because it is hard to talk about such matters without honest reflection convicting our heart of its weakness about such a basic aspect of the Christian life. But the apostle begins to raise our head a bit when he tells us why we should speak truthfully—because we are members of Christ's body (literally, body parts of one another).[4]

Why should the renewed person speak without falsehood? For the sake of the body. If one member lies to another, then the body cannot function. Consider what happens when the eye does not communicate the truth of a hot iron to the hand. Fingers get burned. The body cannot perform its functions if its members do not communicate what is true to each other. The beauty of this analogy is that the apostle is reminding us that our words—what we say—affect the ability of the church body to function. When trust disappears, the work of the body comes to a screeching halt until that trust can be restored. And what is the nature of that body? The apostle has already told us that the church is the body of Christ in which the Spirit dwells and that God will use her to fill the earth with his transforming power (1:23). Our words and the integrity that gives them credibility are the means God uses to flood the earth with the power of the gospel. The apostle makes a vital connection between piety and power that we should never ignore. Piety is not the cause of grace. But gospel grace compels true

4. The Greek "members of one another" clearly associates this passage with how Christians are "members of his [i.e., Christ's] body" (Eph. 5:30; cf. Rom. 12:5), thus drawing on Paul's repeated theme concerning the church as Christ's body (Eph. 1:23; 2:16; 4:4, 12, 16; 5:23).

holiness that is vital to the progress of the gospel. Without piety there is no gospel power. Proclaiming grace without displaying holiness will preclude the spread of the gospel.

The reason that we refrain from falsehood and maintain truth even under pressure is that God lifts our eyes to see that relationships of trust are the wheels on which the ministry of the church progresses. The men with whom I will share my greatest concerns are those I have seen operate with integrity when they were under pressure. In contrast, I must confess there are men I avoid because I have seen them compromise the truth under pressure. Integrity in speech allows us to minister God's grace to others and to ourselves. Paul graciously lifts our eyes to see the impact of our words on the body of Christ and its transforming ministry in the world to teach us how renewed persons should speak.

Thinking as a Renewed Person (4:26–27)

The renewed person should think without uncontrolled or prolonged anger. The apostle carefully words his instruction to help us avoid misunderstanding (Eph. 4:26–27). Note that he does not say that we should never get angry. Such a command would be impossible and even ungodly. There are just causes for righteous anger. Injustice, cruelty, and insensitivity to others stir God's wrath and rightly cause anger in us who are made in his image (e.g., Jesus cleansing the temple, Matt. 21:12–13). Christians sometimes cripple their own emotional health and progress in relationships by refraining from expressing the cause of tensions under the false presumption that all anger is wrong. We can properly, directly, and biblically experience and express anger (Mark 3:5; Matt. 18:34). The apostle does not forbid anger but the sinful expression of it. This means that our emotions are not so to control our actions that they then turn to ungodly and destructive expression (Ps. 4:4).[5] Most counselors have dropped the idea that simply giving vent to anger will result in a healthy psyche. Expressing anger honestly and explaining its source can be helpful and healthy, but simply venting uncontrollably only reinforces anger and further deepens its roots, causing further relational damage.

5. The opening words of Ephesians 4:26 cite Psalm 4:4 (= 4:5 in the Septuagint and Masoretic text), precisely following the Septuagint and Hebrew texts. The psalmist, during his distress while enduring the opposition of those who tell lies, calls his soul to respond without anger-inspired sin and with trust in the Lord.

Due to a misunderstanding, a child of mine recently got angry with me and was further upset that I disciplined her for expressing her anger. My child said, "I need to be able to tell you that I am angry." "I agree," I said. "Your anger was not what caused my discipline but the uncontrolled way that you expressed it. For me to allow you to express anger without respect or control not only will cause damage to our relationship but also will damage you in the future as you deal with friends, employees, and a spouse." Accounts of well-known Christian leaders who have lost their positions for repeated, uncontrolled outbursts of anger should caution us all. Less apparent, but equally dangerous, is quietly harbored anger that slowly destroys relationships with the corrosion of resentment. Of course, there is a place for righteous anger. Expressing legitimate anger without sin is a true Christian virtue that brings blessings and protects relationships, but persons who know God's grace also know the dangers of uncontrolled anger.

Lack of control over anger may be evidenced by how long it is held, as well as by how vigorously it is expressed. Paul tells us not to let the sun go down on our anger (Eph. 4:26b).[6] Early on in our marriage, I misinterpreted this verse. I wanted to be biblical in the way that we handled disputes, so I insisted that we not go to sleep until we had resolved whatever disagreement we were facing. I thought that we had to do this or we would be disobeying God—even if that meant staying up all night. However, at a certain point of tiredness, we discovered that our ability to resolve disagreement became almost zero. In fact our ability to resolve disputes usually is inversely proportional to the lateness of the hour. I simply misread the verse. It does not say, "Do not let the sun go down on your dispute." It says, "Do not let the sun go down on your anger." (The word for "anger" here is rare and communicates response to a particular event that causes exasperation, indignation, or rage.)[7] Even if the matter is not solved, we are not to give such anger long priority in our emotions. Something other than rage—such as love, longing for resolution, the desire to see mercy, even the desire for Christ's justice to rule for the good of others—should ultimately be controlling us. Rage is satisfied only by some

6. Similar ethical counsel can be found in ancient Jewish literature (e.g., from Qumran in 1QS 5:24–6:2) and in Greco-Roman philosophy. Here Paul may implicitly connect this counsel to "not let the sun go down while you are still angry" with the broader context of his citation from Psalm 4:4 (which continues: "In your anger do not sin; *when you are on your beds, search your hearts and be silent*").

7. The term refers to the cause provoking anger in the Septuagint of 1 Kings 15:30; 2 Kings 19:3; 23:26; Nehemiah 9:18, 26. Yet this same word is also used parallel to other terms for anger in Jeremiah 21:5.

form of retaliation. Even if the matter is not fully resolved, the sun should never set on that kind of destructive anger in the heart of a Christian.

Why is the apostle concerned about how and how long our anger is expressed in our hearts? Because he does not want the Devil to gain a foothold.[8] Here again the apostle raises our heads to see the grace that is really behind the rule. Archimedes said, "Give me a lever long enough with a place to stand and I can move the world." Paul says that to allow anger to simmer—the kind of anger that actually desires the suffering of others—gives Satan a foothold in our hearts from which he can begin to control our world. Paul will return to this theme shortly, but for now consider the magnitude of the warning he gives. Even when we have a just cause for our anger, if we let it simmer so that our minds nurse the grudge at night and repeatedly plow the furrows of our own pain, what grows in us is of little use to us and of little attractiveness to others. Our anger spoils us. It has been said that anger is an acid that destroys its container. So the apostle graciously lifts our heads above our own pain so that we can see the consequences of the thought patterns that give Satan a foothold for his corrosive work in our hearts.

Not only does the apostle address aspects of our speech and thought, but he finally gives us rules for our actions.

Acting as a Renewed Person (4:28)

The renewed person acts without selfishness. Specifically, the apostle says that Christians should not steal (Eph. 4:28). More than one commentator seems a bit distressed that Paul puts this instruction in the present tense (lit., the one stealing—present active participle—should steal no more). We find it shocking that those in the church would be stealing in the present tense and need the instruction to stop. Commentators usually remark that theft was so common in the ancient world that Christians of that day, unlike today,

8. "Foothold" renders the fairly common Greek word for "place or position" (*topos*). Here metaphorically it refers to an "opportunity" for the Devil to take root in our lives (cf. Rom. 12:19, "leave room [= opportunity] for God's wrath"; and see W. Bauer, W. F. Arndt, F. W. Gingrich, and F. W. Danker, *A Greek-English Lexicon of the New Testament* [Chicago: University of Chicago Press, 2000], s.v.). The term here for "devil" means "slanderer" (cf. 1 Tim. 3:11; 2 Tim. 3:3; Titus 2:3; and Zech. 3:1–2), and this title is used by Paul to designate the most eminent slanderer (Eph. 6:11; 1 Tim. 3:6–7; 2 Tim. 2:26; also repeatedly in the Gospels and Acts), whom elsewhere he calls Satan (e.g., 1 Tim. 1:20; 5:15; and many other times in the New Testament).

needed such instruction. Of course, such comments simply fail to recognize how common stealing is in our day among Christians.

Unauthorized software usage, file-shared music, and pirated videos are only the tip of the iceberg of a culture whose retail prices can be inflated by a third due to shoplifting, whose employers budget for employee theft, where corporate scandals are so regular as to bore us, and where the government taxes us on the assumption that we will hide resources. Christians are not immune to all this. We, too, can lie to landlords or employers to avoid financial responsibilities. When we feel that we have been taken advantage of, it is easy to rationalize doing personal work on company time. Yet, however soft we may be on our own sin, Paul reminds us that we dishonor the Savior whenever we steal by taking pay for time that we did not spend doing what our employers were compensating us to do.

Paul counters the urge to steal by commanding its flip side: work.[9] Again note the negative imperative followed by its positive counterpart. Note also that the need to work hard and well remains an issue in our culture. Those seeking just to get by in life without working are not only the stereotypical welfare cheaters and idle rich. Studies tell us that more and more middle-class young men are less inclined to work in positions of responsibility (or complete college) because undemanding jobs can provide them all they want: an apartment, a fast car, a flat-screen TV, and a willing partner.

Paul gives a very different reason why we should work: so that in doing "something useful" we may have something to "share" with others. The word translated "useful" has at its root the idea of something "good" or worthwhile. Then Paul says that we are to do that which is of God so that we can "share" (*metadidōmi*—a word that also is used to describe communicating the gospel[10]) with others in need. The spiritual echoes in Paul's words move our minds to consider the impact of not stealing. By moving from the position of being a "taker" to a "giver," our orientation as believers is reversed from our previous way of life. Once we sought to deprive others for our good; now we seek to share with others for their good. Thus, by living in accord with the instruction of the gospel, the "thief" becomes a representative of God's mercy.

9. This is one of the more intense Greek words for "work" (*kopiaō*), perhaps rendered better as "labor" or "toil."

10. 1 Thess. 2:8.

Paul's wording is not explicit, but it contains enough of a spiritual tone to remind us that working, in contrast to stealing, is actually sharing Christ with our neighbor—or, as Martin Luther put it, "becoming Christ to one's neighbor."[11] If we can really see it (and actually very few even in the church seem able to see it), the giving of our gain rather than taking for our gain so reflects the nature of Christ that we are actually sharing Christ. Jesus said of such giving, "Inasmuch as you do it unto the least of these, you do it unto me" (see Matt. 25:31–46).

In so sharing we have the privilege of becoming Christ to our neighbor. Our working in order to share with others is not simply a means of keeping God happy with us (in fact, the works of our hands are never sufficient to merit God's acceptance). Yet such sharing has a far greater purpose, and that is a more powerful motivation than self-protection or self-promotion. Generosity of spirit, concern for mercy, and the willingness to live sacrificially are actually presentations of the grace of Christ as though Christ himself were speaking through us.

Despite my weakness and sin, I may become Christ to my neighbor by sharing generously out of my life. What a privilege! This realization underscores the need for the church to be involved in mercy ministries, but it also challenges us to examine whether we have seriously considered how our lives will exhibit the obedience of selflessness that makes Christ real in us as well as to others. For the fact of the matter is that if I am not Christ to my neighbor, Christ has little reality to me either. Thus, selfless sharing is grace to my own soul in that it makes Christ more real and understandable to my own heart. Obedience does not earn Christ's presence, but in our obedience Christ presents himself to us—his love, his sacrifice, and his grace become the air we breathe, the context of our thought, and the world in which we live. No longer is he a theological abstraction, but he is our life (see Col. 3:4).

The significance of the impact of our obedience on others as well as on us keeps Paul writing. Though he has already addressed how what we say, think, and do is not merely about self-promotion before God or self-protection from God, the idea of representing Christ and his grace stimulates greater intensity of expression. Already the apostle has lifted

11. Paul Althaus and Robert C. Schultz, *The Theology of Martin Luther* (Philadelphia: Fortress, 1966), 135.

our heads in every imperative to show how holiness promotes the grace of God in our lives. He stimulates our obedience as a response to the greatness and wonder of the dynamics of his grace *toward us*. But now the emphasis on the gracious effects of obedience *on others* takes even greater priority in Paul's thought. He returns to the earlier subjects of speech, thought, and action with greater intensity because he is lifting our heads to see beyond the walls of our own lives. Paul's urgency comes from his desire for us to understand the import of our obedience on the lives and souls of others.

Grace for Renewed Witness (4:29–32)

Paul is still the apostle of the heart set free, but he now intensifies his imperatives to teach us to use grace to stimulate personal witness. By "witness" I am not only writing about the expression of evangelistic words; rather, I am addressing how the testimony of our lives makes Christ real to those about us, even those within the covenant community.

Speaking as a Renewed Witness (4:29)

The renewed person speaks for the sake of personal witness without any words that harm. We are told to put off all unwholesome speech (Eph. 4:29). The word "unwholesome" (Greek *sapros*) means "rotten" or "putrid" and refers generally to profanity or obscenity. Paul says literally "all bad speech do not let journey out of your mouth." What interesting and instructive language! Bad language begins a journey of decay when it comes out of your mouth, reverberating with effect upon the lives of others. Elsewhere Paul writes that we should "shun profane and vain babblings: for they will increase unto more ungodliness"—they start a journey leading to a destination less godly than where we started (2 Tim. 2:16 KJV). How different is the apostolic instruction from our common and willing misunderstanding of grace; that is, the attitude that says, "Let me show you how well I understand grace; I can use coarse humor and profane language without feeling guilty." The pervasiveness of profanity in our entertainments and associations has largely desensitized our ears to the apostle's command, but I doubt if this would surprise him. He was in a culture where filthy speech and entertainments were incorporated even into religious practices. He knew how countercultural pure speech was, and perhaps that is why he would insist so upon it. It would be such a powerful witness.

We should not think that God is just a persnickety and prudish old grandmother who gasps and frowns about the syllables that come out of our mouths. How strange it would be to think that God is up in heaven concerned to see if our lips, tongues, and larynxes pump out any puffs of air that offend him. It is not the words themselves but rather their journey that more concerns God.

When I was in graduate school for speech communication, one of our studies exposed people to a series of optical illusions. Depending on their speech background and patterns, they would perceive (actually see) different objects in the optics. Speech is one of the ways that we organize thought, and it even establishes patterns of brain function that affect not just the way that we speak but also the way that we see our world and think about it. This is why persons who are converted as adults often have such a difficult time avoiding profanity. Their thought life has been oriented by such speech, and it is difficult for them to see the world or interact with others and not think in profane terms.

Such observations give deeper meaning to Christ's admonition that it is not what goes into a man's mouth that defiles him, but what comes out of his mouth (Matt. 15:11). Rotten speech in very real ways spoils the world that we can and do perceive. Similar to the way we can get up in the morning with a groan that seems to make the whole day rotten to us, our rotten expression (critical, dark, and unkind comments) can make putrid our world and the world of those who live with us. God has a more glorious plan for our lives and our tongues, and graciously seeks to preserve the beauty of our world by teaching us to guard our speech.

The concern for our tongues is not limited, however, to the effect of our words on us, but extends to the effects of those words on others. The positive command that corresponds to not using rotten speech (that which is ruinous) is: "Do not let any unwholesome talk come out of your mouths, but only what is helpful for building others up according to their needs, that it may benefit those who listen" (Eph. 4:29). This imperative is far broader than we may expect or like.[12] Christians are not allowed to say whatever we desire simply by

12. The imperative notion here is clearly implied from the Greek context, and the Greek conditional and indefinite pronoun function together like an indefinite relative ("but [speak] whatever is good to the building up of the need"). The repetition of "good" and "need" in both verses 28 and 29 emphasizes

rationalizing that we do not cuss or become coarse. We are not even allowed to fall back upon some category of neutrality in rationalizing what we say, as in "It doesn't hurt anyone, so it's all right to say." The apostle's standard is that if it does not build up and benefit, then it is not worthy to be said.

With these edifying qualifications the apostle shows the true colors of his concern. Yes, we are to be concerned for what we say and think and do because of how such matters affect us; and indeed the apostle has graciously lifted our heads to see the grace toward us that motivates such imperatives. But now the grace is driven outward toward others, and we are made to understand that what we say is a form of witness. Our words are an instrument of God's grace toward others by which his own nature is known and shared. Literally the apostle says we are to speak so as to "give grace to the hearers" (Eph. 4:29d).[13] Thus we are to speak only what builds up and benefits others because our lives are not our own but are meant to show forth the One who indwells us.

Thinking and Acting as a Renewed Witness (4:29–32)

The witness aspect of our lives becomes most clear as the apostle now both combines and intensifies the thinking and doing imperatives he previously mentioned. The renewed person thinks and acts for the sake of personal witness without any intention of harm (Eph. 4:29). The apostle gives a long list of negatives to rid from our lives. Many commentators see this list as progressive (as though one allowed to thrive will spawn the next): "bitterness, rage and anger, brawling and slander, along with every form of malice" (Eph. 4:31).[14]

---

how both act (Eph. 4:28) and speech (Eph. 4:29) should be targeted toward the good of the needy recipient. The concept of "building up" has already occurred in Ephesians (Eph. 4:12, 16), drawing on Paul's building metaphor (Eph. 2:21; cf. 1 Cor. 3:9; 2 Cor. 5:1). Paul in his epistles elsewhere repeatedly enjoins such "building up" or "edification" (Rom. 14:19; 15:2; 1 Cor. 14:3, 5, 12, 26; 2 Cor. 10:8; 12:19; 13:10; cf. 1 Cor. 10:23; 1 Thess. 5:11).

13. Cf. Colossians 4:6. Although the conveying of benefit is clearly in view (and this idiom in the Hellenistic world could simply imply some benefit giving), in Ephesians God has repeatedly been the one to give "grace" (*charis*) to his people both in granting saving grace (Eph. 1:6–7; 2:5, 7–8) and in gifting them for service (Eph. 4:7; esp. Paul in 3:2, 7–8). Thus the verbal association indicates in this context that God's gracious generosity is to be imitated by his people. Note that Paul opens and closes this letter by invoking through his own words "grace" on his hearers (Eph. 1:2; 6:24).

14. Cf. Colossians 3:8; 1 Timothy 6:4. Like Ephesians 4:31, in these texts *blasphēmia* is directed not toward God but toward the slandering of other people. "Anger" is further cautioned against in 2 Corinthians 12:20; Galatians 5:20.

You cannot be in the church long without seeing such forms of thought and action in evidence, but that does not excuse them or allow us to tolerate them in ourselves or others. We know intuitively that when such attitudes and actions are allowed among us, the ministry of the church itself is damaged. I remember in our church watching two young brothers engaged in an elbow battle during the singing of "Great Is Thy Faithfulness." Somehow each had decided the other had not allowed him enough space, so while we sang they vied for position with their elbows. Although they did not miss a single word of "Great Is Thy Faithfulness" as they jabbed each other, there was little doubt that God's faithfulness was not on their minds or on the minds of those who observed them. Perhaps it is the power of our squabbles to distract from the grace of God that causes the apostle to reverse his pattern with this set of imperatives and give the motivation prior to the instruction.

Prior to listing the various attitudes and actions that spring from being forgiving, the apostle says, "Do not grieve the Holy Spirit" (Eph. 4:30).[15] The words challenge our theology as much as they encourage our hearts. We are not accustomed to thinking of our thoughts and actions affecting God's heart. There are even aspects of our theology that make us question whether it is proper to think this way. Yet the apostle under the inspiration of the Holy Spirit speaks with wonderful intimacy about the nature of our God and his heart for us. Just as Christ can be touched by the feelings of our infirmities (Heb. 4:15), his Spirit grieves over our failure to love as we should in the Christian community. There is some poignancy in the consideration that the Holy Spirit, the One who is our Comforter (John 14–16), is himself grieved by our sin. The thought is meant to arrest us and correct us. The same Spirit who convicts my heart of sin, generates in me love for God, gives me new birth, provides my apprehension of the beauty of grace in the world, and seals my redemption until the coming of my Lord—this same Spirit who loves me so intimately and perfectly, I can cause to grieve. Not wanting to hurt him is strong motivation for not intending the harm of his people or purpose.

15. This strongly echoes Isaiah 63:10 ("yet they rebelled and grieved his Holy Spirit"), varying slightly from the Septuagint in favor of the Hebrew. Peter O'Brien in *The Letter to the Ephesians* (Grand Rapids: Eerdmans, 1999) suggests here a deep connection between Ephesians and this chapter of Isaiah, arguing that Paul drew typologically on the events of the exodus reflected in Isaiah in order to inform himself about God's eschatological redemption and the work of the Spirit of God.

The purpose of the Holy Spirit informs us most specifically why antagonisms that disrupt the church disturb him. What is the Holy Spirit's purpose? It is to testify of Christ. The Spirit's witness in my heart of the truth of the gospel is the seal on my heart that I am his for the day of redemption.[16] Jesus said, "But when the Comforter is come, whom I will send unto you from the Father, even the Spirit of truth, which proceedeth from the Father, he shall testify of me" (John 15:26 KJV). When we are indwelt by the Spirit but possess attitudes or actions that are not reflective of Jesus, we undermine the ministry of the Holy Spirit. Thus the progression and witness of the gospel require not grieving the Spirit by any form of malice that creates disturbances within our heart or his church.

The emphasis on peaceableness and the absence of malice again causes us to hang our heads. There is too much dissension in us and around us. But the apostle further pierces our heart and punctuates his intent with the final instruction to forgive as Christ forgave us (Eph. 4:32b). In these words there are explanation, example, and encouragement.

First, we have an *explanation* of forgiveness that is very important. Occasionally you hear Christians struggle over whether they need to forgive if someone who has sinned against them has not yet repented or repented well enough. The problem with such an approach is that it confuses pardon and forgiveness. This passage places forgiveness in the context of putting malice aside: "Get rid of . . . every form of malice . . . , forgiving each other" (Eph. 4:31d, 32). One does not have to remove all consequences for sin (i.e., to pardon) in order to forgive. It may be just and necessary for an offender to suffer consequences for wrong, but the motive of the one imposing or requiring the consequences cannot be malicious. We are not permitted to desire the ultimate harm of the offender. The gospel always provides hope, always seeks restoration. Even when the criminal is sentenced, and we properly rejoice to see justice done, the Christian also desires to see the offender recognize the sin, repent, and know spiritual restoration. Forgiveness does not require pardon from consequences; it requires an absence of malice (i.e., no desire for the person's spiritual harm) even in the application of those

16. Paul reidentifies the Holy Spirit as the one who seals believers (Eph. 1:13), guaranteeing their "redemption" (Eph. 1:14), which comes from the forgiveness of our sins through the blood of Christ (Eph. 1:7). Here in Ephesians 4:30 this "day of redemption" looks forward to the eschatological fulfillment of the promised redemption/forgiveness that is already ours in Christ Jesus (Eph. 1:14).

consequences. We may well desire justice, but desires for personal revenge or spiritual damage are not our right as Christians.

We are given the *example* of Christ to remind us why we who represent him are to forgive (Eph. 4:32c). He died for us while we were yet his enemies. He calls us his own and covers us with the benefits of his own blood when we abuse his grace and continue to sin against him. His example tells us the nature of true forgiveness. But who can express such forgiveness, perfectly or fully, when we have been grievously sinned against?

For such a question we also have the *encouragement* of Christ. Even when your forgiveness is not all that he requires, remember "God forgave you" (Eph. 4:32d). He even forgives your lack of forgiveness that dishonors him. When we see the irony of this and the sweetness of it, we are made more willing to forgive—to reflect the Christlikeness that is our own hope that, when expressed, makes him more real in our life and for those people in our life.

The refusal to forgive, in all its forms and manifestations, is fundamentally contrary to the ministry of the Holy Spirit, who testifies of the Savior who gave himself for us while we were yet his enemies (Rom. 5:8–10). This is why the apostle culminates his positive instruction of being "kind and compassionate" (Eph. 4:32a) with the imperative to "forgiv[e] each other, just as in Christ God forgave you" (Eph. 4:32b).[17] This is more than simply a dull obligation to do to others as Christ has done to you because we can never as fully or perfectly love as Jesus does. If this were all that is in the requirement, then we would be burdened rather than helped. Rather, the apostle lifts our heads to see what our commitment to forgiving attitudes and actions accomplishes. By forgiving we do become Christ to others. By bearing in our bodies the weight of unjust accusation, undeserved pain, and unretaliated harm, we are the Holy Spirit's message of Jesus to others. By the practice of forgiveness we have the privilege of being a living witness to the One we most love, and who has loved us eternally and sacrificially. This is the ultimate motivation that gives us joy in our suffering, strength for obedience, and love for his commands. My life will never deserve his love, but my life can reflect his love; and because I love him, I will live for him in what I say and think and do.

17. Cf. Colossians 3:12–13. Just as forgiveness is a character trait of God that is to be emulated in Christian virtue, so also kindness and compassion are fundamental to the character of God (Eph. 2:7; see also Rom. 11:22; Titus 3:4).

Paul's imperatives are so structured as to remind us that ours is not simply a "Don't religion." By obeying Christ's commands we are allowed to participate in his ministry and actually become his witness by his Spirit to others. Although our actions never earn his acceptance, they do gain his approval as he shows the world his own heart through us. How privileged and powerful is this witness? This was powerfully evidenced in the life of a woman named Gladys Staines.

On January 23, 1999, Gladys's husband Graham and her two sons Timothy and Philip, ages eight and ten, were asleep in a vehicle in a remote village in eastern India. The Staines had given their lives there as missionaries to lepers for thirty-four years. They were about to give much more. While the man and his sons were sleeping, a group of militant Hindus doused the car with gasoline and set it on fire. The militants then prevented the Staines from getting out and kept rescuers at bay. The horrific incident brought world attention, but even more did Gladys's response to the terrible murder of her husband and two young sons.

She wrote, "When I learned that my family was dead, I told my daughter: 'We'll forgive, then, won't we?' And she said, 'Yes, Mummy, we will.'"

She explained, "Forgiveness brings healing. It allows the other person a chance to start life afresh. If I have something against you and I forgive you, the bitterness leaves me. . . . Forgiveness liberates both the forgiver and the forgiven.

"How was I able to forgive? The truth is that I myself am a sinner. I needed Jesus Christ to forgive me. Because I have Jesus in my life, it is possible for me to forgive others."

Her words so reflect the apostle's words: "Forgive as God in Christ forgave you," and the results of her forgiveness match the Spirit's intent. Gladys honestly reports that before the murders her family's ministry had been quite localized. But her witness of Christ's love has turned world attention and reform on the persecution of other Christians in India, the militancy of certain Hindu groups, and the plight of the lepers to whom the Staines had ministered.[18]

Of course, such witness for the gospel does not go unchallenged. The progress of the gospel brought about by Gladys's witness of forgiveness has

18. Material from "Once You Forgive, There Will Be Healing," *Christianity Today* (February 1, 2003), 46–48; and related sources.

actually ignited more rage against her in many quarters of India. She writes, "The hate campaign is a part of life." Why then does she endure, and show kindness and compassion? The answer is that kindness and compassion against the backdrop of bitterness and rage are an even greater witness to Christ. If her heart were filled with bitterness and rage toward those who have treated her so badly, her ministry of the gospel would be over.

After the accounts of Gladys's forgiving heart circulated, another missionary reported that a man in India received a gospel tract. After reading it, he asked, "Is this the same Jesus that Gladys Staines believes in?" "Yes," the missionary replied. The man then said, "I want to know that Jesus."

When what we say and think and do is free of "all bitterness, rage and anger, brawling and slander, along with every form of malice," the Holy Spirit is not grieved but grants us the power of the gospel. How dear is that? For the person renewed by God's grace, it is as dear as what is most precious to us.

Some time after the murders, I read Gladys's report on how her daughter was doing—the same young girl who had resolved with her "mummy" to forgive. Gladys wrote that someone approached her daughter at school and said, "I can't understand how you can forgive." Do you know what the daughter said? She said, "Mummy, I can't understand how they can't understand why we have forgiven." Forgiveness had so etched the mind of Christ on this girl that she could not even perceive why others could not understand the need and beauty of forgiveness. The grace the apostle Paul shares with us in this passage is the understanding that when our words, and thoughts, and actions witness of Christ, he privileges and enables our hearts to know most intimately the One most dear. This is great grace. And something in us knows that when such grace is witnessed in us and through us, the Holy Spirit does not grieve but sings.

16

The Smell of Jesus

Ephesians 5:1–7

Be imitators of God, therefore, as dearly loved children and live a life of love, just as Christ loved us and gave himself up for us as a fragrant offering and sacrifice to God. (Eph. 5:1–2)[1]

The title of this chapter, "The Smell of Jesus," is not original with me. It appeared on the sign of a nearby church that announces each week's sermon title to the passing traffic. I know the pastor of that church and chuckled to hear the reaction of his wife. "Your title," she said, "will offend. You should call your sermon 'The Fragrance of Jesus' or 'The Scent of the Savior' or 'The Perfume of Salvation.'"

"'The Smell of Jesus,' she said, "sounds as though you are talking about gym socks, not the Savior of our souls."

1. The best paragraph divisions in Ephesians are hard to discern. The NIV division at Ephesians 5:8 breaks up the clear connection of vv. 8–14 with vv. 1–7 (or, more specifically, vv. 3–7); a very likely break occurs at verse 15, although in reality the whole of chapters 5–6 is bound tightly together (and is also interwoven with ideas from chapter 4). The punctuation in recent Greek text editions tends to keep Ephesians 5:8 with 5:7, but these same Greek editions disagree on general paragraph divisions throughout chapter 5.

Said the pastor in response, "I think I'll keep the title. If it gets half the attention you are giving it, then we will have a full house on Sunday." Perhaps a little humor of that nature is needed to prepare us for this passage. This is a chapter I have both longed and dreaded to write. I struggle to know how to convey the seriousness of the apostle's concern to open our senses to two related sins that are a stench to God, yet too often become a perfume to his people.

The sins that Paul combats in this passage are formidable: lust and greed. Paul writes with some stridency about these because he wants to protect the Christian community, the building that is rising to the glory of God, from these corrupting influences that can rot the church from the inside. Paul knows how quickly God's people can dismiss these sins. So he speaks of the holiness God desires in terms of a sense that will evoke vivid memories and compelling feelings for those raised in a world where religious sacrifices were common. Paul uses recollections of the permeating smell of those sacrifices to bring into the present consciousness of the Ephesians the entire ministry of Jesus as motivation for Christian purity.

God commands purity. That is nothing new. It is not even new in this epistle. Paul has dealt with the theme twice already in the preceding verses, cautioning us to honor God in what we say and think and do. But knowing the command does not always lead to honoring it. So Paul now comes after our heart through our nose.

Savor Your Identity (5:1–2)

Live as the Children of God (5:1)

The apostle tells the Ephesians to "be imitators of God." The words flow from the preceding verses in which the Ephesians are reminded to forgive just as in Christ, God forgave them (Eph. 4:32).[2] As God has treated you, so reflect him in your relations with others, says the apostle. But simply reminding the

2. The connection to Ephesians 4:32 is emphasized by the word "therefore," the repetition of the imperative "be" (*ginesthe*), and the parallel "just as" (*kathōs*) clauses in 4:32 and 5:2. Also, Ephesians 5:1–2 continues the positive admonitions of 4:32 before returning (in 5:3–4) to the rejection of the negative dimensions of fallen humanity (note the repeated pattern of negative/positive in 4:25–32). For these reasons, some commentators and some Greek editions consider 5:1–2 to be a continuation of the preceding paragraph.

Ephesians of what God has done is not the only motivation the apostle uses. He also reminds the Ephesians of the status that they have as a consequence of God's forgiveness. Imitate God "as dearly loved children," Paul says.[3] This is the culminating reality of all that has preceded: "In Christ Jesus you who once were far away have been brought near through the blood of Christ. . . . For through him we both [Jew and Gentile] have access to the Father by one Spirit" (Eph. 2:13, 18). Now the apostle urges these people of God to live in accord with the status that they—and we—have as God's children.

Paul's emphasis on our identity in Christ as the motive for our obedience is as clearly stated in these verses as anywhere in Scripture. Here we can plainly see a demonstration of Herman Ridderbos's oft-quoted observation that in gospel teaching the imperative rests on the indicative and this order is not reversible.[4] The indicative—who we are—is clearly stated here by Paul; that is, by Christ's reconciliation we of all nations and backgrounds are reckoned as God's dearly loved children. God's imperatives, and our obedience, rest on that loving relationship; they do not form the relationship. We obey because we are loved; we are not loved because we obey. The love of our Father precedes and stimulates the obedience of his children. We are to forgive and live and love as dearly loved children imitating the One who already is our Father, not performing to bribe God to become our Father.

The significance of obedience based on the Father's love becomes more apparent when we consider where the apostle will soon head with his imperatives. He will soon address the sins of lust and greed. How would you turn others from such sin? Should you warn? Yes. Should you command to avoidance? Yes. Should you condemn participation? Yes. But what first? First, remind those who love God and are grieving for their failure that they are his dearly loved children. Say to a struggler, "You are a wonderful child, a precious child of God, dearly loved. You are precious to him. Live as one dearly loved. Be what you are in Christ."

3. The *imitatio* theme in Pauline ethics manifests several applications. Here Paul invokes the direct imitation of God (a concept also found in the Jewish author Philo contemporary to Paul). Elsewhere Paul calls believers to imitate his own example as he himself imitates Christ (1 Cor. 11:1; cf. 1 Cor. 4:16; Phil. 3:17; 1 Thess. 1:6; 2 Thess. 3:7, 9; also cf. Heb. 13:7). Similarly churches are to imitate what is Christ-honoring in other churches (1 Thess. 2:14; also Heb. 6:12). While such imitation of God echoes the Old Testament call to "be holy" as God is holy, here Paul focuses especially on imitating in our relationships with others (5:2) the love that we have received as God's children (5:1), for whom Christ died (5:2).

4. H. Ridderbos, *Paul: An Outline of His Theology* (Grand Rapids: Eerdmans, 1975), 253.

Seeing this pattern of Scripture has corrected my ministry and helped me to think in gospel patterns. When ones dear to me have failed to live as God desires, I recognize it is easy to motivate them toward new obedience with shame and fear. But I have learned that for most, shame is a cycle and fear wanes. Weakened by their sense of failure and worthlessness, those who are primarily motivated by shame become only more vulnerable to sin. When time dissipates the sharpness of their guilty feelings, the allure of the sin becomes stronger for those who have been weakened by shame. Fear motivation (by this I mean pressuring people with threats that God will exact his pound of flesh when he has been crossed) ultimately makes us bitter toward God rather than loving of him and his will.

What is more productive and power-instilling than shame or fear is the approach of the apostle. He reminds God's people that they are "dearly loved children." In the knowledge of that love provided by Christ's blood rather than their performance, power for obedience springs. Such power will be needed because of the nature of the command that immediately follows.

Live as the Child of God (5:2)

In savoring their new identity the Ephesians are reminded that they are to live not only as children of God, but also to live as the Child of God. Held before us and the Ephesians is the example of Jesus Christ. We are told to "live a life of love, just as Christ loved us and gave himself up for us as a fragrant offering and sacrifice to God" (Eph. 5:2).[5] Imitating God means imitating his Son, and that means doing whatever is required to make our lives a fragrant offering and sacrifice to God. The smell of Jesus, the fragrance of the Savior that we are to have waft from our lives, also includes offering and sacrifice.

The image that the apostle is bringing to mind, of course, is that of the Old Testament sacrifices where the people brought an offering to God and sacrificed it upon the altar so that its fiery consumption would cause the odor of a sweet sacrifice to God.[6] There is much in the image that is pleasant. But

5. The Greek phrase (translated "live a life of love") literally commands that the Christian "walk in love" (*peripateite en agapē*). As remarked earlier (see notes on Eph. 2:10 and Eph. 4:1), Paul frequently enjoins the command to "walk" as a metaphor for daily Christian living (Eph. 4:1, 17; 5:2, 8, 15; cf. 2:2, 10).

6. The allusion to the Old Testament sacrificial system is apparent not only in the terms "sacrifice" and "offering," but especially in the mention of a "fragrant offering" (better rendered a "pleasing aroma"), which in the Old Testament repeatedly refers to a variety of sacrifices made to the Lord (e.g., Gen. 8:21; Ex.

it also reminds us that the fragrance from an altar does not come without some giving of self (an offering) and some dying of another (a sacrifice). There is no life of love without a degree of giving and dying.

As intimidating as that sounds, it may also be a source of comfort to us. In a world where we are tempted to advertise the earthly benefits of the faith, the Scriptures remind us of the theology of the cross. All who would be like Jesus must offer and sacrifice themselves. Luther taught that if we are truly to imitate Christ, then we must also in some measure suffer for the sins of others. The Reformer did not mean that we can atone for others' sin, but we do suffer for their sake as we endure suffering so that they might know him.

In a world full of people caught up in sinful practices and attitudes, living like Jesus for the sake of others will involve both the giving of ourselves and the dying of self. Why is this a comfort? Because it allows me to confess that there is nothing unusual or odd in me when the purity and integrity to which God calls me also hurt me. Christian young men and women are too often ill-prepared for battle and weakened in spirit by the sense that they should not have to struggle much with the temptations of physical lust and personal gain. Such persons are tempted to think that if they were really holy, mature, and Christian, then it would not be difficult or painful to please God. But what is fragrant to God involves a giving *and* a dying of self—there is going to be some pain. If there were no pain involved, there would be no sacrifice. The fact that your obedience involves pain and struggle does not necessarily mean that God is displeased with you or that you are less spiritual than others. In fact, without the pain of giving and sacrifice there could be no fragrant offering to God. What enables us to bear and offer this pain is savoring our identity as children of God, and remembering that we are called to live as the Child of God who offered and sacrificed himself for us.

Savor Your Purity (5:3–4)

We should savor the privilege of being children of God who are called to live as the Child of God. But what we savor does not always characterize our lives. Purity is a struggle, so Paul continues his instructions by telling us how to experience the purity our heart desires.

29:18, 25, 41; and many times in Leviticus and Numbers). Paul elsewhere employs the idea of a sacrificial fragrant offering in Philippians 4:18 (there in regard to the gift from the Philippians sent to Paul).

Starve Impurity (5:3)

We can experience purity only by denying ourselves impurity. This means that we must deal radically with sins we are tempted to excuse such as immorality and greed. For such the apostle urges a starvation diet.

Paul first commands us not to indulge any *immorality* (Eph. 5:3–4). It would not particularly surprise us if the apostle would simply say, "Do not allow immoral activity among you." But instead he says, "But among you there must not be even a hint of sexual immorality, or of any kind of impurity"—literally, "but fornication (*porneia*) and all kinds of uncleanness . . . let it not even be named among you" (cf. Eph. 5:12).[7] Not merely is impurity not to enter the Christian's life and the Christian community, but it is not even to be mentioned in our speech. And lest we question what that means, the apostle continues, "Nor should there be obscenity, foolish talk, or coarse joking" (Eph. 5:4).[8]

Paul's instruction to avoid even small compromises should teach us much about how sin progresses and how it can be overcome. When I counsel others regarding sexual sin, I say God rarely flips a switch in us and turns off sexual lust or inappropriate attractions. When powerful, destructive lust forms in our lives, it is most often like a flame on a gas stove that grows more intense the more it is fed fuel. The way that the lust becomes manageable is not with the presumption that God will simply take lust away (though that is in

7. The Greek word for "sexual immorality" or "fornication" (*porneia*) generally designates any immoral sexual intercourse (including adultery, prostitution, and any other form of sex outside of marriage); in some contexts its meaning may extend to incestuous marriages. Paul repeatedly rebukes all such sexual immorality (e.g., 1 Cor. 5:1; 6:13, 18; 7:2; 2 Cor. 12:21; Gal. 5:19; Col. 3:5; 1 Thess. 4:3), and he frequently connects sexual immorality with "impurity" (2 Cor. 12:21; Col. 3:5; cf. 1 Thess. 4:3–7). Both sexual immorality and impurity are elsewhere listed in sequence as works of the flesh (Gal. 5:19). The Septuagint employs the Greek for "impurity" (*akatharsia*) to refer to any ritual uncleanness (including that produced by sexual sin; e.g., Lev. 20:21; Hos. 2:10); furthermore, Paul elsewhere can refer to "impurity" broadly (1 Thess. 2:3), and some scholars argue that in this verse "any kind of" (*pasa*) impurity includes more than sexual sin. However, the connection with sexual immorality in this context (and frequently elsewhere in Paul) indicates that the term "impurity" especially designates sexual sin here (cf. also Rom. 1:24).

8. These three Greek terms for such vulgar speech are found only here in the New Testament and Septuagint. The first emphasizes any shameful obscenity (likely including both talk and gesture), the second designates foolishness in word, and the third implies a comical risqué wit. The fact that the third item (risqué wit) could be viewed with both positive and (less often) negative nuances by pagan Greek authors shows that Paul calls Christians to be more careful in their speech than even good Greek society might demand. Note that Paul emphasizes their Christian position as saints ("because these are improper for God's holy people"). Those who are already deemed "holy" are to act in keeping with their position in Christ (see further below).

his power). We should remember that God made us as sexual beings who should long for one another within the bonds of marriage—we are made to be "lusty" creatures. What turns down the intensity of improper lust is starving it of improper fuel. Indulging sexual impurities of speech, thought, and entertainment will feed the power of sin in our lives.

The ways that impurity leads to improper lust are not new or more acceptable because they suddenly seem less avoidable. Paul writes to Ephesians whose common markets and main streets were no less full of immorality than our own. Greco-Roman gods were celebrated for sexual conquests, and there is no perversion present today that was not accepted in some form in that ancient world.[9] We may think of ours as an oversexualized culture, but the Ephesians' church was not less tempted.

The apostle knew how the flames of desire could burn out of control among God's people, and so he urges them to starve the flames by denying the desires their fuel. He says that there must not even be a hint of immorality among God's people. What is immoral is not even to be mentioned. Not only does he forbid what is filthy—we expect that—but also what is foolish or unprofitable (not serving our best interests or God's glory). But what if it's humorous—not harmful, just a jest? The apostle of God says that even if the coarse reference is funny, it is not to be mentioned.

Paul says all forms of impurity "are out of place" among God's people—his temple (Eph. 5:4). Here Paul echoes the ethic of the writer of Proverbs who urges his son not to walk on the path of the wicked and not even to go near it but to turn from it and walk the other direction (Prov. 4:14–15). Prophets and apostles know that the tolerance of any sin leads to greater sin, and therefore it must be starved of all that would feed its indulgence.

Paul's words should encourage us that we are not strange if we struggle with impurity; giving and dying of self have always been needed to overcome it. Some of that giving and dying will involve starving the flames of lust by identifying its sources in our life, sources that may be culturally accepted and even endorsed by fellow Christians.

We must confess what is not right for our heart, and give it no place in our life. We may need to seek the counsel of a confidential mentor or group of

9. While not every Greco-Roman cult involved sexual promiscuity, at least some of the mystery cults did so. Sexual images were common in Greco-Roman art, and Greco-Roman literature abounded with stories of sexual intrigues.

friends to develop accountability and honest assessment of habits. And if we are with Christian brothers and sisters whose movie, music, and television habits have been unexamined, we may need to stir up the love and courage to question whether the Bible or the culture is guiding their lives. We should be willing to be thought odd for the sake of Christ, for if we cannot stand for our convictions among Christians, then it is unlikely that we can be a witness in the world.

The apostle continues to describe our sin-starvation diet by commanding us not to indulge *greed* (Eph. 5:3, 5). This is the second category of sin that Paul forbids in this passage. They seem an unlikely duo: lust and greed. Why link them? Some explain that in New Testament usage the word for greed here may be laden with sexual connotation, as in being greedy for another person's body or beauty.[10] That dimension of greed is certainly included in this text. But the separate listing of the sin of greed seems to indicate that Paul's reach may also be broader, as though he wants us to recognize the commonalities of sexual lust and material greed. In essence, both are the consequence of concluding that what God provides is not enough. When either controls us, we conclude that God's provision for our lives is inadequate. Whether we pursue a lust for persons or things, we profess that his supply is insufficient and deny his lordship over that aspect of our lives. Thus Paul says that all impurity and greed are idolatry (Eph. 5:5). Yet such idolatry, which we would wish to deny is true of us, is startlingly present among us.

Believers wrestle with the idolatry of greed when they envy a person who has a nicer car and apartment; a pastor may wrestle with similar idolatry when he sees the more luxurious lives of laypersons in his church, or other ministers in larger or more affluent churches. The influence of greed (in its sexual and material forms) even on church leaders was made plain in a conference workbook recently provided by the *Embers to a Flame* ministry. Listed as the top two reasons that ministers leave their pulpits were sexual and financial pressures. Greed of all kinds—sexual and material—is a destructive force of great power. A telltale sign of such idolatry is growing

10. Paul earlier connected impurity with greed (Eph. 4:19); and the terms for sexual immorality, impurity, and greed appear together again with "passion" and "evil desire" in Colossians 3:5. As here in Ephesians 5:3 so also in Colossians 3:5 he identifies the trait of greed with "idolatry." The relative pronoun ("*which* is idolatry") in both Ephesians 5:5 and Colossians 3:5 is singular, probably pointing most directly to "greed," but not excluding the thought that immorality and impurity are also a forsaking of God and thus constitute idolatrous acts.

discontent with God's provision for our lives. When we borrow, spend, or pout for more than we have, often we are bowing to the idol of greed. And by listing greed in the list of sins we must starve, Paul urges contentment with God's provision.

Feed Praise (5:4)

Throughout this portion of Ephesians, the apostle confronts sin with its substitute. Christians are exhorted not to lie but to tell the truth (Eph. 4:25), not to steal but to work (Eph. 4:28), not to express bitterness but rather kindness (Eph. 4:31–32). That pattern now continues as Paul exhorts believers not to speak what is filthy, foolish, or coarse, but rather to offer thanksgiving (Eph. 5:4).

Why is thanksgiving the proper substitute for impurity? Because it is the replacement of idol worship with worship of God. I have a pastor friend who has a special ministry to brothers and sisters struggling with various addictions. He has a novel approach to helping Christians sense the nature of their sin. He has them study the Old Testament temple worship. What did such worship involve that would prompt him to recommend its study? It involved coming away from the rest of the world to a place of solitude, taking delight in a sacred place to which one could return again and again, and elevating the appreciation of divine faithfulness above earthly priorities. My pastor friend says that study of the temple ultimately helps Christians see their addiction for the idolatry it truly is—worshiping in the temple of a foreign god whose promises are empty. That is why Paul so insightfully calls the pursuits of lust and greed "idolatry," and seeks to counter it with thanksgiving for God's provision.

Simply seeing sin's deceptive nature will not in itself create the praise that Paul wants to substitute for idolatry. In order for Paul to elicit the thanksgiving that he believes will provide spiritual power for the Ephesians, he must also make clear the nature of God's provision. To do so, Paul calls sin idolatry (Eph. 5:5), and he calls the people saints (Eph. 5:3). That second identifying term seems improbable, yet it is the believer's ultimate power. At the beginning of Paul's discussion of why lust and greed are improper (Eph. 5:3) and out of place (Eph. 5:4), he makes sure we know for whom such things are wrong. We are to rid ourselves of all forms of impurity because "these [things] are improper for God's holy people" (Eph. 5:3b). There it is again:

the indicative. Before discussing impure actions that make us ashamed, Paul reminds us of God's prior actions that make us holy. Not only are we God's children, we are saints, holy people (*hagioi*).

Paul is not talking to those who have perfect lives. If the Ephesians were perfect, there would be no reason to write to them of their idolatries of lust and greed. Yet Paul addresses these people, among whom great sin must be present, as holy ones. They are not holy by their actions, but by God's forgiveness in Christ—the root concept motivating all imperatives in this passage. Praise to God—not simply lip service or religious ritual but profound gratitude and love for what Christ has done—fills the heart that knows God's love. And the heart that is filled with a responsive love for God has no place for idolatry. When we fully understand the love that makes us holy, then we live as God has already reckoned us to be.

Paul teaches us to provide power over sin by proclaiming the holy status of those who are in Christ Jesus. When I know that I am not made for sin, that I am a fundamentally different creature in Christ Jesus—still sinful but reckoned holy so that no sin will satisfy me or have ultimate power over me—then I am filled with thanksgiving. And because God inhabits the praise of his people, when we are filled with his praise, we are filled with his power.

Savor Your Security (5:5–7)

Though we gain strength for the Christian life by savoring our purity and savoring our identity, we ultimately must face the dangers of sin. If we do not recognize the danger, then we are not prepared to live the holy lives God desires. Thus the final dimension of Paul's exhortation against impurity is warning! But as he warns, he further strengthens us by enabling us to savor our security.

Heed the Warnings (5:5–6)

We feel more secure when we know that we will be clearly warned of danger. Paul provides such warnings in telling us both what is denied idolaters and what is promised them.

What is denied idolaters: inheritance. Paul says that "no immoral, impure or greedy person . . . has any inheritance in the kingdom of Christ and of

God" (Eph. 5:5).[11] In other words, you may think that you will gain by pursuing your lusts and your greed but, in fact, you will lose everything. Certainly Paul is thinking of the kingdom of God in primarily eschatological terms, but the knowledge that Christ is building his kingdom now (Eph. 1:23) makes us mindful that such pursuits will make our lives empty now also. This is made even more clear in the wording of the next verse of this passage about what is inherited as a consequence of these idolatries.

What is assured idolaters: wrath. Paul does not only warn about the denial of an inheritance, but also about what is inherited by those whose lives are idolatrous pursuits of lust and greed. "Let no one deceive you with empty [i.e., void of truth] words, for because of such things [i.e., these vices] God's wrath comes on those who are disobedient" (Eph. 5:6).[12] The word "comes" is in the present tense. While Paul could have isolated the ultimate consequences of sin in the eschaton, he includes the present.[13] Aspects of God's wrath come against sin now. This does not mean that the sinful now will face all the consequences of their idolatry, but the emptiness of such pursuits already denies the joy and fulfillment of a life with God.

What better letter could there be for our age to heed? Consider what Paul has written about immorality and greed in the light of the sins of this age. We live in a culture immersed in immorality and greed. Spiritual warning signals blare from many directions, but, in apparent sensory overload, we

11. A similar warning is found in 1 Corinthians 6:9–10 (cf. Gal. 5:19–21; Rev. 21:8). As is rightly emphasized in the NIV translation, the order "sexual immorality, impurity, and greed" in verse 3 is paralleled in the kinds of people who practice these acts in verse 5 ("immoral, impure or greedy person"); and the stems of these parallel terms are identical in Greek. Paul emphatically introduces this sentence with an unusual syntactical combination of two different verbs for "knowing"—rendered in the NIV "of this you can be sure." The language here of the "kingdom of God," which is repeatedly employed by Jesus himself, is also frequently found in Paul (Rom. 14:17; 1 Cor. 4:20; 6:9–10; 15:24, 50; Gal. 5:21; Col. 4:11; 1 Thess. 2:12; 2 Thess. 1:5), while the idea of the "kingdom of Christ" is less often mentioned (Col. 1:13; 2 Tim. 4:1, 18; cf. 1 Cor. 15:24 where it may focus on Jesus' current reign). On "inheritance" see comments on Ephesians 1:14.

12. The mention of "wrath" and of the "sons of disobedience" reminds the readers of the danger of their pre-Christian state (Eph. 2:3). See also Colossians 3:6, which similarly references God's wrathful judgment while warning Christians to reject pagan sin (Col. 3:5–9; cf. Rom. 1:18).

13. An eschatological connection is clear in the context (Eph. 5:5), and is expected due to the frequent use in the New Testament of "comes" (*erchomai*) in the futuristic present to indicate coming eschatological judgment. However, the inaugurated eschatology of Paul reminds us that the end times, and the threat of judgment, are already present with the death and resurrection of the Messiah, even if they await consummation in the Messiah's return.

grow more blind and deaf to the seriousness, pervasiveness, and destructiveness of our indulgences.

In an airport recently I watched as a woman walked down a concourse toward a passenger transport cart approaching from the opposite direction. The cart had a flashing light, a loud beeper warning of its approach, and was full of people, yet the woman kept walking on a direct collision course. Finally, the driver slammed on the brakes and, still, the woman walked into the cart. She was not blind, or deaf, or deranged. I learned from others that drivers of these carts are trained to deal with persons such as this woman. In a busy airport, the senses of such persons can become so overloaded by all the warnings and alarms that the signals are no longer processed in the brain. Evidence grows that we are increasingly such people. The many reports about the consequences of sexual sin and materialistic greed in our culture are shouting their warnings to us. Yet, at the same time, we continue to expose ourselves and our children to the sinful entertainments and materialistic priorities with fewer and fewer pangs of conscience.

We may tell ourselves and each other that such things do not really matter, that we are unaffected, that we have an adequate worldview to deal with such things, and that mature Christians—grace-filled and culturally engaged—will not be bothered. To such explanations Paul responds, "Let no one deceive you with empty words, for because of such things God's wrath comes" (Eph. 5:6). Paul is not here threatening that God will abandon or destroy his children (see discussion of Eph. 5:7 below), but he is pointing to the wrath that will come upon those whose ultimate choice is idolatry and using their punishment as an object lesson to warn his children to steer clear of sin. Even if its consequences are not ultimate for the child of God, his discipline of idolatrous pursuits should be sufficient to turn us from evil.

Expose the Darkness (5:11)

What many will now want (and fear), in light of Paul's warnings, is some standard measurement of the amount of skin, the number or kind of profanities, or the plot categories that will make it clear which entertainments are acceptable and which unacceptable. We may also want to know the maximum amount of personal spending that is allowed before it qualifies as greed. Such rules for all times and places, of course, cannot be constructed. One reason is in this very passage. Down a few verses, we will see that Paul encourages these same Ephesians, "Have nothing to do with the fruitless deeds of darkness, but rather expose them" (Eph. 5:11). How simple life would be if Paul said only the first half of that verse: "Have nothing to do with . . ." Then we could simply resign and retreat from our culture. But Paul also says, "rather expose the fruitless deeds of darkness." How can you do that if you do not know something of the culture?

The requirements to heed the warning against sin and to expose the darkness in which it thrives, put every Christian in the so-called Puritan dilemma of needing to be "in the world but not of it." Seeking to engage, rebuke, and redeem our culture remains a battle of conscience and responsibility. The battle will test us until Christ returns. But we cannot achieve any measure of victory in the battle if we simply abandon biblical instruction. Sociologist Alan Wolfe in *The Transformation of American Religion* writes, "Christians and Jews . . . have ignored doctrines, reinvented traditions, switched denominations, redefined morality, and translated their obligation to witness into a lifestyle."[14] As a result he concludes that America is pervasively religious but that religion is neither reshaping the culture nor providing any danger warnings to its adherents.

Paul cautions instead that there can be no true morality without piety, no real witness without purity, no significant revival of the soul when there is regular compromise of the heart. The kingdom does not progress where idolatries of lust and greed predominate. We have to decide, as one writer puts it, whether we will "practice the culture" or "practice the faith." Deciding how to engage in the battle for our hearts, our culture, and our children will not be easy, but we have an authority and the witness of the Spirit in our hearts. Paul says that in order to expose the darkness, we will need to give of ourselves and die to self, but such is the nature of war. Our identity as well as God's warning motivates us to pursue holiness, but the warning will not accomplish its purpose if we do not fully understand its context. Even the warning comes out of a heart of love.

Love God's Warning (5:7)

As we read these awful warnings against impurity, we must put ourselves in the place of the Ephesians. They are surrounded by sexual and material

14. Alan Wolfe, *The Transformation of American Religion* (New York: Free Press, 2003), 215.

temptations that have captured them in the past and tempt them in the present. Without question there are those in the churches who are continuing to struggle with these idolatries, or else there would be no reason for Paul to address such matters. But how are the Ephesians to deal with these warnings? They are to receive the warnings with love because they are expressed with care and measure.

What is the motive of God's warning? Remember that he is warning his children, his holy ones. He is warning those dear to him of their danger, but this is itself a sign of his love. If he did not love, he would not warn. Always we are to understand that an aspect of the grace of God is his zeal to warn us of the consequences of sin. Were he only a God of retribution, then he would relish the harm that comes to those who cross him. But here he speaks to those already bought by the blood of his Son, and who yet trample his blood underfoot by their sin, warning them to flee from the consequences of their sin. The motive for such a warning to such people as these can only be love.

The love is underscored by the careful measurement of the warning. What is its extent? The warning never extends to rejection. Consider carefully the final words of this passage. Paul warns the Ephesians that God's wrath comes upon idolaters and says, "Therefore do not be partners with them." Note the careful use of the third person "them." Paul does not say, "Therefore disinheritance and eternal wrath will come upon *you*." He clearly warns that idolaters will experience wrath, and so he warns the believers to stay away from—not partner with—them and their practices.[15] But even though the Ephesians surely have sin in their lives, the apostle does not say, "You are one of them."

Paul spares the believers the greatest consequence of sin, which is being identified by it. Paul never makes idolatry the identity of the believers. They remain holy ones who are the children of God. The words echo those from John's epistle: "How great is the love the Father has lavished on us, that we should be called children of God! And that is what we are!" (1 John 3:1). In

15. In 1 Corinthians 5:9–13 Paul indicates that those who claim to be brothers, yet who flagrantly and habitually practice immorality, ought to be expelled from the congregation. The parallels in the broader context of 1 Corinthians (especially 6:9–10) with this section of Ephesians may indicate that Paul is also warning the Ephesian congregation against partnering with such people. Note that in 1 Corinthians 5:9–10, Paul carefully does not say that one should therefore flee from the world; rather the goal is to keep Christians from sharing as participants in sinful activities.

a similar way Paul speaks here to the Ephesians as if to say, "Behold what manner of love the Father has lavished upon you that you should be God's children, his holy ones. That is what you are."

In Flannery O'Connor's short story "A Temple of the Holy Spirit," an adolescent girl is visited by two older teenage cousins who want to introduce her to more sophisticated and adult interests. At one point the girl overhears her older cousins mock a nun who has suggested a formula to help young women stop the advances of young men. Sister Perpetua advises that the way to fend off a young man in the back of a car is to say, "Stop, sir! I am a Temple of the Holy Ghost!" The older cousins find this advice hilarious. The younger girl, however, is deeply moved. The news that she is the dwelling place of God fills her with a sense of awe. She savors what it means to be so special to God that he would give her such a gift, and the knowledge of being so treasured by God makes her desire to live her life in thanksgiving to him. The adult sophistications that were so appealing still have their allure, but now she knows that they are out of place for one made to be the holy dwelling of God.

Paul has said to these Ephesians already that they are a temple of God (Eph. 2:21), and now he says that they are his children, his holy ones (Eph. 5:1, 3). This is the knowledge that is to fill them with praise and make out of place the impurities and idolatries of the world. They are no longer made in such a way that these things of the world can bring satisfaction; these things will, in fact, bring greater pain. These same dynamics will occur in our lives, so Paul seeks to overwhelm us with the savor of our identity, the blessings of purity, and the warnings of grace. We are to imitate God because we are his children. Nothing else will do any more; nothing else will satisfy. Paul tells us that as an odor of a sweet savor to God, we should be what we are. We are his children and we are saints. So we should live that way!

17

The Light Bearers

Ephesians 5:8–21

For you were once darkness, but now you are light in the Lord. Live as children of light (for the fruit of the light consists in all goodness, righteousness and truth) and find out what pleases the Lord.
(Eph. 5:8–10)

Staring up into the darkness of a star-studded sky, my friend John Dozier strained to see the goose he had heard honking overhead. A full moon rising over a ridge of the Colorado Rockies gave the sky a vanilla glow. John's eyes adjusted to the ambient light, and he suddenly realized there was not just one goose overhead, but thousands. Scores of flocks were filling the sky from mountain to horizon. One strand after another of migrating birds threaded through the starry night. And in the strands closest to him, John was able to make out the white underbelly of each bird, so that the flocks of birds in V-formations were like strings of lights outlining Christmas trees flying across the sky.

The beauty and wonder of the sight were a gift of the Creator to John, causing him to marvel that God could make these ordinary creatures bear such dramatic witness to the glory of their maker. But it was not until years later that John wrote of the greater wonder that the event brought to his mind and heart. He realized that he had been able to see each goose because its breast was reflecting light off the snow, which was reflecting light off the moon, which was reflecting the light of the sun on the other side of the earth millions of miles away. The light from each creature that provided such beauty and wonder was not from the goose but was derived from a vastly distant sun sharing its glory at the will of the heavenly Father.

The glorious light of the Son in creatures like us is Paul's theme in this portion of Ephesians. The message is all the more important when we recognize how dark must have been the hearts of the Ephesians at this stage in Paul's letter. He has just finished admonishing these early believers with two rounds of challenges regarding what they do and say and think. Then he tops off this instruction with a remarkably frank warning against sexual sin, telling the Ephesians in their pagan culture that among the believers there must not be even a hint of sexual immorality (Eph. 5:3). We can imagine how those listening either hung their heads in remorse or shook their heads in resistance to the apostle's apparent lack of cultural realism. "Not even a 'hint' of sexual immorality?" they must have questioned. "Then how is anyone supposed to live?" We recognize these attitudes; shame and resistance are the natural responses to strong spiritual challenge in every age, including our own. Either because of what we wish we had not done, or wish to continue to do, we conclude, "No one can be what God requires; no one can reflect his glory. It's not possible. It's not realistic. There is no hope." Paul replies to such dark reasoning by telling the Ephesians there is a ray of hope: "For you were once darkness, but now you are light in the Lord."[1]

Reflect the Light of the Son (5:8–17)

Paul tells the Ephesians to live as children of light (Eph. 5:8b). The terminology intentionally plays off the "darkness" themes of earlier passages. There Paul speaks of the darkness of a pagan existence. Now he wants to remind the saints of their privileges and responsibilities because they worship a God who is and provides light. Humble gratitude beacons behind the choice of terms. These believers are not the light; they are the

1. The word "for" (*gar* in Greek) links verses 7 and 8. The connection here is strong enough that some Greek editions treat verse 8 as a continuation of the preceding sentence.

children of light. Their lives are to be reflections of a greater light in what they express and in what they expose.

Express Light (5:8–10)

Paul expects the Ephesians to express the light of their God in what they do and in whom they please.

What the children of light are to do is to bear God's fruit. The apostle says, "Live as children of light (for the fruit of the light consists in all goodness, righteousness and truth)" (Eph. 5:8b–9). This is a continuation of the earlier theme that, as Gentiles, these Ephesian believers were "darkened in their understanding" (Eph. 4:18) and given over to "sensuality" and "every kind of impurity" (Eph. 4:19).[2] In contrast, those not darkened in understanding but "made new in the attitude of [their] minds" and "created to be like God in true righteousness and holiness" (4:23–24), should bear fruit in keeping with their identity.[3] Paul here summarizes the fruit that he has been describing over the last several paragraphs: *goodness* (i.e., good-heartedness toward others in contrast to malice, Eph. 4:26–27, 29–32); *righteousness* (i.e., honoring God's standards especially as in living a separated life as opposed to indulging the culture's sensuality and selfishness, Eph. 4:19; 5:3–5; 6:14), and *truth* (i.e., displaying integrity, dealing honestly, and speaking truthfully, as opposed to old habits of lying and deceit, Eph. 4:25; 6:14).[4]

2. Believers must also battle the evil forces of this dark world (Eph. 6:12). As in other epistles Paul refers to the darkness that captivates the unbeliever (Rom. 1:21; 2 Cor. 6:14; Col. 1:13; cf. Acts 26:18, 23) and the need for believers to flee from that darkness (Rom. 13:12; 2 Cor. 6:14; 1 Thess. 5:4–11). God is the one who exposes the darkness of men's hearts through his light (1 Cor. 4:5), and thus his is a kingdom of light (Col. 1:12). There are Old Testament roots to such language (e.g., Prov. 2:13) especially in Isaiah (e.g., Isa. 2:5; 5:20; 10:17; 42:16; 50:10; 60:1–3); and the metaphor of darkness and light was also known in Second Temple Jewish literature (e.g., Sir. 50:9; Wis. 5:6; 7:26; 18:4; and especially in the War Scroll [1QM]; cf. perhaps Rom. 2:19). Earlier above it was noted that Jesus himself employed language of light and dark (e.g., Matt. 5:14–16; 6:23; Luke 11:34–36; John 8:12; 12:35–36, 46; cf. John 3:19–21).

3. Their present identity in verse 8 is emphasized by "now" (cf. Eph. 2:2; 3:5, 10), and contrasted with their former pagan lives ("once" or *pote* in the Greek text; cf. Eph. 2:2–3, 11, 13). Thus before salvation all people were "objects [literally 'children'] of wrath" (Eph. 2:3), but now in Christ those who are saved are "dearly loved children" (Eph. 5:1) and "children of light" (5:8).

4. Paul frequently employs metaphors about fruit (e.g., Phil. 1:11), most notably in his discussion of the "fruit of the Spirit" (Gal. 5:22–23), which overlaps significantly with his list of Christian traits here in Ephesians. Some early manuscripts of Ephesians actually read "fruit of the Spirit" in 5:9 (likely due to scribal assimilation to Gal. 5:22), but "fruit of the light" is more likely original, found with wider early testimony among the manuscripts and fitting the context better.

Living as children of light is determined not only by what we do, but also by whom we please. Paul says, "Live as children of light . . . and find out what pleases God" (Eph. 5:8c, 10).[5] With this brief wording the apostle reminds us that living as a child of light is a matter of the motive of the heart as well as the works of the hands. Not only are we to do what God commands for fruitfulness, we are to do so out of a desire to please him. We should delight in his delight. Mere outward conformity to the law is not what God requires. The person who does what God says with a resentful heart and begrudging obedience does not bear the mark of the true child of light. The heart renewed by the Spirit desires to please God, is anxious to find out what he desires, and is motivated by the sense of bringing God pleasure.[6]

It is almost impossible for me to think of being motivated to bring God pleasure without thinking of the words of the devout athlete Eric Liddell, who was made famous in the movie *Chariots of Fire*. Why did he strive to run so fast and so well? He said, "God made me fast, and when I run, I feel his pleasure." But the record of one who has performed splendidly from the desire to please God likely does not occupy the mind of the apostle. He writes to Ephesians of multiple and shameful backgrounds in a corrupt and profane culture who are still struggling to live as children of light. Why does he tell them to "find out" (i.e., prove, as in testing a metal) what pleases God?[7] The apostle desires that even in their weakness and frailty the Ephesians will know they *can* please God.

Some time ago in a southeastern town a man told me of a grandchild he and his wife had watched during working hours for the first three years of the child's life. A daughter's difficulties had made them the caretakers while she worked. The daughter and her husband ultimately got back on their feet through a job that opened in California, causing them to move there. Some time later neighbors of the grandparents were vacationing in California and

5. Again here the command to "live" (Eph. 5:8) translates the Greek expression to "walk" as children of light (note comments on *parapateite* in Eph. 5:2).

6. Paul in several important places speaks of the Christian goal of pleasing God (Rom. 12:1–2; 2 Cor. 5:9; 1 Thess. 4:1; cf. Rom. 14:18; Gal. 1:10; Phil. 4:18; Col. 1:10; 3:20).

7. This use of the verb for "finding out" (*dokimazō*, "to test, examine, discern") in Ephesians 5:10 echoes Romans 12:2, where Christians are likewise commended to *test* what is God's good, *pleasing*, and perfect will (cf. Phil. 1:10; 1 Thess. 5:21; also note 2 Cor. 13:5 and Gal. 6:4 where Christians are to examine themselves). Here the verb *dokimazontes* is a participle, adverbially explaining what it looks like when Christians "live" (i.e., "walk" in 5:8) as children of light, intently pursuing that which pleases God (thus the participle is best understood as a participle of result, or possibly of manner or means).

happened upon the daughter and her son in a large discount store. The grandson was shy, but fished in his jeans pocket for a while before pulling out a little mass of lint. "Would you give this to my Grandma?" he asked. The neighbor took the lint, but discarded it before telling the grandmother back home about the "silly gift." The grandmother said, "I wish you had not thrown it away. I would have been so pleased to get it because it was all that he had to give me." When he matures and knows how much his Grandma would have appreciated a gift as humble as lint given from a heart of love, consider how much more this child will want to please her.

When we know that our meager offerings to God—the little thoughts, words, and acts of righteousness that are all that we have to give—bring him pleasure despite their inadequacies and our shame, we want to bring him better gifts. The desire to please One so delightfully pleased with us becomes our passion and our power, our highest and strongest motivation. We want to keep finding out what pleases him—to express light for his sake.

Expose Darkness (5:11–17)

Being children of light means not only that we express light, but also that we expose darkness. The apostle says, "Have nothing to do with the fruitless deeds of darkness, but rather expose them" (Eph. 5:11).[8] We must consider these words in light of what has preceded. In an interesting botanical lesson we have the contrast of what light and darkness produce. Light produces fruit that pleases God (Eph. 5:9); but darkness, a denial of the sun (such as when a tarp is left on a lawn), is fruitless, yielding nonproducing (literally barren, or sterile) deeds (Eph. 5:11). Though sin may be pleasant for a season, it ultimately fails to produce the harvest of fulfillment that it promises—it is fruitless.

The puzzle of the passage, of course, is not that sin is fruitless but that we are told both to "expose" it and to "have nothing to do with" it. This instruction seems something akin to telling your child to clean up the garage but don't touch the dirt. One command seems at cross purposes with the other.

8. Although the verb *elenchō* ("expose") can indicate conviction, reproof, or correction, lexicons recognize a separate category of public exposure or demonstration with implications of censure (John 3:20; see W. Bauer, W. F. Arndt, F. W. Gingrich, and F. W. Danker, *A Greek-English Lexicon of the New Testament* [Chicago: University of Chicago Press, 2000], s.v.), and the "exposure" meaning seems particularly apt here due to the metaphors of light and darkness.

In our English translations, the exhortation "have nothing to do with the fruitless deeds of darkness" echoes the earlier command "among you there must not be even a hint of sexual immorality" (Eph. 5:3). This perception is strengthened by the words that follow: "For it is shameful even to mention what the disobedient do in secret" (Eph. 5:12). The apostle seems well aware that allowing the sinful and profane practices of the surrounding culture into the conversation of Christians will plant destructive images and considerations in the mind. These will ultimately desensitize us and make us accept what we should abhor, tolerate what tempts, or actually desire what displeases God. When we are so familiar with the profane that it no longer offends and we have forgotten how to blush because of it, then we are in grave spiritual danger. The apostle's words remind us again to beware of giving sin—even sin of which we disapprove—entry points in our lives through too little awareness of how even its mention (in speech, entertainments, jesting, and discussion) actually gives it a place to grow in our hearts.

Still, the problem remains: how do we have nothing to do with dark deeds, not even making mention of them, and still expose them? When Graham Waterhouse, a young missionary, explained to a group in my home that she was planning to go to Thailand to take the gospel to women in the red-light district of Bangkok, the gasps were audible. I could not help but remember the difficulties that Amy Carmichael had in raising support for her ministry of exposing temple prostitution of children in India because of the Victorian sensibilities that made it impolite for her to mention the horror that thousands of children faced. How can we have nothing to do with the fruitless deeds of darkness and yet expose them?

1. *Consider context.* First, we must consider the context. The words "have nothing to do with" are from a Greek term (*synkoinōneō*) that means partnership or partaking together (Eph. 5:11). You are not to take part in the darkness, that is, not to partake of it. The words come in the context of Paul warning against what will involve Christians in evil, but even he makes mention of sensuality, every kind of impurity and lust (Eph. 4:19). The warning to us is to consider whether our exposure to such matters comes as a consequence of trying to expose them or to enjoy them. The temptation for Christians in exposing darkness is to forget the exposure. We talk about redeeming the culture, but on the journey we can simply join in with the

rest of the culture. Its entertainments, speech, and habits become our own, and we blithely talk about them in our contexts without even realizing they have no place in the life of the children of light (Eph. 4:27). Perhaps the best test is whether we are bold enough to call the darkness truly dark and expose it as evil.

2. *Consider the motive.* Secondly, we must consider the motive of our mentioning the matter. Whether our actions lead us to enjoy or to expose the darkness leads to a question of motive. Here the essential question has already been put before us by Paul. Are we trying to "find out what pleases the Lord" (Eph. 5:10)? Is our motive to figure out what will make us more holy and Christ's name more hallowed in this world? Such questions cause us to examine the deep recesses of our heart for true answers. These questions must consistently be asked and honestly answered: Are we pleasing God or self?

3. *Consider the instruments.* Thirdly, we must consider the instruments of the exposure. What will help us answer the question of whether or not our actions are truly devoted to exposing the darkness? We must determine what instruments we are using and should be using to expose the darkness. And what exposes darkness, according to the apostle? He says, "But everything exposed by the light becomes visible, for it is light that makes everything visible" (Eph. 5:13–14a).[9] What composes the light that is the instrument of exposure? Already we have been told that "the fruit of the light consists in all goodness, righteousness and truth" (Eph. 5:9). The words remind us that darkness is best exposed by light rather than more darkness.

Even in Christian circles there will be those that beckon us to the darkness, claiming that we will there better learn the darkness that we are to expose. Paul states the opposite, making it clear that the radiance of holiness will make the fruitlessness of evil more apparent. In essence, he claims that it is better to shine a light in a closet than to stumble around in the darkness so

9. The phrase "by the light" can in Greek modify either "becomes visible" ("be made manifest"; so KJV) or "exposed" (so NIV, RSV, NASB, ESV). The sense of the passage changes little with this decision. The more complex interpretive issue concerns whether the deeds exposed by the light are those of unbelievers or Christians. It appears that the focus is particularly on the deeds done by unbelievers (connecting this with 5:11–12 and 5:5–7), although Christ's light ultimately is to shine on all.

that you may know its dimensions. A faithful marriage, a chaste life, a frugal lifestyle, and gracious speech will do far more to expose the fruitless deeds of evil than partnership with the culture in its futile pursuits of darkness. Paul said to the Romans, and to us, "I want you to be wise about what is good, and innocent [simple] about what is evil" (Rom. 16:19). It is important to know and to believe that in worldly innocence there can be more power for the exposure of evil than in becoming an expert in the matters of Satan.

Writer Marva Dawn tells how the pursuit of what is right exposes what is wrong:

> The playwright-president of the Czech Republic, Vaclav Havel, was once asked why the "Velvet Revolution" against the communists in the former Czechoslovakia was successfully nonviolent. Havel answered somewhat like this: "We had our parallel society. And in that parallel society we wrote our plays and sang our songs and read our poems until we knew the truth so well that we could go out to the streets of Prague and say, 'We don't believe your lies anymore'—and Communism *had* to fall."[10]

4. *Consider the danger.* Fourthly, we must consider our awareness of the danger. The necessity of understanding the power of evil provides the basis for Paul's final set of guidelines for how we are to have no partnership with darkness and yet expose it. He quotes a Christian hymn whose source is unknown, calling the church to an awakening from the dead (Eph. 5:14b): "Wake up, O sleeper, rise from the dead, and Christ will shine on you."[11] Today we talk about someone needing "a wake-up call" when one seems oblivious to imminent consequences. Paul issues this poetic wake-up call in the middle of warning the church about the compromises with darkness. Not only does he call the church to wake up, but also to "rise from the dead." The obvious reference to resurrection is a reminder that not to wake up to the dangers of the culture is to persist in what is fruitless and dead. But the

10. Marva Dawn, "Worship to Form a Missional Community," *Direction* 28.2 (Fall 1999): 141.

11. In 5:14 the formula *dio legei* ("this is why it is said") indicates that some traditional material is being introduced (see Eph. 4:8 where the Old Testament is cited; cf. James 4:6). The quotation does not conform precisely to any Old Testament passage, and thus it is usually considered by commentators to be a piece of Christian tradition from the time of Paul (i.e., a hymn). Nonetheless the wording of the hymn has strong connections to the thought of Isaiah (26:19; 60:1–2), and these Isaiah-like concepts (especially the juxtaposition of light and darkness in 60:1–2) undergird the overall context of Eph. 5:8–14 as well. Hence Paul's citation here of this early Christian hymn was particularly apt.

contrary is also clear; that is, if you wake up from your slumber, Christ will shine on you. Living as though there is real danger in darkness and staying away from it will make Christ's light shine more radiant. For the children of light there is no greater desire or blessing.

5. *Consider the aim.* Lastly, in order properly to balance separation from sin and exposure of it, we must consider if the aim of our actions is Christ's glory. If you are a child of light, your highest aim will be to make Christ shine—on us and before the world (Eph. 5:14d). The evidences of having this aim are that you will, first of all, live with care. With an awareness of the ever-present danger of darkness, the apostle warns, "Be very careful, then, how you live—not as unwise but as wise" (Eph. 5:15).[12] The children of light have awakened to the danger of the darkness and live accordingly. They do not pretend that there are no real dangers in their world or in their patterns of behavior. They are constant in giving rigorous, wise examination to their mind, heart, and behavior, knowing that the darkness can always encroach upon their lives. They live carefully for the sake of the light shining on them.[13]

They also live carefully—with a mission—for the sake of the light shining on others. Paul urges them to do this by "making the most of every opportunity, because the days are evil" (Eph. 5:16).[14] The words "making the most" or "redeeming" (KJV) come from a Greek term (*exagorazō*) meaning "to

12. This verse begins with the common Pauline admonition "be careful," or literally "watch out" (*blepete*; see 1 Cor. 3:10; 8:9; 10:12; Gal. 5:15; Phil. 3:2; Col. 2:8), here heightened in attentiveness via the adverb "carefully." Although this imperative can indicate the beginning of a new paragraph, the connections with the preceding instructions are significant, reminding us that Paul's depiction of Christian living in chapters 4–6 flows together effortlessly.

13. Once again "how you *live*" translates the Greek *parapateite* ("how you walk"; see verse 5:8 and the note on 5:2). Paul had previously prayed that the all-wise God (Eph. 3:10; Rom. 16:27) would dispense the wisdom of his Spirit to the Ephesian believers (Eph. 1:17; cf. Col. 1:9). The significance of wisdom in holy living is certainly demonstrated in the Old Testament (especially in Proverbs), and was emphasized in early Judaism. Wisdom is also important in Pauline theology (see esp. 1 Cor. 1–2), and Paul elsewhere admonishes Christians to wise action (e.g., Rom. 16:19; Col. 4:5).

14. The day is also called "evil" in the midst of the spiritual battle of Ephesians 6:13. This draws on the broader Pauline notion of Christians, who await the consummation of the kingdom at the return of Christ, living out that kingdom in this "present evil age" (Gal. 1:4; Eph. 2:2; 1 Cor. 2:6–8). In Colossians 4:5 Paul similarly calls believers to "make the most of every opportunity" (i.e. to "redeem the time"). Here the participial form of "redeem" (*exagorazomenoi*) adverbially informs the readers what wise living looks like (Eph. 5:15); it is a participle of result or possibly manner/means (cf. the note on 5:10).

recover from the power of another by paying a price." Knowing that the days are evil, we pay the price needed in our lives to have Christ shine on us and through us. We live with zeal for him, rather than for ourselves. The word chosen for "time" (*kairos*) is noteworthy, too, because it implies a specific moment rather than an extended period of time (*chronos*). In his own way, Paul says, "Seize the day; don't let this opportunity pass; take advantage of the moment God provides." Having been redeemed by his blood, we now redeem the time for him, making the most of every opportunity so that his name will shine in all the earth.

Those whose aim is the shining of Christ also live with understanding. With this care and with this mission as our priorities for Christ's sake, we are not foolish but seek to "understand what the Lord's will is" (Eph. 5:17—both a summary of the preceding verses and a launching pad for what follows).[15] Elsewhere the apostle writes, "It is God's will that you should be holy" (1 Thess. 4:3). God desires a holy people to reflect his holy light. The children of light so desire to be such a people that they give their minds to understanding what God's will is so that they will not live foolishly.

So that his children might reflect the light of the Son, the Lord has given us clear instructions regarding how we should live and think. These are necessary and vital aspects of the Christian life that the children of light must know. As ministers, counselors, missionaries, parents, and friends, you cannot hope to be a reflector of Christ's light if such matters are not part of your own instruction. In order to have the light of Christ shine into the lives of those we love and he loves, they also must know how to live and to think.

Paul does not stop explaining our need to live for the glory of Christ with these general principles for Christian living. What will follow in the book of Ephesians is much more practical instruction on marriage, the household, and Christian warfare. Still, something new and vital connects these general principles and practical instructions. It is the link that follows and can perhaps be explained through the observation of a friend of mine who is a

15. Understanding the Lord's will here reemphasizes the idea of "find[ing] out what pleases the Lord" (Eph. 5:10). Paul has already referred to his ministry as one granted him "by the will of God" (Eph. 1:1; cf. 1 Cor. 1:1; 2 Cor. 1:1; Col. 1:1; 2 Tim. 1:1), and he also affirms that God's salvation-historical plan and its individual application in the life of believers are according to God's will (Eph. 1:5, 9, 11). Therefore the phrase "God's will" can emphasize God's sovereign plan (also see Rom. 1:10; 15:32; 2 Cor. 8:5; Gal. 1:4). Paul also directs Christians to perform the "will of God" (Eph. 6:6; cf. Rom. 12:2; 1 Thess. 4:3; 5:18; Col. 4:12) and thus to participate in God's prescriptive design for his holy children (i.e., in that which pleases the Lord).

college campus minister. He notes that when people come to the Lord Jesus Christ there is a common path that they follow with regard to Scripture. First they use the Bible as a guide to good behavior. Their constant use of the Bible is to have it tell them what to do. At some point, however, they get the what-to-do down, and the next phase of their lives gets devoted to determining what to think. At this stage, the Bible may simply become a book of doctrines used to validate our logic and to beat others in debate.

At some point, however, if spiritual growth continues, the new believers discover that as important as are right behavior and thought to the Christian, the Bible ultimately is neither a Boy Scout manual nor a debater's index. Some Christians (in fact, entire movements of Christians) can get stuck in one or more of these modes, believing that living as the children of light is essentially about right behavior or about right thought. But the Bible is about more than right behavior or even right thought. Mature believers discern that God's Word is the means by which God makes himself known so that we might live in union with him. The ultimate aim of Scripture is making known to the heart the reality of God, who is himself the ultimate desire, power, meaning, and hope of the children of light. And the ultimate aim of the apostle as he seeks to rescue us from darkness is to encourage us not only to reflect the light of the Son, but actually to live as the light of the Son.

Live as the Light of the Son (5:18–21)

Paul expresses a truly remarkable expectation in the next portion of his letter. He urges first that we not get drunk on wine that leads to excess or reckless living (Eph. 5:18).[16] At first glance, this appears simply to be more moral instruction. And there certainly is a moral dimension to these words. The children of light are not to drink to excess. Then, as now, being drunk lowers inhibitions and resistance to sin so that many kinds of darkness are

16. The term *methyskō* is used of literal drunkenness in Luke 12:45; John 2:10; 1 Thessalonians 5:7 (and metaphorical drunkenness in Rev. 17:2), and it is frequently found in the Septuagint (e.g., Gen. 9:21; 1 Sam. 1:14; 2 Sam. 11:13). This same command against drunkenness is found in the Septuagint of Proverbs 23:31, which varies significantly from the Hebrew text (and English translations) although the Hebrew also clearly warns against drunkenness. Such Old Testament warnings against drunkenness likely inform Paul's command here and elsewhere (see esp. Rom. 13:12–14; 1 Thess. 5:7–8; cf. Titus 1:6; also see 1 Peter 4:1–5), expressing his concern against the abuse of alcohol in the Greco-Roman world (possibly including its use in Dionysiac religion). The present imperative probably indicates that these Christians should never be drunk (rather than that they should stop getting drunk).

often the consequence. But there is a subtle turn in the apostle's words. If he were simply following the negative/positive substitution pattern that he has presented in the preceding paragraphs of this letter, then we would expect him to say, "Do not get drunk on wine, but abstain from intoxication." Instead he says, "Do not get drunk on wine. . . . Instead, be filled with the Spirit" (Eph. 5:18).[17]

The language of "filling" is too significant in the book of Ephesians for this reference to be incidental. At the end of the first chapter of this epistle, we learned that the church is Christ's body, "the fullness of him who fills everything in every way" (Eph. 1:23). In the third chapter Paul prayed that the Ephesians would know all the dimensions of the love of Christ, so that they "may be filled to the measure of all the fullness of God" (Eph. 3:19). In the fourth chapter we learn that he "ascended higher than all the heavens, in order to fill the whole universe" (Eph. 4:10) and put his gifts in the church so that we might "become mature, attaining to the whole measure of the fullness of Christ" (Eph. 4:13). Now we are urged to put away something in the world that holds us under its influence—excess wine—and instead to be filled with the Spirit by which we have already learned the fullness of Christ comes (Eph. 3:16–17). In summary, the apostle is encouraging and urging God's people to be filled with the Spirit of him who fills up everything with the purpose of renewing and redeeming the universe for his glory.[18] Paul is encouraging and urging us to recognize that we have the privilege not merely of reflecting the light of the Son, but also of living as

17. In scriptural thought, what fills you also controls you (e.g., Acts 5:3).

18. The same verb for "filling" with the Holy Spirit is found in Acts 13:52, where "the disciples were filled with joy and with the Holy Spirit." Luke frequently emphasizes this "filling" (Luke 1:15, 41, 67; Acts 2:4; 4:8, 31; 9:17; 13:9), and in Luke's writings many people are so filled (Jesus, Elizabeth, Zechariah, Peter, Paul, and large groups of Christians), with some being repeatedly filled (especially Peter in Acts 2:4; 4:8; and probably Paul in 9:17; 13:9). Thus in Luke the filling of the Holy Spirit is not a "once for all" occurrence nor is it limited to certain leaders. Also in Luke the results of such filling can vary (most often involving speaking the Word of God, but also including speaking in tongues at Pentecost and prophesying). Paul's language here differs slightly from Luke's, since Paul employs the preposition *en* (translated "with," although perhaps better rendered "by") and does not include the adjective "holy." Nonetheless, this is consistent with Paul's earlier language for the Holy Spirit's work (Eph. 2:18, 22; 3:5). This New Testament language clearly draws on Old Testament instances where individuals are filled by the Spirit in order to build divine structures (see Ex. 31:3; 35:31), to lead (Deut. 34:9), or to prophetically declare God's Word (Mic. 3:8). Some claim that such filling must be a repeated event since the command to "be filled" is a present imperative in Ephesians, yet the syntax of the present imperative itself does not necessitate that conclusion, even if the context shows that the filling by the Spirit is to be an ongoing part of the Christian community and family.

the light of the Son. We are to be the light of the Son, both reflecting him and also shining the light of his indwelling presence that is our life. Paul speaks to believers with the understanding that we can be so filled with Christ's radiance, power, and being that we have his identity and bear it to others.

This is the deep truth of our union with Christ that is so difficult, but necessary, to fathom in order to experience the deepest joys and greatest light in the darkness of this world. We should understand that, fundamentally, our faith is not about what we do (as important as that is), nor is it about what we think (as important as that is). Our faith is fundamentally strengthened by understanding who we are through the indwelling Christ. We are who we are because of our union with him. Nothing else can be the integration point (the place where the promises of Scripture and our identity intersect) of true spirituality. If we make what we do (right actions) the integration point of our faith, then we become fundamentalistic and Pharisaical, with the judgment of others' misbehaviors the preoccupation of our religion. If we make what we think (right doctrine) the integration point of our faith, then we become rationalistic debaters with judgment of others' faulty doctrine the preoccupation of our religion.

Only when the integration point of our faith is knowing and living out the fullness of the person of Jesus Christ will his person and witness be the true preoccupations that fill our lives. Right doing and thinking are necessary for this proper filling, but Christ alone is the aim, the object, and the goal of what we do and think. When we confuse the means (what we do and think) with the goal (the reality of the indwelling Christ), then religion becomes sterile, fruitless, and, in the most sad of ways, merely human.

Emptied of the World (5:18a)

To keep our faith from being merely about human doing and thinking, the apostle says, "Do not get drunk on wine." This command is a synecdoche (a part for the whole), referring to emptying our lives of excess wine but also—in contrast to the filling of the Spirit—emptying ourselves of anything in this world that would hold us under its influence. Such influence, whether by wine or other intoxicants, leads to reckless living that would darken the very life of light the apostle has been advocating.

Filled with the Spirit (5:18b–21)

Not only are we to be emptied of the control of worldly intoxicants, we are to be filled with the Spirit. The play on words is striking, for just as Paul warns against worldly inebriation, he wants to charge us with L.U.I. (living under the influence) of the Spirit. What does it mean to be filled with the Spirit? To answer we must first remember the context that already indicates those filled with the Spirit are radiating the presence of Christ to the world around them. Four sets of participles in the Greek text then describe the characteristic activities of those who are Spirit-filled (i.e., under his influence): (1) speaking, (2) singing (and making music), (3) thanking, and (4) submitting.[19]

1–2. *Speaking and singing (5:19)*. Seemingly entering right into the heart of contemporary worship discussions, Paul exhorts us to speak to one another in psalms, hymns, and spiritual songs (Eph. 5:19a).[20] The instruction first endorses gathering our expressions of worship from numerous sources: the psalms of the Old Testament; hymns (i.e., the songs of the New Testament church, presumably such as the one he has just quoted in verse 8); and spiritual songs (i.e., personal songs of the heart that in this Spirit-filling context are apparently an expression of the Spirit's ministry in the individual). But these worship expressions are not simply for the individual. The musical expression of the church involves "speaking to one another." In contrast to some contemporary teaching that says that our worship is to be directed entirely to God, Paul presumes that there is a horizontal dimension to our worship. In praising God we consciously should be directing our worship to the edification of others. As Christ ministers to others by extending himself for them, when we worship with

19. The four sets of participles are clearly connected adverbially to the imperative "be filled" in verse 18 (see the translation in the KJV, ESV). Some translations treat them as imperatival participles, though usually inconsistently (NIV; cf. RSV, NASB); yet, like the participles earlier in the chapter (Eph. 5:10, 16), they are more likely adverbial participles of result (or possibly manner) expressing what it looks like when one is filled by the Spirit.

20. Colossians 3:16 mentions the same three categories of music. All three terms are used for worshipful music in the Septuagint. "Psalms" typically refers in the New Testament to the Old Testament Psalter (Luke 20:42; 24:44; Acts 1:20; 13:33; with a possible exception in 1 Cor. 14:26). The word for "song" is also found in worship contexts in the book of Revelation (Rev. 5:9; 14:3; 15:3). The word "spiritual" (*pneumatikais*) in "spiritual songs" is omitted in two quite early Greek manuscripts, although the overall meaning changes little with the omission.

the needs of others as our concern, then we are ministering Christ and consequently being filled with his indwelling Spirit.

But the music of our worship is not exclusively a horizontal ministry. To be filled with the Spirit, Paul also says, "Sing and make music in your heart to the Lord" (Eph. 5:19b).[21] Our worship is not to be merely formulaic and perfunctory, but a true expression from the heart of our love for God. We are singing to the Lord. We are honoring him in our worship. He is the audience and object of our praise and, thus, we are filled with his Spirit in our worship. This understanding of being filled with God's Spirit in worship, however, creates an additional glorious perspective of our privileged vessels. Since in true worship we are filled with the Spirit, our God is both the audience and the voice of our praise. We are the instrument by which God becomes present in praise to himself, a concept that brings rich meaning to the psalmist's observation that God inhabits the praise of his people (Ps. 22:3 KJV). This realization that we are generating the voice of God for the praise of God in our worship makes our praise more glorious than we normally imagine, and should give our sinful hearts much hope in the realization of the spiritual power by which he can use us to praise him as well as speak to his people.

The power of praise both to glorify God and to minister to his people recently shined brilliantly in our town. We faced the tragic and, as yet, unexplained death of a dear young woman. Her college and high school friends packed the largest church in our town for her funeral. During the service a young couple sang to us of their abiding faith through the words of a contemporary song: "the valley of the shadow will lead to the river of joy." As the couple sang, a row of the deceased woman's friends rose from their seats at the front of the church and stood together as a stirring affirmation that this song was their faith, too. At one point, one of these young women even raised her fist as if to say in defiance of death, "We will not let even this darkness conquer the light of our faith or the testimony of our friend who is now with the Lord."

21. Again this clause is paralleled in Colossians 3:16. The Greek verbs here for "sing and make music" are etymologically related to the nouns for "songs" and "psalms" earlier in the verse. These verbs are elsewhere used of musical worship in Romans 15:9; 1 Corinthians 14:15; Ephesians 5:19; James 5:13; Revelation 5:9; 14:3; 15:3 (and frequently in the Septuagint). That such worship is addressed to the "Lord" (contrast "to God" in Col. 3:16) has been taken as further evidence of early Christian hymns exalting Christ as deity (cf. Rev. 5:9–13).

I wept then at their courage and faith made so evident, knowing that the young people who joined in the presentation of that song were speaking to the rest of us of the beauty of faith and, at the same time, were praising God for the eternal promises that made their faith so precious. But the young friends were not the only ones speaking and singing. As they spoke to us and sang to God, they were being filled with God's Spirit, so that he himself was ministering to us and glorifying his name. One glory reflected a greater glory, as our God filled the praises of these young people to speak comfort to the rest of us and to make his name great so that we would all know the light of heaven that we so desperately needed in the darkness of that tragedy.

3. *Giving thanks (Eph. 5:20)*. Thanksgiving is another natural outflow of hearts made melodious by God's great grace. We have been redeemed from the darkness and made a part of the eternal song. God himself sings through us to himself. This is cause for much thanksgiving. Because abundant thanksgiving is a natural response to such supernatural grace, the apostle says that we are to be "always giving thanks to God the Father for everything" (Eph. 5:20a).[22] Doing this is completely unnatural to us. It may even strike us as wrong.

How can we always give thanks for everything? We easily understand how and why we should express godly gratitude for the blessings in our lives, but apparent blessings are not the only things that enter our lives. Are we to give thanks for murder and abuse, for cruelty and hate? Despite the contrary insistence of some well-meaning commentators and churches, the answer must be, No. We cannot speak with God's Spirit and at the same time praise him for what he hates. Yes, the *extent* of our praise is to be expansive: "always" and "for everything," but there is a *context* for this thanksgiving. It is to be "in the name of our Lord Jesus Christ" (Eph. 5:20b).[23] We are filled with

22. Paul elsewhere instructs congregations to give thanks (Col. 3:17; 1 Thess. 5:18), a practice which Paul himself models in nearly every letter (see notes on Eph. 1:16). Furthermore, Paul frequently speaks of how he "always" (*pantote*) gives thanks for the churches (1 Cor. 1:4; Eph. 5:20; Col. 1:3; 1 Thess. 1:2; 2 Thess. 1:3; 2:13; Philem. 4). Paul directs praise here "to the [=our] God and Father" (for this phrase see 1 Cor. 15:24; also see Gal. 1:4; 1 Thess. 1:3; 3:11, 13; and cf. Rom. 15:6; 2 Cor. 1:3; 11:31; Eph. 1:3).

23. "The name of our Lord Jesus Christ" appears elsewhere in Paul (1 Cor. 1:2, 10; 5:4; 6:11; Col. 3:17; 2 Thess. 1:12; 3:6; cf. Phil. 2:10), and like "the name of God" (Rom. 2:24; 1 Tim. 6:1; cf. Acts 15:14; Rev. 3:12) it designates who Jesus is and what he does/has done (Acts 4:10; 8:12; John 1:12; 3:18; 20:31; 1 Peter 4:14; 1 John 5:13).

the Spirit when we praise God for everything that hallows and magnifies the name of our Savior.

To the extent that tragedy makes us dependent on our Lord, and enables others to see his comfort and seek his eternal promises, we can give thanks. As stars shine brighter in the desert and a diamond is more beautiful on black velvet, so the name of our Savior—his glory, honor, and redemption—beacons more brightly and intensely in the darkness of the world. We give thanks even for the darkness that makes the glory of Christ's name more evident. The thanksgiving, however, is not for the horrors of a fallen world but for the name of the Savior that alone can answer and redeem those horrors.

My friend John Dozier, the one who wrote about the snow and the geese at the beginning of this chapter, wrote of another experience in the snow that occurred one Christmas:

> The time was about 8:30 p.m., Christmas night, 2002. As I stood up to walk away from my Dad's body lying in the snow, and dying from a self-inflicted gunshot wound, [in my mind] I heard some very familiar words from the Bible that I had clung to for many years before this most dreadful night: "I know that my Redeemer lives, and that in the end He will stand upon the earth" (Job 19:25), and "We know that in all things God works for the good of those who love him, who have been called according to his purpose" (Rom. 8:28). [It was as though] the voice inside me said, "Have faith, John, this night too I will redeem. Have faith, my beloved." And for me, God began to fulfill His promise that very evening last Christmas as I stepped into the police station and began a conversation with a young police officer that ended in the affirmation of his faith. . . . Then and there God gave me the gift of a down payment on his redemptive promise. . . .

Even the darkest darkness God will redeem by his light. In my friend's recognition of the promise and need of the Lord's redeeming the darkness of that Christmas night is seen the source of thanksgiving that we can offer always and for everything. God promises to redeem all things in Jesus' name. Because he shall stand upon the earth as the Lord of all things for all time, we can thank him always for all things as all will be made glorious by him. We can praise him now for the down payments of the fulfillment of his promised kingdom even in this present darkness, in Jesus' name.

4. *Submitting (Eph. 5:21).* In addition to offering praise to God on that awful Christmas night, my friend John also submitted his pain in faith for the eternal well-being of a young policeman he did not even know. By so shining the light of Jesus, the babe that was born on a Christmas night two thousand years ago was made present again on that Christmas night in 2002.

In submitting ourselves for the good of others, our crucified and risen Savior shines powerfully through us and we are filled with his Spirit. Perhaps that is why the apostle finishes his definition of what it means to be filled with the Spirit with the encouragement to "submit to one another out of reverence for Christ" (Eph. 5:21),[24] a phrase that sets the stage for the rest of this epistle's instructions about human relationships (see chapters 5 and 6 on husbands and wives, parents and children, masters and servants).

The natural and simplest reading of the final words of this passage is that we should honor the command to submit to others out of reverence for Christ's authority over our lives.[25] Unquestionably this is part of the meaning, but there is an additional richness in these words in light of what has already been said. When we perceive the Spirit of God as present in his children, then submitting to them is submitting to Christ in them. And when we submit to them as Christ submitted himself for us, then we are Christ to them.

When we submit ourselves for the good of others by the Spirit of Christ in us, we do not merely reflect the glory of the Son; we become the glory of the Son to them. As we minister in his name, submitting to one another—not out of anyone's deserving—out of reverence for Christ, then we are filled with his Spirit and so is the marriage, or the home, or the workplace, or the church in which such submitting occurs.

Subsequent chapters of this commentary explore the connection between this verse and home life (Eph. 5:22–6:9). At this stage it is important to note

24. The question as to whether the Greek participle is in the middle voice ("submitting yourselves to") or in the passive voice ("being submitted to") likely has only slight exegetical payoff; however, the fact that the preceding adverbial participles in Ephesians 5:19–20 are all active in meaning would indicate an expectation in the context that the subject performs the action here as well (i.e., the middle voice interpretation).

25. The Greek word for reverence here is *phobos*. While this word essentially means "fear," it is often used in the Greek Old Testament concerning a reverence for God (e.g., Ex. 20:20; 2 Sam. 23:3; Neh. 5:9, 15; Ps. 36:1 [Septuagint 35:2]; Prov. 1:7; Isa. 11:3). Such usage continues in the New Testament (Rom. 3:18; 11:20; 2 Cor. 5:11; 7:1; cf. Phil. 2:12). Thus Paul implies a high Christology when he directs reverence to the "Lord [Jesus]" in 2 Corinthians 5:11 (cf. Acts 9:31; Col. 3:22) and here. In Ephesians such reverence is to be relationally echoed in marriage (Eph. 5:33) and in house servitude (Eph. 6:5)—see comments on these verses in subsequent chapters.

that this verse is also applicable to church relations as a whole, for this verse (and the participle verb it contains) clearly is connected to the command to "be filled with the Spirit" and to that command's application in the worship and life of the church (Eph. 5:18–21). Equally critical to note is the use of the verb *hypotassō*, with its meaning of subjection to an appointed order (see the extended discussion in the notes of chapter 19). Here the word emphasizes that church members are especially to subject themselves to those who are deemed of more authority in the church and in the family (even if all are to interact humbly and sacrificially with one another; see Eph. 5:1–2; Phil. 2:1–11; 1 Peter 5:5–6). Thus, with this verb, "one another" designates each member's responsibility to submit to those with appointed authority in the church (1 Cor. 16:16; 1 Peter 5:5) rather than an indiscriminate submission of every person to everyone else.[26] Such submissive sacrifice is powerful reverence for, reflection of, and expression of our Savior. By such presentation of him, his indwelling Spirit is demonstrated and he is present.

Many times in the course of my preaching, I have told the account of my first trip to college. I was going to a school that I had never visited in a town that I had never seen. My father drove me the five hours to the campus. As we approached the college, our conversation became increasingly difficult. I became more and more quiet. Finally, my father looked directly at me and said, "You are frightened, aren't you?" I confessed that I certainly was. Immediately my father pulled to the side of the highway and stopped the car. He turned toward me with words that I pray I will never forget. He said, "I do not know if things will go well or poorly for you. I do not know if you will succeed or fail. But I want you always to remember that you are my son, and nothing will ever change that. No matter what happens, I will love you and there is a place for you in my home." The words did not take away all the challenges of college, or remove all the darkness of some events, but my father's words were a beacon of light and hope through it all. They were strength to me, as his willingness to submit his heart and home to the assurance of my welfare became Christ's own witness of care for me.

Much more recently my own son faced intense struggles at college because of the untimely death of a close friend. My son's loving heart kept him from sleeping at night and being able to focus on his studies. When he came home

26.Compare for example "carry each other's burdens" in Galatians 6:2, where each member looks to help those who have burdens, rather than every member carrying everyone else's loads.

for the funeral of the friend, the funeral activities and arrangements kept my son's energies and thoughts occupied for a few days. Then the time came to pack the car and return to school. I sensed his concern beginning to grow again, but other traveling companions were soon to arrive and we were running out of time to talk. Desperate to offer some help, I followed my son into the garage as he packed the last load of books and clothes into the car. "Jordan," I said, "I do not know how things will go for you back at school—whether you will do well, or whether you will not be able to continue. But whether you finish or flunk, I want you to remember that I am your father, you are my son, and nothing will change that. There will always be a place for you here, no matter what." As I said the words, they had a familiar sound in my ears and later I recognized that I was echoing the words of my own father to me. I was reflecting my father's love in my life to my son. Still, my words were more than a reflection. At the same moment that they reflected my father's love, my words were also an original, real, and authentic expression of my own love *and*, by his Spirit in me, of my Savior's love to my son. As I submitted all that was in my heart to try to be light in my son's darkness—in ways beyond my full understanding—Christ was present to my son through his Spirit in me. God made me Christ to my son.

Such ministry of the Savior is the ultimate aim of our lives that we must never forget. We are not put in relationship with others primarily to tell them some*thing* to do, or to teach them some*thing* to know, although each of these is vitally important. Ultimately the aim of all our doing and all of our knowing is to bring to God's people the person, ministry, and glory of our Savior. May he who fills us with his Spirit so that we might know him and make him known fill each heart with his light so that even in this dark world his glory would shine in us and through us for the sake of his people and his glory.

18

The Sacrificial Head

Ephesians 5:21–33

The husband is the head of the wife as Christ is the head of the church, his body, of which he is the Savior.... Husbands, love your wives, just as Christ loved the church and gave himself up for her.
(Eph. 5:23, 25)

The passage above is familiar, and it is controversial. In the last half century, differing philosophies regarding gender, sex, and marriage have revolutionized the way many perceive marriage roles and responsibilities in Western culture. As a result, centuries-old perspectives about how men and women should relate in marriage have been questioned, and sometimes rejected. No husband or wife in modern society has been spared the need to examine presuppositions about how God calls us to live together in this relationship, which is second in blessing only to our salvation. Thus we need to examine carefully this passage where the apostle Paul gives the Bible's lengthiest instruction for husbands and wives. First, we will deal with those portions speaking to husbands. The important discussion dealing with wives we will save for the next chapter.[1]

1. This passage forms the beginning of what has been called a "household code" where social roles in the household are addressed, including those of husband/wife, parent/child, and household master/

The importance of Paul's words for marriage can be illustrated in the experience of a couple who came to my office. They knew their marriage was coming apart when they came to see me, but they did not know why. Both were Christians. Both had come from families that frequented church, and both were well schooled in the Bible. They had met while attending the same Christian college.

I detected nothing in their background that could account for the tensions they were now experiencing. Then I asked the young man for his own explanation of why their marriage was troubled. He expressed genuine consternation. He said that he had tried to be a good husband. Because his college had strongly emphasized the importance of following biblical family models, he had committed himself to being a biblical leader in his home. So I asked him to explain in everyday terms how he fulfilled his biblical leadership. As I have recorded elsewhere, this is what he said:

> In order to make sure there is no question about who is the head of our home I try to make sure both my wife and I let Scripture rule our actions. For instance, if I come home from work and am trying to relax by watching TV or reading the paper, my wife may ask for some help with something in the kitchen, or with the kids [he had three preschoolers, including a set of twins]. . . . To make sure that we both know who is the head of our home, I flip a coin in my mind. If it comes up heads, I help. If comes up tails, I don't. That way there's no question of who's in charge.[2]

When he said this, I thought I was beginning to get an idea of where some of the problems in this marriage might lie. But why? Does not the Bible say that the husband is the head of the home? Does not this Scripture give a husband a right—even a responsibility—to keep family roles and responsibilities clear? What fundamentally is wrong with the

---

slave (see also Col. 3:18–4:1; Titus 2:2–10; 1 Peter 2:18–3:7; cf. 1 Tim. 6:1–2). There were rough parallels to such codes in Greco-Roman literature, although the similarities to Hellenistic Jewish literature were perhaps more pronounced. Such roles cohere on the surface with the patriarchal orientation concerning submissive roles in broader Greco-Roman society; however, Paul addresses mutual commands to all parties and thus limits the excesses of pagan patriarchalism. Moreover, it is important to recognize here that Paul grounds his advice not in social norms, but in Old Testament interpretation (e.g., Eph. 5:31; 6:2–3), in the Christian filling with the Holy Spirit (5:18), and in the work of Christ (Eph. 5:23–33; 6:5–9).

2. This passage is discussed in greater length and detail in this author's book *Each for the Other: Marriage as It's Meant to Be* (Grand Rapids: Baker, 1998; rev. 2006). Materials reappearing here and in chapters 19 and 20 are used with permission of Baker Book House.

definition of arbitrary rule for headship adopted by this husband? The answer is that this husband's definition did not submit to Scripture. In the Bible being a Christian husband requires Christlike love—a sacrificing of self in accordance with the role, reasons, and resources that God assigns to male headship in a biblical marriage.[3]

The Role of a Christian Husband: Headship (5:21–24)

The role to which God calls Christian husbands emerges from a puzzle in this passage. How can Paul seem to endorse mutual submission in one verse (Eph. 5:21) and, in the next, talk about wives submitting to their husbands "for the husband is the head of the wife" (Eph. 5:22–24)? Trouble brews around this word "head." Our culture demands that we determine both what it means and what it requires.

There are those in our day who try to dismiss concerns about this troublesome term by claiming that the concept of headship Paul advocates is either (1) specific to Paul's culture or (2) subject to his own chauvinism. The latter—which simply asserts Paul erred—I cannot assume because the Scriptures claim to be (and are) divinely inspired. The argument for cultural specificity I will deal with more in the next chapter, but note here that Paul is establishing the nature of the church in both its macro and micro components. If what he says here about so basic a building block of the human community is false for our times, then we really have no reason to think that anything he here designs for our homes and churches conforms to God's plan. The uncertainty to which such a conclusion enslaves us is all the more apparent when we recall that Paul says that "the husband is the head of the wife as Christ is the head of the church" (Eph. 5:23). The present force of these two comparative statements denotes that if the husband is no longer head of the wife, then the headship of Christ over his church

3. While the submissive role of the wife in marriage is clearly addressed here in Ephesians, it also must be noted that this whole passage focuses especially on the husband: (1) much more space is spent talking to the husband, (2) the husband bears the weight of being the analog of Christ, (3) Paul's command is highly individualized to each husband by the emphatic *hoi kath' hena hekastos* ("each one" in Eph. 5:33), and (4) the only actual Greek imperatives in the passage ("love" in Eph. 5:25 and 5:33) are addressed directly to husbands. While such advice to husbands was not wholly lacking in Greco-Roman writings, the call to love appears much less emphasized in such literature than pagan patriarchal assumptions concerning submissive wives and all-powerful husbands (as the *paterfamilias*). Hence, Paul especially emphasizes to his readers the imperatives most at variance from their surrounding culture.

is also now uncertain. The significance of this uncertainty cautions us against cavalier dismissal of this text. Thus the chief task I assume is not to defend the presence or significance of the term "head" in this text, but to define its meaning.

What Headship Does Not Mean (5:23–24)

Let us begin by establishing what headship does not mean. The term "head" (*kephalē*) *cannot* mean nothing. When Paul says that Christ is "head" of the church (Eph. 5:23), we know the term is important—it is *not* nothing. Because Christ is the head of the church, his bride, he acts as her Savior (Eph. 5:23).[4] Jesus gave himself out of love to make the church holy, radiant, and blameless (Eph. 5:25–27). Thus, at some level, headship conveys the sense of taking responsibility for that which God commits to one's care.

I do not offer this description of headship merely to argue against modern philosophies that would seek to dismiss these words. I write with the greater intention of addressing those husbands who may use headship as an excuse for passivity in their marriages. Those husbands who will not expend the effort to do anything responsible in their homes may claim they are exercising the prerogatives of headship, but they are in fact abandoning their biblical role. Abdication of responsibility is more common than domination.

A friend of my wife once reported, "My husband hasn't made a decision regarding our family in two years. He doesn't decide how to discipline the children—that's left to me. He never consults me about taking out-of-town work assignments. He comes and goes seemingly without any regard for my feelings or the children's needs. They don't even know him. All he does is come home from time to time and break our routine before leaving again. I don't have three children; I have four."

This wife complains to her husband frequently about his habits, and he tells her that in a few weeks he will work out a time when they can talk about it. But he never does. Here is a man whose headship is defined by passivity—choosing not to act responsibly in behalf of his family. However, indifference to the needs of one's family is not biblical headship. As Paul's letter to the

4. Paul elsewhere depicts Christ as husband and the church as his bride (2 Cor. 11:2; cf. Rom. 7:2–4), an image also known in the early church (Matt. 9:15; 22:2; 25:1 [and parallels]; John 3:29; Rev. 19:7–9; 21:2, 9; 22:17). The image picks up Old Testament parallels with Israel as the bride (e.g., Isa. 54:5–8; 62:4–5; Jer. 2:2–3; 31:31–32; contrast Israel as an adulterous wife in Isa. 50:1; Ezek. 16, 23; Hos. 1–3).

Ephesians has made abundantly clear, Jesus did not choose to do nothing in his care of us—his family (Eph. 1:7; 2:17–18; 5:1–2).

The reason I mention that headship does not justify passivity is that while popular media and feminist objections to biblical headship frequently revolve around male dominance, my experience as a counselor is that wives are frequently distressed by their husband's passivity—avoidance of responsibility. This is often more acute in troubled marriages where the woman (typically the more verbal) constantly complains to the husband about what he is not doing with the man responding by going into a shell of nonresponsiveness.

Even in abusive marriages a typical pattern includes long periods of passivity interspersed by brief episodes of rage. In those brief moments of aggression the man asserts himself only to become passive to family needs and verbal needling much of the rest of the time. Such men's default mode of relating to their families is self-absorbed, self-contained, and nonresponsive. Yet being a biblical head of a home is not a passive role of doing only what is not bothersome, disquieting, or upsetting. A husband's abdication of authority is as unbiblical as his abuse of it. Biblical headship does not mean *nothing*.

The *something* that headship means may also need to be described negatively. First, headship does not merely mean "source" as some modern-day exegetes have claimed because they dislike the second-class status they feel is necessarily implied by the traditional rendering of *kephalē*. When New Testament scholar Wayne Grudem catalogued 2,336 instances of this term in ancient Greek literature, he could find no clear instances where the word carried the idea of "source" or "origin."[5] Even if such were the case, we should recognize that it would hardly be less offensive to modern sensibilities for Paul to say that man is the source of woman. Changing the meaning of *kephalē* to "source" really solves nothing.

Headship also does not connote spiritual or personal superiority for husbands in the sense that it grants them the right of arbitrary, selfish, prideful,

5. See Wayne Grudem, "Does *Kephalē* ('Head') Mean 'Source' or 'Authority Over' in Greek Literature? A Survey of 2,336 Examples," in *The Role Relationship of Men and Women*, ed. George Knight III (Chicago: Moody, 1985), 49–80; reprinted in *Trinity Journal*, n.s., 6 (1985): 49–80. See further his article "The Meaning of *Kephalē* ('Head'): A Response to Recent Studies" in John Piper and Wayne Grudem, *Recovering Biblical Manhood and Womanhood* (Wheaton, IL: Crossway, 1991), 425–68. The counterexamples others use typically relate either to the "source" of a river (in Greek either end of a river is called a *kephalē*; thus in such metaphorical language with rivers it probably does not emphasize a "source" but an extremity) or to an ambiguous phrase from the pagan cosmology of Orphic worship ("Zeus the head, Zeus the middle, and from Zeus all things are made").

or capricious rule. This should be clear from the apostle's wording: "Husbands, love your wives" (Eph. 5:25). Nowhere does the Bible define love as taking advantage of others for personal gain—as is made clear by the words that follow in this same verse: "love . . . just as Christ loved the church and gave himself up for her." These words should call to our minds Jesus' sacrificial ministry: giving up of heavenly glory, living in poverty, washing feet, and suffering upon a cross. Headship is not lording one's position or power over another for personal gain.

What Headship Does Mean (5:23–24)

Headship in this context clearly is an expression of authority. This conclusion seems unavoidable when you see that Paul indicates that just as the church submits to Christ as its head, so the headship of a husband becomes the rationale for the wife's submission (Eph. 5:23–24).[6] Even if there is not an exact congruence between Christ's authority and the authority of the husband, Paul's intention to communicate some aspects of the husband's authority is undeniable.[7] The apostle gives an expectation based on the husband's headship ("wives should submit to their husbands"), gives an example of what this means ("as the church submits to Christ"), and finally extends the expectation as broadly as is possible ("in everything").[8] Paul clearly wants to express a concept of wide-ranging authority.

At the same time the use of the term "headship" is an expression of service. This conclusion also becomes inescapable when the structure of the passage is analyzed. First note that these verses about husbands and wives follow the conclusion of one long sentence in the Greek text (Eph. 5:18–21 in our English translations). In this extended sentence Paul urges those in

6. Paul elsewhere identifies Christ as the "head" (1 Cor. 11:3; Eph. 1:22; 4:15; Col. 1:18; 2:10, 19), and in each location Christ's authoritative role is emphasized (while a corresponding supportive role also appears simultaneously in certain verses, e.g., Eph. 4:15). Especially important in this context is Ephesians 1:22, where Christ is "head over everything" (with *hyper* and the accusative indicating "over" or "above"), and all things are "placed" (literally "submitted" from *hypotassō* as in Eph. 5:24) under his feet.

7. The appearance of the Greek conjunction *alla* (rendered "now") at the beginning of verse 24 is better understood with its normal meaning "but." Paul compares the submissive (Eph. 5:24) and headship (Eph. 5:23) relationships between Christ/church and husband/wife, but he also contrasts them.

8. The verb "submit" is supplied in the Greek from the participle in Ephesians 5:21, and this is confirmed by the use of the same verb in the comparison with Christ and the church in Ephesians 5:24 (cf. Col. 3:18–19).

the church to be "filled with the Spirit" (Eph. 5:18) and, then, in the same sentence uses four adverbial participles to indicate how this filling reflects in our lives: (1) "Speak to one another with psalms, hymns and spiritual songs"; (2) "Sing and make music in your heart"; (3) "always giv[e] thanks to God"; and (4) "Submit to one another out of reverence for Christ" (Eph. 5:19–21). Submitting to one another is the last result of being filled with the Spirit and serves as the launching pad for Paul's thought over most of the next two chapters.[9]

The verses that follow this last participle contextualize what it means to "submit to one another" in various relationships. These relationships can be divided into three groups: wives and husbands, children and parents, slaves and masters. Note that in each grouping the first individuals Paul mentions (i.e., wives, children, and slaves) are those that his culture would already consider to be in a submissive role. Paul does nothing particularly unsettling for his culture by telling these individuals to continue to submit—although he does add a new motive for their submission; that is, reverence for God. However, Paul also never annuls the authority of those his culture considered to be in authority roles. For example, parents still have authority over children, and slaves are not encouraged to take a vote to decide whether to obey their masters.[10] Paul does not reposition those in traditionally submissive roles, nor does he invalidate the role of those with authority.[11] Instead he insists that those in submissive roles be faithful in their submission, while simultaneously telling those in authority to use their authority for the benefit of those in their care.[12] All parties are called to sacrifice, to use their gifts and privileges for the sake of others. In this way the apostle echoes the sacrifice

9. Commentators debate whether these participles (lit., "speaking . . . singing . . . giving thanks . . . submitting . . .") are imperatival or simply consequential in relation to being filled with the Spirit. There is no debate, however, that Paul expects these practices to result from the Spirit's presence in the lives of believers.

10. Paul does suggest a different nuance to the submissive role of child and slave, since they are called not merely to "submit" but to "obey" (*hypakouō* in Greek). Paul pens a parallel shift in verbs in Colossians 3:18–4:1, although he does not always maintain such a sharp distinction (1 Tim. 2:11; 3:4; Titus 2:5, 9; cf. 1 Peter 2:18; 3:1, 6).

11. The fact that Paul could use terms for male headship (1 Cor. 11:3–10; Eph. 5:23–24) alongside his proclamation of how Christian redemptive freedom equally applied to male and female, slave and free (e.g., Gal. 3:28), indicates that he found no tension between the dignity accorded equally restored image-bearers of God and the distinct roles assigned each in marriage, home, and the church (compare 1 Cor. 12:13; 7:20–24 and 11:3–10; and compare Col. 3:11, 18, 22).

12. See also the discussion prior to note 26 in chapter 17 and note 1 in chapter 19.

theme that began this section of thought and again calls all to "Be imitators of God, therefore, as dearly loved children and live a life of love, just as Christ loved us and gave himself up for us as a fragrant offering and sacrifice to God" (Eph. 5:1–2).

Paul's words are particularly weighty for those who have authority because they are the ones with the most to learn and adjust in this biblical social order. Husbands, parents, and masters must learn how their authority must be exercised to serve the needs of wives, children, and slaves. Paul is not removing authority, but he is redefining it in terms of Christ's sacrifice. Here is the radical nature of the church at its most culturally cutting edge, slicing away at traditional notions of authority to establish the concept of a servant/leader, one whose authority is dedicated and directed toward the service of others' good.

The world will not understand this servant/leader role, but since it is a reflection of the ministry of our Savior/Lord (the One who totally submitted himself to our needs, though he had absolute authority), those in the church should have at least an inkling of its implications.

The Reasons for a Christian Husband's Servant/Leader Role (5:25–31)

We must identify the purposes that God intends for those in this servant/leader role to clarify the definition of biblical headship. Not until we understand God's reasons for husbands' servant/leadership will we truly understand their biblical responsibilities. By seeing husbands' responsibilities through the lens of Christ's ministry, we should understand that the role of Christian husbands is redemptive. Husbands represent Christ to their spouses. Husbands cannot understand their daily responsibilities in a marriage without understanding that their primary purpose as heads of households is to help all persons in the home fully apprehend the Lord's grace in their lives.

To Glorify the Wife (5:25–28)

The exercise of biblical headship should enable a wife to know the fullness of God's grace in her life. This redemptive purpose should be apparent in Paul's description of Christ's care for his bride, which the apostle calls Christian men to make the model of their husbanding. "As Christ [the authoritative Lord of the universe] loved the church and gave himself up for her to make her holy, cleansing her by the washing with water through the word, and to present her to himself as a radiant church, . . . in this same way, husbands ought to love their wives" (Eph. 5:25–28).[13] I do not have the space to deal extensively with every word of this instruction. Still, Paul's central point should be clear: husbands should follow the example of Christ who gave of himself to glorify the church.[14] The radiant beauty that God desired for his spiritual spouse, he purchased with the price of his own blood. Our Lord submitted his life to glorifying his bride.

In light of these words, we must not excuse that type of marital headship which, with the most selective and self-serving of biblical proof texts, ignores its biblical purposes and makes wives feel worthless, degraded, and incapable. The reason I know this is wrong is that Christ's love, on which the husband's love is supposed to be modeled, never makes me feel devalued or insignificant. Headship modeled on Christ's redeeming work should instill in another the sense of divine value that God purposes for all his people. Headship that does not confirm this value is actually a form of robbery because it takes from a person some measure of the knowledge of grace that God intends for one to possess.

Robbing another of one's sense of value sounds awful, yet it is extremely common. Whether such robbery is deliberate or not, it is almost always the result of an insecurity that compels us to establish our own sense of worth by exerting power or control over another. Some evil kind of math in us seems to reason that if we have managed to reduce another's sense of worth, then our own value increases.

My wife is one of the most competent, capable people I know. Her grades were far better than mine in school. For two years straight she

13. Repeatedly in Ephesians Paul has emphasized the love of God the Father (Eph. 1:4; 2:4; 5:1; 6:23) and the love of Christ the Son (Eph. 3:17–19; 5:2, 25–32; 6:23) for the church. The church is to respond by loving one another (Eph. 4:2, 15–16; 5:1–2), and here this is specifically applied to husbands loving their wives.

14. Christ's sacrifice is here portrayed as "giving himself up" or "handing over/betraying himself" (from *paradidōmi*). Paul elsewhere refers to the "delivering over" of Christ (esp. Eph. 5:2; also Rom. 4:25; 8:32; 1 Cor. 11:23; Gal. 2:20). In Galatians and Ephesians Christ hands himself over, while elsewhere God the Father does the handing over (e.g., Rom. 8:32)—clearly both Father and Son in love mutually initiated this ultimate sacrificial act. Paul personalizes both this sacrifice, and Christ's love for him, in Galatians 2:20: "The life I live in the body, I live by faith in the Son of God, *who loved me and gave himself for me.*"

was selected as the outstanding musician among all music majors at her university. Numerous academic and professional honors and awards have come her way. After we had been married for a short while, an event forced me to recognize that my headship was not benefiting her sense of personal worth. We had a washing machine that broke. I was busy and asked her to call the repairman. She did not, and when I asked her about it that evening, she confessed in tears that she did not feel capable of making the call. We both remember the event vividly. She remembers because the conversation so stressed her. I remember because it scared me. I thought to myself, "Kathy, what is wrong with us that after a year of being married to me, one who is as able and intelligent as you thinks so little of herself that she cannot make a phone call? What have I done to make you think so little of yourself?"

I cannot say that answers came immediately to these questions. Neither my thought nor my theology was mature, but I will tell you of an image that regularly flashed into my mind for months after that moment. In my mind's eye I saw a framed print in my grandmother's home. The picture shows a young man at the wheel of a great ship during a storm. Wind whips the sails and waves crash over the deck, but the boy's face remains calm and confident. The reason is clear: the artist depicts Jesus standing with his hand on the boy's shoulder. The caption beneath the picture is "Jesus is my co-pilot." The words and the image communicate that when we sense the presence of the Savior our confidence grows to meet any challenge. The opposite was happening in my relationship with my wife.

I had to recognize that my presence often made Kathy's self-confidence vanish. She felt like a capable driver only when I was not in the car. She doubted her competence in social gatherings only when I was in the conversation. In a thousand ways (some of which I recognized and others I did not) I made my wife question her adequacy, and thus I robbed her of a sense of the fullness of her worth. I had to reexamine myself in the light of Christ's model for the church. My role is to build up my wife, to enable her to sense fully and deeply her infinite worth to me and to her Savior. She cannot readily know of her worth to God if the husband he provides somehow diminishes her.[15]

15. The epilog to the story is that when our washer again broke a few years later, Kathy took the machine apart, ordered a new part from the appliance store, and repaired the machine herself.

Ephesians 5:25–31 gives various hints of how husbands should build up their wives' esteem and faith:

First, Paul says Jesus cleansed his bride by the washing with water through the Word. Though this is an obvious reference to baptism, the core idea—of communicating the cleansing forgiveness available in Christ Jesus through the Word—is that the Word of God is to be a present voice in our homes that consistently speaks of the reality of God's provision for his people. Drawing on the Old Testament sacrificial vocabulary, Paul speaks of this provision in terms of sanctification (*hagiazō*, "make her holy") that requires cleansing (Ex. 29:36–37; Lev. 8:15; 16:19; Heb. 9:13; see also 1 Cor. 6:11; 2 Tim. 2:21). Sanctification is the act that renders those in the church holy (Acts 20:32; 1 Cor. 1:2; 6:11), so that they can be called saints. There is a positional component to this vocabulary in Paul, and also the expectation that church members will grow progressively in sanctification as they live Christian lives (1 Thess. 5:23; 2 Tim. 2:21). Paul now indicates that it is the husband's responsibility to aid his wife in sanctification by making sure that the Word of God is present in the home. Living and reading Scripture in the home, as well as making sure the family regularly worships where Scripture is honored, are ways that this expectation is fulfilled.

The word Paul uses for "washing" (*loutron*) here, he also uses in Titus 3:5 ("He saved us through the washing of rebirth and renewal by the Holy Spirit"). In Ephesians 5:26 the washing is done "with water"; baptism with water was done from the inception of the church (e.g., Acts 8:36–39; 10:47; Heb. 10:22; 1 Peter 3:20–21). Paul earlier mentioned such baptism (Eph. 4:5; cf. Rom. 6:3–4; Gal. 3:27; Col. 2:12; 1 Cor. 1:13–17). Some argue that this washing should instead be seen as a bridal bath (Ezek. 16:9); perhaps the readers' individual baptisms invoked for Paul a corporate notion of a purified church cleansed from sin via baptism and prepared for marriage. Still, it is clear that the "washing" that sanctifies is primarily related to the ministry of the Holy Spirit in the Word of God.

The mention of the "word" (*rhēma*) here is analogous to Ephesians 6:17 which refers to the "word of God" that is power against evil that threatens both the individual and the home (cf. the saving word of faith/Christ in Rom. 10:8, 17–18). Paul here uses *rhēma* as he might more often use *logos* (e.g., Eph. 1:13; Rom. 9:6; 13:9; 15:18; 1 Cor. 1:18; 14:36; 15:2, 54; etc.). Again the point is that using various means to ensure that wives and families have a regular diet of Scripture is a responsibility of the heads of households, and a key way we reassure our families of God's goodness. I am consistently surprised how, in premarital counseling, young women ask me to impress upon their husbands the importance of devotional reading; they want their husbands to carry out this ministry of the Word in their homes, but do not want to pressure their husbands into doing it. Husbands who are aware of the importance the apostle places on Scripture for the blessing and protection of the home will take steps to ensure its witness without pressure from their spouses.

Secondly, Paul also says that husbands are to follow the example of Christ who made his bride (the church) "radiant to himself" (Eph. 5:27). The adjective *endoxos* here indicates "glorious, radiant" (cf. Isa. 60:9); it is the opposite of being dishonored (1 Cor. 4:10). In biblical narratives this word can indicate both clothing and miracles (see Luke 7:25 and 13:17 respectively) by which one's glory is made apparent. Here in Ephesians 5:27 the physical metaphor is first extended ("without stain or wrinkle or any other blemish" [the last literally "or some of such things"]), and it is then followed by the sacred analogy ("holy and blameless"). Earlier the church was chosen before the creation of the world to be "holy and blameless in his sight" (Eph. 1:4; cf. Col. 1:22). The ultimate "presenting" of the church in this glorious state refers to an eschatological act, as indicated in this context by the church's perfection ("holy and blameless"; see esp. 1 Cor. 11:2 and Col. 1:22, 28), and by the eschatological associations with the verb "to present" (see also 2 Cor. 4:14).

In all of this, Paul communicates Christ's appreciation for the beauty of his bride. The obvious application is that husbands are to express their appreciation for the beauty (internally and externally) of their spouses. We must recognize that making wives question their beauty or encouraging them to be dowdy is one way that some husbands exercise control in their marriages. But this is contrary to Christ's example. God intended us to be attractive to one another, and one way that we affirm his blessing, as well as build up one another, is by affirming our spouse. We diminish our wives and our marriages when we do not tell our wives of their beauty (external and internal) as part of our rejoicing in what God has provided.

Thirdly, verse 31 speaks of a husband's willingness to make his union with his wife take precedence over other family relationships, even that of his own parents. Because counselors tell us that relationships with in-laws are one of the chief sources of tension in marriage, husbands should make it very clear that the concerns of a wife are valued over the concerns of the man's parents. This does not mean that the man need not honor his parents, but it does mean his wife's needs take a higher priority.

Fourthly, verse 29 speaks of feeding and caring for one's wife as one does for one's own body.[16] The word "feed" can be translated as "nourish" (KJV) or "bring to maturity."[17] "Care for" can be translated as "cherish" (KJV) and means to nurture with tender care.[18] These terms remind us that in order to love one's spouse biblically, one's physical resources should not be used selfishly. Money and goods are to be used for the nurture of others.

But none of these hints is more critical than the first words of verse 25: "Husbands, love your wives."[19] Nothing more communicates the grace of God to our spouses than our love of them. When a husband communicates Christlike, unconditional appreciation of his spouse, the nature of the grace of God informs and builds up the wife's understanding of her preciousness.

I recognize that some reading these words about a husband's headship having the purpose of glorifying his wife will feel that what I have just said is demeaning. Indeed, much of what is written in popular Christian literature about men "discipling their weak wives" and "tolerating their hormones" is demeaning and wrong. The notion that women are hopelessly needy creatures who will wilt without a man to build them up can perpetuate stereotypes destructive to our marriages. According to Scripture, neither men nor

16. The argument does not refer merely to our self-serving tendency to care for our bodies (even if it is true on that level), but ultimately draws on the analogy with the church as the body of Christ. As Christ cares for his body/church, so ought a husband to care for his body/wife (Eph. 5:28) with whom he is "one flesh" (Eph. 5:31; cf. Eph. 5:29). The metaphor of the church as the body of Christ is common in Paul, but here it takes on a new application (see Eph. 4:12, 25; also Rom. 12:4–5; 1 Cor. 6:15; 12:12–27; Col. 3:15).

17. The same verb (*ektrephō*), which etymologically is related to the term for "feed" (*trephō*), is used in 6:4 of children: "instead, *bring them up* in the training and instruction of the Lord." Frequently it is found in the Septuagint for raising children (e.g., 2 Sam. 12:3; 1 Kings 11:20; 12:8, 10; 2 Kings 10:6; 2 Chron. 10:10; Hos. 9:12; Zech. 10:9; Isa. 23:4; 49:21), and it even appears in Psalm 23:2 (Septuagint 22:3), "He *nourishes* me upon still waters."

18. This verb in its literal sense means "to warm up" (*thalpō*, see Septuagint Deut. 22:6; 1 Kings 1:2, 4; Job 39:14), but it is used metaphorically in the New Testament for caring for another (see 1 Thess. 2:7, where it speaks of a nursing mother caring for her baby).

19. "Love" (*agapaō*) is the predominant word in this passage, being the only imperative in Ephesians 5:25, 33 (and also being obligated in Eph. 5:28).

women (except those gifted for celibacy) will be all that God intends without their spouses. What this means is that biblical headship not only is designed for glorifying the wife, but it also has the redemptive purpose of sanctifying the husband.

To Sanctify Self (5:28–31)

A sanctifying process enables us to become what God intends. What does God intend for husbands to be? He intends for us to be complete, as mature in personal and spiritual development as we can be before we are with him (James 1:2–4). But how will this wholeness come about? Paul says, "For this reason a man will leave his father and mother and be united to his wife, and the two will become one flesh" (Eph. 5:31).[20] This is a reference to the physical union of a man and woman in marriage—but much more also.

The language of verse 31 puts before us the creation plan to make us whole persons. The wife was made to complement and complete the husband. Lest this sound too demeaning for her, think of what it connotes for him. Unless the man is gifted for celibacy, he is ever incomplete—incapable of realizing the divine potential God intends for him in this life—apart from the ministry of his wife in his marriage. Further, because the two are to be one, if one of those parties to the union is damaged, demoralized, or degraded, then neither will be completely whole. Just as a basketball deflated on only one side still cannot fulfill its purposes, so a marriage with one side diminished will deprive both persons of the full potential God intends.

A few years ago when Kathy and I lived in an apartment complex among seminary students, we invited a couple over to our house for an evening of table games. We were playing Uno, a game that requires animated conversation, when we realized the guest wife was not really participating. In fact, she was so quiet that the situation became rather uncomfortable. Finally, when the embarrassment was intolerable, the husband explained to us that the reason his wife was not speaking was that he had occasionally been embarrassed by things she said in the company of others. As a result, they had agreed that since he was the head of the house she should not speak in public unless he

20. This citation from Genesis 2:24 largely follows the Septuagint with only slight variation in wording but not in meaning (i.e., omitting the possessive "his," and using the preposition *anti* in place of its synonym *heneken*). Jesus quoted Genesis 2:24 (Matt. 19:5; Mark 10:7); and Paul cited it elsewhere (1 Cor. 6:16).

granted her permission. They were serious about this! As you might guess there were other problems, too.

Some months later the husband began to suffer from severe depression and left seminary. We have never heard from them again. Still, I have occasionally considered what this man did to himself. The Lord had provided him with a wonderful spouse. Yet by manipulation and intimidation he had so weakened her that when he needed her support, she was incapable of providing it.

Husbands are incomplete without their wives. If a husband does not build up his wife, then he who is made whole only by the expression of his wife's gifts and graces is himself diminished. I have needed to learn this biblical principle. I was raised in a troubled home, and I needed my wife's tenderness to learn what it means to be caring and expressive. Although I was sensitive by nature, I did not know how to express affection. I did not know how to express appreciation. In my early adult years, I was out of touch with my emotions, having forgotten how to laugh or how to cry. Yet I was trying to be a husband and a minister of the gospel. Were it not for my wife helping me to understand and express tenderness, I dread to think of what my "ministry" would be. The Lord taught me much through the spouse he provided, but mostly he helped me to find the real me that had gotten lost in the family tensions of my youth.

I must be careful not to imply that it is just my ministry to others that has been affected by my wife's completing of my personality. In a profound way my wife not only helped me find myself, she helped me to find the deeper dimensions of my God. This is because the ability to experience intimacy is closely connected to the ability we have to experience the transcendent. If you cannot share intimacies with the people God has placed in your life, then it is nearly impossible to share an intimate relationship with him. By her love and patience my wife made me more whole than I could be apart from her. I had and have much to learn from her. Had I for too long intimidated, unappreciated, and belittled her, I would have lost myself—and I would not have begun to fathom how wide, and long, and high, and deep is the love of my Savior.

I thank God for the great grace of helping to sanctify me by my wife and of reminding me that if I do not build her up, then I diminish myself. My sanctification, my wholeness before God, cannot be complete without glorifying her. No wonder Paul says that the man who loves his wife loves himself (Eph. 5:28–29, 31).[21] The apostle describes husbanding as nurturing and feeding one's own body because self-preservation and growth are the derivative consequences of building up our wives. In the application of a husband's authority to the nurture of his wife, he ultimately discovers his own spiritual health and fulfillment. Close to almost all of us is the proof of this truth. Simply by examining the lives of our acquaintances we recognize that men who respect and cherish their wives are typically whole people. And we see that those husbands whose views of headship allow them to diminish or despirit their wives are men whose lives are typically emotionally and relationally unhealthy on other fronts as well. When a husband weakens the wife the Lord has designed for his support, the man endangers the human and spiritual potential of both parties in the marriage.

THE RESOURCES FOR A CHRISTIAN HUSBAND'S SERVANT/LEADER ROLE (5:32–33)

Thus far we have discerned that biblical headship involves expressing authority in such a way that God's redemptive purposes for both parties in a marriage are fulfilled. But how do husbands do this? This passage offers no specific "this-is-what-you-are-to-do" instruction for husbands regarding the division of household tasks, deciding when to move for whose job, determining who holds the TV remote control. Yet by uncovering the resources cited in this text that are available for the carrying out of the husband's role, we get a clear idea of what should be weighed when making these decisions.

What could God have given husbands to enable them to exercise their authority? He could have provided license to use force, rules, and punishments to establish male authority—some religions provide such. In the light of how human authority is often expressed and enforced, such instructions might be expected. But such expressions of power will not produce a healthy

21. Note the echo of this expression in verse 33 ("each one of you also must love his wife as he loves himself"). The latter phrase echoes the words of Leviticus 19:18 ("love your neighbor as yourself"), was well known to Paul (Rom. 13:9; Gal. 5:14) and in the early church (Matt. 19:19; 22:39; Mark 12:31; Luke 10:27; James 2:8); and, ultimately, the phrase reminds us that love of both husband and wife must be selfless to fully benefit self.

marriage relationship of two people who love each other as Christ loves us. So how does God tell husbands to fulfill their role as heads of households?

Self-sacrifice (5:25)

Paul says, "Love your wives, just as Christ loved the church and *gave himself up* for her." An essential resource that husbands are to use for enacting their headship is selflessness.

A leader not only in his home but also in the evangelical world is J. Robertson McQuilkin. In 1990, however, he resigned prematurely from the presidency of Columbia Bible College and Seminary because his wife Muriel, afflicted with Alzheimer's disease, needed his care. During his last two years as president he wrote that it was increasingly difficult to keep Muriel at home. When she was with him she was content, but without him she became distressed and panic-stricken. Although the walk from their home to the school was a mile round trip, Muriel would often try to follow her husband to the office. Seeking him over and over she would sometimes make that trip ten times a day. When he took her shoes off at night, McQuilkin sometimes found her feet bloodied from all the walking. Washing her feet prepared him for a similar Christlike act that he ultimately performed for her. He sacrificed his position to take care of her.

This is the leadership of humility, the headship of service—husbanding by sacrifice. To it God calls men who would be biblical heads of their homes. A Christian husband leads by service. He heads his family through selfless love. He has the primary biblical responsibility in the home to set a spiritual standard by his own sacrifice to make God's grace evident.

What kind of authority is this? There is no easy way to describe it. I often hear Christians try to define male headship in the home by saying that the husband has the last word or is the final authority in decision making. This is certainly true, but without an understanding of biblical priorities such a definition can be terribly misused. Does it mean that even if the wife hates the idea of moving to a distant town, doesn't want a particular home, thinks that a child does not need another after-school activity, doesn't want a certain kind of love-making, disagrees with a husband's discipline of their children, or believes an investment is unwise, that the husband should insist on his wishes anyway because he is the head of the home and has the final word? If having the final word means that others' view and feelings do not have to be considered, then I do not see such a definition ever provided for biblical headship.

Far from encouraging a husband to exercise his authority for personal privilege, the Bible takes care to direct a Christian husband to use his authority for the benefit of his spouse and family. Thus biblical headship shifts the focus of husbanding from taking charge to taking responsibility, and from asserting one's will to giving one's self to the good of another. Headship is more a function of controlling our nature than controlling our wives. We are always "Christ's ambassadors, as though God were making his appeal through us" (2 Cor. 5:20). To represent him we must be willing to suffer for his name, stand for his principles, and support his people—even if the place for doing so is in our own homes.

With great wisdom the Bible mandates no particular style, manner, or set of behaviors that alone qualify as biblical headship. In fact, if this aspect of the believer's life holds true to other mandates for Christian character, then there are probably as many legitimate expressions of headship as there are variations of personality. Biblical headship is simply the exercise of God-given authority whereby a man does all that is within his power to see that love, justice, and mercy rule in his home even when fostering such qualities requires his own personal sacrifice.

Christ's Sacrifice (5:32–33)

How can we live so? How can we sacrifice so? By recognizing that ultimately the resource provided for Christian husbanding is not simply self-sacrifice, but Christ's sacrifice. It may seem disingenuous that Paul—so obviously speaking in this passage about Christian marriage—nonetheless says, "This is a profound mystery—but I am talking about Christ and the church" (Eph. 5:32). It is tempting to accuse Paul of joking here. My instinctive response is to say, "C'mon, Paul, you know you are really talking about marital, not spiritual, relationships." Yet, as I study more I see that the apostle must be serious about his words here.

Commentators debate whether this "mystery" speaks to the act of marriage itself (which in Catholic theology is a sacrament) or to the relationship between Christ and his church. The occurrences of "mystery" elsewhere in Ephesians (1:9; 3:3–4, 9; 6:19) indicate that this term relates to the deep purposes of God as revealed in Paul's gospel. Also the phrase "for this reason" in verse 31 naturally refers to Christ and his body in verse 30. Furthermore, Paul actually tells us he is talking about the church (in Eph. 5:32). Thus the "mystery" is certainly not limited to human marriage. However, the broader context implies that the whole notion of the church as both Christ's body and bride is mirrored in the one-flesh relationship between a husband and his bride. The mystery then is how Christ, through the gospel, calls a bride to himself, and how Christian marriage is to illustrate this great sacred act. For this husband, this ultimately means that a husband's love for his wife is intimately tied to his knowledge of Christ's love for us.[22]

If a husband or a wife is not secure in Christ's love—if we need control over another to have some confidence in ourselves—then we cannot love as Christ requires. We will have no resources to serve another if we are not sure of our standing in him. His love is our relational fuel. If we are running on empty (not filled with the knowledge of his love for us), then we will inevitably suck personal energy from the life of our marriage.

Only when our hearts are brimming with the knowledge of his grace do we have the resources we need to maintain a Christian marriage. Without a sure relationship with the Lord Jesus Christ, we simply do not have the security or strength necessary to sacrifice for the good of another. Ultimately the only resource we have that enables us to love as Christ requires is his own love. That is why Paul is so careful in this passage to spell out the assurance we have of God's love for us through the sacrifice of his Son. Only when we rest in his love can we reflect it. The degree of confidence we have in the strength of his care for us will largely determine the measure of selfless tenderness we can express.

I know I have not answered here all the questions today's husbands and wives have about how Christian headship is to be expressed in marriage. I still have much to learn, but I do not consider the path to my learning to be obscure. If a husband's constant effort, consistent motivation, and deep desire are to love as Jesus loves him, then that husband's choices are neither as mysterious nor as harsh as we may be tempted to imagine.

When Robertson McQuilkin recounted in *Christianity Today* his decision to resign his leadership of one of the nation's prestigious evangelical institutions to care for his wife, the response was overwhelming.[23] Husbands and

22. And deep knowledge of Christ's love is tied to mature love for one's spouse.

23. Robertson McQuilkin, "Living by Vows," *Christianity Today* (October 8, 1990), 38–40.

wives who read the account renewed their marriage vows; pastors told the story to their congregations; young people attested to a rekindled desire for a marriage commitment their culture had previously taught them to minimize and devalue. McQuilkin said, "It was a mystery to me [how so many were responding] until a distinguished oncologist, who lives constantly with dying people, told me, 'Almost all women stand by their men, but few men stand by their women.'"[24]

How curious that in dying to self and becoming a servant to his wife this man became a leader of men and women throughout this nation. But then, it is not really curious at all. It is really only the heart of the gospel, a mirror of Christ's ministry that should be reflected in all of our marriages: we lead most clearly, most effectively, most authoritatively, and most like Christ when we live most sacrificially.

God calls us to believe that just as this one husband became a leader to many when in active obedience to Christ he applied his gifts, talents, authority, and calling to the nurture and care of a loved one, so also we become leaders in our families when we exercise our gifts, abilities, and rights in the service of our loved ones. The Lord who submitted himself to the cross in your behalf calls us husbands to servant/leadership no less submissive to his will in our homes. There, too, taking the lead in dying to self are our Christian mission, our marital joy, and Christ's glory. The path to Christian leadership in the home is always the way of the cross.

24. See McQuilkin, "Living by Vows," 40; and Robertson McQuilkin, "Muriel's Blessing," *Christianity Today* (February 5, 1996), 34.

19

The Submissive Wife

Ephesians 5:22–33

Wives, submit to your husbands as to the Lord. For the husband is the head of the wife as Christ is the head of the church, his body, of which he is the Savior. Now as the church submits to Christ, so also wives should submit to their husbands in everything. (Eph. 5:22–24)

When Sarah Ferguson (Fergie) married Britain's Prince Andrew, the world marveled at the days of pageantry surrounding the wedding. But what more remember is the moment when their vows were taken. Fergie was supposed to say to her groom, "I promise to love, honor, and *obey*. . . ." She did say the phrase, but not without a sideways grin at the prince that said much more. Her look could hardly have articulated more clearly the new duchess's thought: "You've got to be kidding. Nobody really believes those anachronisms about wifely submission anymore, and you had better not!" She repeated the vows, but with a toss of her head Fergie as clearly tossed away the content of those words. In hindsight, her smirk of bemused lip service to traditions not intended to be honored has become a sad metaphor for a royal marriage gone awry. But it is not merely royalty to whom the metaphor applies.

If we strip away the party platforms and lip service, we too readily give to the official positions of our churches, political parties, families, or traditions, we will also find that large questions remain about the responsibilities of women in marriage. A campus minister at Vanderbilt University tells me, "It does not matter whether the intelligent women on this campus are liberal feminists or conservative traditionalists—if you can get them to talk honestly about their deepest concerns, most will say they still wonder if their choices are right. Deep down they are desperate for a credible authority to tell them what women are supposed to be."

Sadly, our churches have not proved to be a credible enough authority to settle the issue—even among themselves. I know of some churches that have urged women who are fed up with abusive husbands to leave their marriages. Other churches—under the assumption that the abuse is a result of women not being submissive enough—have used discipline to try to force women to submit to husbands guilty of the same offenses. I hear confusion among my own relatives as women deeply committed to marriage and sincerely desiring to honor Scripture have, after decades of sacrifice, cried out in spiritual agony, "I know the Bible says to submit, but I can't continue to live this way. I have tried, but I can't keep on. I just can't."

From palaces to campuses to churches to our homes and hearts the questions echo: How, really, is a wife supposed to love, or to honor, or to obey? I cannot handle all the complexities of these important questions in these few pages. I do know, however, that our God is too concerned for his people to leave us without principles to guide and govern our most precious relationships. Many of these principles appear in Ephesians 5 to address the ultimate question we have to ask: "What is a Christian wife to be?" The inescapable answer here (for those who believe that the Bible is authoritative) is this: a Christian wife is to be submissive. However, lest that simple answer betray the wisdom and sensitivity of Scripture, we must carefully define what submission means in terms of its biblical requirements, nature, and goals.

The Duty of a Christian Wife (5:22–33)

The duty to which God calls Christian wives could hardly be more clearly stated by the apostle. "Wives, submit to your husbands as to the Lord" (Eph. 5:22). However, simply repeating the word "submit" or even giving its Greek origin (a compound verb that could be rendered "to arrange under") does not tell us all we have to know.[1] What does Paul intend for us to understand by submission?

Submission Does Not Mean Nothing (5:22–24)

We know that submission cannot be an incidental term without meaning because of the comprehensive ways in which it is addressed. Consider the scope of the apostle's words. They are quite encompassing. The apostle first gives a comparison analogy. Wives are to submit to their husbands "as to the Lord" (Eph. 5:22). As all persons should arrange their lives under the righteous purposes of their Lord, so also wives should prioritize their lives relative to their husbands' purposes in God's kingdom. Lest that comparison prove insufficient, the apostle then adds a more compelling example of his thought based on the relationship of Christ and the church. As the church submits to Christ, her head, so also wives should submit to their husbands' headship (Eph. 5:23–24).[2] As the church could never fulfill its purposes without submission to the holy will of her Lord, the apostle reminds women that they cannot fulfill their divine purposes if they are not submitting to the biblical purposes of their husbands. Finally, lest we assume Paul means these standards to apply only to some narrow part of life, the apostle clarifies the extent of his instruction by saying that "wives

1. Paul elsewhere applies this verb (*hypotassō*) to wives in 1 Corinthians 14:34; Colossians 3:18; Titus 2:5 (also see 1 Peter 3:1, 5; and the cognate noun in 1 Tim. 2:11). In Ephesians the verb earlier depicts Jesus' role as the head of all things in 1:22 ("God placed [literally: subjected] all things under his feet"; see also 1 Cor. 15:27–28; Phil. 3:21; cf. Heb. 2:5, 8; 1 Peter 3:22). Such subjection certainly can be honorable and can involve a subordination of role without a diminishment of worth, and this is particularly seen in how God the Son "submits" to God the Father (1 Cor. 15:28). A further list of all New Testament occurrences of this verb substantiates that the translation "submit" is appropriate, along with its connotation of one person placing himself or herself under the authority of another. The verb designates both those who submit to God (Heb. 12:9; James 4:7) and those who fail in this duty (Rom. 10:3; including "the flesh" in Rom. 8:7). Christians should submit to governing authorities (Rom. 13:1, 5; Titus 3:1; cf. 1 Peter 2:13) and to authorities in the church (1 Cor. 16:16; cf. 1 Peter 5:5). In the church the spirit of prophets submits to prophets (1 Cor. 14:32). Slaves submit to masters (Titus 2:9; cf. 1 Peter 2:18). In narratives the young Jesus submits to his parents (Luke 2:51), and the demons submit to the apostles (Luke 10:17, 20). Finally, metaphorically the creation is currently in submission to "frustration" (Rom. 8:20), since after the fall creation was so stationed by God himself. See also the discussion of *hypotassō* prior to note 26 in chapter 17, and the discussion of headship in chapter 18.

2. See 1 Corinthians 11:3–10 and the previous chapter on the meaning and import of "headship" language.

should submit to their husbands in everything" (Eph. 5:24). These really are comprehensive words.[3]

Consider, too, the scope of Scripture's witness. As comprehensive as these words seem, we might still consider them inapplicable today if the passage containing them were unique or exceptional. Then our culture (as well as Christians applying biblical interpretation principles of letting more clear passages interpret less clear passages) might do well to conclude that these "submission" concepts do not really apply to us.

However, we cannot draw such a conclusion in light of the consistent commitment of Scripture to these concepts. Note that wives are instructed three times in this passage alone to subject their priorities to their husband's authority (see Eph. 5:22, 24, 33). Paul uses the same or related terminology about husbands and wives in at least five other books (1 Corinthians, Ephesians, Colossians, 1 Timothy, and Titus).[4] The apostle Peter also tells wives, "Be submissive to your husbands so that, if any of them do not believe the word, they may be won over without talk by the behavior of their wives" (1 Peter 3:1). Peter then ties this "gentle and quiet spirit" to Israel's earliest history, saying it was with such a demeanor that "Sarah . . . obeyed Abraham" (1 Peter 3:4–6). Paul goes back even further in the Ephesians and Corinthians passages by relating this order of family relationships to the events of creation (Eph. 5:31; 1 Cor. 11:7–12). The instruction for wives to submit to husbands is not limited to one unique passage. It is spread across the Pauline material, echoed by another apostle, extended to Israel's origins, and cited throughout human history. Instruction so comprehensive in its scope and duration cannot mean nothing.

Submission Does Mean Something (5:25–33)

The something that submission means is perhaps most obvious in light of the purposes it fulfills.

3. On "in everything" (*en panti*), Peter T. O'Brien, *The Letter to the Epheisans* (Grand Rapids: Eerdmans, 1999), 417, notes that this refers to "every area of life": "Just as the church is to submit to Christ in everything, so in every sphere wives are expected to submit to their husbands."

4. Especially Ephesians 5:22–33; Colossians 3:18–19; Titus 2:2–8 and the discussion of headship in 1 Corinthians 11:3–12; 14:34–36; 1 Timothy 2:8–15 address gender roles in worship; and the church leadership of male elders and deacons requires that they be a "husband of one wife" in 1 Timothy 3:2, 11–12 and Titus 1:6 (compare the converse language in 1 Timothy 5:9).

First, submission fulfills the purpose of *completing another* (Eph. 5:31–32). Paul refers to the genesis of the marriage relationship (Gen. 2:24), saying, "For this reason a man will leave his father and mother and be united to his wife, and the two will become one flesh. This is a profound mystery" (Eph. 5:31–32).[5] These words tell us that submission is the pouring of oneself into the completion of another. It is the sacrificing of self to make a relationship and those in it whole. Paul says this is a profound mystery, and we can well attest to that. It is beyond our explaining (and yet so obvious to us) that God has made those of us not gifted for celibacy such that we are never quite whole—in our relational maturity, in our personal development, or even in our spirituality—without those he intends to complement and complete us in marital oneness.

We will look at another individual (or even at ourselves) after a few years of marriage and say, "That person has so matured, so leveled out, or become so less self-absorbed since marrying so-and-so." At least, that is what we say if the marriage is functioning well. If the marriage is going poorly, we typically recognize that self-absorption, immaturity, or character flaws may be even more prominent than they were before marriage. When the real oneness God intends for marriage does not occur, the people themselves become less whole. Though this is a mystery, it fits precisely with the pattern of Scripture which tells us that since God designed marriage to sanctify its members by their union, the abuse or neglect of that union must damage us.

Knowledge of these ways that God intends for our lives to affect each other directs our understanding of the apostle's instructions. To the husband God gives authority for biblical headship that is designed to lead a family in paths of sacrificial service to God. To the wife God commits a willingness to honor and support the husband's leadership so that he can carry out these responsibilities. Each has responsibility for the other to the end that the family unit is whole and healthy before God.

Note that this goal of wholeness before God is emphasized in Scripture far more than any specific set of behaviors. Every couple will have differing personalities, gifts, and situations. We are not obligated to some simplistic set of rules that determines who takes the garbage out, who washes the dishes, or how many hours outside of the home a spouse may work or play without

5. See the notes on 5:31 in the preceding chapter concerning this citation from Genesis 2:24.

crossing some biblical threshold of marital correctness. The responsibilities of marriage are determined at the deepest levels of the Christian heart, and call for the most diligent, honest, and conscientious questions of self-examination. The husband not only must ask, "Am I leading my family to a better knowledge of God?" but also, "Is my leadership self-serving or sacrificial?" The wife must similarly ask not only "Do my actions, words, and attitudes enable my husband to lead my family to a better knowledge of God?" but also, "Have I truly in everything submitted my life to this highest priority?"

Submission also fulfills the purpose of *glorifying another* (Eph. 5:25–27, 33). These questions of the heart cannot be answered by arbitrary, cultural, or merely traditional role assignments regarding such things as who gets to talk first, who writes the checks, or who gets to drive. Of course, a marriage goes awry if the husband abdicates responsibility in all of these areas, or if a wife assumes authority by arranging to control the family in all these areas. Still, the inappropriateness of imposing arbitrary or cultural rules on all Christian homes is obvious when we understand that submission (in addition to requiring the pouring of oneself into the completion of another) involves the exercising of gifts for the glory of another. The infinitely rich and varied ways God dispenses gifts to bless his people should alert us to the futility and wrong of trying to make all spouses glorify one another the same way.

This requirement to use one's gifts to glorify another becomes most apparent when we recognize the balanced construction of the instruction Paul gives wives *and* husbands in this passage. Paul instructs husbands to use their headship as Christ used his for the glory of his bride, the church (Eph. 5:25–27). The effect is to remind husbands that they must never abuse their authority so that they rob their wives of "radiance" (see Eph. 5:27). At the same time wives are told not to disregard submission so that they rob their husbands of "respect" (Eph. 5:33). Submission necessarily honors, and teaches others in the family to honor, the authority of the head of the home, or else "respect" is an empty and misleading word.

Discerning how wives fulfill the obligation to respect their husbands requires us to unroll further the implications of Paul's comparison of marriage to the relationship of Christ and the church. First the church obeys the godly standards of the Savior, as a wife should honor the godly authority of her husband (1 Peter 3:6). But we need also to remember that the church never dispenses with the gifts and graces God provides. The church does not submit to Christ by singing a little softer, exercising intelligence a little less, or seeking to be of little influence in the world. Rather she is called to arrange all her energies and abilities under the grand purpose of glorifying the Savior. To do less would not be submission; it would be disobedience. By this line of thought we grow to understand the wisdom of Paul's terminology. Biblical submission does not call women to suppress their gifts any more than the church is called to suppress her gifts. The gifts of the church are to be fully exercised for the glory of another. In the same way women should fully express (not suppress) their gifts for the good of another. This truly is an "arranging under" of one's own gifts for the glory of another.

Such submission is never an abdication of responsibility for another's welfare, nor is it an abandonment of gifts to fit a culturally determined role. Such abdication and abandonment can actually have the opposite effect from biblical submission that is designed to bring God's grace more fully into the life of the husband. Limiting headship and submission to a certain set of behaviors that suppress a wife's gifts can actually undermine the biblical priorities of godly submission. By underutilizing her gifts a woman may also be abandoning her husband to faults or weaknesses that God put her in the marriage to help address.

Proper submission of gifts to the good of another may actually involve challenging another with the insights or righteousness that God has provided. A wife who suppresses all comment or action while a husband abuses a child or destroys himself with unwise choices is not exercising biblical submission. Simply abandoning another to his or her faults is not God's purpose for one he places in the marriage to make the other whole and glorious to himself. Challenge must still be expressed with love and respect. Still, submission ultimately cannot be simply the suppression of gifts but rather is *full expression of them in behalf of another*. God does not expect anyone to minimize the gifts he grants for the praise of his glory or for furthering his glory in the lives of others.

The Dignity of a Christian Wife (5:21–24, 31)

This expression of gifts in behalf of another further defines submission not only in terms of duty, but also in terms of dignity. To see how biblical submission grants dignity we must examine the precise wording of this passage. Such an examination may initially create shock. Where our translations say, "Wives, submit to your husbands" (Eph. 5:22), the word "submit" does not appear in the original language of the text.[6] The very word we are so ready to debate is not actually present—in this verse. Interestingly, its absence not only underscores the necessity of submission, it also confirms the dignity of a Christian wife.

The Value of a Christian Wife (5:21)

The place where the word "submit" does appear is in the preceding verse where the apostle concludes his instruction on how to "be filled with the Spirit" by saying believers should "submit to one another out of reverence for Christ" (Eph. 5:21). Then Paul directly applies these words to wives (lit., "Wives, as unto the Lord") in verse 22. As indicated in previous chapters, the meaning of *hypotassō* requires submission of one person to a person of greater authority. But this instruction to wives entails only the first constituency among Christians to whom the submission mandate applies. Next will follow similar instruction for children and slaves. But husbands, parents, and masters, while retaining greater authority, are not without obligation to give of themselves for another. All are under the divine constraint to live as Christ, giving themselves in love and sacrifice for those in their care (Eph. 5:1–2): husbands, by giving themselves for their wives, as the Lord gave himself for the church (Eph. 5:25–33); fathers, by not exasperating their children (Eph. 6:4); and masters, by treating slaves with respect and fairness since even the master is a slave of Christ (Eph. 6:9).

Each person is to express whatever gifts, rights, or authority he or she has for the good of another in order to honor Christ and build up his kingdom. The reason this structure confirms the dignity of a Christian wife is that it proves that her submission does not lessen her value or diminish her place in the kingdom. All Christians are to submit to proper authority and to give of themselves for the good of others God has placed in their lives (e.g.,

6. As noted in the previous chapter, in Greek the verb "to submit" must be supplied in verse 22 from the context in verse 21. Supplying "submit" in verse 22 is certainly correct contextually, and also correct given that the verb "submit" occurs again in verse 24 (where Paul's condensed language places the verb in only the first clause of verse 24, clearly implying it in the second). Also note that the parallel passage in Colossians (3:18–19) commands submission of wives (*hypotassesthe*) and love from husbands.

1 Peter 5:5). Although the apostle clearly assigns differing purposes to husbands and wives, he just as clearly exempts no one from the requirement of having the attitude that was also in Christ Jesus who made himself nothing and became obedient to God's call for selfless sacrifice (cf. Phil. 2:5–8).

In Christ's kingdom submission does not lessen believers' standing; it confirms their place. Christians' responsibilities vary; their value does not. To conclude otherwise is to reason that Christ becomes inferior in the Godhead when he submits himself to the Father (John 6:38; 1 Cor. 15:27–28), though Jesus proves himself to be equal with God (John 5:18); or that the Spirit deserves less glory because he performs the purposes of the Son (John 16:7). By his trinitarian nature our God has made it abundantly clear that an equality of value does not require an identity of roles.[7]

The Glory of a Christian Wife (5:31)

The dignity of a Christian wife shows not only in the sacrificial calling she shares with all God's people, but also in the glory of purpose God grants her. By her gifts and calling, she completes her husband and enables him to fulfill God's purposes for himself and the family (see chapter 18 discussion of Eph. 5:31). To understand the dignity of this "completing-another" purpose, consider the goals our society often advocates for women. In contrast to the biblical perspective that a woman fulfills heavenly purpose in marriage, the modern perspective, taken to extreme, shackles women's (as much as men's) worth to mere standards of income, title, and accomplishment. This perspective teaches women that if they have not sufficiently risen in corporate stature or professional recognition, then they are less valuable than those who have achieved more. Worth becomes directly tied to a row of figures in a bankbook or a line of ink in a year-end report.

While the Bible offers no support for denying women equal opportunity in the workplace, God clearly wants women (and men) to gauge their significance by measures of greater consequence than material possessions or societal pecking order (Matt. 16:26; 1 Tim. 6:17–19). When personal worth gets linked to personal success, then one's dignity exists simply in comparisons to others. And it rests on transient personal and

7. See also note 11 in chapter 18 and note 1 of this chapter.

economic factors beyond anyone's control. God wants us to base our dignity on his eternal regard.

A subtle, yet spiritually debilitating, change occurs in a woman when her dignity is measured by wealth, number of children, size of house, personal accomplishments, or a husband's prestige. Such measurements turn a woman's attention from God's purposes to her own.

The indignity of this self-focus can become apparent in as unlikely a source as an avant-garde women's magazine. A book reviewer in just such a magazine noted that early feminist books had been about women gaining access to power and opportunity. But in assessing newer books, she concluded: "Feminism is no longer a battle for equal opportunity in a male-dominated society, but a kind of 12-step recovery program for wounded women. . . . 'There is an endless appetite for self-help books. . . .' They do not offer women still struggling in an unfair world any clarion call to arms. Instead they urge women to redefine their inner lives."[8] This review was written by an advocate of modern feminism. How sad (and revealing) that, at least in this reviewer's estimation, a cause that began with advocacy of others has deteriorated into just another journey into me-ism. Everyone recognizes the indignity of pouring one's life and demands into the vain, cloying pursuit of "what's-in-it-for-me."

Whether man or woman, no one is more disrespected than an individual driven by selfishness. We sense this truth in the comic-book life of a Donald Trump, who gains power and wealth at the expense of our respect; and we see the opposite in the life of a Mother Teresa, who received the honor of the world though she had nothing. Such examples enable us to understand the dignity God grants to the wife who submits herself to the good of her husband and family. The Bible says they will rise up and call her blessed (Prov. 31:28). Her dignity is assured in the blessing of the ones to whom she gives herself. Her glory resides in her unwillingness to be driven by any priorities other than God's. Heaven is reflected in her focus on others.

One of the great failings of the church is that we have done so little to let women know how valuable and glorious their family ministry is. My wife has said to me, "Bryan, you must understand that all my choices

8. Phoebe Hoban, "Women Who Run with the Trends," *Harper's Bazaar* (January 1994), 42.

are attackable. It does not matter which choices I make—there are some women in the church who will criticize me for not fulfilling what they say is my proper role. If I stay at home all the time, some will say that I have abandoned my gifts. If I go to work full time, some will say I have abandoned my children. And if I try to divide my time wisely, then I am open to attack from all." Thus I am obligated to assure my wife that I value her and the decisions she makes according to biblical priorities. I must conscientiously affirm that nothing is more precious to me, and that nothing is more valuable to our family, than my wife's fulfillment of her biblical responsibility, so that she is not improperly swayed by trends or traditions.

Our church simply cannot expect to be heard in this society without trumpeting the glory and value of the biblical purposes women serve. We cannot even expect women in the church to believe our assertions of their spiritual equality if what they also hear within our church walls is derision over their questions, insensitivity to their predicaments, flip answers, needless exclusion from the use of biblical gifts, and political put-downs (whether intended or not).

It can be so disconcerting and discouraging in churches that hold the truth of Scripture dear and that speak clearly of the preciousness of women in God's family economy for women to find themselves the object of the jests, jibes, and insensitivity of men. We may understand (but cannot accept) the explanation that those in biblically conservative churches are only reacting to the feeling that we are under siege from the forces of our society. If we really think that we will uphold biblical priorities by embarrassing, intimidating, and demoralizing those God places among us, then we are doing much more to reveal our insecurity than to promote orthodoxy. We cannot expect Christian wives to desire the role God has designed for them if the church does not vigorously defend the dignity of that responsibility and give honor to those who assume it.

A Christian woman said to me recently, "I understand why so many women struggle with what the Bible says about submission, but I have never struggled with submitting to my husband because he lets me know how much he respects me." When Christian women know they are respected for honoring their biblical responsibilities, then they are fulfilled and dignified by the expression of their gifts in behalf of another.

The Desire of a Christian Wife (5:33)

Only as we in the church defend and proclaim the dignity of the duty God gives Christian wives can women be expected to desire this vital biblical ministry. The nature of this desire Paul also unfolds with the most careful choice of terms.

To Respect Her Husband (5:33)

Paul concludes this address to husbands and wives with the instruction for men to "love" their wives and for wives to "respect" their husbands (Eph. 5:33). Here the apostle seems to be dealing with each gender at the weak points of our relational tendencies. Often a man's great temptation is to use the power of his position and physique to enforce dictatorial rule or to indulge passive self-absorption. A woman's comparable temptation is to use the power of words and emotions to diminish a husband's influence so that she has control of the home. Paul allows neither "power play" by commanding men to love their wives sacrificially and commending women who respect their husbands.

Something in us instinctively knows the power of the forces the apostle is seeking to curb. When Kathy and I were first married and living in an apartment in a poor part of our city, the paper-like walls and floors of the complex gave us an ear-opening perspective on the way some people live. The violence in so many of the families around us was particularly shocking. Most curious was the minister's family below us. Most of their fights were about who was the "better witness." We usually tried to ignore the shouts and slaps until he started choking her so she could not respond, and then we would have to find some way to intervene—phoning, knocking, or borrowing a cup of sugar.

The fights were awful. But as Kathy and I, night after night, would try to close our ears to the conflict as it built, we would sometimes turn to one another and say, "Why does she taunt him so? She knows he is going to hit her." We did not know then what we have now learned about abusive homes: that as often as a man will try to dominate a woman with strength, a woman will try to control a man with shame.

Even if violence is not a part of our home (although it is a part of many Christian homes), we must learn by listening to the ways spouses try to get their way, even in Christian marriages. With intimidation or intransigence—both of which are expressions of power—men often exert their control. Women, by a look, a cutting remark, an accusation, or some embarrassing reminder may seek to diminish their husband so that he becomes less sure of himself and, thus, more controllable. Sadly these factors often then turn cyclical, as insecure men react to their sense of being diminished by becoming more dominating, which then gives a wife more opportunity to needle and shame, which subsequently triggers more abuse. When this cycle is operating at any level, each party in the marriage is vying for power; but note, Paul crusades for love (5:1–2). Love permits none of this grappling for spousal control. A Christian husband has not been granted the privilege to intimidate or ignore his wife; a Christian wife has no right to diminish or shame her husband.

Early in our marriage my wife and I agreed not to belittle one another in public, even in jest, because we noticed how many of our friends used ridicule (often quite innocently disguised in teasing) to get an edge over one another. I had to be honest with my wife and say simply that I need her respect. Too few Christian women seem to know how much husbands need their wives' respect. There have been moments in my life when I felt the only significant things I could claim as my own were the respect and love of my wife. When a church's leadership was convinced I was wrong, when I felt I had sacrificed my career for a cause everyone about me seemed to think was foolish, when fellow churchmen have made me doubt my own competence, when I have delivered an awful sermon, when I have been guilty of sin that I knew exposed the weakness of my faith—in each of those moments the respect of my wife meant everything. I could not do, or be, what I believe is important (and at times frightening) in the life of the church were it not for my wife's consistent faithful regard for me.

To Reverence Her Husband (5:33)

Paul's careful choice of words indicates that he knows the importance of a wife's regard for her husband. The translators of the New International Version tiptoed gently past our modern sensibilities when they used the phrase "the wife must respect her husband" (Eph. 5:33). The word translated "respect" is actually of the same origin as the word Paul uses to say we must "reverence" Christ in the verse that opened this discussion of Christian submission (Eph. 5:21). In both places the word communicates the idea of holy awe.[9]

We readily understand how and why we are to "reverence" Christ, but why would Paul say that a wife should "reverence" her husband? I can remember the objection of a woman in our church who was seeking to divorce her husband without biblical cause. When leaders urged her to find new cause to love her husband, she replied, "Love him! I can't even stomach him. Just the thought of him makes me ill." I wonder how she would have felt if we had urged her to "reverence" him!

I cannot tell you with certainty why Paul uses this term. One likely reason is that the husband, as the spiritual head of the home, is the one who must give account to God for the spiritual nurture of the family. Much as an Olympian's parents can be almost awestruck by their own child who will perform before millions under the scrutiny of human judges, so wives who see with spiritual eyes may perceive the glory of the responsibility the Judge of the universe assigns to husbands who must stand before the hosts of heaven to give an account for their families.

Still, a more certain reason that Paul uses this term is that it points a wife back to the source of her esteem for her husband. The word "reverence" in these final words of instruction must have been intended to echo the apostle's opening words that root all aspects of submission in Christ's purposes (Eph. 5:21). The effect is to encourage wives in this way: "Your relationship for your husband finds its source not in who he is, or what he does, or how deserving he is. The relationship to which God calls you has its source in your relationship with the Savior. The desire for fulfilling your responsibility must be rooted in the desire you have to please God."

This divine-source motivation is more evident when we consider the structure of this entire chapter. This startling imperative for "holy awe" addressed to wives at the end of this passage is actually the bloom of thoughts planted at its beginning: "Be imitators of God, therefore, as dearly loved children and live a life of love, just as Christ loved us and gave himself up for

9. In Ephesians 5:21 the noun *phobos* appears, and in 5:33 the verb *phobeomai* (for comments on *phobos* in Eph. 5:21 see chapter 17). Both are general words for fear that take on the special meaning of "reverence" in reference to God or Christ. The Greek verb *phobeomai* is used for such reverence for the "Lord" Christ in Colossians 3:22 (and for God in Luke 18:2, 4; 23:40; Acts 10:2, 22; 13:16, 26; 1 Peter 2:17; Rev. 11:18; 14:7; 19:5). This verb is employed often in the Greek Old Testament for the reverence of God (e.g., Gen. 22:12; Pss. 55:19 [Septuagint 54:20]; 66:16 [Septuagint 65:16]; Eccl. 8:12; 12:13).

us as a fragrant offering and sacrifice to God" (Eph. 5:1–2). The confidence and joy we take from the Lord's love is the strength and motive for our own. Wives are to reverence their husbands (and husbands are to give themselves for their wives) out of reverence for what Christ has done for us. Ultimately each of us is to be continuing Christ's sacrificial work in each other out of love for him. Just as Jesus' sacrifice was a fragrance of love that pleased God, so our ultimate desire to fulfill our marital responsibility comes from the knowledge that it, too, brings pleasure to the God of grace.

I sensed a bit of this divine pleasure when an elderly couple sat before me in church. They have been lifelong in the church and wed for more than sixty years. The husband's Bible should be collected for a museum of the saints. He has taken and cross-indexed sermon notes in that Bible for most of the sixty years of the marriage. It is a masterpiece of Bible love and knowledge. Yet, despite that legacy of love for the Lord's Word, the man has faced health challenges in recent years that have sometimes challenged his memory. On that particular Sunday that the couple sat before me, he could not find the book of Esther when the pastor announced the text for the sermon.

I watched him flip pages, look confused, and then turn more pages with a look of desperation growing on his face. His frantic motions caught his wife's attention. And with a movement of her hand as subtle as a whispered kiss, she reached over and turned his Bible to the appropriate page. Then, without looking at him she smiled and patted his knee in reassurance.

The gestures were so simple, but they well demonstrated a love that had matured in the Lord for more than sixty years. She used the gifts and abilities that were hers to help her husband, to support him in his worship, and to show respect for him even when his limitations meant that he may no longer have deserved such honor. The gestures would have been easier if she had not strained to be so subtle, but her goal was his glory. In preserving that, she dignified herself, and surely brought pleasure to God.

Who witnessed this wife's giving of herself in that caring touch? Perhaps no one on earth beyond my wife and me witnessed this dear woman's reverent care for her husband. Yet I pray that on that day she sensed heaven's regard for the beauty of her service. And I pray that she, along with all Christian wives, will know and claim the eternal value and scriptural glory of every wife who so submits to her husband out of reverence for Christ.

20

The Godly Household

Ephesians 6:1–9

Fathers, do not exasperate your children; instead, bring them up in the training and instruction of the Lord. . . . And masters, treat your slaves in the same way. Do not threaten them, since you know that he who is both their Master and yours is in heaven, and there is no favoritism with him. (Eph. 6:4, 9)

I was staying in the home of a pastor, a man well known for the scholarship of his ministry and the significance of his church. As a guest speaker for the multiday conference hosted by his church, I generally spent the afternoons working on the message for the evening. One afternoon as I was working in the pastor's study, I could not help listening to the sounds of his children playing outside the window. I guess you could call it "playing." One child, the nine-year-old son of the pastor, dominated the other children with cruelty, profanity, and intimidation.

The son's performance was hard to listen to and even harder to study through, so after a while I walked out of the office to take a break. The room opened at the bottom of a stairway, and as I crossed the threshold, a movement at the top of the stairs caught my eye. I glanced up to see the boy's mother watching him out a window overlooking the yard. Her silhouette against the window made her obvious pain a more poignant picture. With shoulders drooped and head down she flinched at the latest profanity from her son. Then she heard me too, and as she turned toward me I realized she was crying. From where I stood she knew I had heard her son, and through her tears she said, "I don't know what's wrong with my son. His father doesn't know either. All we know is that we have failed. Our son is only nine years old and we have already failed. We just don't know what we should do."

The statements were a cry of despair as well as a confession of failure. Yet hidden in the words was an understanding that still revealed a biblical hope. The mother said, "*We* just don't know what *we* should do." Though they were unsure what to do, these parents still recognized that an obligation rested upon them. Despite their child's antics and the aching he was causing them, these parents acknowledged they still were responsible for their child's nurture. This is the essence of biblical parenting: not acquiescing to our children's demands, but serving their ultimate need to live as God requires. Sometimes this service is pleasant and other times painful, but it is always characterized by the selfless application of one's resources, insights, and energies to the formation of a child's Christlikeness. Parents honor God when by a compassionate embrace or a controlled discipline they cultivate or correct the spiritual development of their children. Parental service is not a matter of giving in to a child's whims but using our authority and resources for our children's spiritual welfare. We lead by using authority to serve the best interests of others.

This servant/leader principle directly flows from the truths already articulated in this section of Paul's epistle (see the "headship" discussion in chapter 18) and now is applied to other household relationships discussed in this chapter. Paul begins by applying this principle to parenting (later he will speak to masters of households). Despite this important instruction, however, I cannot help but wonder if the mothers and fathers he addressed in that decadent Roman culture were tempted to a bit of exasperation with the apostle. Maybe they shared the disappointment we feel over the brevity of his instruction. For despite the cultural perils our children face and the scores of consequent questions we must address, Paul's direct words to parents in this passage are limited to a scant single verse (v. 4). Is that enough? A positive response will elude us unless we consider the building blocks Paul makes foundational for families before he constructs instructions for a child's nurture.

Foundations for Godly Parenting (6:1–3)

The building blocks undergirding a child's construction become apparent when we consider the expectations that God has for the foundation of a child's life. This little instruction to parents follows a host of instructions for the household of faith. A child is raised in a context, and God's expectations for that context are clear as we consider the relational building blocks that provide biblical foundation for the rearing of our children.

1. The first building block parents should lay for a child's biblical foundation is the parents' own love relationship with the Lord. Paul assumes he is speaking to people in the body of Christ. The preceding content of much of this letter to the Ephesians is addressed to understanding the nature of the church. This should not be merely a passing observation. It means the Lord's expectation is that biblical parenting occurs in a church context.[1] This has the immediate practical implication of communicating that we can learn much about parenting from those in the church—through the preaching of the Word, the example of elders, and conversation with peers. Especially when my wife and I were first-time parents, we took many cues about raising our children from other couples in the church whose families we respected.

Beyond these practical implications, however, there is a more fundamental reason why Paul waits to discuss parenting until after his discussion of the church. The formal relationship one has with a church should be indicative of a personal relationship with the Lord. It is this intimate love relationship with the Lord that is the most basic building block of Christian parenting. To sense the close tie of this love relationship with the Lord to Christian parenting you have only to return to the beginning of the previous chapter and see how Paul began his instruction to Christian households: "Be imitators of God, therefore, as dearly loved children and live a life of love, just as Christ loved us and gave himself up for us" (Eph. 5:1–2). You could even back up to the beginning of the book where Paul greets the Ephesian church in terms of our divine parenting:

> Grace and peace to you from God our *Father* and the Lord Jesus Christ. Praise be to the God and *Father* of our Lord Jesus Christ, who has blessed us in the

1. Note that the children are directly addressed here, as if Paul expects them to be present in the church congregation while his letter is read aloud.

> heavenly realms with every spiritual blessing in Christ. For he chose us in him before the creation of the world to be holy and blameless in his sight. In love he predestined us to be *adopted* as his *sons* through Jesus Christ, in accordance with his pleasure and will. (Eph. 1:2–5)

Paul assumes that in order for us to be good parents we must have a solid understanding of our relationship with our heavenly Father. There are at least two reasons for this foundation block of a love relationship with God for Christian parenting. The first relates to our own need for a model and the second to our need for security.

It is more than a truism that we tend to become our parents. For good or ill we tend to follow our parental models. Abusers raise abusers, alcoholics raise alcoholics, adequate parents raise well-adjusted children. Of course, there is comfort in this equation only if you are on the positive side. Fear and despair press in, however, if you recognize your own parents' modeling was inadequate or horrid. How can we hope to raise our children well if our own models are broken? The words of the apostle rescue every Christian parent from hopelessness by reminding us we are all on the positive side of the parental-model equation. Our Father is the Lord. For some of us the grace in this simple fact is beyond measure. We are not bound to the patterns of our earthly parents. We have a heavenly parental model to guide us.

The reality of the heavenly Father's love can be more real, more powerful, and more motivating than biology and learned behavior. For this reason, an intimate relationship with him does more to establish what we will be as parents than any other single fact in our existence or background. What we perceive him to be as our Father is more determinative than any other factor of the types of parents we will be. This realization that *the Father we perceive our God to be shapes the parent we are able to be* challenges us to make sure that our understanding of, and consequent relationship with, our God is biblical. To ensure this, Paul says much about the nature of this heavenly parent in his letter to the Ephesians.

When Paul says that God has been a Father to us since before the foundation of the world, the apostle directly reinforces the security we must have in order to be effective Christian parents. Our greatest failings as parents usually result from our insecurities. I recognize this in myself when I confess what typically upsets me most with my children. What makes me angriest? The things that embarrass me or make me look bad are most likely to make me mad. I find that I too easily discipline out of my concern for me rather than out of a primary concern for my children's welfare. At its root such selfish discipline is a fear of others' rejection or disregard.

Conversely, my wife (among many others) often struggles to discipline because of the fear that a child will feel badly toward her or reject her love. Of course, these are not gender-specific traits. There are plenty of fathers who will not discipline for fear of a child's rejection, and many mothers who serve their own egos through managing the performance of their children.

The sum of these truths is that anxious parents do not make good parents. So Paul assures Christian parents that God dearly loves us now and has so loved us since before the creation of the world. These assurances take concern for self out of one's motives in parenting. Our security in our relationship with God frees us to parent for our children's good rather than for our own—giving to them our security rather than taking it from them (Eph. 5:2).

No doubt this necessity of parenting from personal security further explains why Paul has placed instruction regarding the relationship between spouses before that regarding the relationships of parents and children (Eph. 5:22–33). There is more than a biological order here. There is also a relational priority. My relationship with my wife should so confirm her personal security with the Lord that she can afford to do what is best for our children even if that action threatens her sense of need for a child's acceptance. My wife's relationship with me should be such a reinforcement of my own security with the Lord that I do not need to discipline my children for my sake.

2. A second building block that establishes the relational foundation for biblical parenting is a love relationship with one's spouse. Paul lays down instructions for relating to spouses before giving imperatives for parents (Eph. 5:22–33). Again, the implicit understanding here is that biblical child-rearing is built on a healthy relationship between a husband and wife. This does not mean that children cannot be well raised by single parents whom the providence of God has placed in sole charge of children, but this is not the regular pattern of Scripture.

The reasons that such a spousal pattern is needed include having a united front when it comes to discipline, but more is at stake here. Through his parent's marriage a child learns the joys of intimacy not just with another person, but with God. The ultimate goal of the husband's headship and the wife's submission is making Christ's love a reality for everyone in the family. As the parents make Christ real to each other, they also teach the child what intimacy with the Lord means. Patterns of intimacy in the home are a direct path to transcendent understanding. As a result, the greatest earthly gift a parent can give a child is a loving relationship with one's spouse.

Nothing more clearly indicates to me the impact of a parent's marriage on a child's nurture than the family history of a close Christian friend. He was raised in a large family with siblings whose ages are widely separated. He reports that a line of spiritual and emotional health seems to be drawn in the sand of time separating those children raised in the early, healthy years of his parents' marriage and those raised when his parents' relationship was deteriorating. Emotional health, solid marriages, and spiritual maturity characterize the now-adult, older children. Conversely, troubled psyches, brushes with the law, and spiritual indifference mark the younger children who were raised in that same home during the unraveling of their parents' marriage. No one can prove a direct cause and effect for the differences in these siblings. Healthy marriages do not guarantee well-adjusted children, and healthy children sometimes emerge from the unhealthiest home environments. Still, Scripture affirms what our own experience and instincts attest: healthy marriages typically are the soil from which healthy children spring.

This conclusion is not merely anecdotal. In a *Christian Century* article, William Willimon reports on a sampling of students at Duke University. More than 45 percent of these students cited their parents' divorce as their "most determinative life-changing event."[2] Their stories and statistics join with Scripture to testify that safeguarding the parents' marriage relationship remains an essential element of a child's nurture.

Because the relationship between parents is a primary conduit of God's grace into a family, a parent who slights a spouse for career advancement, unnecessary economic advantage, or even ministry concerns ultimately hurts the child. To pursue career or wealth at the expense of a healthy home costs way too much. The gain is temporal, the loss eternal. The love of one's spouse must take precedence even over the concerns of the children. A parent

2. William Willimon, "Reaching and Teaching the Abandoned Generation," *Christian Century* 11, no. 29 (Oct. 20, 1993): 1018.

who pours affection and attention into children at the expense of honoring a spouse may seem to be serving the children, but such priorities actually jeopardize the ultimate welfare of the children. Because God intends for the parents' relationship to bring the reality of Christ's love into the home, a spouse who sacrifices the marriage even out of concern for a child jeopardizes the spiritual welfare of that child.

A loving relationship with God and a loving relationship with a spouse form the foundation of biblical parenting. When we assume the responsibilities of biblical parenting, we submit ourselves to the consequences of these truths. This means we commit ourselves to honoring God and our spouse for the sake of children even when such commitments prove to be trying, difficult, and seemingly undesirable.

Comfort can be found within these foundational relationships for parenting. By affirming that good childrearing occurs within a context of Christian living rather than through a precise set of right or wrong parental behaviors, the Bible assures us that a child's nurture is not determined by a set of rules that we mysteriously divine from Scripture's relatively few statements on specific parenting practices. This conclusion flies in the face of some handbooks of Christian parenting that teach there is one correct way to affirm, or show affection, or discipline. Not only does such teaching defy the liberties of Scripture and deny the dignity of individual differences, such rigid instruction also seems to imply that children can be ruined if we make a mistake in some particular aspect or moment of a child's upbringing. This is precisely what Scripture does not attest.

We will all make mistakes as parents. This does not automatically make us bad parents, or immediately threaten the ultimate welfare of our children. There are actions, moments, and practices where I know my wife and I have made mistakes with our children. There are moments of improper discipline, impatience, and poor judgment that I hope they will not recall in years to come. Yet, if I fear that some particular mistake will ruin my children, then I will ultimately be paralyzed, or I will refuse to examine my parenting patterns lest I have to confess I have warped my children by past mistakes. However, the fact that God places the foundations for biblical childrearing in a spiritual- and marital-life context means that no single act of well-intentioned parenting is determinative of a child's future. The grace that a Christian heart embraces and a Christian's marriage should foster allows

Christian parents the privilege to fail, seek forgiveness, and try again. The Father's unconditional, eternal love erases dread that a momentary lapse in judgment will ruin our children or destroy our own relationship with him. This grace of God frees Christians to parent without second-guessing every act of discipline or denying past errors.

Of course, the fact that we can fail and make mistakes does not mean that God does not have some specific expectations for our children. To make that clear the Bible not only reveals the relationships that form the foundation of Christian parenting, it also describes the responsibilities that should direct the actions of both parents and children.

3. A third building block necessary for a biblical foundation is clear understanding of the responsibilities of the child.[3] We will parent well only if we know what God expects us to nurture in our children. What does God expect children to do? The simple answer: obey (Eph. 6:1).[4] Children should submit to their parents "in the Lord" (Eph. 6:1b)[5]; that is, do whatever parents require so long as their instruction does not lead outside God's will or Word. Paul also makes it clear that this submission is to be more than just doing what a parent requires. Sullen, angry, begrudging fulfillment of duty is not acceptable. The apostle says an obedient child must "honor" father and mother (Eph. 6:2). Children must submit in action and attitude to their parents' instruction.

Paul supplies two reasons for such submission. First, children are to obey "for this is right" (Eph. 6:1).[6] What a peculiarly simple and, at first glance,

3. The term for children here (*tekna*) can designate young children, and it can also refer to children well into adulthood. Nonetheless, the parallel clause in Ephesians 6:4 about "training and instruction" seems to focus primarily (if not exclusively) on preadult children.

4. Note the shift in verb here from wives "submitting" (Eph. 5:22, 24) to children "obeying" (cf. Col. 3:18, 20). "Obey" (*hypakouō*) refers to following the directives of another, and it most often speaks in the New Testament to the proper following of God's gospel directives (Rom. 6:16–17; 10:16; Phil. 2:12; 2 Thess. 1:8; cf. Acts 6:7; Heb. 5:9; 11:8; contrast Rom. 6:12, 16). Even nature itself obeys Jesus' commands (Mark 4:41; cf. Mark 1:27; Luke 17:6). Nonetheless, this verb can also be applied to people obeying those in authority (Eph. 6:5; Col. 3:22; 2 Thess. 3:14; 1 Peter 3:6).

5. The phrase "in the Lord" is lacking in a few early (but widespread) manuscripts, yet most manuscripts (including many early ones) include it. The parallel command in Colossians 3:20 indicates that the obedience of children "pleases the Lord" and, therefore, children also obey parents out of respect for the Lord. This is a close parallel to the earlier "Wives, submit to your husbands as to the Lord" (Eph. 5:22).

6. The Greek word for "right" (*dikaios*) is also thought to have this meaning ("right") in Philippians 1:7 (also cf. in the NIV Matt. 20:4; Luke 12:57; Phil. 4:8; Col. 4:1); nonetheless, *dikaios* more often denotes "just" or "righteous." Here in Ephesians 6 it is right (or just) for the child to obey because this is what the righteous commandment requires (Eph. 6:2).

unnecessary statement! Still there is great wisdom in the apostle's simple affirmation of the rightness of a child's obedience. We will feel the weight of it when we face our struggles to hold our children to these standards of Scripture. Consider that moment when a little three-year-old bundle of sugar and spice bedecked in the finery of a new Easter dress ignores her daddy's "No," and grabs a handful of candy from the table treats intended for coming guests. Then, when Daddy patiently again tells this precious package of lace and sweetness to put the candy back, she says "No." Now Daddy knows that if he does anything about this rebellion he will feel like the Grinch who stole Easter. What should this father require? What does the Bible say? "Children, obey your parents *for this is right*."

Surely it is because God knows how we as parents are so easily torn by our love for our children and our insecurities about ourselves that he graciously speaks so plainly here. To the question that sometimes almost tears our hearts out, "Should I insist my child obey?" God answers, "Yes, 'for this is right.'" When a young mother cannot bring herself to discipline her child, when a father will not supply the time or attention to discipline, when the latest childrearing book has made us question whether we should just ignore some improper outburst from a child—in each of these moments we need the straightforward simplicity this Scripture supplies.

If we love our children too much to require them to do what is right, then we have not really loved them enough. Paul explains why this is so when he gives the second reason for children to submit to their parents. Not only is it right for our children to obey, it is good for them (Eph. 6:2c–3). God promises obedient children *blessing* (i.e., "that it may go well with you") and *safe-keeping* (i.e., "that you may enjoy long life on the earth"). This last statement does not guarantee that obedience will ward off all disease and accidents.[7] It is rather Paul's proverbial (a general truth that can have exceptions) rendering of the promise that accompanies the fifth of the Ten Commandments (Ex. 20:12; Deut. 5:16).[8] In this way the apostle communicates that a disobedient child endangers himself physically and spiritually.

7. The fifth commandment promises long life on the "earth," but the Greek word (*gē*) can also mean "land." The "land" in the Pentateuchal context likely designated the Promised Land, which God gave to Israel; here in Ephesians this meaning appears extended to encompass more broadly God's promise of blessing to his covenant people.

8. Note, however, that the promise can have an eschatological fulfillment in that children who honor God with their lives will be kept safe for eternity on this earth when it is renewed by Christ's return. Also

The damage disobedience causes was well demonstrated to my family on a trip to an amusement park years ago that is now legendary for us. We were waiting in line for a train ride. As the wait lengthened, a five- or six-year-old child in front of us decided to climb on a fence railing to a position that made it hard for the remaining people in line to pass. His mother reacted quickly, saying, "Johnny, come down from there." Johnny did not even move an eyelash. Were not the damage being done so evident, the litany of correction attempts that followed would have been comical:

> "Johnny, come down from there, right now!"
>
> "Johnny, come down. I won't tell you again."
>
> "Johnny, I am going to count to three."
>
> "One, two, . . . two and a half. . . . Now, Johnny, I mean it."
>
> "Johnny, I am going to tell your father when we get home."
>
> "Okay, Johnny, just stay there. I'm going to leave you if you don't come down."
>
> "Johnny, please, please, come down. I'll buy you an ice-cream cone."

We squeezed by the child when it was our turn to ride the train, but for all we know Johnny is now twenty years old and still sitting on that fence rail.

If you can re-create that incident in your mind's eye, think not only of the stone-cold look on Johnny's face. Consider the countenance of the surrounding people. What do their faces reflect? They are all frowning at the child. Responsible parents must dare to look at these faces because they prophesy

---

note that Paul's citation of this promise follows with slight variation the Septuagint of Exodus 20:12 (which is quite similar to the Septuagint of Deut. 5:16). The Septuagint accurately represents the intent of the Hebrew of Deuteronomy 5:16. Jesus also quotes this commandment (Matt. 15:4; 19:19 and parallels). Second Temple Jewish literature evidences frequent use of this commandment in moral instruction (e.g., Philo, *Special Laws* 2.224–33; Josephus, *Against Apion* 2.206; Pseudo-Phocylides 8); yet this could be carried to an extreme in such literature, as when respect for parents "atones for sin" in Sirach 3:1–5. Paul remarks that this is "the first commandment with a promise"; although other of the Ten Commandments can be rooted in depictions of God's character (especially the second and fourth), this is the only one with a promise. Paul's observation also points to the prominent position of the fifth commandment at the beginning of the human-to-human (horizontal) commands in the Ten Commandments (these Ten Commandments themselves function as the most important and first commandments of the Mosaic law).

the future of an uncontrolled child. A child who will not obey a parent's authority only sees the world's frown. Not only does such a child inherit a parent's frustration, he also reaps the disapproval of teachers, neighbors, other parents, friends, future employers, and ultimately his own heart. A child who consistently sees his reflection in the frown of the world can only view himself as despised. This is one reason the book of Proverbs wisely says that parents who will not discipline hate their child (Prov. 13:24). Such parenting can subject the child to a lifetime of misery—a fate we typically desire only for our enemies.

Not only is a disobedient child a bother to the world, but he is also a danger to himself. Only a few days ago in a nearby park I witnessed a child running away from his father who was frantically calling, "Jason, don't run that way!" "Why, Daddy?" said Jason as he kept running, and tumbled headlong over a hill into a concrete culvert only his taller father could see. The child's bloodied forehead was a painful corroboration and a vivid object lesson of this Scripture's truth. We are to raise obedient children because this is right for them and it is good for them, protecting from the consequences of disobedience that are both earthly and eternal. For, ultimately, a child who does not know obedience cannot know the Lord. Paul elsewhere contends that "disobedience to parents" is indicative of sinful pagan society (Rom. 1:30; cf. 1 Tim. 1:9) and that such disobedience will also be a characteristic of the "terrible times in the last days" (2 Tim. 3:1–2).

4. A fourth building block needed for a child's biblical foundation is clear understanding of the expectations God has for parents. The first expectation can be simply summarized: *We* are to raise our children. The apostle's words carry an implicit understanding of who is to do the raising of a child. Fathers and mothers are mentioned in Ephesians 6:2, not grandparents, not paid services or servants, not institutions outside the home. This does not mean the Bible forbids parents ever to utilize the services of others in fulfilling their biblical responsibilities of child care. Still, Paul's words challenge us all to make sure that we are the chief caregivers.

In this society where social, economic, and spiritual pressures are tearing parents from their home responsibilities, this caution must not be ignored. Too many parents in our churches have virtually turned over the upbringing of their children to daycare, school care, grandparents, or nannies. I want to emphasize here that no one unfamiliar with the specific life complexities that face another family has a right to determine that the family automatically sins by using any version or degree of these nonparental care systems. The question of whether or not *you* are still raising your child is a matter of conscious, conscientious, committed involvement in a child's nurture that defies putting a stopwatch on the hours a child spends here or there. Nevertheless, a husband and wife working long hours in demanding jobs that leave them both exhausted at the end of the day when they pick up kids from grandma's or daycare must question whether they are submitting themselves to the family model the apostle envisions for biblical parenting. Bigger homes, nicer cars, and longer vacations purchased at the price of absent parents cost far too much, and may well indicate submission to values distant from Scripture.

The fact that the parenting God requires is a spiritual discipline helps explain the wording Paul uses to instruct parents. The apostle addresses his imperatives to fathers (Eph. 6:4). This is not because Paul thinks that mothers have no role in childrearing. He clearly identifies maternal responsibilities when he instructs children to honor father *and* mother (Eph. 6:2). By addressing the spiritual head of the home directly, Paul underscores the spiritual challenge and significance of biblical parenting.

The "father" language in this passage, though it is applied to earthly parents, forces into our consciousness the Person for whom the apostle has more frequently reserved that word. In this epistle the word "father" most often refers to God in his relationship with believers.[9] This inspired echo makes us understand that we are to nurture our children as God fathers us, and never to sacrifice their good for our own. Such fathering is in shamefully short supply in our society no matter where we look. Television news specials have recently shifted the blame for our nation's inner-city problems from drugs to the absence of fathers in urban homes. But the fathering crisis is not limited to the poor neighborhoods of our nation's cities.

Recent reports indicate that while 80 percent of African-American children in the United States are being raised apart from their biological fathers, 60 percent of Hispanic children and 50 percent of white children are in the same situation. In that same sampling of students at Duke University that I

9. See Ephesians 1:2–3, 17; 2:18; 3:14; 4:6; 5:20; 6:23. The only exceptions are in this passage and in the Genesis 2:24 citation in Ephesians 5:31.

have already cited, only one of these best and brightest of America's children mentioned a father when asked to list the most life-molding factors in their lives. At all rungs of our society fathers have led the parental abdication of family responsibilities. Paul leads parents back into homes through the headship of fathers. His words and family worldview remind us that parenting is a high spiritual priority we must take care not to slight.

Imperatives for Godly Parenting (6:4)

Having laid the foundation of relationships and responsibilities on which God expects us to build our parenting, the apostle finally issues imperatives for parenting through the instructions he gives Christian fathers (Eph. 6:4).[10] With these imperatives God tells us how his expectations for our children translate into parental action. The imperatives for Christian parents come in both negative and positive form; we are told what not to do, and then what to do.

5. A fifth building block involves taking seriously some negative instruction (Eph. 6:4a). Dedicating ourselves to our children's welfare means first that Christians must not parent with unbiblical patterns or priorities. Paul says, "Do not exasperate your children" (Eph. 6:4). Understanding the special term the apostle chooses for this negative instruction unfolds its broad implications for parenting. The Septuagint usage of "exasperate" (with which Paul would be familiar) does not refer simply to frustration, anger, or anxiety. The term was usually reserved to describe God's own just anger over Israel's idolatry.[11] This is why the King James Version translates this instruction of

10. Greco-Roman society (and much Jewish literature from the period) tended to so emphasize the role of the father that his power (*patria potestas*) could be viewed excessively. Paul again is careful in this context to balance his instruction to children with a warning to fathers not to exasperate their children (cf. Pseudo-Phocylides 207 for similar Jewish advice).

11. This is true in over fifty of the fifty-seven Septuagint occurrences of *parorgizō* (e.g., Deut. 4:25; 31:29; 1 Kings 15:30; 16:2). Even the few exceptions here are informative: so in the Septuagint of Psalm 106:16 (=Septuagint 105:16) the transgressing Israelites "provoked Moses"; and in Deuteronomy 32:21 (quoted in Rom. 10:19) God will "provoke" Israel (via Gentile domination) because they first "provoked" God (for two other exceptions see Ezek. 32:9; Dan. 11:36). The Second Temple book Sirach cautions children against "provoking" their mother lest they be cursed by God (Sir. 3:16; and see other uses in 4:2–3). This verb is related to other terms for anger, and thus it connects to the cautions about anger earlier in Ephesians (Eph. 4:26–27, 31).

Paul as "provoke not your children to wrath." The exasperation described here refers to a righteous resentment of actions or attitudes inconsistent with one's faith commitments. An exasperated child is one who has a right to be provoked because of the incongruities between a parent's stated beliefs and that parent's actual behaviors.

Our children have a right to be upset with us when our parental actions conflict with our spiritual values. We do not have to guess what values the apostle has in mind. We simply need to review the preceding verses that detail his immediate concerns. Authority based on the example of Christ, love patterned after the sacrifice of Christ, and respect expressed out of reverence for Christ have dominated Paul's previous discussion. What then would cause exasperation in terms of parenting inconsistent with these values? One cause would be authority that requires submission but submits to none, as when a mother tells a child to quit whining by whining at him, or when a father compels self-control by throwing a temper tantrum. Another cause would be love that needs sacrifice but seeks self, as when a mother pushes for a child's success to affirm her own worth, or when a father punishes to enforce behavior that secures his own reputation or comfort. We also exasperate our children when we demand respect at the expense of individual dignity, as when a mother shames a child into obedience, or when a father exerts control by comparing the child with others inside or outside the family.

Whether it takes the form of manipulative guilt trips, shaming silent treatments, or abusive denials of worth, the home that rules by guilt undermines biblical obedience. The essence of parental love is recognizing that we are the dispensers of God's grace into our children's lives. They learn to identify and reverence God's character through the way we treat them both in moments of profound pride and in times of intense disappointment.

When one of my children was younger, I struggled with these truths. He bordered on being hyperactive, and was always on the edge of being out of control. I was unprepared to deal with a child who not only seemed unconcerned about his own safety but also appeared oblivious to the concerns of others. His antics consistently endangered him and embarrassed his parents. We are not against disciplining our children in traditional ways, but we were failing to gain his obedience.[12] I was spanking three, four, and more times each day trying

12. Although corporal punishment can certainly be overused and abused, Christians have long accepted spanking as one possible means of discipline (although certainly not the only one). Aside from

to exercise my authority, but to my dismay I discovered I was up against my match. No amount of correction controlled this child. It was frustrating and demoralizing for the whole family. As a result, I found I was sometimes disciplining out of the anger I felt over my own failure. With the anger, resentment began to grow between my son and me. His behavior exposed my own sense of parental inadequacy, and he began to think of himself as a wild child because that was the way I characterized him. My concern for my own reputation and authority was robbing my son of my love, his dignity, and God's grace.

Something had to change. One day I said to my wife, "I can't spank him anymore." This was as much an admission of failure as it was a decision to try something else. Selfish concern for my own authority and respect was damaging my son. Stubborn adherence to discipline measures that had worked with my other children, which were part of my own background, and that demanded the least change in me had, in fact, driven me from what I knew Christian parenting required.

We began to consider alternative ways of compelling our son's obedience because we knew abandoning discipline was not biblically permissible. God was gracious. He put a gifted-child expert in our church who told us that highly intelligent children sometimes crave mental stimulation so much that they cannot control their need for sensations of any type. By physically disciplining our child we were actually heightening his stimulation threshold. The Lord then helped us recall that even in his most excitable moments our child would almost always settle when his mother took him into her lap, stroked his hair, and told him about how thrilled we were the day God brought him into the world. If we could just capture the dynamics of that immobilizing mechanism, we thought we might have a new discipline tool.

So, for the next several months whenever control was needed, instead of spanking we simply made our son sit down wherever he was. He had to stop and be still until we said he could resume his activity. For this active child such time-outs were almost torture, but we insisted. The technique did not work like a charm, but over a period of weeks we began to see results. By allowing him to decompress instead of adding more stimulation to his system when we disciplined, our son was able to get more control over his own actions.

---

the famous "spare the rod, spoil the child" (roughly equivalent to Prov. 13:24), the book of Proverbs frequently suggests spanking as an appropriate discipline (Prov. 22:15; 23:13–14; 29:15; cf. 10:13).

I feel foolish as I now in hindsight examine some of my mistakes with my son. Yet confession of these errors gives me a greater appreciation for the wisdom of Scripture and more understanding of God's grace. By insisting that a child respond to a single kind of discipline in the same manner as his siblings, I was not allowing my son the dignity of being the individual that God made him to be. By not separating discipline for my child's welfare from concern about my own reputation and authority, I was allowing selfishness to motivate my parenting. God's parenting standards reflect a deeper grace. Out of respect for the individual gifts God has granted my children, I must submit myself to the responsibility of discovering ways to discipline that honor the unique ways God has made them and plans to use them. Biblical parenting requires me to respect the dignity of my children's differences, to use my authority selflessly, and to affirm their worth without protecting mine. In short, my parenting must remain consistent with my understanding of the grace God has extended to me. I must not exasperate my child.

6. A sixth building block is the conscientious application of some positive instruction (Eph. 6:4b-d). God does not tell us merely what not to do for our children. He tells us what to do as well. Christian parents should "bring them [children] up in the training and instruction of the Lord" (Eph. 6:4). John Calvin translated this "bring them up" phrase as "let them [children] be fondly cherished." This interpretation reflects how the Bible uses these nurturing terms elsewhere. Paul uses similar wording earlier when he says a husband should cherish his wife as much as he "cares" for his own body and just as Christ does the church (Eph. 5:29). Paul now intensifies these concepts in his instruction to fathers. The effect is that each father must care for his child as much as he "cares" for his own flesh.

As the first husband, Adam, "cared" for his wife as flesh of his flesh, and as Christ "cares" for his bride, the church (which is the product of his sacrificed flesh), so we as parents are to "care" for our children. They are the product of our flesh. Since our life is in them, we are to bring up our children with the care we give to our own bodies. We nurture our children as the essence of our lives. The physical and spiritual vitality God grants us should also thrive in our children through our sacrificial care. Parents are givers. We pour Christ's love into the nurture of those he commits to our care.

How do we express such care? Paul gives two words to guide: training and instruction (Eph. 6:4c). Both of these terms refer to the discipline of children but with slightly different shades of meaning. The first term (training) carries the more positive connotation; we are to model, teach, and encourage godly patterns of life.[13] The second term (instruction) contains a slightly negative nuance; we are to warn away from, admonish, and discipline that which is inconsistent with godliness.[14] You may feel the shades of meaning a bit more clearly in older translations that encourage parents to raise children "in the nurture and admonition of the Lord." Paul's use of such terms in tandem for childrearing reminds us that biblical parenting requires a balance of affirmation and admonition.

This scriptural balance of firm guidance and loving correction finds almost startling corroboration in modern family research such as these studies cited by Bonnidell Clouse in *Teaching for Moral Growth*:

> Criminologists at Harvard Law School studied the characteristics of over 2500 male offenders in reformatories, correctional schools, jails, and prisons; matching them with nondelinquent boys and men by age, ethnic origin, intelligence, and place of residence. They wanted to see how the two groups differed. The kind of homes the men grew up in appeared to be the most important factor. "If one is looking for a point of impact in which a multiplicity of criminogenic factors are involved, it will be found in the household, in parent-child relationships," . . .
>
> Delinquents and criminals tend to come from homes in which discipline is *overstrict or erratic*, supervision is unsuitable, neither parent shows warmth or love, and there is little or no closeness of family members. Nondelinquents are more apt to come from homes in which discipline is *firm but kindly*, supervision is suitable, parents show affection for the child, and the family does many things together. . . . [emphasis added]

13. This Greek word (*paideia*) was a common term in Greco-Roman society for education and training. In the New Testament it can be used of discipline/correction (Heb. 12:5, 7–8, 11), or more broadly it can indicate how Scripture "trains" the Christian in righteousness (2 Tim. 3:16). Both the "correction" nuance (used frequently) and a broader sense of "training" can be evidenced in the more than one hundred occurrences of *paideia* in the Septuagint and in the many uses of the cognate verb *paideuō* in the New Testament and Septuagint.

14. This Greek noun (*nouthesia*) is also found with the sense of "warning" in 1 Corinthians 10:11 and Titus 3:10 (in the Septuagint see Wisdom 16:6). Its cognate verb usually means to warn or admonish (Acts 20:31; 1 Cor. 4:14; Col. 1:28; 3:16; 1 Thess. 5:12, 14; 2 Thess. 3:15; though possibly "instruct" in Rom. 15:14).

> As was mentioned, in comparison with noncriminals very few criminals came from homes in which the discipline is "firm but kindly." Research in the area of child development shows that "firm but kindly" is optimal. Diana Baunrind (1970), in a ten-year study of parent-child relationships, found that *authoritative* parenting in which the parents exert firm control without hemming the child in with too many restrictions is more apt to produce a motivated, friendly, moral, and cooperative child than either *authoritarian* parenting in which the parent attempts to shape, control, and evaluate all the activities of the child, or *permissive* parenting in which few demands are placed upon the child who is permitted to do whatever he or she pleases. . . . The children of authoritarian parents tend to be discontented, distrustful, and lacking in warmth, while the children of permissive parents tend to be the least self-reliant and self-controlling of all three groups. Children reared permissively are often said to be spoiled and may become tyrants who rule over their own parents. . . .
>
> Authoritative parents use a unique combination of high control and positive encouragement of the child's autonomy and independence. There is no question but that the parent is in charge. Guidelines and rules are given within which the child must operate, and standards for future conduct are set. But parents share their reasons for the rules and encourage verbal give-and-take on the part of the child. Both the rights and interests of the parents and the rights and interests of the child are taken into consideration.[15]

How do we achieve this balance of training and instruction, of affirmation and admonition, of kind but firm parenting? The answer lies in the final words of Paul's instruction. We are to raise our children in the training and instruction "of the Lord" (Eph. 6:4d). The chief goal of parenting is to create a life that knows and honors God. This means we are constantly to be examining whether our words, our manner, our correction, and our home environments nurture an understanding of the Lord. Such godly parenting requires more than the application of a specific technique of discipline, or setting a curfew in accord with the standards of the latest parenting seminar. No single set of techniques or rules will make us good parents. Our sins and our children are far more perplexing than any book, seminar, or sermon can comprehensively cover. There are, of course, many helpful things that we can learn from Christian authors and other experienced parents. Still, we must

15. Bonnidell Clouse, *Teaching for Moral Growth* (Wheaton, IL: Victor, 1993), 67–68.

understand that the complexities of each child's nature and situations will not allow template responses.

This uniqueness of each child should not frustrate or bewilder us. Rather, we can take it as a biological affirmation of the beautiful creativity God has applied to making each of our children special. Not only does the uniqueness of each child affirm individual dignity; it has the additional benefit of driving each conscientious Christian parent back to where we started: prudent application of scriptural principles discerned by a heart in tune with the Lord. The fundamental step of parenting is a loving relationship with God. This is especially obvious when we are talking about discipline. For if we do not have a grip on grace, we will not have the courage to discipline, but if grace has no grip on us, there will be no constraint to our discipline.

Grace for the Whole House (6:5–9)

The constraint that grace puts upon discipline allows the apostle to deal with the last and most difficult of subjects for the ancient household: master and slave relationships. In the contexts more familiar to modern Christians, master/slave relationships are about work—unfair work! But Paul addresses this subject in the context of the Christian household. The relationships of husbands, wives, parents, children, slaves, and master are all considered in the context of this household discussion because all were considered members of the household—those for whom the family was responsible. Slaves were not family in terms of having equal rights, but neither were they simply employees or property. They were considered part of the family unit; thus they are discussed in this portion of Paul's letters that scholars call the "household codes." As members of the household, slaves' lives were both the instrument and the obligation of their master's efforts, choices, and concerns. We do not have categories that readily capture the ancient worldview, but Paul uses the complexities of these household obligations to press important spiritual priorities for all.

Household Slaves (6:5–8)

Paul presses on the conscience by leveraging the understanding that a master bore spiritual as well as physical responsibility for a slave. In Paul's time, a slave assumed the religious obligations of a master. This applied in

Christian households, too. When a master became a Christian, he or she baptized everyone in the household (e.g., Acts 10:47–48; 16:15, 30–33; 1 Cor. 1:16). This followed Old Testament patterns in which slaves received the sign of circumcision when the head of the household entered God's covenant (Gen. 17:23; Ex. 12:43–48).

Such total control of another's existence was easily abused, so Paul seeks to regulate the master-slave relationship along with the other household relationships. He tells slaves to be witnesses for the gospel by working well (Eph. 6:5–8). And he tells masters to treat their slaves well (Eph. 6:9). We appreciate the evenhandedness, but these words of the apostle still do not feel right. We want him to outlaw slavery. Our contemporary sensors do not detect adequate contempt for slavery in Paul's words.

One way of dealing with our distress regarding Paul's dealings with slavery is to transfer all notions of slaves and master to modern contexts of employees and employers. Yet, while there certainly are principles of obedience and fair treatment that apply in the modern workplace, we should never pretend that employment readily compares to slavery. An employee has the obligation to demonstrate Christ's integrity and service, and an employer has the obligations to demonstrate Christ's justice and mercy. Each has the obligation to be the face of Christ to the other in the workplace, but neither experiences the difficulty of being such in the context that a master/slave relationship imposed.

Another way of dealing with the difficulty of Paul's seeming indifference to the injustice of slavery is to note that ancient forms of slavery were quite varied (a slave might be a stablehand, a handmaid, a captured enemy, or the treasurer of a city). According to Old Testament law, the bonds of slavery could not extend beyond six years. All of these factors remind us that the slavery Paul addresses cannot be directly compared to the chattel slavery of American history. Still, this soft-pedaling of the evil of slavery ultimately rings false to any who know the pain and degradation of denied freedom. Surely the apostle knows this, too, as he turns his attention to masters and reminds them of the gospel that binds them to higher priorities than their society has recognized.

Gospel-bound Masters (6:9)

As difficult as it for us to do, it remains best to keep the evil of slavery in mind and recognize that Paul was simultaneously dealing with immediate cultural realities and preparing for cultural transformation. Here is how he approaches the subject: The sacrifice/submission principles evident in Paul's instructions to parents (in this chapter) and to husbands (in chapter 18), he now applies to slaves and masters. The application of these principles will not differ greatly from what has been said regarding the other household pairings Paul has already addressed. Slaves, for the moment, would need to continue in their condition, faithfully serving their masters for the sake of giving credibility to the gospel and honor to God (Eph. 6:6–8). As with wives and children, this instruction on submission would create few ripples of objection in the ancient world.

On the other hand, the radical nature of Paul's gospel priorities becomes apparent when he directly addresses masters. The apostle commands masters to exercise their authority in such as way as to ensure the Christlike treatment of their slaves (Eph. 6:8). This would have upended the worldview and daily practices of virtually all slave-owning households. Knowing this, the apostle charges masters to make no threats, and bolsters his instruction with the reminder that the slave and the owner have the same Master in heaven (Eph. 6:9).

With inspired wisdom the apostle enables the gospel to progress in a society that approves slavery while planting seeds for its destruction. Similar steps are evident in the book of Philemon where the apostle does not command a master to release his slave, but rather to think of him as Paul's "son" (Philem. 10) and to treat him "as a dear brother" (Philem. 16). Elsewhere Paul reminds all that "he who was a slave when he was called by the Lord is the Lord's freedman" (1 Cor. 7:22). Thus it is apparent in the households where Paul's instruction for masters and slaves was followed that the bonds of slavery were broken and that the freedom of Christ would reign.

The applications to us are not difficult. If slaves and masters were obligated to demonstrate Christ to each other in a context of such great inequity, then how much more should we be willing to represent him in our work contexts. If our employer is unfair, that no more excuses us from acting with integrity than a slave was excused from Christlikeness in a society of unfairness. If an employee is difficult, that gives a boss, who represents Jesus, no more option of retribution or arbitrariness than a master. Even where difficult economic or employment decisions must be made, all who represent Christ to one another must act with his truthfulness, integrity, and charity.

The complexities of properly exercising authority in the Christian home and workplace drive us back to consideration of the foundations and purposes of all authority in the home. The way the apostle structures his presentation of these issues makes it clear that all expressions of authority (spousal, parental, or master) are to reflect the character of our Savior. As a consequence, leadership in the home and workplace should lead us to greater dependence on him and to a greater appreciation of him. By using our authority for the good of others we discover our own most noble purposes and are drawn most closely to the divine nature.

News reports of the actions of two parents aboard Amtrak's Sunset Limited revealed these truths of divine reflection with a powerful poignancy. Gary and Mary Jane Chancey were riding on the Limited on a foggy September morning in 1993 when it plunged off a railway bridge into a bayou outside Mobile, Alabama. The Chanceys were traveling with their eleven-year-old daughter Andrea, who has cerebral palsy and requires a wheelchair. As their train car sank into the bayou, water rushed into the Chanceys' capsized compartment. Fighting the flow of water rushing through their window, the two parents combined their efforts to lift Andrea to a rescuer. Then the water pressure overwhelmed them, pushed them deep into the darkness of the train cabin, and they were gone.

These parents gave their lives to lift their child to safety. God gives all Christian parents and leaders a similar calling. Under what is sometimes intense pressure and pain, we are to lift those in our care to the Lord. By the ways we model the Lord and mold others' perception of him, we discern the love we require as well as the love we must give. By lifting others to the Savior we become like him, and thus discover more of the love of the Savior who lifts us to heaven by his sacrifice.

21

The Armor of Faith

Ephesians 6:10–24

Finally, be strong in the Lord and in his mighty power. Put on the full armor of God so that you can take your stand against the devil's schemes. (Eph. 6:10–11)

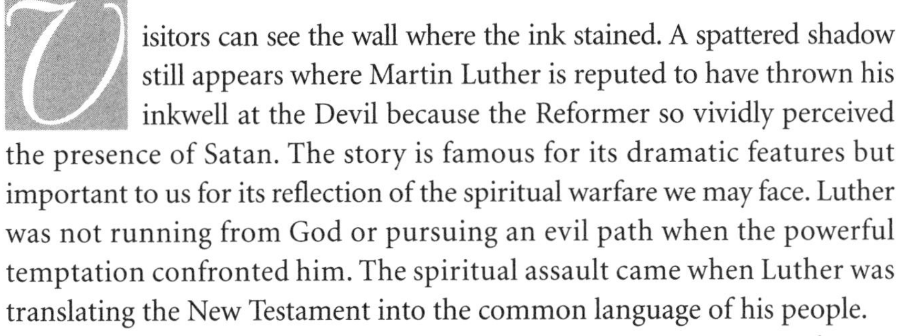

Visitors can see the wall where the ink stained. A spattered shadow still appears where Martin Luther is reputed to have thrown his inkwell at the Devil because the Reformer so vividly perceived the presence of Satan. The story is famous for its dramatic features but important to us for its reflection of the spiritual warfare we may face. Luther was not running from God or pursuing an evil path when the powerful temptation confronted him. The spiritual assault came when Luther was translating the New Testament into the common language of his people.

After enduring great personal sacrifice and while engaging in a religious effort that would change the face of the Western world, Luther's faith was severely tested. The attack of the spiritual enemy was intense despite Luther's noble activity. At the time of great spiritual endeavor, Satan never seemed more real.

Luther's experience teaches us that we are not immune to spiritual assault even when we have personally sacrificed and deeply immersed ourselves in noble spiritual endeavor. In fact, these are the moments that may bring the most intense spiritual battles. Neither personal resolve nor church walls insulate us from Satan's threats.

The realities of spiritual warfare remain in every spiritual condition. Consider the pressures that face modern Christians despite centuries of refining biblical thought and fighting for biblical principles. The fortresses of fundamentalism that artificially kept potential temptations at arm's length by demonizing all forms of alcohol, tobacco, card playing, and theater going are crumbling throughout the evangelical world. At the same time, the accessibility and allurement of the Internet have put sexual temptation, material indulgence, gambling entertainment, personal disengagement, and ungodly communication within a mouse-click of persons of every age and social station. The expectations of business travel, the interactivity of genders in the workplace, the "freedoms" of the pill, the anonymity provided by our closed-apartment lifestyles (even when living in million-dollar homes), the personal isolation allowed by multithousand-seat worship centers, the enticements of consumerism endlessly promoted by amoral Western prosperity—all combine to create a culture where sin is crouching at the door of even the most socially respectable.

At the same time that these winds of external change blast us, changing patterns of family and church relationships make our spiritual footing unsure. A short list of the cultural gales that have swept over our traditions would include divorce, domestic partnerships, abortion, single-parent homes, the booming daycare business, the busyness of soccer-moms and career- or hobby-dads, the media preoccupation of teens, the recreation orientation of Sundays, and the decline of biblical literacy. The breakdown of traditional structures that nurture families and faith not only have robbed us of models of how to live godly lives, but also have removed even from Christians the ordinary restraints against temptation that past generations of believers had built (sometimes through inappropriate legalism) into their lives.

The consequences of wandering from God's path are evident in the moral "freedoms" of our fracturing society. With all of this personal liberty, we have discovered great bondage—not merely to occasional temptation, but to ingrained patterns of spiritually destructive behavior. Our slavery becomes apparent in our prayers for release from compulsive, addictive, and repeated sin. We pray, "God, please help me to stop . . . to stand against this temptation . . . to resist this sin . . . to change this habit . . . to act differently . . . to be rid of this compulsion . . . not to fall again, to yield again, or to be this way again." But how do we stop the impulses that so powerfully war against our righteous resolve? How do we progress in the battle against sin and self when Satan attacks us through our own lusts, weaknesses, and ambitions? The apostle Paul provides the answer in the passage under consideration.

In Ephesians 6:10–18, Paul equips us for spiritual warfare. He assures us that we can stand against the Devil's schemes (Eph. 6:11). There is hope of spiritual victory over our compulsions when we use the apostle's instruction to understand the nature of our enabling, our Adversary, our weaponry, and Christ's empowering love.[1]

Our Enabling (6:10)

With the simple word "Finally" (Eph. 6:10), the apostle reminds us that there has been instruction preceding this immediate plan for spiritual battle.[2] This plan cannot operate in isolation but presumes a grasp of matters previously addressed in the book of Ephesians. These matters include an understanding of the divine source of our relationship with the God who eternally loved us and made us his own (chaps. 1–2), the need for a unified relationship with others in the church whose varying gifts help make us spiritually mature (chaps. 3–4), and the beauty of loving and sacrificial relationships in our families that help us incorporate and reflect Christ's grace (chaps. 5–6). Implicit in these preceding instructions are all the patterns of belief and behavior that we would expect the apostle to say equip us for godly living.

Godly Patterns

There are no shortcuts to the spiritual battle preparation identified here but, thankfully, there is no mystery either. Doing as Paul has instructed

1. Material for this chapter is used with permission from Crossway Books and is adapted from the author's *Holiness by Grace: Delighting in the Joy That Is Our Strength* (Wheaton, IL: Crossway, 2001), 135–56.

2. The Greek for "finally" (*tou loipou*) also appears in Galatians 6:17, and in related forms in 2 Corinthians 13:11; Philippians 3:1; 4:8; 1 Thessalonians 4:1; 2 Thessalonians 3:1 (cf. 2 Tim. 4:8). Each seems summative, and each introduces instructions (they can also appear mid-letter, so Phil. 3:1; 1 Thess. 4:1).

in preceding passages—putting ourselves under sound teaching, seeking prayerful association and accountability to others in the church, and serving one another in healthy family relationships—nourishes Christlikeness in us. Following these well-worn paths to godliness informs and aids Christian living. Ours is not a magic religion full of mysterious incantations, secret handshakes, and arcane codes. Thus we have a duty to challenge others and ourselves to be faithful in these ordinary patterns of spiritual preparation if we are to progress and persevere in spiritual maturity as God intends. Our immersion in, and integrity with, these patterns of Christian association and accountability are the ordinary means by which we grow in godliness.

Of course, we fear that these ordinary means of growth are not enough. And, in truth, they are not. If all we are depending on to help us overcome Satan are our own right beliefs and behaviors, then we are in grave danger. Perhaps we have discovered this when we have altered our patterns and renewed our personal resolve to master a sinful practice in our lives, only to struggle and fall again. Then what should we do? Paul answers in what follows with his gentle reminder of the necessity of godly patterns in our lives. Paul does not annul the necessity of the patterns, but he places them in their proper context.

Godly Power (6:10)

Ultimately God's power alone equips us to grow spiritually by motivating our hearts and enabling our wills to follow the patterns of godliness his Word commands. God expresses this power by embracing us and energizing us so that we can do as he requires.

We can begin thinking how this empowering process works by acknowledging the reservations we may have about the biblical patterns already mentioned. We may feel cautious about these ordinary means of grace not because we question their goodness, but because we fear that we are not good enough to practice them faithfully enough. Our Lord's care shines in how he deals with this concern in Paul's initial words.

The apostle begins his instruction by urging us, "Be strong in the Lord" (Eph. 6:10).[3] The "in the Lord" phrase is Paul's common way of referring to

3. Each time Paul uses this verb ("be strong") he locates the source of that strength in God and in Christ (Rom. 4:20; Phil. 4:13; 1 Tim. 1:12; 2 Tim. 2:1; 4:17). Note also the passive occurrence of the synonymous "be strengthened" (*krataiōthēnai*) in Ephesians 3:16.

our relationship with God made possible through our union with Christ. We are *in* him: covered by his blood, robed in his righteousness, members of his household, sons and daughters, in union with him, beloved. We may dread the exposure of our weaknesses in our battle against sin, but the apostle reminds us that the strength of our relationship with our God is provided by Christ. Because we are in him, we have access to a power that is greater than we.

My five-year-old daughter decided to play soccer with her much older siblings and cousins at a Thanksgiving gathering. She quickly tripped and got trampled. In tears she ran off the field, determined to enter the fray no more. So I picked her up, hugged her to my chest, and played the rest of the game with her in my arms. Knowing that she was in my embrace renewed her zeal for the battle, and she could not have been a more enthusiastic team member. In a similar way we gain strength for spiritual battle from knowing that even if we have failed and fallen, we are "in the Lord." Because knowledge of our unchanging relationship grants us the will to fight and to reenter the fray when we have fallen, we understand why Paul first urges that we "Be strong in the Lord." In God's embrace we will battle with renewed zeal and strength.

After these words of relational encouragement, Paul identifies the source of the power that we will need for spiritual battle: "Be strong in the Lord and in his mighty power" (lit., "the power of his might," Eph. 6:10). God not only provides us support but also the actual strength that we need for spiritual battle. The nature of this strength that comes from God should not be mistaken for mere internal energy, as though God were promising to dispense spiritual vitamins or pep pills. Paul's specific wording indicates that God does not want us merely to supplement our strength with his, but so to invigorate the new life that he has regenerated in us that he *is* our strength.

The phrase that Paul here uses to refer to God's might, he has used previously in this epistle. In the first chapter, Paul writes that he wants the saints to know God's "incomparably great power for us who believe" (Eph. 1:19a). That incomparable power the apostle then describes as "the power of his might" (Eph. 1:19b) that God "exerted in Christ when he raised him from the dead and seated him at his right hand in the heavenly realms" (Eph. 1:20). Then Paul goes on to say that this power also "made us alive with Christ even when we were dead in transgressions. . . . And God raised us up with Christ and seated us with him in the heavenly realms in Christ Jesus" (Eph. 2:5–6). All of this background makes it clear that the "mighty power" in which Paul urges us to "be strong" is resurrection power—the divine power that makes the dead live and reign in heaven.

The powers of resurrection and rule have special significance in this passage where Paul indicates that believers war not against flesh and blood but against authorities and powers of this dark world (Eph. 6:12). Since Paul has earlier said that the risen Christ is above all authorities and powers (Eph. 1:21), then we who are in union with Christ are spiritually seated with him in heaven and thus have rule with him over the authorities and powers of Satan. The present effects of this power have been carefully described in the early passages of Ephesians. Because of the power of God's might, we who were once dead in our transgressions and sins are now alive (Eph. 2:1, 5). Once we followed the ways of this world and were under the dominion of the ruler of the kingdom of darkness, but now by virtue of the definiteness of his sovereign choice we reign with Christ in the heavenly realms (Eph. 2:2, 6). Once we were by nature objects of wrath, but we are now his glorious inheritance (Eph. 2:3; 1:18). Once we were foreigners and aliens, but now we are fellow citizens with God's people and members of God's household (Eph. 2:19).

We can further understand the power of God's mighty work in us by identifying the differences that distinguish our past spiritual status (before Christ indwelt us) from our present status (due to his indwelling Spirit):

Once We Were	**Now We Are**
Dead (2:1)	Alive (2:5)
Under the dominion of Satan (2:2)	Seated in heavenly realms (2:6)
Objects of wrath (2:3)	His glorious inheritance (1:18)
Separate (2:12)	Brought near (2:13)
Foreigners (2:19)	Fellow citizens (2:19)
Aliens (2:19)	Household members (2:19)
Denied gospel mystery (3:5)	Understanding gospel mystery (3:4)
Infants (4:14)	Maturing in Christ (4:15)
Old self (4:22)	New self (4:24)
Darkness (5:8)	Light (5:8)

These contrasting descriptions reiterate with startling clarity that God's resurrection power has made us fundamentally different creatures than we were in our unregenerate state.[4]

Through the power of God's might, we have a new nature. Whereas the old nature was not able to resist the wiles of Satan and the lusts of our flesh, the new nature operates with the power of the risen Lord and thus has abilities never before attainable nor apprehensible. Sinclair Ferguson summarizes,

> While we continue to be influenced by our past life, "in the flesh," it is no longer the dominating influence in our present existence. We are no longer in the flesh but in the Spirit (Rom. 8:9). Christ's past (if we may so speak) is now dominant. Our past is a past "in Adam"; our present existence is "in Christ," in the Spirit. This implies not only that we have fellowship with him in the communion of the Spirit, but that in him our past guilt is dealt with, and our bondage to sin, the law, and death has been brought to an end.[5]

Biblical truths examined previously in this epistle now ring with greater clarity and significance (see Eph. 1:21–22; 2:4–10, 22; 3:16; 4:7; 5:8, 18). Because of Christ's resurrection power at work in us, greater is he that is in us than the Evil One who tempts us (1 John 4:4). We enter spiritual warfare with strength born of the confidence that no temptation will assault us that is greater than our ability to resist—because we face our trials with that same indomitable force that raised Christ from the dead (1 Cor. 10:13). Isaac Watts wrote of the resurrection victory that we have over Satan's attacks:

> Hell and your sins resist your course;
> But hell and sin are vanquished foes:
> Your Jesus nailed them to the cross,
> And sang the triumph when he rose.[6]

Our minds protest, "This is not the way that I feel. I feel that I am not able to resist. I have fallen before and have resolved with all my willpower that I will not fall again, but then I have. I do not feel that this resurrection power is mine." We feel this way because no greater vestige of our former nature clings to us than the

4. See earlier notes on Ephesians 4:17–24.
5. Sinclair Ferguson, *The Holy Spirit* (Downers Grove, IL: InterVarsity, 1996), 112.
6. Isaac Watts, "Stand Up, My Soul; Shake Off Your Fears," 1707.

doubt that our new nature is real and that the God who gave it is more powerful than any foe. That is why the apostle prepares us for spiritual battle with the truth of God's certain relationship and the reality of our resurrection power. Faith in these is essential if we are to enter the battlefield with confidence.

Faith that God has made us new, has made us his, and has made us able is essential before we will experience God's victory over compelling and compulsive sin. I thought of these truths as I listened recently to my wife working with a thirteen-year-old doing an algebra problem. The answer was not coming easily, and before too long my straight-A-student daughter was crying, "I will never get this. I can't do it. I'm so dumb."

My wife, with a voice made stern enough to cut through the tears, said, "You are not dumb, and I never want to hear you say that. Now look back two pages in your book and see what you already know is right and then come back to this problem." Our daughter is not dumb. The sternness in her mother's voice was actually a loving affirmation of our daughter's true nature and ability. Only the lack of confidence that she could handle the problem kept her from pushing through to the answer. When her mother refused to allow this child to characterize herself by that powerless nature, the capability our daughter actually had came to the fore and she solved the problem.

God speaks in a similar fashion to his children through the apostle Paul. The Lord hears us crying, "I am so weak, evil, stupid, and incapable that I cannot overcome this sin." We are lovingly corrected: "'Be strong in the Lord and his mighty power.' The One who has loved you gives you a nature that makes you capable. You must have faith in the power of his might. Your Adversary, who says that you cannot resist, lies and seeks your harm. Do not believe him."

Our Adversary (6:11–16)

So able is our Adversary that the apostle takes some time to describe him. The Devil schemes (Eph. 6:11). Since we are new creatures in Christ Jesus, our struggle is not fundamentally against our own impulses anymore. The Devil uses forces beyond mere flesh and blood as his instruments.

His Nature (6:12)

Paul says that Christians wrestle "against the rulers, against the authorities, against the powers of this dark world" (Eph. 6:12). Terms such as these designate dark spiritual forces in Ephesians (1:21; 2:2; 3:10) as also elsewhere in Paul (Rom. 8:38; 1 Cor. 15:24; Col. 1:13, 16; 2:10, 15; cf. 1 Peter 3:22). Many attempts have been made to classify these demonic forces of darkness identified by Paul. Most of these identifications are speculative and based on traditions clouded by history. Paul's varied language in his writings also cautions us against delineating a labeled hierarchy of demonic forces; rather, his purpose is broadly to remind readers of the spiritual battle that rages in the heavenlies and wars against us. Christ's triumph over these forces is assured and inaugurated (Eph. 1:21), even if, during these evil days (Eph. 5:16) before the consummation of Christ's triumph, the believer must act wisely and be careful not to give the Devil a foothold (see notes on Eph. 4:27).

When Paul states that we must be prepared to stand in "the evil day" (Eph. 6:13; contrast Eph. 5:16), he likely has in mind a time of particularly strong spiritual battle for the believer (possibly even as the consummation of the kingdom of God approaches). All of these warnings tell us that the apostle clearly wants us to prepare for spiritual realities the rest of the world may not see. Satan is at work through dark forces that are in the world before our eyes: evil leaders, decadent pursuits, poverty, injustice, racism, promiscuity, and materialism. The Evil One who parades as an angel of light blinds us to the devastating effects of these forces. He deludes or distracts us with selfish interests to convince us that we must accept these evils for the sake of personal liberty, pleasure, and power that are supposed to bring happiness.

Still, the apostle does not limit the evil of Satan to the world we know. Instead, he adds that we are also wrestling against "spiritual forces of evil in the heavenly realms" (Eph. 6:12; cf. 3:10). We are not used to thinking of evil in the "heavenly realms." Paul uses this term broadly to characterize the spiritual world where evil schemes develop to ensnare the heart, confuse the mind, and entrap the soul.[7] Our natural, physical orientation does not normally allow us to perceive this unseen world, and yet the Devil is so clever and able that he operates on both the worldly and spiritual plane in his endeavor to destroy God's kingdom and people. The Bible thus alerts us that the deceit of Satan powerfully and pervasively influences every sphere of life.

7. See Ferguson, *Holy Spirit*, 167: "This work of the Spirit in uniting us to Christ brings the Christian life into an eschatological atmosphere. It is lived out in the heavenly realms (Eph. 1:3; 2:6). But these are also the realms of eschatological conflict where the evil day is faced (Eph. 6:12–13)."

Our Concern (6:13, 16)

Characterizing the delusions of evil is quite painful but necessary:

At the cultural level. Women and children are abused while our entertainments are filled with sexual stimulation that supposedly hurts no one. Racism retreats from the national agenda while one in five young black men is in prison. Recreational spending increases while families in poverty multiply and missionaries struggle for funds. Care for the victims of war and disease increasingly becomes an imposition while our own economy flourishes.

At the family level. Pursuit of higher incomes causes parents to decrease their involvement with the children whose lives they are supposedly improving. In hopes of finding financial heaven in a jackpot people in the United States now spend more on gambling than on food. In the pursuit of personal freedom divorce, promiscuity, AIDS, and abortion mercilessly entangle the lives of virtually every family.

At the spiritual level. More open attitudes toward enjoying the freedoms of Christian liberties—fueled by accelerating changes in societal norms and the erosion of family and church authority—make struggle with compulsive, secret sin more common among us each year. These pursuits further stimulate the selfishness and insecurities that impoverish our relationships and lead to greater struggles with family and community breakdown. All of this pain, fear, frustration, and disappointment are part of Satan's scheming in the spiritual as well as the material world.

The Bible attributes such power to our Adversary in order to make us regard him with proper seriousness and ourselves with proper significance. At the location of the ink-stained wall of Martin Luther, the current curators of the historical site have hung a little monkey with pointed ears and tail to represent "the Devil" Luther supposedly resisted. How convenient were it so. We could then dispense with any real concern about the Adversary who has lived for thousands of years and known the counsels of heaven. We only invite harm to ourselves by making our Adversary small and unintimidating. R. Kent Hughes writes,

> I am no genius at mathematics, but even with my limited capabilities I could be terrific at math if I worked on it for 100 years (maybe!). If I labored at it for 1,000 years and read all the learned theories, I would be a Newton or an Einstein. Or what if I had 10,000 years? Given that time, any of us could become the world's greatest philosopher or psychologist or theologian or linguist. . . . Satan has had multiple millennia to study and master the human disciplines, and when it comes to human subversion, he is the ultimate manipulator.[8]

Beyond these capabilities, the certainty of Satan's attack (Eph. 6:13) and the viciousness of his fiery assault (Eph. 6:16) add to our causes for concern. If Satan is so capable and his evil is so definite and destructive, then we had better regard him seriously. We must also recognize our limitations in confronting him. No one is ready for spiritual warfare until, in view of the nature of this Adversary, we freely confess that apart from God we cannot repel the assaults he will bring through our circumstances and our weaknesses. This is the second great need of spiritual warfare: along with faith in our new nature, we must confess our helplessness without God.

Our Weaponry (6:10–20)

Confession of our helplessness prepares us—even compels us—to don the weapons of spiritual warfare.[9] Paul identifies two major aspects of

8. R. Kent Hughes, *Ephesians: The Mystery of the Body of Christ* (Wheaton, IL: Crossway, 1990), 217.

9. Paul elsewhere employs the image of spiritual warfare when he commands us to "put on the armor of light" (Rom. 13:12; in context this is parallel to putting on Christ, Rom. 13:14), and when he says that the weapons of our warfare are not fleshly since they come with divine power (2 Cor. 10:4). The imagery in such passages varies, so while the "helmet" is "salvation" in both Ephesians (6:17) and 1 Thessalonians (5:8, "the hope of salvation"), the "breastplate" in Ephesians is a "breastplate of righteousness" (6:14) but it is a "breastplate of faith and love" in 1 Thessalonians (5:8—note that "faith" is a "shield" in Ephesians and "love" goes unmentioned among the panoply in Ephesians). This cautions against undue speculation as to why each piece of armor is identified as it is; likely the overall impression one should draw is simply an awareness of the broad array of spiritual weaponry that God has provided. All the specific armor terms are standard ones for Roman military weapons (so the "shield" would be the large door-shaped shield, and the "sword" would be a smaller hand-to-hand combat sword, etc.), but each term also appears repeatedly in the Greek Old Testament. Also important for Paul are the Old Testament associations. In Isaiah 59:17 God himself puts on righteousness as a breastplate and dons the helmet of salvation (also taken up in Wisdom 5:18). In Isaiah 52:7 and Nahum 1:15 there is mention of the "feet of those who bring good news" and "who proclaim peace" (cited in Rom. 10:15). The girding of the waist/loins with truth (depicted as a "belt" in the NIV, Eph. 6:14) is reminiscent of Isaiah 11:5 ("righteousness will be his belt and faithfulness [=Septuagint 'truth'] the sash around his waist")—for the idiom of girding the waist see also Luke 12:35; 1 Peter 1:13. A less clear

this arming process: putting on the full armor of God and praying in the Spirit. We humbly seek these heavenly provisions when recognition of the potency of our enemy rightly erodes our confidence in our own resources to repel him.

Putting on God's Armor (6:11–17)

Confession of our helplessness apart from God must precede putting on our armor lest our preparations be perceived as righteous works we do that qualify us to resist Satan. As Rose Marie Miller writes:

> The first "real enemy" in your life is always your own unsubmitted self-life (James 4:1–10). To struggle against your own agendas and passions is at the heart of spiritual warfare. The second "real enemy" is Satan. The one who hates you without compromise is always the power of darkness (Eph. 6:12). Wherever there is self-praising pride the Devil has much, much influence.[10]

The metal of God's armor is not a product of our energies and efforts, although we can unearth much erroneous teaching that implies otherwise.

The apostle carefully identifies the source of the strength in our armor. He says, "Be strong in the Lord and in *his* mighty power" (Eph. 6:10). How are we to be strong in his power? We "put on the full armor *of God*" (Eph. 6:11). After identifying the magnitude of Satan's power, Paul again tells us to "put on the full armor of God" (Eph. 6:13). The apostle repeatedly emphasizes the divine source of our protection. We take our "stand against the devil's schemes" (Eph. 6:11) and "stand [our] ground" (Eph. 6:13) not primarily by more vigorous performance of good deeds or by greater exercise of our willpower and resolve, but through confidence in and dependence on God's provision.

This perspective does not encourage spiritual sloth. After reminding us twice that our armor is of God (Eph. 6:11, 13), the apostle first says to "put

---

association may be found with Psalm 7:13 (7:14 Septuagint) where "flaming arrows" are mentioned (cf. Ps. 11:2). Swords are associated with words from God in Isaiah 49:2; Hosea 6:5 (cf. Heb. 4:12). Such spiritual characteristics are found thematically throughout the book of Ephesians: e.g., "truth" (1:13; 4:21, 24–25; 5:9), "righteousness" (4:24; 5:9), "gospel" (1:13; 3:6; 6:19), "peace" (1:2; 2:14–15, 17; 4:3; 6:23), "faith" (1:15; 2:8; 3:12, 17; 4:5, 13; 6:23), "salvation" (1:13; 2:5, 8; 5:23), "word" (1:13; 5:26) and especially God's "Spirit" (1:13; 2:18, 22; 3:5, 16; 4:3–4, 30; 5:18; cf. 1:17). Therefore, this passage forms a fitting finale to the epistle.

10. Rose Marie Miller, *From Fear to Freedom: Living as Sons and Daughters of God* (Wheaton, IL: Harold Shaw, 1994), 116.

on the full armor of God, so that . . . you may be able to stand," and then he says, "after you have done everything" that is required, "to stand" (Eph. 6:13). God's armor enables the stand that spiritual warfare requires, but we are also required to take a stand. These instructions maintain the importance and necessity of our efforts, but simultaneously keep us from believing that our works are sufficient to protect us from Satan's assaults.

No matter how excellent was his armor, we would not expect a soldier to do well in battle if his previous diet and exercise had not prepared him to fight. In a similar way the spiritual disciplines and godly patterns of life Paul has previously described help prepare us to battle our Adversary. But "after you have done everything" by way of those preparations, we still must stand and fight. Of course, we would still be vulnerable without armor. So preparing for battle must also include donning armor. That what protects us in the battle is the armor of God should remind us that our confidence is not ultimately in our efforts but in God's provision.

Though there is a great human inclination to do so, if we interpret "putting on the full armor of God" as greater human righteousness or resolve, then the metaphor that Paul is using will ultimately fail. That failure becomes apparent when we consider each instruction of Paul as it is sometimes taught with a well-intended, but misguided zeal to equip Christians to resist Satan through their own efforts. Paul says, "Stand firm . . . with the belt of truth buckled around your waist" (Eph. 6:14). This often is interpreted either as studying the truth so that you know it well, or speaking the truth with integrity. "Stand firm . . . with the breastplate of righteousness in place" (Eph. 6:14). This may be interpreted as acting righteously in as many situations as possible. "Stand firm . . . with your feet fitted with the readiness that comes from the gospel of peace" (Eph. 6:15), which, of course, commends proclaiming the gospel in as many places and ways as possible.[11] "Stand firm . . . [by taking] up the shield of faith, with which you can extinguish all the flaming arrows of the evil one" (Eph. 6:16). Interpreters find various ways to demonstrate that these words require stirring up as much internal sureness,

11. These sorts of explanations have led to debates as to whether the Greek (literally "readiness of the gospel of peace") means "readiness which comes from the gospel" or the "readiness to [proclaim] the gospel." The likely Old Testament origin of this phrase (Isa. 52:7; cf. Nah. 1:15) speaks of the messenger who brings good news and announces peace, and thus such gospel announcement by the believer is probably what is intended here in Ephesians as well (note further the messianic associations with Eph. 2:17).

willpower, or belief as we can, so that Satan cannot penetrate our psyche with doubt or our lives with harm through a chink in our faith.

This kind of interpretation, however, becomes quite troubling with the following set of instructions. Paul next says, "Take the helmet of salvation and the sword of the Spirit, which is the word of God" (Eph. 6:17). How do we supply the helmet of salvation? In the Old Testament, God himself has a helmet of salvation, and we are certainly not able to don such by our efforts (Isa. 59:17). Eternal salvation is not something that our hands control. And how could we be responsible for the sword of the Spirit, which is the Word of God? Yes, I can quote from Scripture, as Jesus did to resist Satan, but I do not provide the Spirit. The oft-cited note that the sword of the Spirit is the one offensive piece of armor Paul mentions still does not imply that the power of the Word comes from us. We wield the Word to fight Satan's influence, but the power of the Word is from the Spirit who inspired it.

How can we equip ourselves with salvation and the Spirit? The solution lies in discovering that such interpretations—whereby we arm ourselves by our actions—miss the point of the apostle. That point eludes us when we question, "How can I provide truth, righteousness, the gospel of peace, faith, salvation, and the Spirit?" The apostle's point becomes evident when we ask, "Who supplies truth, righteousness, the gospel of peace, faith, salvation, and the Spirit?" The answer is: our God, the One who provides our armor.

These weapons against evil are what our God, not our hand, supplies; therefore we can and must trust our armor. The precise language of the apostle furthers this understanding. A literal translation indicates that we put on the full armor of God and stand, "*having* the belt of truth buckled" about our waist, and "*having* the breastplate of righteousness in place."[12] The armor that we use God has already put in place. We stand firm *because* God has already supplied our armor, not *in order to* receive the armor. We stand because we are confident of what God has done, not because of our confidence in our doing what God requires. If my only armor in the battle against Satan is my sufficiency, then I am doomed. I am no match for him, but my God is. Safeguarded by his armor, I can and do stand against the Adversary.

12. Following the initial imperative, "Stand firm," is this series of aorist (i.e., completed action) participles.

This was the point from the beginning: we stand firm against the assaults of Satan because we have strength "in the power of God's might." God provides the power that enables us to stand against Satan's attacks (Rom. 13:12; 1 Thess. 5:8). The Old Testament passage that stimulates Paul's thought on these images makes it clear that these pieces of armor are God's (see Isa. 59:17). Thus we battle with the confidence that we are protected—armored—by his truth, by his righteousness, and with the gospel of peace, with the faith, with the salvation, and with the Spirit that are from him.

Because God provides each aspect of our armor, we need not fear its failure against Satan's attacks. Our confidence is not in our abilities, but in the ability of our armor to withstand assault. It is certainly true that Christian disciplines can further our confidence in and ability to use God's armor. However, if we begin to believe that our spiritual protection rests on our degree of spiritual discipline, then our virtues become tools of unbelief in which we deny the need of grace and assert the rule of self. We do not put on the armor of God by trusting in the more vigorous performance of our duties, but by relying on God's provision for our protection. We gain the confidence to rely on God's armor and utilize it when, on Scripture's authority, we perceive his protection to be as real as the armor Paul observed on the soldier guarding him in prison when the apostle penned these words.

Thus, when the day of evil comes and our temptation is great, we should not say, "Satan cannot touch me because of how truthful, righteous, and faithful I have been." Rather we should say, "I am protected by the truth that though I feel weak, I am strong; though I may fall, I possess Christ's righteousness.[13] And though I am not perfect, I have peace with my God who has provided the faith I could not conjure (for faith, too, is a gift of God),[14] the salvation I could not earn, and the Spirit I daily need." The spiritual disciplines and godly practices of our lives are not what protect us against Satan; they are the means of grace by which God builds within us greater understanding and confidence in him, so that we will stand on his promises and provisions when the day of battle comes.

13. Note that in the armor imagery, it is the belt of truth that holds all the other pieces of armor in place. Trust in the ultimate truth of Scripture enables us to keep the rest of our spiritual defenses ready.

14. See Paul earlier in this same epistle, Ephesians 2:8–9; and also Acts 13:48; Philippians 1:29; 2 Peter 1:1; Westminster Shorter Catechism 30: "The Spirit applies to us the redemption purchased by Christ by working faith in us, and thereby uniting us to Christ in our effectual calling."

The way I visualize this truth—that we are enabled by confidence in the armor that God provides—follows the imagery of the apostle (though confessedly with the image of a medieval knight more in my brain than that of a first-century Roman soldier). I can imagine looking out through the faceplate of the helmet of salvation that God has given me. Coming toward me I see the assaulting forces of the Evil One with all his dominions, powers, and authorities. Simply seeing the approaching cloud of darkness from this mighty enemy, I fear that I cannot stand. The ground shakes and my knees begin to buckle.

Then the apostle Paul, like a general on the field of battle, calls out, "Steady now. Do not retreat. Take your stand. Be strong in the power of his might. Forget the strength that you thought you could provide. But always remember the power of the armor that God has given you. Resurrection power has given you a breastplate of his righteousness, the shield of faith, feet that are shod with readiness that comes from being at peace with the Sovereign of the universe. Beyond all of these defenses, he has given you an ultimate weapon, the sword of the Spirit that is the Word of God. Now, confident of the strength and integrity of the armor that you have been given, stand firm."[15]

Is there any degree of human effort in resisting sin? Yes, of course. In his previous discussion of faith, church, and family patterns, Paul clearly indicates that faithful living is preparation and defense in spiritual battle. In addition, study of God's Word, commitment to righteousness, and the proclamation of the gospel are patterns of life that ready us to repel Satan. Richard Foster personally articulates the responsibility that every maturing believer assumes: "Through the Holy Spirit's guidance and strength, I will order my life according to an overall pattern that conforms to the way of Christ. Over time this process will develop deeply ingrained habits in me so that, at the moment of crisis, inner resources to act in a Christlike manner are available."[16] Our habitual godliness is a means that the Holy Spirit uses to increase our faith, inform our minds, and strengthen our wills for God's

15. This military analogy is clearly implied in the present context, and the repetition of "stand" (Eph. 6:11, 13, 14) indicates that this is our principal calling in the war. Elsewhere (outside specific military contexts) Paul also encourages the churches to "stand firm" (e.g., 1 Cor. 16:13; Gal. 5:1; Phil. 1:27; 4:1; Col. 4:12; 2 Thess. 2:15).

16. Richard Foster, "The Daring Goal: What to Expect When We Accept Christ as Our Life," in 1997 Seminary and Graduate School Handbook (Carol Stream, IL: Christianity Today, 1997), 47.

purposes. We cannot neglect the daily disciplines of holiness and expect to be well muscled for spiritual warfare.

Still, the core steel of our resistance when we "have done everything" (to use the words of Eph. 6:13) is to take up "the shield of faith" in what God has provided so that we can withstand the fiery darts of the Devil (v. 16). "Satan has not changed his strategies. *His approach is always to insinuate that God is not good, and that he is not for us.*"[17] Thus our primary power in spiritual warfare resides in faith because, as Pastor Don Matzat writes: "It is the primary task of the Devil to remove from us the Word of God, primarily the good news of the Gospel. He attacks our faith. In the parable of the sower, our Lord Jesus identified the birds who steal the newly sown seed as the Devil. He does not want us to believe, confess, and stand upon the Word of God."[18] Satan wants to rob us of our confidence in God's acceptance based on the righteousness of Christ alone, knowing that the freedom, joy, and courage provided by the unyielding love of God unleashes the Spirit's power in us to repel Satan's wiles and warfare.

Praying in God's Spirit (6:18–20)

Since the power to stand is ours, then why do we not stand? The gospel answer is not that our enemy is too strong, because Satan is defeated. Neither is the answer that we are too weak, because resurrection power indwells us. Rather the answer is that we do not have sufficient desire to resist. It sounds contrary to the cry of the heart to say that we do not have a desire to stand. We desperately desire the dismissal of the sin from our lives. Yes, we want it gone, but until then we still want it. The sin still appeals. Our armor is not too weak to withstand Satan's attacks unless we let him in, but we do. For this reason, the final instruction of the apostle is not to add more armor, but rather to seek to stir within us the will to use it.

Having discussed the armor that we should put on, the apostle urges us to do one more thing: pray in the Spirit (Eph. 6:18).[19] Why? "Praying in the

17. Miller, *From Fear to Freedom*, 120.

18. Don Matzat, *Truly Transformed* (Eugene, OR: Harvest House, 1992), 186.

19. In Greek the two verbs in verse 18 are participles that link the prayer in this verse to the imperative "stand firm" in the armor of God (v. 14). Paul frequently calls his readers to pray (e.g., 2 Thess. 3:1; 1 Tim. 2:8), even to pray in all circumstances and for all people (Phil. 4:6; 1 Tim. 2:1) with perseverance (Col. 4:2–3; 1 Thess. 5:17; cf. Luke 18:1). Here such prayer is done "in" or "by" the Spirit (*en pneumati*, cf. Jude 20). Paul does not elsewhere specifically call for prayer "in the Spirit" (the dative *pneumati*

Spirit is prayer that conforms to the will and purpose of the Spirit."[20] By humbly submitting our wills and desires to God's, the Spirit takes the limited wisdom and zeal of finite creatures and uses them with infinite wisdom and power to work all things together for good (Rom. 8:26–28). In terms of our sanctification, the "good" the Spirit brings is accomplished by transforming us continually into Christ's likeness (Rom. 8:29).

What do we seek when praying in the Spirit? Such prayer is not a plea for magical power, so much as it is a prayer for the Spirit to stir up within us (i.e., ourselves and others in the body of Christ) a greater zeal for God—an inner stirring to stand for his purposes when the enemy approaches. We utter this prayer when we sing,

> Breathe, O breathe thy loving Spirit into every troubled breast;
> Let us all in thee inherit, let us find the promised rest:
> Take away the love of sinning; Alpha and Omega be;
> End of faith as its Beginning, set our hearts at liberty.[21]

We understand why Paul urges such prayer in the context of spiritual warfare by seeing where the concept of praying in the Spirit receives fuller explanation in this epistle to the Ephesians. While Paul is now urging the people of God to pray for the Spirit's work, the apostle has previously prayed the same in their behalf:

> For this reason I kneel before the Father, from whom his whole family in heaven and on earth derives its name. I pray that out of his glorious riches he may strengthen you with power through his Spirit in your inner being, so that Christ may dwell in your hearts through faith. And I pray that you, being rooted and established in love, may have power, together with all the saints, to grasp how wide and long and high and deep is the love of Christ, and to know this love that surpasses knowledge—that you may be filled to the measure of all the fullness of God. (Eph. 3:14–19)

---

in 1 Cor. 14:15–16 refers to "my [human] spirit" as in 14:14), although he does elsewhere declare the important role of the Spirit in prayer (Rom. 8:26–27). Moreover, the Holy Spirit's work in the believer is well recognized in Paul, and extends to all areas of Christian living. So, if we limit ourselves just to instances of *en pneumati* in Ephesians, God lives in the believer by his Spirit (2:18, 22), the Spirit reveals God's mysteries (3:5), and the Christian life is one lived filled by the Spirit (5:18).

20. Ferguson, *The Holy Spirit*, 188.

21. Charles Wesley, "Love Divine, All Loves Excelling," 1747.

Paul's prayer culminates with the petition that the Ephesians would be strengthened with power by the Spirit in their inner being. This power will enable them to grasp how high and long and wide and deep is the love of Christ, so that through this love they will be filled with the fullness of God.

The power that the Spirit communicates comes as a result of the love he stirs in our hearts. Our desires are transformed by what Thomas Chalmers (1780–1847) called "the expulsive power of a new affection."[22] The Spirit renews and cleanses our desires, creating an appetite for a closer and more mature relationship with God. By the Spirit's work in us this appetite overwhelms and drives out unhealthy previous appetites. As Ezekiel beautifully expressed it, those in whom the Spirit works become "careful to do" the Lord's will.

The Holy Spirit takes hearts that are hard and then softens them toward God (Ezek. 11:19–20; 36:25–27). The Spirit changes our priorities, our affections, our cravings—and makes us have a love for God that is greater than a love for the things of the world that attract us even as they attack us. Hearts formerly cold toward God do not become warm toward his people and purposes by a mere act of willpower. While we can will a change in behavior, we do not by an act of will change what we find attractive, appealing, and lovely. The Spirit accomplishes what willpower cannot in reconstructing the affections of our hearts. This is a supernatural work that is facilitated by the means of grace, but is not able to be accomplished by them apart from the Spirit.

We should understand that there is many a cold heart ritualistically praying and reading Scripture in the vain expectation that the labor itself will produce godly love and spiritual power. We pray in the Spirit because we believe that the Spirit alone can so radically change the heart as to make it truly desire the things of God.

As I am writing, three oak trees outside my back window are waving their leaves in the cold midwinter winds. The waving is a sign of their obstinate nature. All of the other trees in our neighborhood have long since shed their leaves. These oaks, however, will keep the brown, shriveled vestiges of their former life all winter. While the winter blasts and freezes will strip the leaves

22. Thomas Chalmers, *Sermons and Discourses*, vol. 2 (New York: Carter, 1846), 271.

from some stems and even make bald some sections of their limbs, the trees will not entirely shed the deadness that clings to them.

Only when the warmth of spring activates the hidden energies in the oaks and that life presses to the surface will the new leaves push out the old. "The expulsive power of our new affections" operates similarly. As the vestiges of our old nature cling to us through the shriveled but still potent desires of a past way of life, no amount of natural effort will eradicate their presence. Though the rigor of our disciplines may remove some habits and change the appearance of large portions of our lives, only forces within us stimulated by the Spirit of God will truly replace vestiges of the old life with the vitality of the new.[23]

The human will is engaged in spiritual warfare, but it is not human willpower that will defeat the forces of Satan. Rather Satan is defeated by the supernatural process in which the Spirit makes his will our will by renewing within us a consuming, overwhelming, compelling love of God. Then, as the forces of evil come and our resistance to them requires the weapons (means) of grace that the apostle has spelled out in this epistle, we willingly take up our arms with the confidence that our God has provided everything that we need to do what he requires.

Love for God provides the zeal needed to employ the weapons he provides. This does not mean that the battle will be without effort or without pain. It is, after all, spiritual *warfare* that the apostle here describes. But, with the faith that God has given us sufficient armor to resist the assault of Satan, we can stand so long as we truly desire to do so. That desire is also the gift of God, as his Spirit for which we pray stirs within us the love for God that is more compelling than the love for sin.

Full and consistent apprehension of why we love God is the most effective piece of armor in the Christian arsenal because the Devil always begins and presses his attack with an alienation of our affections. Thus the most powerful tool we have to equip others for spiritual battle, and the most effective participation we have in the work of the Spirit, is consistent adulation of the beauties of the grace of God. We "preach the gospel to our own hearts,"[24] tell-

23. I trust my readers will appreciate this modern rewrite of a very old but very useful illustration.

24. The phrase is Jack Miller's paraphrase of Luther's oft-repeated urging to return to the essential message of Christ's justifying work as the basis and strength for daily Christian living. See Miller's phrasing as found in Jerry Bridges, *The Discipline of Grace: God's Role and Our Role in the Pursuit of Holiness* (Colorado

ing others and ourselves of God's eternal love, Christ's humble birth, sinless life, selfless sacrifice, and coming glory. We provide the power of the gospel by reminding believers of the manifold ways in which an infinitely loving Father has made the wonders of heaven the certain inheritance of children as wayward as we.

As the Spirit uses the revelation of God's grace to change hearts, affections change, lives change, and, where disciplines remain needed, they become willingly and lovingly exercised. John Murray beautifully summarizes,

> The Holy Spirit is the Spirit of truth and therefore as the Spirit of love he captivates our hearts by the love of God and of Christ to us. In the diffusion of that love there flows also love to one another. "Beloved, if God so loved us, we ought to love one another" (1 John 4:11). The biblical ethic knows no fulfillment of its demands other than that produced by the constraint and claim of Christ's redeeming love (cf. 2 Corinthians 5:14, 15; Galatians 2:20). Our love is always ignited by the flame of Christ's love. And it is the Holy Spirit who sheds abroad in our hearts the igniting flame of the love of God in Christ Jesus. The love that is ignited is the fruit of the Spirit.[25]

The Word of God is the sword of the Spirit not because the Bible has magical power to charm Satan, but because its content from beginning to end is the revelation of God's love that compels the human heart to seek him (Eph. 6:17). The message of grace is the instrument of power in spiritual warfare.

We don the armor of God by faith, repenting of our own weaknesses and believing that each element of divine protection can resist the assaults of Satan as God has promised. And, having received the promises represented

---

Springs: NavPress, 1994), 8; and Luther's Introduction to his Commentary on Galatians: "It is necessary that this doctrine [of grace] be kept in continual practice and public exercise, both of hearing and reading.... The most excellent righteousness of faith, which God through Christ, without any works, imputes to us, is neither political, nor ceremonial, nor the righteousness of God's law, nor consists of works, but is clean contrary to these; that is to say, it is a mere passive righteousness, as the others are active.... This 'passive righteousness' is a mystery that someone who does not know Jesus cannot understand. As a matter of fact, Christians do not completely understand it and do not take advantage of it when they are tempted. So we have to constantly teach it over and over again to others and repeat it to ourselves, because if we do not understand it and have it in our hearts, we will be defeated by the enemy, and we will be totally confused. There is nothing that gives us peace like this 'passive righteousness.'" (For clarity I have included a portion of the translation of Erasmus Middleton, edited by John Prince Fallowes [Grand Rapids: Kregel, 1979] and the paraphrase of World Harvest Mission in the workbook *Discipling by Grace* [1996], lesson 2:1.).

25. John Murray, *Principles of Conduct* (Grand Rapids: Eerdmans, 1957), 226.

by each aspect of the armor, we relish and rely upon the love of God to stir up within us by his Word and Spirit a large and loving heart for his glory and purposes. Then we act as that heart inspires and enables.

Empowering Love (6:18–24)

This vision of the true nature of spiritual warfare explains why there must be such an emphasis upon the grace of God in our lives and ministries to others. We do not proclaim grace so that any will make light of sin or of our duty to resist it. We herald God's amazing mercy to join with the Spirit in stirring up such a love for God in his people that when the day of evil comes, they will gladly put on the full armor he provides to fight for his purposes. Then, despite the hardships and the pain that God's people may face in the battle, they will stand strong in the power of his might.

Paul prepares the Ephesians for such battles first by telling them that they must stay alert for Satan's attacks (Eph. 6:18), and then by urging them to pray for Paul himself to remain strong in the battles that he is facing (Eph. 6:19–20). By urging the Ephesians to pray for him, the apostle underscores that spiritual battles are not won by superior human knowledge or status, but by the Spirit. By humbly asking for personal prayer he also recruits the Ephesians for his own spiritual warfare, and simultaneously communicates how much he values their role in his life.

Paul expresses his regard for others to both echo and reinforce the love of God that empowers us in spiritual battle. Tender words build strong hearts. Love changes and recharges the will. Thus Paul's final words to the Ephesians are a flood of affection. Paul says he is sending Tychicus, "the dear brother and faithful servant in the Lord" (Eph. 6:21), to the Ephesians in order to share news about "how we are" and so "that he may encourage you" (Eph. 6:22). Then the apostle communicates God's care for the Ephesians: "Peace to the brothers, and love with faith from God the Father and the Lord Jesus Christ" (Eph. 6:23). Finally, Paul communicates his own love for the churches of Ephesus mixed with a final challenge for them to maintain their love for Christ: "Grace to all who love our Lord Jesus Christ with an undying love" (Eph. 6:24). Thus, in his parting words, Paul again uses the grace and love of God to stimulate love, hope, and zeal for his purposes in our battles. The message is clear: love is power. Those who most grasp the grace of God are those made most willing and able to fight for him.

Some years ago I enjoyed watching "iron man" competitions on TV. Watching those who swim, bike, and run multiple-marathon distances in the grueling triathlon makes me dream of what I might be able to do if I had more time, opportunity, and a different body. More inspiring to me than the usual stories of the big-name competitors, however, was the 1999 account of the father-and-son team of Dick and Ricky Hoyt. The two have run together in more than eight hundred races.

More remarkable than the fellowship this father and son enjoy is the fact that the now adult son, Ricky, was born with cerebral palsy. To race, he must be pulled, pushed, or carried by his father. There is a part of us that might jump to the conclusion that Ricky does not race at all . . . that his father does all the work. But tens of thousands of viewers saw the son's role in this competition when wind, cold, and an equipment failure made progress hard on Ricky, even though his father was the one pedaling the modified tandem bike. Dick knelt down to his son, contorted and trembling in the cold, as the two were still facing many more miles of race on the defective bike. Said the father to the child belted to the bicycle seat, "Do you want to keep going, Son?"

The father would be the one enabling and providing the means to overcome, but the son still had to have the heart to finish well. To the son were given the privilege and responsibility to desire to continue to make progress. Though the example is not perfect, it explains much of what the Bible teaches about our spiritual battles. We have a Father who has already given the power to enable us to resist all the challenges of our Adversary. We can prevail through the means and strength our Father provides, but we must still have the heart to do so.

In light of this need for a heart that beats for him, our God bids us feed on his Word and seek the Spirit that opens our minds to the knowledge of the Savior and renews our will with a compelling love for him. By God's Word and Spirit we are filled with the knowledge and love of him that give us the desire to run with him (and to him) more than anything else in the world. The grace he pours into our heart enables us "to grasp how wide and long and high and deep is the love of Christ, and to know this love that surpasses knowledge—that [we] may be filled to the measure of all the fullness of God" (Eph. 3:18–19).

Index of Scripture

Genesis
2:24—283n, 294, 294n, 316n
8:21—238n6
17—94n
17:23—324
22:12—303n
24:27—19n2
31:14—68n
38:17–20—54n5

Exodus
4:21—205n
4:22—25n10
6:6—34n
12:43–48—324
15:13—34n
18:10—19n2
19:5—54n4
19:6—11n7
19:22—101n
20:12—313, 314n
20:17—207n
20:20—267n25
22:31—11n7
24:2—101n
29:18—239n
29:25—239n
29:36–37—280
29:41—239n
31:3—261n18
35:31—261n18
40:34–35—132

Leviticus—239n
1:3—118n
1:10—118n
4:32—23n8
8:15—280
11:44–45—11n7
16:19—280
18—203n3
19:2—11n7
19:18—285n
20:7–8—11n7
20:21—240n7
25:23—123n1
26:1—95n
26:30—95n

Numbers—239n
15:40—11n7
18:6–7—188n
36:2—68n

Deuteronomy
4:7—101n

4:20—47
4:25—317n11
5:16—313, 314n
6:4—185n
7:6—11n7
7:6–7—57
7:9—47
9:5–7—47
9:29—47
10:16—94n, 95n
14:2—54n4
15:7—205n
26:18—54n4
30:6—94n, 95n
31:29—317n11
32:8–9—47
32:21—317n11
34:9—261n18

1 Samuel
6:6—205n

2 Samuel
7:5–13—126n4
23:3—267n25

1 Kings
8:10–11—132
8:39—132n
8:43—132n
8:49—132n
8:51—47
12:16—68n
15:30—223n7, 317n11
16:2—317n11

2 Kings
19:3—223n7
23:26—223n7

1 Chronicles
16:36—179n
29:10—19n2
29:15—123n1

2 Chronicles
6:13—152
6:30—132n
6:33—132n
6:39—132n
30:27—132n
36:13—205n

Ezra
9:5—152n

Nehemiah
5:9—267n25
5:13—179n
5:15—267n25
8:6—179n
9:18—223n7
9:26—223n7

Job
5:9—143n
9:10—143n
19:25—266
25:6—39n

Psalms
4:4—222, 222n, 223n6
7:13—338n9
11:2—338n9
13:3—66
19:8—66
22:3—264
23:2—282n17
28:6—19n2

29:3—65n3
33:12—47
33:14—132n
34:18—101n
36:1—267n25
39:12—123n1
41:13—179n
55:19—303n
66:16—303n
66:20—19n2
68—188, 188n, 189, 190n
68:9–10—68
68:18—188n
72:18–19—19n2
72:19—178n, 179n
74:2—68
76:2—132n
78:62—68
78:71—68
79:1—68
89:52—179n
94:5—68
94:14—68
95:8—205n
106:5—68
106:16—317n11
106:40—68
106:48—179n
118:6—22
118:22—127n8, 128
119:151—101n
145:18—101n
148:14—101n

Proverbs
1:7—267n25
2:13—252n2
4:14–15—241
8:20—79
10:13—319n
13:24—315, 319n
22:15—319n
23:13–14—319n
23:31—260n
28:14—205n
29:15—319n
31:28—299

Ecclesiastes
8:12—303n
12:13—303n

Isaiah
1:2—25n10
2:5—252n2
2:18—95n
5:20—252n2
6:3—140
8:14–16—128
9:1–7—96
9:6—108
10:11—95n
10:17—252n2
11:3—267n25
11:5—337n9
16:12—95n
19:1—95n
21:9—95n
26:19—257n11
28:16—127n8, 128
31:7—95n
41:14—39n
42:16—252n2
46:6—95n
49:2—338n9
50:1—273n
50:10—252n2
52:7—117n7, 337n9, 339n

54:5–8—273n
57:19—101n, 117n7
59:17—337n9, 340–41
60:1–2—257n11
60:1–3—252n2
60:9—281
62:4–5—273n
63—230n
63:10—230n
63:17—205n
64:4—170

Jeremiah
2:2–3—273n
4:4—95n
12:5—209
21:5—223n7
31:31–32—273n

Ezekiel
11:19–20—345
16—273n
16:9—280
23—273n
32:9—317n11
36:25–27—345

Daniel
5:4—95n
5:20—205n
5:23—95n
11:36—317n11

Hosea
1–3—273n
1:10—25n10
2:10—240n7
6:5—338n9

Micah
3:8—261n18
5:5—108
7:18—38

Nahum
1:15—337n9, 339n

Zechariah
3:1–2—224n
8:1–15—219n
8:16—219, 219n
8:16–19—219n

Matthew
5:9—25n10
5:14–16—252n2
5:45—25n10
6:5—152n
6:12—113
6:23—252n2
7:15–20—161n
7:24–27—161n
9:15—273n
10:2—187n6
15:4—314n
15:11—228
16:26—298
18:16—72n10
18:20—72, 72n10
18:34—222
19:5—283n
19:19—285n, 314n
19:29—54
20:4—312n6
21:12–13—222
21:42—127n8, 128
22:2—273n

22:39—285n
23:37—101
25:1—273n
25:31–46—226
25:34—54
25:40—116
26:39—152n

Mark
1:27—312n4
3:5—205n, 222
3:14—187n6
4:41—312n4
6:52—205n
8:17—205n
10:7—283n
11:25—152n
12:31—285
14:58—95n

Luke
1:15—261n18
1:41—261n18
1:67—261n18
2:51—292n1
6:13—187n6
6:35—25n10
7:25—281
10:17—292n1
10:20—292n1
10:27—285n
11:34–36—252n2
12:35—337n9
12:45—260n
12:57—312n6
13:17—281
15:10—153
16:2–4—136n4
17:6—312n4
18:1—343n19
18:2—303n
18:4—303n
18:11—152n
18:13—152n
20:42—263n20
23:40—303n
24:44—263n20
24:49—189

John
1:12—265n23
2:10—260n
3:18—265n23
3:19–21—252n2
3:20—254n
3:29—273n
5:18—298
6:38—298
6:44—50
6:65—50
8:12—252n2
9:25—90
12:31—80n3
12:35–36—252n2
12:46—252n2
14–16—230
14:15—165
14:17—65
14:20—205n
14:30—80n3
15:5—159, 197
15:26—65, 231
16:7—298
16:11—80n3
16:13—65
20:31—265n23

Acts
1:20—263n20
1:26—187n6
2:4—261n18
4:8—261n18
4:10—265n23
4:11—127n8, 128
4:28—47n
4:31—261n18
5:3—261n17
6:7—312n4
7:2—65n3
7:5—68, 68n
7:48—95n
7:59–60—152n
8:12—265n23
8:36–39—280
9:4—142
9:4–5—13
9:17—261n18
9:22—13
9:31—267n25
10:2—303n
10:22—303n
10:45—12n
10:47—280
10:47–48—324
13:9—261n18
13:16—303n
13:26—303n
13:33—263n20
13:48—341n14
13:52—261n18
14:14—187n6
15:14—265n23
16:15—324
16:30–33—324
16:38–39—123
17:24—95n
19:11–12—7
19:30—7
20:4—5n2
20:31—321n14
20:32—54, 68n, 280
21:5—152n
21:26–32—108n3
21:28—147
21:29—147
22—136n3
26:18—54, 252n2
26:23—252n2
28—xv

Romans
1:2—127n7
1:4—71n8
1:7—13
1:8–10—61n
1:9–10—64n
1:10—259n
1:12—252n2
1:18—245n12
1:18–32—206n5
1:20—69
1:21—204
1:24—240n7
1:25—179
1:29—206n6
1:30—315
2:19—252n2
2:24—265n23
2:25–29—95n
3:9—112n
3:18—267n25
3:21—127n7
3:22–24—85n
3:24—34n
3:25—34

4:10–12—95n
4:20—330n
4:25—278n14
5:1–2—188n
5:8—82
5:8–10—232
5:9—34
5:10–12—112n
5:15—85n
6:3–4—280
6:3–5—83
6:4—79
6:6—211n12
6:11—211n12
6:12—312n4
6:16—312n4
6:16–17—312n4
7:2–4—273n
7:5—80n4
7:7–13—108n4
7:18—80n4
7:25—80n4
8:1–17—80n4
8:4–5—65
8:6–9—55
8:7—292n1
8:9—65, 333
8:13–14—65
8:14–23—25n10
8:15—25
8:20—292n1
8:23—25, 34n
8:26–27—344n19
8:26–28—344
8:26–39—26
8:28—266
8:28–30—67n
8:29—344
8:29–30—26, 47n
8:32—24, 85, 170, 278n14
8:33—26
8:35–39—162n
8:38—335
8:38–39—71n9
9—80
9:1—210n10
9:4—25n10
9:5—179
9:6—280
9:22—80
9:26—25n10
10:3—292n1
10:8—280
10:15—337n9
10:16—312n4
10:17–18—280
10:19—317n11
11:5–6—85n
11:7—205n
11:13—5n1
11:15—112n
11:20—267n25
11:22—232n
11:25—37, 140n5, 205n
11:29—67n
11:33—36n4, 88, 143n
11:33–36—168
11:36—179, 185n
12:1—182n
12:1–2—253n6
12:2—213, 253n7, 259n
12:3–8—186n
12:4–5—282n16
12:4–8—184n, 194
12:5—72n11, 221n
12:6—187n5
12:19—224n
13:1—292n1

13:9—108n4, 280, 285n
13:12—252n2, 337n9, 341
13:12–14—260n
13:13—206n5
13:14—80n4, 211n12, 214n16, 337n9
14:15—79
14:17—245n11
14:18—253n6
14:19—229n12
15:2—229n12
15:6—265n22
15:9—264n
15:13—69
15:14—321n14
15:18—280
15:32—259n
15:33—179
16:7—187n6
16:13—26
16:19—257, 258n13
16:25–27—140n5, 168, 168n, 169
16:27—179, 258n13

1 Corinthians
1–2—258n13
1:1—6n, 259n
1:2—265n23, 280
1:3—13
1:4—265n22
1:4–9—61n
1:10—265n23
1:10–17—183n2
1:13–17—280
1:16—324
1:18—280
1:23—209
1:26–31—67n
1:30—34n
2:1—140n5
2:4–5—69
2:6–8—258n14
2:6–16—65, 140n5
2:7—47n
2:9—170
2:12—79
2:14—55
3—126n5
3:9—161n, 229n12
3:10—258n12
3:16–17—132n
3:17—211n12
4:1—140n5
4:1–2—136n4
4:5—252n2
4:10—281
4:14—321n14
4:16—237n3
4:20—245n11
5:1—240n7
5:4—265n23
5:5—80n4
5:9–10—248n
5:9–13—248n
5:11—207n
6:9–10—54, 245n11, 248n
6:10—207
6:11—265n23, 280
6:13—240n7
6:14—71n8
6:15—282n16
6:16—283n
6:18—240n7
7:2—240n7
7:18–19—95n
7:20–24—276n11
7:22—325
8:6—185n
8:9—258n12

9:5–6—126n6
9:17—136n4
10:11—321n14
10:12—258n12
10:13—333
10:16—34
10:23—229n12
11:1—237n3
11:2—281
11:3—72n11, 275n6
11:3–10—276n11, 292n2
11:3–12—293n4
11:7–12—293
11:23—278n14
11:25—34
11:27—34
11:32—79
12:4–6—122
12:4–31—184n, 186n
12:8–10—191n10
12:12–27—72n11, 282n16
12:13—276n11
12:14–20—193
12:21–26—192
12:28–29—127n7, 187n6
12:28–30—191n10
13:4—183n2
14:1–5—187n6
14:3—229n12
14:5—229n12
14:12—229n12
14:14—344n19
14:15—264n
14:15–16—344n19
14:16—179
14:26—229n12, 263n20
14:29—127n7
14:29–37—187n6
14:32—127n7, 292n1
14:34—292n1
14:34–36—293n4
14:36—280
14:37—127n7
15:2—280
15:7—187n6
15:7–9—187n6
15:9—142n10
15:10—142n9
15:12–19—191n12
15:24—71n9, 245n11, 265n22, 335
15:27–28—292n1, 298
15:28—292n1
15:33—211n12
15:43—71n8
15:50—54, 245n11
15:51—140n5
15:54—280
16:13—342n15
16:16—268, 292n1

2 Corinthians

1:1—6n, 259n
1:2—13
1:3—65n3, 265n22
1:3–4—19n2
1:19—209
1:20—179
1:22—54n5
3:14—205n
3:18—174
4:4—80n3
4:6—66, 174
4:7—69
4:14—281
5:1—229n12
5:5—54n5
5:7—79
5:9—253n6

5:11—267n25
5:14—347
5:15—347
5:17—109n5, 112, 211
5:18–21—112n
5:20—287
5:21—24
6:14—252n2
6:15—12n
6:16—132n
6:16–18—25n10
7:1—267n25
7:2—211n12
8:5—259n
8:9—85n
8:22–23—126n6
8:23—187n6
10:1—136n3, 183n2
10:4—337n9
10:8—229n12
11:2—273n
11:3—211n12
11:13–15—191n12
11:31—65n3, 265n22
12:9—69
12:12—187n6
12:19—229n12
12:20—229n14
12:21—206n5, 240n7
13:4—71n8
13:5—253n7
13:10—229n12
13:11—329n2
13:14—122

Galatians—11n7
1:3—13
1:4—79, 258n14, 259n, 265n22
1:5—168, 178–79
1:6—67n
1:6–9—191n12
1:10—253n6
1:11—140n5
1:16—140n5, 209
1:19—126n6
2:7–9—126n6
2:20—278n14, 347
2:21—85n
3:26—25n10
3:27—214n16, 280
3:28—276n11
4:3—79
4:4–7—25n10
4:5—25
5:1—342n15
5:2—136n3
5:2–6—95n
5:5—65
5:13–26—80n4, 211n12
5:14—285n
5:15—258n12
5:16—65, 79
5:19—206n5, 240n7
5:19–21—245n11
5:20—229n14
5:21—54, 245n11
5:22—183n2, 252n4
5:22–23—252n4
5:23—183n2
6:1—183n2
6:2—268n
6:4—253n7
6:8—80n4
6:10—124
6:12–16—95n
6:17—329n2
6:18—179

Ephesians

1—xvi, 157n
1–2—xvi, 329
1–4—xvi
1:1—xv, 4–5, 9, 28, 176n, 209n9, 259n
1:1–2—3
1:1–14—145
1:1a—4, 6
1:1b—6, 9
1:1b–c—9
1:1c—12
1:2—13, 21, 24, 142n9, 229n13, 338n9
1:2–3—316n
1:2–5—308
1:2–14—33
1:2a—5, 13
1:3—19–20, 21n5, 24, 30, 33, 65n3, 176n, 265n22, 335n
1:3–6—17
1:3–12—19
1:3–14—17n, 26, 26n, 65
1:3a—19
1:3b—20
1:4—22, 26, 29n15, 41, 46, 77, 172, 176n, 199, 278n13, 281
1:4–5—22, 26, 162
1:4–6—17, 26
1:4b–6—29
1:5—6n, 24, 26, 28, 29n15, 38, 47n, 124, 259n
1:5–6—17n, 19, 25–26, 185n
1:6—29–30, 33–34, 175
1:6–7—142n9, 229n13
1:7—17n, 34, 102n, 143n, 146, 157, 172, 176n, 212, 231n, 274
1:7–8—34
1:7–10—32
1:7a—34
1:7b–8—35
1:7c—35
1:8—36
1:9—6n, 37, 47n, 140n5, 259n, 287
1:9–10—32, 176n
1:9a—37–38
1:9b—38
1:10—40–41, 47, 50, 136n4, 172
1:10a—40
1:10b—40
1:11—17n, 25, 46, 49–50, 54, 68, 68n, 77, 144, 259n
1:11–12—6n, 45
1:11–14—44
1:11a—45–46
1:11b—47
1:12—19n3, 46n1, 48–50, 67n, 175
1:12–13—176n
1:13—17n, 45, 49–50, 55, 55n, 141n7, 210n10, 231n, 280, 338n9
1:13–14—44
1:13a—49
1:13b—50
1:13b–14—54
1:14—19n3, 25, 33, 34n, 51, 68, 68n, 140n7, 158, 175, 231n, 245n11
1:15—61, 146n, 199, 338n9
1:15–16—19n2, 60
1:15–16a—61
1:15–23—59
1:15–2:22—145
1:15a—61
1:15b—61
1:16—63, 265n22
1:16a—62–63
1:16b—63
1:17—36n4, 63, 65, 175, 258n13, 316n, 338n9
1:17–18—64
1:17–19a—64

1:18—25, 47, 54, 67n, 140n7, 143n, 157–58, 172, 175, 183, 332
1:18–19—68n
1:18–20—157
1:18a—63, 66
1:18b—66
1:18c—67
1:19—70, 142n9, 157n
1:19–20—69, 146, 212
1:19–21—189
1:19–22—70
1:19–23—70, 172
1:19a—69, 331
1:19b—123, 331
1:19b–22—71
1:20—20, 20n, 21n5, 83, 144, 176n, 331
1:20–21—144
1:20–22—158
1:20–23—19–20
1:21—69, 332, 335
1:21–22—190n, 333
1:22—192, 275n6, 292n1
1:22–23—59
1:22c—71
1:22c–23—72
1:23—73, 141n7, 157n, 164, 176, 184n, 191, 221, 221n, 245, 261
2:1—78n, 79, 79n, 158, 332
2:1–2—46n1, 79, 203
2:1–3—78, 100n, 112n
2:1–5—157
2:1–6—86
2:1–7—78n
2:1–10—77, 78n, 79n, 219n
2:2—71n9, 90n13, 183n1, 203n2, 238n5, 252n3, 258n14, 332, 335
2:2–3—252n3
2:3—46n1, 79n, 80, 112n, 211n12, 245n12, 252n3, 332
2:3–5—77
2:4—78n, 199, 278n13
2:4–5—81, 100n, 106, 146
2:4–7—81, 157
2:4–10—333
2:5—78n, 79n, 83, 85, 142n9, 229n13, 332, 338n9
2:5–6—332
2:5–7—83
2:5a—83
2:5b—83
2:6—20n, 21, 83–84, 144, 158, 212, 332, 335n
2:6–7—176n
2:7—84–86, 90, 143n, 232n
2:7–8—85, 142n9, 229n13
2:7–10—85
2:8—78n, 87, 146n, 338n9
2:8–9—61, 87, 146, 212, 341n14
2:8–10—78n, 86
2:10—79, 87, 89–90, 90n13, 91–92, 106, 176n, 183n1, 203n2, 215, 218, 238n5
2:11—5n1, 46n1, 91, 100, 100n, 107, 252n3
2:11–12—122, 203
2:11–13—91
2:11–14—79n
2:11–22—79n
2:11–3:6—46n1
2:11–3:7—5n1
2:11a—91
2:11b—94
2:12—67n, 96, 123nn1–2, 141n7, 146n, 204, 332
2:12–13—67n
2:12a—96
2:12b—96
2:12c—97
2:12d—99
2:13—35, 100, 100n, 107, 110, 117n7, 176n, 212, 237, 252n3, 332

2:13–22—49
2:13a—100
2:13b—100
2:13c—102
2:14—106–8, 112, 153
2:14–15—105, 107–8, 338n9
2:14–15a—108
2:14–16—184n
2:14–18—105
2:14a—108
2:14b–15a—108
2:15—110, 214n16
2:15–16—153
2:15a—108
2:15b—109, 112
2:15b–16—108
2:16—108, 112, 141n7, 221n
2:16–17—111
2:16a—112
2:17—105, 108, 117, 338n9, 339n
2:17–18—101n, 105, 274
2:18—117–18, 122, 145, 145n13, 169, 237, 261n18, 316n, 338n9, 344n19
2:18–19—185
2:19—122, 126, 126n4, 153, 162, 185n, 332
2:19–20—120
2:19a—122
2:19b—123
2:19c—123
2:20—152, 158, 187n6
2:20–21—162
2:20–22—126, 126n4
2:20a—126
2:20b—127
2:21—129, 162, 229n12, 249
2:21–22—151, 158
2:22—122, 129, 131, 158, 184, 199, 261n18, 333, 338n9, 344n19
2:22a—129
2:22b—131
3—140n5
3–4—329
3:1—xv, 5n1, 46n1, 136, 138, 183
3:1–2—136
3:1–6—135
3:1–12—5n1
3:1–13—134, 151
3:2—136, 138, 142n9, 209n9, 229n13
3:2–6—140n5
3:3—138–39
3:3–4—139, 287
3:3–6—138
3:4—139, 332
3:4–5—127, 127n7
3:5—65, 126n6, 127n7, 138–39, 187n6, 252n3, 261n18, 332, 338n9, 344n19
3:6—50, 139, 176n, 338n9
3:7—69, 136, 138, 141, 142n9, 173n
3:7–8—142n9, 229n13
3:7–9—141
3:7–13—141
3:8—142, 142n9, 152, 157, 162
3:8–9—134
3:8–13—141n8
3:9—136n4, 142, 142n11, 185n, 287
3:10—21n4, 36n4, 71n9, 144, 152–53, 162, 252n3, 258n13, 335
3:11—144, 146, 176n
3:12—118n, 145–46, 153, 169, 338n9
3:13—5n2, 146
3:14—151, 157, 316n
3:14–15—151, 157, 185n
3:14–16a—158
3:14–19—149, 344
3:14a—151
3:14b—152
3:14b–15—152

3:16—69, 143n, 156, 157n, 173n, 175, 330n, 333, 338n9
3:16–17—156, 261
3:16a—157
3:16b—157–58
3:17—146n, 158, 162n, 199, 338n9
3:17–19—149, 278n13
3:17a—158
3:17b—159
3:17b–18a—160
3:17b–19—160
3:18—157n, 212
3:18–19—162, 162n, 170, 349
3:18–19a—156
3:18b–19a—161
3:19—73, 156, 157n, 158, 162n, 163, 199, 261
3:19–20—191
3:19a—163
3:19b—163
3:20—69, 169, 212
3:20–21—167–68
3:20a—169
3:20a–b—169
3:20b—170
3:20c—172
3:20c–d—172
3:20d—173
3:21—175, 176n, 179
3:21a—175
3:21b—176
3:21c—178
4—188n, 190n, 235n
4–6—258n12
4:1—5n2, 79, 90n13, 136n3, 183, 203n2, 238n5
4:1–6—183
4:1–16—181
4:2—199, 278n13
4:2–3—185n
4:2–6—198
4:2a—183
4:2b–3—183
4:3—61, 338n9
4:3–4—338n9
4:4—67n, 183–84, 221n
4:4–6—122, 141n7, 183, 185n
4:4–7—181
4:5—184, 185n, 280, 338n9
4:6—185–86, 316n
4:7—187–88, 191, 229n13, 333
4:7–10—187–88
4:7–11—198
4:7–14—186
4:8—188–90, 257n11
4:8–10—188
4:9—189
4:10—73, 189, 261
4:11—126n6, 127n7, 187, 190
4:12—72n11, 141n7, 191, 195, 221n, 229n12, 282n16
4:12–15—190, 198
4:12a—190
4:12b—190
4:13—73, 164, 261, 338n9
4:13a—191
4:13b—191
4:14—191, 332
4:15—72n11, 158, 191, 197, 199, 219, 275n6, 332
4:15–16—141n7, 196, 278n13
4:15–16a—197
4:16—191, 199, 221n, 229n12
4:16a—197–98
4:16b—198
4:17—79, 90n13, 183n1, 201, 203, 203n2, 238n5
4:17–19—204
4:17–24—201, 333n4
4:17a—203

4:17b—203
4:17d—203
4:18—204–5, 252
4:19—206, 242n, 252, 255
4:19a—206
4:20—209
4:20–21—209
4:20–24—208
4:21—176n, 204, 210n11, 218n1, 338n9
4:21b—209
4:22—210, 210n11, 211n12, 214n16, 218n1, 332
4:22–24—201, 210, 210n11, 218, 218n1
4:22c—211
4:23—213, 214n15
4:23–24—212, 252
4:24—109n5, 211n12, 218n1, 332, 338n9
4:24–25—338n9
4:24a—214
4:24b—211, 214
4:25—184n, 210n10, 218n1, 219, 219n, 243, 252, 282n16
4:25–28—218
4:25–32—217–18, 218n1, 236n
4:25a—219
4:25b—219
4:25c—218
4:26—219n, 222n
4:26–27—222, 252, 317n11
4:26b—223
4:27—80, 256, 335
4:28—224, 229n12, 243
4:29—227–29, 229n12
4:29–32—227, 229, 252
4:29d—229
4:30—34n, 230, 231n, 338n9
4:30–32—217
4:31—229, 229n14, 317n11
4:31–32—243
4:31d—231
4:32—176n, 231, 236, 236n
4:32a—232
4:32b—231–32
4:32c—232
4:32d—232
5—235n, 267, 291
5–6—xvi, 235n, 329
5:1—185n, 236, 237n3, 249, 252n3, 278n13
5:1–2—235–36, 236n, 268, 274, 277, 278n13, 297, 302, 304
5:1–7—235, 235n
5:2—79, 90n13, 183n1, 199, 203n2, 236n, 237n3, 238, 238n5, 253n5, 258n13, 278nn13–14, 307, 309
5:3—206n6, 240, 242, 242n, 243, 245n11, 249, 251, 255
5:3–4—236n, 239–40
5:3–5—252
5:3–7—235n
5:3b—243
5:4—240–41, 243
5:5—54, 68, 68n, 158, 207n, 242–43, 245, 245n11, 245n13
5:5–6—244
5:5–7—244, 256n
5:6—245–46
5:7—235n, 246–47, 251n
5:8—79, 90n13, 183n1, 203n2, 235n, 238n5, 251n, 252nn2–3, 253n5, 253n7, 258n13, 263, 332–33
5:8–10—250, 252
5:8–14—235n, 257n11
5:8–17—251
5:8–21—250
5:8b—251
5:8b–9—252
5:8c—253

5:9—210n10, 252n4, 254, 256, 338n9
5:10—253, 253n7, 256, 258n14, 259n, 263n19
5:11—246–47, 254–55
5:11–12—256n
5:11–17—254
5:12—240, 255
5:13–14a—256
5:14—257n11
5:14b—257
5:14d—258
5:15—79, 90n13, 183n1, 203n2, 235n, 238n5, 258, 258n14
5:16—258, 263n19, 335
5:17—259
5:18—260–61, 263n19, 271n1, 276, 333, 338n9, 344n19
5:18–21—260, 268, 275
5:18a—262
5:18b–21—263
5:19—263, 264n
5:19–20—267n24
5:19–21—276
5:19a—263
5:19b—264
5:20—265, 265n22, 316n
5:20a—265
5:20b—265
5:21—267, 272, 275n8, 297, 297n, 303, 303n
5:21–24—272, 296
5:21–33—270
5:22—291–93, 297, 297n, 312nn4–5
5:22–24—272, 290, 292
5:22–33—290–91, 293n4, 309
5:22–6:9—267
5:23—221n, 270, 272–73, 275n7, 338n9
5:23–24—72n11, 273, 275, 276n11, 292
5:23–33—271n1
5:24—275nn6–8, 293, 297n, 312n4
5:25—270, 272n, 275, 282, 282n19, 286
5:25–27—273, 295
5:25–28—277–78
5:25–31—277, 280
5:25–32—278n13
5:25–33—293, 297
5:26—280, 338n9
5:27—22n, 281, 295
5:28—282n16, 282n19
5:28–29—285
5:28–30—141n7
5:28–31—283
5:29—282, 282n16, 320
5:30—184n, 288
5:31—271n1, 281, 282n16, 283, 285, 288, 293, 294n, 296, 298, 316n
5:31–32—294
5:32—140n5, 287–88
5:32–33—285, 287
5:33—267n25, 272n, 282n19, 285n, 293, 295, 301–2, 302n
6—xvi, 144, 267, 312n6
6:1—312
6:1–3—307
6:1–9—305
6:1b—312
6:2—108n4, 312, 312n6, 315–16
6:2–3—271n1
6:2c–3—313
6:4—282n17, 297, 305–6, 312n3, 316–17, 320
6:4a—317
6:4b–d—320
6:4c—321
6:4d—322
6:5—267n25, 312n4
6:5–8—323–24
6:5–9—271n1, 323
6:6—259n
6:6–8—325

6:8—325
6:9—297, 305, 324–25
6:10—69, 329–31, 338
6:10–11—327
6:10–18—69, 329
6:10–20—337
6:10–24—327
6:11—80, 224n, 329, 334, 338, 342n15
6:11–16—334
6:11–17—338
6:12—21n4, 71n9, 144, 252n2, 332, 334–35, 338
6:13—258n14, 335–39, 342n15, 343
6:14—210n10, 252, 337n9, 339, 342n15, 343n19
6:15—339
6:16—80, 146n, 336–37, 339, 343
6:17—280, 337n9, 340, 347
6:18—343, 343n19, 348
6:18–20—343
6:18–24—348
6:19—140n5, 287, 338n9
6:19–20—348
6:20—xv, 5n2
6:21—348
6:21–22—5n2
6:22—348
6:23—146n, 199, 278n13, 316n, 338n9, 348
6:24—229n13, 348

Philippians
1:2—13
1:3–8—61n
1:7—312n6
1:10—253n7
1:11—252n4
1:15—209
1:27—123n2, 342n15
1:29—341n14
2:1–11—183n2, 268
2:3—183n2
2:5–8—298
2:5–11—183n2, 189
2:10—152n, 265n23
2:10–11—41
2:12—267n25, 312n4
2:15—22n
2:25—126n6, 187n6
3:1—329n2
3:2—191n12, 258n12
3:2–3—95n
3:10—71n8
3:17—79, 237n3
3:20—123n1
3:21—69, 292n1
4:1—342n15
4:6—169, 343n19
4:8—312n6, 329n2
4:13—330n
4:18—239n, 253n6
4:20—168, 178–79

Colossians
1:1—6n, 259n
1:2—12n, 13, 252n2
1:3—64n, 65n3, 265n22
1:3–8—61n
1:6–7—209n8
1:9—64n, 258n13
1:10—79, 253n6
1:11—69, 183n2
1:12—54
1:13—71n9, 245n11, 252n2, 335
1:14—34n, 35n, 61n
1:16—71n9, 185n, 335
1:18—72n11, 275n6
1:19—36n4, 73
1:19–23—112n

1:20—34, 112n
1:21—204
1:22—22n, 281
1:23—136n3
1:25—136n4
1:25–27—140n5
1:26—37
1:28—36n4, 281, 321n14
1:29—69, 142n9
2:2–3—140n5
2:3—36n4
2:6—209
2:8—79, 258n12
2:8–23—191n12
2:9–10—73
2:10—71n9, 73, 164, 275n6, 335
2:11—80n4
2:11–13—83, 95n
2:12—71n8, 280
2:13—80n4
2:13–14—109n4
2:14—23
2:15—71n9, 190n, 335
2:19—197, 275n6
2:20—79
3:1—83
3:4—226
3:5—206n6, 240n7, 242n
3:5–9—204, 245n12
3:6—245n12
3:8—229n14
3:9—211n12
3:9–10—211, 211n12, 219
3:10—109n5, 214n16
3:11—95n, 276n11
3:12—26, 183n2
3:12–13—183n2, 232n
3:13—183n2
3:15—67n, 72n11, 184n, 282n16
3:16—36n4, 263n20, 264n, 321n14
3:17—265nn22–23
3:18—276n11, 292n1, 312n4
3:18–19—275n8, 293n4, 297n
3:18–4:1—271n1, 276n10
3:20—253n6, 312nn4–5
3:22—267n25, 276n11, 303n, 312n4
3:24—54
4:1—312n6
4:2–3—343n19
4:3—xv, 140n5
4:5—36n4, 258nn13–14
4:6—229n13
4:7–9—5n2
4:9—5n2
4:10—xv
4:11—245n11
4:12—64n, 342n15
4:18—xv

1 Thessalonians—11n7
1:1—13
1:2—64n, 265n22
1:2–10—61n
1:3—265n22
1:4—26
1:6—237n3
2:3—240n7
2:5—207n
2:7—282n18
2:8—225n10
2:12—67n, 245n11
2:14—237n3
2:18—136n3
3:10—169n
3:11—265n22
3:13—265n22
4:1—182n, 253n6, 329n2
4:3—240n7, 259

4:3–7—240n7
5:4–11—252n2
5:7—260n
5:7–8—260n
5:8—337n9, 341
5:11—229n12
5:12—321n14
5:13—169n
5:14—183n2, 321n14
5:17—64n, 343n19
5:18—265n22
5:19–22—187n6
5:21—253n7
5:23—280
5:24—67n

2 Thessalonians
1:2—13
1:3—265n22
1:3–10—61n
1:5—245n11
1:8—312n4
1:9—69
1:11—64n
1:12—265n23
2:8–12—191n12
2:13—265n22
2:13–17—85n
2:14—54n4, 67n
2:15—342n15
3:1—329n2, 343n19
3:6—265n23
3:7—237n3
3:9—237n3
3:14—312n4
3:15—321n14

1 Timothy
1:4—136n4
1:5–7—191n12
1:9—315
1:12—330n
1:15—142n10, 143
1:17—168, 178–79
1:20—224n
2:1—182n, 343n19
2:5—185n
2:7—5n1
2:8—343n19
2:8–15—293n4
2:11—276n10, 292n1
3:2—293n4
3:4—276n10
3:6–7—224n
3:11—224n
3:11–12—293n4
3:15—124
3:16—140n5
4:3—12n
4:10—12n
4:12—12n
5:8—124
5:9—293n4
5:15—224n
5:16—12n
6:1—265n23
6:1–2—271n1
6:2—12n
6:4—229n14
6:12—67n, 168
6:16—69, 179
6:17–19—298

2 Timothy
1:1—6n, 259n
1:3–7—61n
1:7—69
1:8—136n3

1:9—26, 67n
1:9–10—85n
2:1—330n
2:10—26
2:16—227
2:21—280
2:25—183n2
2:26—224n
3:1–2—315
3:3—224n
3:16—321n13
4:1—245n11
4:2—183n2
4:3–4—191n12
4:8—329n2
4:12—5n2
4:17—330n
4:18—168, 178–79, 245n11

Titus
1:1—26
1:6—12n, 260n, 293n4
1:14—109n4
2:2–8—293n4
2:2–10—271n1
2:3—224n
2:5—276n10, 292n1
2:9—276n10, 292n1
3:1—292n1
3:2—183n2
3:4—232n
3:4–7—85n
3:5—280
3:10—321n14
3:12—5n2

Philemon
1—136n3
3—13
4—64n, 265n22
4–7—61n
9—136n3
10—325
10–14—5n2
16—325
19—136n3

Hebrews
1:14—54
2:5—292n1
2:8—292n1
2:11—124n
4:12—338n9
4:15—230
4:16—145
5:9—312n4
6:12—237n3
9:11—95n
9:13—280
9:15—54
9:24—95n
10:19—145
10:22—280
11:8—312n4
11:13—123n1
12:5—321n13
12:7–8—321n13
12:9—292n1
12:11—321n13
13:7—237n3
13:21—168, 178

James
1:2–4—283
1:26—221n
2:8—285n
4:1–10—338
4:6—257n11

4:7—292n1
5:13—264n

1 Peter
1:3—65n3
1:3–5—19n2
1:4—54
1:13—337n9
1:14—203n3
1:18—203n3
1:18–19—35
1:19—23n8
1:21—12n
2:4–5a—131
2:6—127n8
2:9—54n4
2:11—123n1
2:13—292n1
2:17—303n
2:18—276n10, 292n1
2:18–3:7—271n1
3:1—276n10, 292n1, 293
3:4–6—293
3:5—292n1
3:6—276n10, 295, 312n4
3:18—188n
3:20–21—280
3:22—292n1, 335
4:1–5—260n
4:11—168, 178
4:14—265n23
5:5—268, 292n1, 298
5:5–6—268
5:11—168

2 Peter
1:1—341n14
2:10—80n4
3:18—168

1 John
2:15–17—79
3:1—248
4:4—333
4:11—347
5:13—265n23

Jude
17—187n6
20—343n19
24–25—169

Revelation—178
1:6—168
3:12—265n23
4:11—168
5:9—35, 190, 263n20, 264n
5:9–13—264n
7:9—110
7:14—110
11:15—40
11:18—303n
13:8—35
14:3—263n20, 264n
14:7—303n
15:3—263n20, 264n
17:2—260n
19:5—303n
19:7–9—273n
21:2—273n
21:8—245
21:9—273n
21:14—187n6
22:17—273n

Index of Subjects and Names

abortion, 8, 336
abuse, 291, 301–2, 308
access to God, 122, 145
accountability, 242, 330
Adam, 53, 88, 320, 333
addictions, 213
administration, of God's grace, 136, 138–39, 142
adoption, 24–25
adversary, 334–37
African-Americans, 114–15, 118
AIDS, 336
al-Amreekee, Jibreel, 135
alienation, 96–99
  from God, 99–100, 122
aliens, 122–23, 126, 332
"all things," 50
Al Qaeda, 135
already and not yet, 21, 34n1, 211n12
"amen," 179
Amerding, Hudson, 181–82
angels, 152, 153
anger, 222–24, 229, 234, 317
  sinful vs. righteous, 202
apostles, 5, 126–27, 187
Archimedes, 224
armor of God, 338–43, 347
Artemis, 7
asking, 169
assurance, 57
Augustine, 78
Auschwitz, 173
authorities and powers of Satan, 332
authority, 268, 291, 297, 318–19
  and character of Christ, 326
  and headship, 275–77
  of husband, 293, 295
  of masters, 325
authorship, of Ephesians, xv-xvi
autism, 70
autonomy, 198
awe, 305

baptism, 280
Barker, Frank, 197–98
barriers, removal of, 110–11, 116–17, 128, 141
Baunrin, Diana, 322
Bayer, Hans, 8
belief, and seal of Spirit, 55–56, 58
belt of truth, 337n9, 341n13
benediction, 57
benefits, of Christ, 102
bigotry, 111, 115
bitterness, 229, 234, 243
blameless, 22–23
blessing, 19–22, 265, 313

blood of Christ, 34–35, 102–4, 107–19, 158, 248
blue whales, 64–65
boasting, 88–89
body of Christ, 74, 190–91
boldness, 145–46
brawling, 229, 234
breastplate, 337n9
brothers and sisters in Christ, 186
brought near, 100–101, 107
Bruce, F. F., 68–69, 218n2
building others up, 228
Burnham, Martin, 138–39, 141

Calhoun, David, 88
calling, 67n5, 90n13, 165
  of church, 182–83
  and pain, 143
  true vs. counterfeit, 137, 138
callousness, 206
Calvinism, 51
Calvin, John, 51, 78, 88, 320
capstone, 127n8
Carmichael, Amy, 255
ceremonial law, 108–9
challenges, 4–6, 14
Chalmers, Thomas, 164, 345
Chancey, Gary and Mary Jane, 326
change, 120–22
Chariots of Fire (film), 253
charismatic gifts, 55
cheating, 219–20
childrearing. *See* parenting
children, 276, 312–15
  care for, 320–23
  exasperating of, 297, 317–18
children of God, 236–39, 248–49
children of light, 151–60, 253, 260
chosen, 32–33, 46–47
Christian community, 236
Christian life, 45, 49, 158, 202, 210, 213, 218, 221
Christlikeness, 306, 325, 330, 344
Chrysostom, 110
church
  as body of Christ, 74, 184, 190–91, 282n16
  as bride of Christ, 273
  calling of, 182–83
  as family, 185–86
  and glory of God, 175
  and parenting, 307–8
  power of, 71–72
  submission to Christ as head, 275
  transformation of world, xvi, 73–76, 173–74, 183, 186
  as witness to glory, 144–48
circular letter, Ephesians as, 9n4
circumcision, 95–96, 110
citizenship, 123
  in kingdom, 96–97
clothing image, 211, 214n16
Clouse, Bonnidell, 321–22
Colossians, xv
comfort, 239, 266
commendation, 62–63
community, 101, 114
  alienation from, 96–97
compassion, 232n17
"completing another," 294, 298
confession of sins, 41
confidence, 7–9, 22, 45, 57, 152–56
confrontation, 42
consumerism, 328
contentment, 192, 243
context, 255–56
control, of spouse, 302
cornerstone, 126, 127–29, 130

correction, 63
corrupting influences, 236
counseling, 166
counterfeit callings, 137–38
covenant, 49, 50–51, 97, 122–23
covenant community, 219
Covenant Seminary, 161
covetousness, 207n6
creation, 172, 292n1
criminals, 321–22
culture, 42–43, 247, 255–56, 336

Damascus, road to, 13, 28, 135, 141
darkened minds, 204–5
darkness, 151, 247, 252, 254–58, 260, 266
Dawn, Marva, 257
day of redemption, 231n16
death, 188
delinquents, 321–22
Demetrius, 7
demonic forces, 335
denominations, 184
dependence, 196–200
deposit, Holy Spirit as, 54, 58
de Sales, Francis, 192
despair, 74
Devil, 334–37, 343
differences, attitudes toward, 192
discipline, of children, 318–20, 323
disciplines, 165
disobedience, 79–80
    of children, 313–15
diversity, in the church, 183, 186–92
divine causation, 47. *See also* predestination
divorce, 310, 336
doctrine, 262
dominions, 190n9
doubt, 53
doxology, 88, 168–69
Dozier, John, 250, 266, 267
drunkenness, 260–61, 262
Duke University, 310, 316
dwelling, 132n9
Dye, Laura, 131
dying to self, 137, 141, 239, 289

edifying words, 202
Eighteen Benedictions, 19n2
election, 33
    as corporate and individual, 26
Eliot, T. S., 170
emotions, 39
encouragement, of Christ, 232
enlightenment, 66
Ephesus, xv, 9–11, 12, 26–27, 40, 50
equipping the saints, 191, 195–96
eschatology, 211n12, 219n3, 245
established, 160
eternal life, 83
eternal plan, 51–53, 58
eternity, as present reality, 84
evangelicalism, 198
evangelism, 30
evil, 26, 258–59, 335–36
exodus, 230n15
exposing darkness, 254–58
eyes of the heart, 66

faith, 61, 159, 337–38n9
fall, 34, 53, 292n1
false teachers, 191n12
falsehoods, 202, 219–22
families, 153, 328, 330, 336
family of God, 101, 123–25, 130, 185–86
fathers, 316–17
Faulkner, William, 91
fear, 238, 267n25
fellow citizens, 122–23, 332

feminism, 299
Ferguson, Sarah, 290
Ferguson, Sinclair, 333, 335n7
Ferrandino, Vincent, 106
fetal alcohol syndrome, 36
filled with the Spirit, 261, 262, 263–69, 276
filling, 261–62
"finding out," 253
flaming arrows, 338n9
flesh, 80n4, 92, 100, 211n12, 333
Fogelberg, Dan, 27
foolishness, 240n8
foothold, 224n8
foreigners, 122–23, 332
forgiveness, 34, 41, 113, 232–33, 237, 280
fornication, 240
Foster, Richard, 342
foundation, of apostles and prophets, 126–27, 130, 152
fragrant offering, 238–39
freedom, 145, 153, 328
free will, of Adam, 88
French Reformation, 75–76
fruit of the Spirit, 62, 252
fullness of Christ, 191, 261
fullness of God, 73, 163–64, 261
fundamentalism, 262, 328
futility, 203–4, 214

Gauguin, Paul, 95
gender, 270, 293n4
generosity, 226
Gentile audience, of Ephesians, 5n1
Gentiles, 45–46, 49, 96, 105. *See also* Jews and Gentiles
- as fellow citizens, 122–23
- in the flesh, 92
- inclusion of, 50–51, 139–40
- manner of life, 203–5

gentleness, 183n2
gifts, 300
- of the church, 296, 297
- despising of, 192–93
- neglect of, 194–95

girding the waist, 337n9
glory, 145, 148, 281
God
- alienation from, 99–100
- faithfulness, 45–53
- as Father, 18, 152–53, 185–86, 307–8
- glory, 48, 152, 175–80
- kindness of, 86–87
- love of, 26–27, 28, 29, 33, 47, 59, 81–83, 149, 163–66, 170, 199, 248–49
- and passions, 39
- plan of salvation, xvi
- power of, 70–71, 81, 83–85, 164, 168, 172–75, 330–34, 341
- rule of, 40–42
- sovereignty of, xvi, 8–9, 40n2, 51, 57, 71, 164, 172, 178, 259n15
- wisdom of, 168, 174

godliness, 215, 321–22, 329–30, 339, 341, 342
good pleasure, 38
good works, 90, 142
goodness, 252
gospel, 338n9
gospel pattern, 238
grace, 13, 16, 21, 29, 31, 43, 82, 85, 87, 88–89, 213–14, 218, 248
- as character of God, 177
- enraptured by, 141–43, 147
- and obedience, 226–27
- renewal by, 218, 219
- and spiritual warfare, 348–49
- vast riches of, 35–37

Graham, Billy, 193

gratitude, 33, 251
Gray, Rick, 3–4, 15–16
Greco-Roman culture, 11, 241
greed, 207n6, 213, 236, 237, 242–44, 245–46
grieving the Holy Spirit, 231–32
Grudem, Wayne, 274
guilt, 34, 238, 318

hallucinations, 215–16
hardened hearts, 205–6
Havel, Vaclav, 257
Haynes, Lewis, 215–16
headship, 271–83, 293n4, 296
  of fathers, 317
  passivity in, 273–74
  as robbery, 278
healing, through forgiveness, 233
hearing, 209–10
heart, 66
  change of, 345–47
  circumcision of, 94n1, 95n2
heart for God, 349
heaven, power of, 208
heavenly realms, 20–21, 84, 144, 332, 335
hedonism, 207
heirs together, 140
helmet, 337n9
helmet of salvation, 340, 342
helplessness, 160
Hindus, 233
holiness, 23–24, 79, 213, 215, 218, 236, 244, 247, 256, 343
Holy Spirit, 338n9
  changes hearts, 345–47
  faithfulness of, 54–58
  and forgiveness, 232
  gifts of, 188
  grieving of, 231–32
  indwelling of, 131–32
  power of, 69, 157–58
  testimony of, 58
  and wisdom, 65
hope, 61, 66–67, 70, 183, 251
horses, running with, 208–9, 210, 216
hostility, 113, 116, 118
household code, 270–71n1, 323
household of God, 124, 126, 127, 332. *See also* family of God
households, 305–26
Hoyt, Dick and Ricky, 349
Hughes, R. Kent, 336–37
Huguenots, 75–76
humility, 33, 39–40, 86, 87–89, 90, 152, 154–56, 183n2, 286
husbands, 270–89
  respect for, 295, 301–4
  submission to, 291–97
hymns, 263

identity, 104, 184, 237, 248–49, 252
idolatry, 50, 95n2, 242–46, 249, 317
image of God, 34
imagining, 170
imitating Christ, 238–39
imitating God, 236–37, 238, 249
"immeasurably" more, 169–75, 180
immorality, 240–41, 245–46
impurity, 92–93, 206–7, 240–41, 243, 244, 247, 249, 252, 255
"in Christ," 19, 26, 49, 100, 176, 333
indicative and imperative, 237, 244
inheritance, 25, 46–47, 54, 67–69, 244–45, 332
injustice, 335
insecurities, 336
  and parenting, 305–6
inspiration, 126–27

instruction, of children, 321–22
instruments, of exposure, 256–57
integration point, of faith, 262
integrity, 221–22, 252, 325
intercession, 63–64
internet, 328
"in the Lord," 312n5, 330–31
intimacy, alienation from, 97–99
Ironside, Harry, 164–65
Isaiah, 128, 230n15
Islam, 106, 135
isolation, from promises, 122
Israel, covenant with, 45–46

Jerusalem, 108
Jesus Christ
 ascension of, 188–89
 authority of, 188–89
 as cornerstone, 127–29, 130, 152
 defeat of sin, 190
 dwells in heart of his people, 158
 as example, 232, 238
 generosity of, 189
 headship over church, 272–73
 incarnation, 189
 love for bride, 277–78, 280–81, 295, 320
 love of, 161–63, 288
 obedience of, 23–24
 provides life, 158
 resurrection of, 83–84
 righteousness of, 159
 sacrifice of, 277, 287–88, 298, 326
 sanctity of, 22–24
Jews, 5n1, 95–96
Jews and Gentiles, 46, 49, 105–6, 108–10, 112, 118, 128, 139–40, 158
Joe and the Volcano (film), 48
Josephus, 108
joy, 111
judgment, 80
justice, 82

Keillor, Garrison, 124–25
Keller, Tim, 61
Khmer Rouge, 95
kindness, 232n17, 243
kingdom of God, 41, 42–43, 244–45
kneeling, in prayer, 152, 155
knowing God, 89
knowledge, head vs. relational, 209
Korea, 185
Kuyper, Abraham, 41–42

land, 313n7
language, 227–28
Lazarus, 81
leaders, leadership, 195, 198, 289. *See also* servant/leader
 greed of, 242
 uncontrolled anger of, 223
legalism, 218
Lennon, John, 106
Lewis, C. S., 201–2, 204, 208, 211, 216
Liddell, Eric, 253
light of the Son, 251–60, 262, 267
Lilly Endowment, 14
living for others, 138–41
lizards, 201–2, 204, 208, 216
Lordship, of Christ, 41–42
Lord's Prayer, 40
love, 30, 199
 for Christ, 164–66
 for God, 151, 155–56, 165, 346
 as power, 150–51, 349
 for spouse, and parenting, 309–12
 surpassing knowledge, 163
 for things of this world, 164
 unites church, 61

Luke, 7
lust, 98, 100, 104, 206, 213, 236, 237, 239, 240–41, 243–44, 255
Luther, Martin, 212, 226, 239, 327, 336, 346–47n24

malice, 229–31, 234
manifold wisdom, 144
marriage, 241, 270–88
  as mystery, 287, 294
Marx, Karl, 95
masters. *See* slaves and masters
materialism, 12, 60, 335
maturity, 143, 191–92, 282, 330
Matzat, Don, 343
McQuilkin, J. Robertson, 286, 288–89
Mead, Margaret, 95
means of grace, 330, 341, 346
memory, 91–100
mercy, 38–39, 43, 50–53, 157
mercy ministries, 226
merit, 26, 29
Messiah, 5, 96, 117n8, 140
military analogy, 342n15
Miller, Jack, 346n24
Miller, Rose Marie, 338
Mintz, Gene, 199–200
missionary zeal, 59–60
mold, 44–45
money, 209
morality, and piety, 247
mortification, 208, 211, 214, 216
Moses, 47
Mother Teresa, 299
motive, 256
Mount Zion, 188–89
Mr. Holland's Opus (film), 195–96
Murray, John, 347
music, 263–64
mystery, 142n11
  of marriage, 287, 294
  of revelation, 37–38
  of salvation for Gentiles, 138, 139–40

neighbor, becoming Christ to, 226
Nelson, Mary, 170
new affections, 345–46
new creation, 172
new identity, 100–104, 105
new life, 83, 90n13, 346
new man, 109, 112, 211–12, 214, 215
New Orleans, 27
Nidingeye, Zack, 114
non posse non peccare, 212
non posse peccare, 212

obedience, 226–27
  based on Father's love, 237–38
  of children, 312–15
  and identity, 237
  as witness, 233
O'Brien, Peter, 230n15
obscenity, 227, 240n8
O'Connor, Flannery, 249
offerings to God, 254
old self, 210–12, 214, 346
one another, 268
Onesimus, 5n2
opposition, 9–12
optical illusions, 228
order and plan to universe, 48–49
Owen, John, 154

pagans, paganism, 11, 96, 203
pain, 239
parenting, 166, 305–23, 326
passions, 39, 150
passive righteousness, 347n24

pastor-teacher, 187
patriarchalism, 271n1
Patrick, 159
Paul
  apostleship of, 6–7
  authority of, 7
  authorship of Ephesians, xv-xvi
  calling of, 135–38
  conversion of, 8, 13
  imprisonment of, xv, 5, 14, 146–47
  love for churches of Ephesus, 348
  as prisoner of Christ Jesus, 135–36
peace, 13–16, 21, 30, 31, 106–19, 120, 168, 183, 338n9, 347n24
peaceableness, 231
"perfecting the enemy," 221
persecution, 75–76
personality, 192–93
Peterson, Robert, 24, 89
Pharaoh, 205n4
Pharisaism, 262
piety
  and morality, 247
  and power, 221–22
plagiarism, of preachers, 219–20
Planned Parenthood, 114
Plantinga, Cornelius, 172
pleasure, 208
pluralism, 107
pornography, 12
posse non peccare, 212
poverty, 8, 335, 336
power, 69–70, 76, 156–60, 163, 172, 207–8, 209
  love as, 150–51
  in marriage, 302
  over sin, 161, 244
  sacrifice of, 136
powers, 190n9, 332
pragmatism, 12
praise, 244, 264
prayer, 18, 63, 151–52, 172, 343–45, 348
predestination, xvi, 6n3, 24, 27, 28–30, 33–34, 47, 77–78, 86, 89
prejudice, 104, 107, 111, 140, 141
present evil age, 79, 258n14
prestige, 136, 207–8
pride, 29, 33, 39, 41, 43, 50, 88–89, 92, 104, 107, 213
Prince of Peace, 108, 117n8
privilege, sacrifice of, 136, 137
profanity, 227–28
promiscuity, 335, 336
promise, 97
propaganda, 221
prophets, 126–27, 187
psalms, 263
Puritans, 208, 211, 214, 247
purity, 236, 239
purposes of God, 49

race, 118–19
racism, 101, 111, 115, 118–19, 335, 336
rage, 223, 229, 234
rainbows, 52–53
readiness, 339
rebuke, 63
reckless living, 260, 262
reconciliation, between races, 41, 112, 117–19
redeeming the time, 258–59
redemption, 34–35, 43, 231n16
remembering, 92–100
remission of sins, 34, 35, 43
renewal, by grace, 218, 219
repentance, 143, 159, 216
responsibility, in marriage, 273–74
restoration, 37

resurrection power, 71, 83–84, 212, 332–33, 342
retribution, 248
revelation, 37–40, 43
reverence, 267, 276
  for husband, 302–4
riches of Christ, 142–43
Ridderbos, Herman, 237
righteousness, 23–24, 212, 215, 252, 338n9
risqué wit, 240n8
Roman emperor cult, 10
rooted, 160

sacrifice, and submission, 276–77
sacrifices
  fragrance of, 236, 238–39
  in temple, 110
safe-keeping, 313
saints, 9, 11–12
salvation, 26, 28–30, 338n9, 340
sanctification, 22, 344
  of husband, 283–85
  of wife, 280
Satan, 79, 188, 224, 335, 343
Saul, 13, 136
seal, 54–56
seated with Christ, 212
Sebastian, David, 128–29
second blessing, 55
secularism, 52–53, 60, 106–7
self-denial, 208
self-fulfillment, 194
selfishness, 224, 299, 336
selflessness, 226, 286
self-sacrifice, of husband, 286–87
sensitivity, 206
sensory overload, 245–46
sensuality, 206–7, 252, 255
separated life, 203
separating from darkness, 254–58
September 11 terrorist attacks, 60–61, 93, 138
servant/leader, 277, 285–89, 306
servant of the gospel, 136–37
service, and headship, 275
sex, 209, 270
sexual addictions, 98
sexual immorality, 240–41, 246, 251, 255
shame, 23, 34, 238, 301–2, 318
Sharp, Granville, 127n6
Shekinah glory, 132, 175
shield, 337n9, 343
simul justus et peccator, 212
sin, 12, 35, 80, 155–56, 212–13
  dangers of, 244
  defeat of, 188, 190
  enticement of, 216
  imprisonment of, 34–35
  indulgence of, 214
  indwelling, 201–2
  of leaders, 198
sinful nature, 80, 211–13
singing, 263–64
slander, 229, 234
slaves and masters, 276, 292n1, 297, 323–26
sloth, 338
Sonship, 24–25
sons of disobedience, 245n12
sound teaching, 330
source, headship as, 274
sovereignty, and human responsibility, 78, 86, 89
spanking, 318–19
speaking, 263
speech, unwholesome, 202, 227–28, 240n8
spiritual citizenship, 96–97
spiritual death, 79–81, 83
spiritual disciplines, 339, 341, 343

spiritual gifts, 189
spiritual insight, 64–65
spiritual songs, 263
spiritual support, 60–61
spiritual warfare, 247, 259, 327–46
spirituality, 262
Staines, Gladys, 233–34
standing firm, 339–40, 342n15, 343n19
starvation diet, for sin, 240, 242
stealing, 224–26, 243
stewards, stewardship, 136n4, 140n5, 142n11
submission, 267–68, 272, 275–76, 297
  of children, 312–15, 318
  of wives, 290–304
subordination, 292n1
suffering, 53, 104, 147, 239
sword, 337–38n9, 342

tabernacle, 132
temple, 126n4, 129–30, 132, 162, 243, 249
  of living stones, 160, 162
temptation, 150, 207, 248, 328–29
Ten Commandments, 207n6, 313, 314n8
testimony, 184, 203, 227
thanksgiving, 61–63, 171, 243, 265–66
theology of the cross, 239
Thousand Clowns (film), 149
time, 259
Tolkien, J. R. R., 172
tongue, 228
traditions, 184
tragedy, 266
training, of children, 321–22
Trajan, 10, 40
trespasses, 35, 36
trials, 21–22, 68, 104
Trinity, 13, 122, 156, 158, 161
Trophimus, 147
Trump, Donald, 299
trust, 221–22
truth, 209–10, 243, 252
  vs. falsehood, 202, 219–22
Tychicus, 5n2, 348

Uganda, 3–4, 15–16
understanding, 36
union, of heaven and earth, 40
union with Christ, 12, 19–20, 22–24, 25, 84–85, 87, 100–101, 102, 144, 146, 158, 176n6, 212, 262, 331, 332
unity, of church, 5n1, 41–42, 115–16, 183, 184–85, 191–92
USS *Indianapolis*, 215–16

Van Tholen, John, 82, 89–90
Vertical Horizon (musical group), 67
violence, in the home, 301–2
vivification, 214

Wailing Wall (Jerusalem), 108
walking, 79, 90n13, 203, 238n5, 253n5
warfare. *See* spiritual warfare
Warfield, Benjamin, 87
warnings, 244–49
washing, 280
Waterhouse, Graham, 255
Watts, Isaac, 39n6, 333
weakness, 82, 104
weapons, of spiritual warfare, 337–43
Wesley, Charles, 344n21
Westminster Confession of Faith, 39, 101
Westminster Shorter Catechism, 88, 341n14
Wheaton College, 181–82
wickedness, 26
Willimon, William, 310
will of God, 6–9, 38, 259n15
Winter, Richard, 98

wisdom, 36, 65, 258n13, 344
witness, 227–29, 233–34
wives
  desire of, 301–4
  dignity of, 296–300
  duty of, 291–96
  glorifying of, 277–83, 295, 298
  sanctification of, 280
  submission of, 272n3, 290–304
Wolfe, Alan, 247
women, gifts of, 296
Word of God, 6, 8–9
  in households, 280–81
working, 225–26, 243
workmanship, 87, 92, 218
works of service, 191
world
  opposition to God, 79
  transformation of, xvi, 73–76, 172–74, 183, 186
worldliness, 214, 262
World War II, 118
"worm theology," 39n6
worship, 121, 243, 263–64
wrath of God, 80, 81, 245–46
wrestling, 18, 31

Young, Sarah Moore, 131

zeal, 346

Available in the Reformed Expository Commentary Series

New Testament

The Incarnation in the Gospels, by Daniel M. Doriani, Philip Graham Ryken, and Richard D. Phillips
Matthew, by Daniel M. Doriani
Luke, by Philip Graham Ryken
John, by Richard D. Phillips
Romans, by Daniel M. Doriani
Galatians, by Philip Graham Ryken
Ephesians, by Bryan Chapell
Philippians, by Dennis E. Johnson
1 & 2 Thessalonians, by Richard D. Phillips
1 Timothy, by Philip Graham Ryken
2 Timothy & Titus, by Daniel M. Doriani and Richard D. Phillips
Hebrews, by Richard D. Phillips
James, by Daniel M. Doriani
1 Peter, by Daniel M. Doriani
1–3 John, by Douglas Sean O'Donnell
Revelation, by Richard D. Phillips

Forthcoming

Mark, by Douglas Sean O'Donnell
2 Corinthians, by Trent Casto